SECOND CORINTHIANS

Sacra Pagina Series

Volume 8

Second Corinthians

Jan Lambrecht, S.J.

Daniel J. Harrington, S.J.
Editor

A Michael Glazier Book
THE LITURGICAL PRESS
Collegeville, Minnesota

Cover design by Don Bruno.

A Michael Glazier Book published by The Liturgical Press.

1	2	3	4	5	6	7	8

Library of Congress Cataloging-in-Publication Data

Lambrecht, Jan.
    Second Corinthians / Jan Lambrecht ; Daniel J. Harrington, editor.
        p.   cm. — (Sacra pagina series ; vol. 8)
    "A Michael Glazier book."
    Includes bibliographical references and indexes.
    ISBN 0-8146-5810-5 (alk. paper)
    1. Bible.   N.T.   Corinthians, 2nd—Commentaries.   I. Harrington,
Daniel J.   II. Title.   III. Series: Sacra pagina series ; 8.
    BS2675.3.L36   1998
    227'.2077—dc21   98-19294
                                                                   CIP

CONTENTS

Indexes

EDITOR'S PREFACE

Sacra Pagina is a multi-volume commentary on the books of the New Testament. The expression *Sacra Pagina* ("Sacred Page") originally referred to the text of Scripture. In the Middle Ages it also described the study of Scripture to which the interpreter brought the tools of grammar, rhetoric, dialectic, and philosophy. Thus *Sacra Pagina* encompasses both the text to be studied and the activity of interpretation.

This series presents fresh translations and modern expositions of all the books of the New Testament. Written by an international team of Catholic biblical scholars, it is intended for biblical professionals, graduate students, theologians, clergy, and religious educators. The volumes present basic introductory information and close exposition. They self-consciously adopt specific methodological perspectives, but maintain a focus on the issues raised by the New Testament compositions themselves. The goal of *Sacra Pagina* is to provide sound critical analysis without any loss of sensitivity to religious meaning. This series is therefore catholic in two senses of the word: inclusive in its methods and perspectives, and shaped by the context of the Catholic tradition.

The Second Vatican Council described the study of the "sacred page" as the "very soul of sacred theology" (*Dei Verbum* 24). The volumes in this series illustrate how Catholic scholars contribute to the council's call to provide access to Sacred Scripture for all the Christian faithful. Rather than pretending to say the final word on any text, these volumes seek to open up the riches of the New Testament and to invite as many people as possible to study seriously the "sacred page."

DANIEL J. HARRINGTON, S.J.

AUTHOR'S PREFACE

Scholars and students of Paul know all too well that his second letter to the Corinthians is not easy. There is not only the question of the integrity of 2 Corinthians as a letter, but also the fact that adequate information is lacking about the concrete situation at Corinth and the identity of Paul's opponents. Moreover, the Greek of this letter is difficult, partly due no doubt to Paul's emotional style. Yet 2 Corinthians is of utmost importance, especially because of Paul's ongoing reflection on his ministry.

The writer of this commentary has tried to adhere to the guidelines of the *Sacra Pagina* series by offering here a one-volume commentary without footnotes and without expanded surveys of the history of interpretation. Brevity of exposition has been a primary goal. A new translation has been prepared. A distinction is made between the verse-by-verse exegesis (Notes) and the more theological explanation (Interpretation). Finally, only a few titles, mostly English, have been added for reference and further study.

My translation is as literal as possible and is intended to help readers to detect precisely what Paul has in mind, his reasoning and the flow of his thought. More than once it was necessary to add some words and even phrases in parentheses to conform to English grammar. In the notes the translation is repeated clause by clause for the sake of easier discussion. Greek words and constructions are given in transliteration followed by the translation in parentheses. For passages from the Septuagint I have sometimes used the translation by L.C.L. Brenton, *The Septuagint with Apocrypha: Greek and English* (repr. Grand Rapids: Zondervan, 1982). As is further explained at the end of the Introduction, the material in the interpretation is divided into four (unequal) sections. The readers will notice that this commentary argues for the integrity of 2 Corinthians. On this position well-known commentators such as C. K. Barrett, Rudolf Bultmann, Maurice Carrez, Victor P. Furnish, Hans-Josef Klauck, Ralph P. Martin, Alfred Plummer, Margaret E. Thrall, Hans Windisch, and Christian Wolff differ. These authors, however, along with many other commentators and writers of monographs or articles, are gratefully remembered here.

I am very much indebted to two of my former students at the Katholieke Universiteit in Leuven, both of whom are now professors and specialists in Pauline studies. Dr. Veronica Koperski, S.F.C.C., Barry University (Florida), has corrected and refined the English and made a number of useful suggestions pertaining to the content. Dr. Reimund Bieringer, Katholieke Universiteit of Leuven (Belgium), carefully read a first version of this commentary and in protracted discussions reacted critically to it. I am convinced that neither would have written the text in the way I did, yet I remain deeply grateful to them for their generous and time-consuming help. I wish also to thank the students in Leuven, as well as those in Rome, who by their interaction during classes and seminars took part in the preparation of this work. It is an honor for a non-American and, moreover, one who is not a native English speaker to have been invited to write in *Sacra Pagina*. For this I want to thank Michael Glazier and the editor of the series, Daniel J. Harrington, S.J. Finally, I also extend thanks to my religious superiors in Belgium for their support, and I am likewise grateful to the staff of the Pontifical Biblical Institute in Rome for repeated invitations to teach on 2 Corinthians and other letters of Paul. Life in the Jesuit community of the Institute and use of its excellent library have proven no small help during the last stages of the composition of this commentary.

The Second Letter to the Corinthians is theologically and autobiographically highly significant. May this most personal of Paul's "weighty and strong" (10:10) letters continue to contribute toward the "building up" (13:10) of its readers.

January 25, 1998   Jan Lambrecht, S.J.
Feast of the Conversion of   Pontifical Biblical Institute, Rome
   Paul, Apostle

ABBREVIATIONS

Biblical Books and Apocrypha

Gen	Nah	1–2–3–4 Kgdms	John
Exod	Hab	Add Esth	Acts
Lev	Zeph	Bar	Rom
Num	Hag	Bel	1–2 Cor
Deut	Zech	1–2 Esdr	Gal
Josh	Mal	4 Ezra	Eph
Judg	Ps (*pl.:* Pss)	Jdt	Phil
1–2 Sam	Job	Ep Jer	Col
1–2 Kgs	Prov	1–2–3–4 Macc	1–2 Thess
Isa	Ruth	Pr Azar	1–2 Tim
Jer	Cant	Pr Man	Titus
Ezek	Eccl (*or* Qoh)	Sir	Phlm
Hos	Lam	Sus	Heb
Joel	Esth	Tob	Jas
Amos	Dan	Wis	1–2 Pet
Obad	Ezra	Matt	1–2–3 John
Jonah	Neh	Mark	Jude
Mic	1–2 Chr	Luke	Rev

Periodicals, Reference Works, and Serials

AB	Anchor Bible
ABR	*Australian Biblical Review*
AnBib	Analecta Biblica
BA	*Biblical Archaeologist*
BBB	Bonner biblische Beiträge
BBR	*Bulletin of Biblical Research*
BEThL	Bibliotheca Ephemeridum theologicarum Lovaniensium
Bib.	*Biblica*
BNTC	Black's New Testament Commentaries
BTB	*Biblical Theology Bulletin*

BU	Biblische Untersuchungen
BZ	*Biblische Zeitschrift*
BZNW	Beihefte zur *ZNW*
CBC	Collegeville Bible Commentary
CBQ	*Catholic Biblical Quarterly*
ChiSt	*Chicago Studies*
CNT	*Coniectanea neotestamentica*
CNT(N)	Commentaire du Nouveau Testament. Neuchâtel
EtB	Etudes Bibliques
EThL	*Ephemerides theologicae Lovanienses*
EvTh	*Evangelische Theologie*
FRLANT	Forschungen zur Religion und Literatur des Alten und Neuen Testaments
FS	Festschrift
FzB	Forschung zur Bibel
GNS	Good News Studies
HNT	Handbuch zum Neuen Testament
HNTC	Harper's New Testament Commentaries
HThR	*Harvard Theological Review*
ICC	International Critical Commentary
Interp.	*Interpretation*
IVP	The InterVarsity Press New Testament Commentary Series
JBL	*Journal of Biblical Literature*
JJS	*Journal of Jewish Studies*
JSNT	*Journal for the Study of the New Testament*
JSNT.S	Journal for the Study of the New Testament Supplement Series
JSSt	*Journal of Semitic Studies*
JThS	*Journal of Theological Studies*
KEK	Kritisch-exegetischer Kommentar über das Neue Testament
LeDiv	Lectio Divina
LouvSt	*Louvain Studies*
MSSNTS	Monograph Series. Society for New Testament Studies
NCeB	New Century Bible
Neotest.	*Neotestamentica*
NIC	New International Commentary on the New Testament
NT	*Novum Testamentum*
NT.S	Novum Testamentum Supplements
NTA	Neutestamentliche Abhandlungen
NTMes	New Testament Message
NTS	*New Testament Studies*
RB	*Revue Biblique*
RevScR	*Revue des sciences religieuses*
RHPhR	*Revue d'histoire et de philosophie religieuses*
RivBib	*Rivista Biblica*
SBL	Society of Biblical Literature
SBL.DS	Society of Biblical Literature Dissertation Series

SBL.SBS	Society of Biblical Literature Sources for Biblical Study
SBT	Studies in Biblical Theology
SJTh	*Scottish Journal of Theology*
SNTU.A	*Studien zum Neuen Testament und seiner Umwelt (Linz).* Series A
StANT	Studien zum Alten und Neuen Testament
StEv	*Studia evangelica*
TANZ	Texte und Arbeiten zum neutestamentlichen Zeitalter
ThBeitr	*Theologische Beiträge*
ThF	Theologische Forschung
ThHKNT	Theologischer Handkommentar zum Neuen Testament
ThQ	*Theologische Quartalschrift.* Tübingen
ThZ	*Theologische Zeitschrift*
TU	Texte und Untersuchungen zur Geschichte der altchristlichen Literatur
TynB	*Tyndale Bulletin*
WBC	Word Bible Commentary
WdF	Wege der Forschung
WMANT	Wissenschaftliche Monographien zum Alten und Neuen Testament
WUNT	Wissenschaftliche Untersuchungen zum Neuen Testament
ZNW	*Zeitschrift für die neutestamentliche Wissenschaft*
ZThK	*Zeitschrift für Theologie und Kirche*

INTRODUCTION

Paul's second letter to the Corinthians is rightly called his most personal letter. In 2:4 he speaks of his love for the Corinthians, which is "beyond measure." He stresses his sincere and generous way of acting with them; he has spoken frankly to them; his heart is wide open to them. There is no restriction on his affection (6:11-12a). He calls for reciprocity: "Make room for us" (7:2a). The whole letter is characterized by the emotional and pleading tone of a Paul who appears to be not too certain of the Corinthians' reactions.

This writing, moreover, arrests the readers' attention by its rich content. Of course, in this letter Paul also deals with the community's current (yet not unimportant) affairs. He wants to justify the twofold change of his travel plans. Thus, though his coming to Corinth had been postponed he insists that he is and remains a trustworthy person (1:15-24). He refers to a previous letter (2:4). He alludes to an incident in which he himself was the offended party. The wrongdoer has been punished, and Paul says in this letter that the punishment is enough; they should now forgive and console that person (2:5-11). Furthermore, in two chapters he deals with the great collection for the poor Christians of Jerusalem. Corinth, too, can participate in it, and the Corinthians should take that undertaking to heart (chs. 8 and 9).

Nevertheless, the whole letter, more particularly 2:14–7:4 and chs. 10–13, is impressive above all for its exposition of the apostle's identity: it is God "who reconciled us to himself through Christ and gave us the ministry of reconciliation, as (it is well known to you that) in Christ God was reconciling the world to himself, not counting their trespasses against them, and that God entrusted the word of reconciliation to us" (5:18-19). This is, no doubt, a grandiose vision. In this letter Paul also defends his apostleship; he more than once fiercely counters the attacks of his opponents. He extensively describes both the quality and circumstances of his apostolic existence: the sufferings he endures, the opposition he encounters, his continual care for the churches. Second Corinthians is, therefore, highly significant theologically as well as autobiographically.

1

This writing is an often implicit yet undeniable plea that Paul addresses to the Christians of Corinth. They must take his side; they should reconcile themselves with him; they should no longer listen to the intruders, the "false apostles, deceitful workers" (11:13). Moreover, many Corinthians must repent from vices and immorality (12:20-21; cf. 6:14–7:1).

The emotional language is certainly one reason why it is not always easy to follow the flow of Paul's argument. The main reason, however, is our insufficient familiarity with the concrete situation at Corinth. Still, this cannot prevent 2 Corinthians from being a letter both profound in its content and fascinating in its style, for the original addressees and for today's readers alike.

1. *Corinth and Paul's Visits*

Corinth, devastated by the Romans in 146 B.C.E., was refounded as a Roman colony in 44 B.C.E. by Julius Caesar and in 29 B.C.E. became the capital of the Roman province of Achaia, which was erected in that year. "New," prosperous Corinth was a cosmopolitan city with a Roman, Greek, and Near Eastern population. Its geographical position at the "isthmus," a narrow corridor between the Peloponnesus and the northern remainder of Greece, enabled it to function as a link between North and South and, through its ports at Lechaeum and Cenchreae, equally between the West (the Gulf of Corinth) and the East (the Aegean sea). Old Corinth had a reputation for immorality. New Corinth was no doubt characterized by cultural and religious syncretism. Many authors, however, consider it to have been little better and little worse than similar ports or cities of those days. However, T. B. Savage may be quoted:

> . . . first-century Corinth differed greatly from other Mediterranean cities. Little in the city was more than a century old: traditions were few, the aristocracy fluid, the society open. This suited the populace, mostly ambitious people of ultimately servile descent, eager to win respectability and power. In their hands the economy exploded, and at a time when neighbouring cities were in decline . . . Corinth had become the envy of the Empire—a city of pleasure, a tribute to human-made splendour, a place where assertiveness and pride reaped great reward (*Power Through Weakness* 52).

Paul's first visit took place during the course of his second missionary journey and is recorded by Luke in his own free way in Acts 18:1-18. These are the details. In Corinth Paul lived and worked with the Jewish couple Aquila and Priscilla and preached to the local Jews in the synagogue. After the arrival of his companions Silas and Timothy (and perhaps the brethren from Macedonia who brought with them financial aid, cf. Phil 4:10-20 and 2 Cor 11:9) he devoted more of his time to proclaiming the word of God. It was only after his rejection by the Jews that he went over to the house of Titius Justus, "worshiper of God," and more specifically addressed the Gentiles. Paul's visit meant the foundation of the Christian community in that city (cf. 1 Cor 3:6: "I planted, Apollos watered, but God gave the growth"; see also 2 Cor 10:14: ". . . even to you were we the first to come with the gospel of Christ"). Paul stayed in Corinth a year and six months, probably from the end of 49 to the middle of 51. From 1 Cor 1:26-29 ("Consider your own call, brothers and sisters: not many of you were wise by human standards, not many were powerful, not many were of noble birth . . .") we must conclude that most members of the community were poor, although some may have been rather wealthy and not without power. This church cannot have been that numerous—a total membership of two hundred has been suggested. The majority of Christians in Corinth were most probably of Gentile origin.

Possible evidence for one later visit to Corinth comes from Acts 20:1-3. Upon leaving Ephesus—after a long stay there during his third missionary journey—Paul set out for Macedonia and Greece, where he stayed for three months. While this passage does not mention Corinth by name it is almost certain that Paul would have paid a visit to the Corinthian community. This visit, however, is not his second but his third. Between the visits described in Acts 18 and suggested by Acts 20 there must have been an intervening visit, the fact of which has to be postulated in view of some data in 2 Corinthians. We can assume that Paul's first visit of eighteen months was a successful one in which the community grew in faith and strength. In 2 Cor 2:1 we find a reference to a "painful" visit (a past second one) and in 12:14 and 13:1-2 the announcement of a future "third" visit: "This (is) the third time (that) I am coming to you . . . I said to those who sinned before and to all the others, and now while absent I say, just as (I did) when present the second time, that when I come again I will not refrain . . ." (13:1-2).

2. *Paul's Corinthian Correspondence*

In the NT canon we have two letters to the Corinthians. There is, however, evidence that strongly suggests the existence of at least two other letters of Paul to this community. In 1 Cor 5:9 we read: "I wrote to you in my letter not to associate with sexually immoral persons." This must be a reference to a lost letter that Paul has written before our 1 Corinthians; that lost writing is now commonly called the "previous" letter. Second Corinthians 2:3-4, moreover, points to a "severe" or "painful, sorrowful" letter that can hardly be identified with 1 Corinthians: ". . . I have written to you out of much distress and anxiety of heart, with many tears. . . ." This last letter, then, falls between 1 and 2 Corinthians and must have been the third letter of Paul to the church at Corinth. While scholars more or less agree that the first letter is lost in its entirety, there is a still ongoing debate as to what became of the third letter, the so-called letter of tears. Some say—and probably rightly so—that it is totally lost as well, while others claim that it has been incorporated, either wholly or in part, into 2 Corinthians (e.g., chs. 10–13).

The three visits and the four letters (= A, B, C, D) fit into the following diagram, which we provide with dates. The dates, however, are unavoidably uncertain. Admittedly some may find them rather early.

First visit (49–51)
    (A) Previous letter (53)
    (B) 1 Corinthians (spring 54; cf. 16:8)

Second brief, painful visit (54)
    (C) Letter of tears (54)
    (D) 2 Corinthians (54)

Third visit (54–55).

3. *Christianity in Corinth*

Can we have an idea of the spiritual and moral situation of the Corinthians? First Corinthians is primarily devoted to emphasizing the unity in diversity that must prevail within the Christian community, yet the root of the problem is not factionalism as such. The manifold and quite different dangers the Christians face appear to find their common origin in the difficulty of living a truly Christian life in a Hellenistic pagan milieu. Paul seems to be concerned with the surfacing of a gnostic-like element in the community. With their wisdom speculations and enthusiasm some members were likely to claim a gross moral freedom or, quite the opposite, some practiced an exaggerated sexual asceticism. Furthermore, must the emotional spiritual manifestations during public worship not be linked to a still-persisting influence of pagan cults? Apart from that, dualistic Greek philosophy does not allow for a bodily resurrection. It is not easy to define whether some abuses affected the whole community and others only part of it and whether or how the various positions on issues pointed to later in 1 Corinthians are to be assigned to the specific factions mentioned in the first four chapters of 1 Corinthians.

Although Paul's arguments in dealing with the difficulties are mostly theological and christological, the problems in Corinth concern above all the ethical behavior of the Christians. Therefore 1 Corinthians should in the first place be read as a hortatory letter. Its style is mainly "deliberative," its concern future-directed. First Corinthians aims at behavioral changes in the life of the Christian community. Moreover, it would seem that in Corinth already at that early period the apostolic authority of Paul has been attacked; several passages of this letter possess an apologetic tone.

The mildly admonishing tone of 1 Corinthians is absent in 2 Corinthians, which is much more defensive and at times very passionate. The problem Paul faces in Corinth now is not only one of broken unity or, in the first place, that of the absence of appropriate moral conduct. Rather he is pleading for a reconciliation between the Corinthians and himself and he is defending himself; he is justifying his authority and ministry against attacks of opponents, clearly false apostles, intruders. They must have been active in Corinth after Paul's first and second visits. What, then, has occurred since the writing of 1 Corinthians?

4. *The Events Between 1 and 2 Corinthians*

During his first visit, when he founded the Corinthian church, Paul stayed a long time in Corinth (probably about eighteen months in 49–51 C.E.). In 1 Corinthians 16 he briefly discusses the collection (vv. 1-4), mentions among other things also the coming of Timothy to Corinth (vv. 10-11) and announces his future travels: "I will visit you after passing through Macedonia—for I intend to pass through Macedonia—and perhaps I will stay with you or even spend the winter. . . . But I will stay in Ephesus until Pentecost . . ." (vv. 5-9). Paul, however, did not carry out that plan. What was the reason for this? For what happened in Corinth after he left we have to rely on the minimal data present in 2 Corinthians.

Other missionaries arrived in the city; they did not respect the work of Paul. A certain person offended Paul and a situation arose that must have upset him so that he went back (by boat) to Corinth. This was presumably a short visit, the painful second visit. Back in Ephesus Paul writes his third (severe) letter, which may have been carried by Titus whom he sends to Corinth to complete the collection (see 2 Cor 8:6). Apparently that letter, as well as Titus' presence, had the desired effect. After his second visit Paul experienced great affliction in Asia: "we were utterly weighed down, beyond (our capability of) resistance, so that we despaired even of living" (1:8).

In the meantime Paul had altered his original travel plans: not through Macedonia to Corinth, but first back to Corinth, then to Macedonia and from there back to Corinth "in order that you might have a second grace (later)" (1:15), i.e., a second visit. The Corinthians would then send him on to Judea (1:16). Yet this altered route is not followed either. Paul leaves Ephesus but does not go to Corinth ("it was to spare you that I have not come to Corinth again" [1:23]). He has made up his mind not to make them another painful visit (2:1). He travels to Troas to meet Titus there on his return from Corinth. Titus, however, has not yet arrived and, although the preaching in Troas offers a positive prospect, Paul is deeply worried. So he says goodbye to Troas and goes on to Macedonia to meet Titus in that region (2:12-13).

Even after Paul arrives in Macedonia he does not have any rest. There are many troubles: disputes with others and fears in his heart. However, all this changes with the coming of Titus: God consoles Paul (7:5-6), for Titus brings good news. The person who offended Paul has been punished. The Corinthians are again ready to listen to Paul. Have they turned away from Paul's opponents? Have these intruders perhaps left Corinth? Paul now writes our second (in fact his fourth) letter to the Corinthians, presumably in the fall of 54. Possibly it was Titus again who brought that letter to Corinth (see 8:16-17).

5. *Paul's Opponents*

It is not completely evident who the opponents of Paul were. Our information about them is almost completely dependent on 2 Corinthians; Paul's remarks may be somewhat biased. Five concrete proposals have been put forward; none of them is generally accepted. (1) For a long time it has been suggested that the opponents are Judaizers, the same Jewish Christians Paul met in Galatia (cf., for example, 2 Cor 11:4-6 with Gal 1:6-9). Yet in 2 Corinthians there are no polemics against circumcision and the works of the Law, nor any mention of justification by faith. (2) A few interpreters still claim that the opponents are Jewish Christian Gnostics: their identity is pneumatic in the gnostic sense. This sounds rather anachronistic. The main features of Gnosticism are not known before the second century. It is not clear if or to what extent an early Gnosis has taken root in first-century Judaism (and Jewish Christianity). (3) A third hypothesis considers Paul's opponents to be Hellenistic Jewish Christians. More concretely they would have been itinerant missionaries who preach in Asia Minor and Greece. They are talented and eloquent personalities who take pride in their visions and miraculous power; as "divine men" they compare themselves with Moses, himself a divine man. Yet this attractive but bold depiction remains extremely hypothetical. (4) Some want to distinguish between "super-apostles" (11:5 and 12:11) and "false apostles" (11:13). The first term points to the Jerusalem apostles, the second to Paul's opponents in Corinth. The false apostles are early Christian missionaries who refer to the authority of Jerusalem and may have been sent by Jerusalem (or, for that matter, Antioch). They question Paul's legitimacy. Yet the initial distinction cannot be accepted and one rightly doubts that the stern opposition is the result of a conflict between

Paul and the Jerusalem authorities. (5) Recently it has been suggested that the tension between Paul and his Corinthian enemies must be seen in the Hellenistic social context. Paul's enemies are "hybrists," intruders as well as powerful Christian people who accuse Paul because, bound by his vision of Christ, he does not observe the social conventions of friendship, refuses financial help and ridicules commendation, and despises rhetorical standards, Greek wisdom, and miracles. Yet even if all this is true we must ask whether the opposition on the part of the Corinthians and the intruders is not motivated by deeper, more christological grounds.

It seems preferable simply to admit that Paul's portrait of his opponents remains vague. Let us listen to what Paul himself says. The most pertinent text is 2 Cor 11:22-23a: "Are they Hebrews? So am I. Are they Israelites? So am I. Are they descendants of Abraham? So am I. Are they servants of Christ?—I am talking as out of my mind—I am more." For Paul these people are decidedly Jewish Christians, even ministers of Christ. They should, however, be considered "false apostles" (11:13). They preach another Jesus, a different gospel from the one Paul preaches, a different Spirit (11:4-5). They are intruders coming from elsewhere (11:4). They accept support and are a burden to the community (11:7-12). They commend themselves and compare themselves with one another (10:11); they value letters of recommendation (3:1). They are well trained in speech and knowledge (11:6). Perhaps they also appeal to visions (5:13 and 12:1-4) and miracles (12:12).

The opponents were probably not very numerous. It is, we think, not completely impossible that there were connections between them and the Jerusalem authorities (see our discussion of 10:12-18), nor, as most scholars hold, is it absolutely certain that they are wholly different from Paul's opponents in Galatia, those who compelled the Gentile Christians to live like Jews (Gal 2:14; see our discussion of 2 Cor 10:4-6; cf. Gal 1:7-9). Yet since Paul himself does not pay much attention to the religious origin and historical provenance of his opponents, identifying them may remain impossible. One could even ask whether this is really necessary in order to understand Paul's main concern. Many Christians of Corinth must have taken sides with the intruders and detached themselves from Paul, at least during a certain period of time. Second Corinthians shows us a Paul who, above all, wants to win them back.

6. One Integral Letter?

The majority of exegetes today readily assume that Paul's second letter to the Corinthians consists, as a matter of fact, of several (fragmentary) letters. There are four main reasons that are brought forward for rejecting or questioning the integrity of 2 Corinthians.

1. When chs. 10–13 are read immediately after ch. 7 (or 9) one cannot but notice the suddenly much sharper, more vehement tone as well as the difference of content. Is it really conceivable, one asks, that Paul would speak so fiercely after the joy and jubilation attending the good news brought by Titus (ch. 7)? Therefore it is often proposed that chs. 10–13 are a reaction to a situation of opposition against Paul, not one of reconciliation with him. The Corinthians seem to have been taken in by the intruders. Some defenders of this view assume that these chapters are written before 2 Corinthians 1–9. Others, however, suppose that after the reconciliation mentioned in ch. 7 matters in Corinth went wrong again. They claim, therefore, that the four final chapters were composed not before but after 2 Corinthians 1–9, at a later critical juncture.

2. Both chs. 8 and 9 deal with the collection and each of them could have been written independently of the other. Furthermore, some repetitions in these chapters are pointed out as well as tensions. Were these chapters perhaps addressed to different people? Chapter 8 appears to be sent to the Corinthians, while ch. 9 could have been meant for the (other) churches in Achaia (see 9:2).

3. One cannot deny that in 2:14 Paul drops his narrative and begins a lengthy theological reflection, which is an apologetic excursus as well. The narrative thread is taken up again in 7:5. Some scholars are of the opinion that originally 7:5 followed immediately after 2:12-13: "When I came to Troas to preach the gospel of Christ, although a door had been opened in the Lord, I had no relief for my spirit because I did not find Titus my brother. So, having said farewell to them, I went to Macedonia." In 7:5 one reads: ". . . when we came to Macedonia, our flesh had no relief, but (we were) afflicted in every way, with strife outside, fears from within." Is the interruption of 2:14–7:4 not a later insertion?

4. A majority of commentators see 6:14–7:1 as a genuine, almost incontestable insertion, a really foreign body. They point out that 7:2 can easily be read and should be read after 6:13. A number of ideas, as well as the vocabulary, of this "fragment" seem to be un-Pauline. Was this so-called foreign fragment added later, or was it Paul who picked up this pre-existing text and integrated it into his letter?

In view of these four considerations some rather radical interpreters distinguish six (or even more) letters or fragments in 2 Corinthians: (1) the letter of reconciliation: 1:1–2:13 and 7:5-16; (2) the "apology": 2:14–7:4; (3) ch. 8 (the collection); (4) ch. 9 (again the collection); (5) the *Vierkapitelbrief* (four-chapter letter) or second apology: chs. 10–13; and (6) the "fragment" 6:14–7:1. Less radical interpreters usually admit the existence of two letters (except for 6:14–7:1): 2 Corinthians 1–9 and 10–13. There is no consensus regarding the sequence of letters or fragments.

Notwithstanding the majority view denying its integrity, other considerations rather suggest that 2 Corinthians is one letter. There is first of all the critical evaluation of the partition proposals. Let us return to 2:14–7:4 (cf. point 3). One should take note of the fact that some words and phrases of 7:5-16 also occur in 7:2-4. This may reveal that 7:5-16 was written soon after 7:2-4. In 7:5 Paul does not use the first person singular as he does in 2:12-13, but the first person plural: the difference may betray an interval between the writing of 2:12-13 and 7:5-16. Paul can hardly have written "our flesh had no relief" (7:5) immediately after "I had no relief for my spirit" (2:13). Moreover, readers familiar with Paul know that he more than once breaks off his narrative (or, for that matter, his argument) to come back to it later, with the consequence that *a b a'* structures are present in his writings, usually, however, with a middle part *(b)* that is shorter than is here the case: see, for example, the "insertion" of 1:19-22 and also the *a b a'* structure in 1 Corinthians 8–10 (*a:* ch. 8; *b:* ch. 9; *a':* 10:1–11:1) and in 12–14 (*a:* ch. 12; *b:* ch. 13; *a':* ch. 14). Analogous remarks, of course, not all equally peremptory, can be brought in against the other so-called arguments (see points 1, 2, and 4).

Three more general considerations should be added. First, nothing in the text tradition (no manuscript) betrays a lack of integrity. Second, those who assume a post-Pauline combination of originally independent parts are forced to work out hypotheses, not always very convincing, to explain the origin of 2 Corinthians as the text now lies before us. The defenders of the radically composite nature of the letter face an especially difficult problem here. Third, modern interpreters may be inclined to require from Paul too great a consistency. After all, we are dealing with a letter, not a systematic exposé. In addition, we do not know how much time—was it perhaps days?—the writing of this letter took nor are we certain that a possible change of mood in Paul or a rhetorical strategy on his part have to be excluded. No break in the narrative or argument, no change in the vocabulary or tone appears to be so great that the parts could not have stood originally, one next to the other, in a single letter.

7. A Structured Survey of the Letter

As with most of his other letters, Paul also begins his second letter to the Corinthians with a salutation and a (type of) thanksgiving (1:1-2 and

1:3-11) and closes it with some last exhortations, greetings, and a benediction (13:11-13). In 2 Corinthians five major parts, although unequal in size, can easily be distinguished: 1:12–2:13 (Paul's reliability); 2:14–7:4 (Paul's apostleship); 7:5-16 (the return of Titus); chs. 8–9 (the collection); and 10:1–13:10 (Paul's self-defense).

The first and third parts belong together: Paul narrates what has happened since he left Corinth; he defends the change in his travel plans; and he expresses his consolation as well as his joy because of the good news that Titus has brought from Corinth. The division of the long exposition in the second part can be presented as follows: 2:14–4:6 (apostolic ministry); 4:7–5:10 (apostolic suffering and hope); 5:11–6:10 (the ministry of reconciliation); 6:11–7:4 (apostolic appeal). The fourth part consists of chs. 8–9. The fifth part can be divided into seven pericopes: 10:1-11 (Paul's defense of his authority); 10:11-18 (wrong and right commendation); 11:1-15 (Paul, the Corinthians, and the super-apostles); 11:16-33 (Paul's foolish boasting); 12:1-10 (more boasting); 12:12-21 (self-defense and apostolic concern); 13:1-10 (stern announcement and injunction).

It has already been said that part one (1:1–2:13) and part three (7:5-16) belong together; the two parts constitute the so-called letter of reconciliation. Quite often 2:14–7:4 and chs. 10–13 are both termed a self-defense, Paul's first and second apologies. Paul's "foolish boasting" properly begins in 11:22 and continues through 12:10 (= the "Fool's Speech").

In his letters Paul often uses the first person plural. Five different uses of "we" occur. (1) "We" can refer to the whole of humanity. (2) By "we" Paul sometimes points to himself and all Christians. (3) It often happens that "we" refers to all apostles (the so-called "apostolic we"). (4) By "we" Paul can also indicate himself and his co-sender or co-workers. (5) Finally, in 2 Corinthians "we" very often means Paul alone; it is then the equivalent of "I" (sometimes called the "epistolary we"). Usually one knows from the context which "we" is employed; a few uses, however, resist an easy solution. Of course Paul also employs the first person singular (see, for example, 11:1–12:18); this, too, stresses the personal character of 2 Corinthians. Although no remark like that in 1 Cor 16:21 ("I, Paul, write this greeting with my own hand"; cf. Rom 16:22: "I Tertius, the writer of this letter, greet you in the Lord") is present in 2 Corinthians, the use of a secretary is not to be excluded.

A suggested schematic survey of the contents of 2 Corinthians follows:

1:1-2: Salutation of the Saints

1:3-11: Blessing God

I. Paul's Reliability (1:12–2:13)

II. Paul's Apostleship (2:14–7:4)

III. Titus' Return (7:5-16)

IV. The Collection (8:1–9:15)

V. Paul's Self-Defense (10:1–13:10)

13:11-13: Final Exhortation, Greetings, and Blessing

For this commentary the text of the letter is divided into twenty-one pericopes (passages that are more or less self-contained and not too long). For each passage a literal translation is offered first; then exegetical notes are given (Notes); finally a more global interpretation is presented (Interpretation). The interpretation usually contains four sections: (a) structure and line of thought, (b) characteristics and/or particular problems, (c) theological reflection, and (d) actualization and critical remarks.

8. *The Theological Significance of the Letter*

In 2 Corinthians there is a dearth of information about Paul's opponents and the identity of the wrongdoer. Moreover, the readers of the letter do not get a clear picture of the Corinthians' attitude toward Paul and their resistance to him. Yet what Paul is writing in 2 Corinthians contains much profound theology; its significance has enduring value and its applicability is universal.

Without doubt is it possible to detect in 2 Corinthians several polemical remarks; Paul attacks his opponents, often in an indirect way. But the letter is mainly *apologetic*. Paul defends himself before the Christians of Corinth and Achaia. This is not only the case in the two major apologies, parts 2 and 5 of the letter; self-defense is also present in parts 1 and 3. That self-defense leads Paul unavoidably to legitimate his ministry.

Various criteria are brought forward: the very existence of the Corinthian church (3:2), the openness of the apostle (5:12), his moral integrity (2:17; 4:2; 6:4), the presence of the signs of the apostle (i.e., miraculous deeds, 12:12), Paul's preaching free of charge (11:7-12 and 12:14-18), his strength in weakness (12:10), and the anticipatory manifestation in him of Christ's resurrection power (13:3-4). Although boasting is foolish, hardly useful (12:1), and always dangerous, in 2 Corinthians Paul himself is boasting; the opponents and the Corinthians force him to it (12:11). Paradoxically, however, he is boasting of the things that show his weakness (11:30). Precisely when he is weak, he is strong (12:10).

The purpose of Paul's apologetic writing is to win back the Christians of Corinth. He aims at a restoration of their mutual relationship; he wants to bring about a lasting *reconciliation*. On the day of the Lord the Corinthians should be proud of Paul as he hopes to be of them (1:14). Many of them now appear to be under the influence of the intruders. They no longer understand Paul: he changes his travel plans (1:23); he writes a severe letter (2:4); he refuses financial support. The Corinthians seem to compare Paul with his opponents (11:5). Paul lacks rhetorical skill (11:6); his speaking is of no account and his bodily presence lacks boldness (10:1-2 and 10). But Paul pleads and speaks to them as to his children: you are not restricted by me; you are restricted in your own affections; open wide your hearts to me; I have great confidence and pride in you (6:11-13; 7:2-4). The good news that Titus brought on his return from Corinth—news about their grief and their zeal for the apostle—filled Paul with joy and comfort (7:6-13). Paul loves the Corinthians; God knows he does (11:11). Of course a renewed relationship with Paul also means peace in the community (13:11) and, above all, reconciliation with God (5:20).

In 1:20 Paul, as if accidentally, explains that in Christ all the promises of God became reality. In 5:18-19 he writes that through Christ God reconciled the world to himself, and in 5:21 he explains that Christ, who knew no sin, was made a "sinner" by God so that in him all of us might become righteous. The Lord Jesus Christ, though he was rich, for our sake became poor so that through his poverty we might become rich (8:9). Christology is very prominent in Paul's mind. Yet in 2 Corinthians Paul above all reflects upon his *apostleship*. In 5:18-20 he emphasizes the fact that God gave and entrusted the ministry of reconciliation to him. As a servant he preaches Jesus Christ as Lord (4:5); as an aroma he spreads the knowledge of God's glory which is on the face of Christ (2:14-15 and 4:6); he preaches the gospel without cost. He can commend himself in every way (4:2 and 6:4). However, it is a ministry carried in clay vessels (4:7). That ministry is characterized by countless sufferings and trials (4:8-9; 6:4-10; 11:23-27), by sincerity in the sight of God and openness to everyone's conscience (4:2), as well as by an exemplary moral behavior (8:21).

This ministry is qualified by a continual care for the churches (11:28). At great length Paul insists that the Corinthians complete the collection for the poor of Jerusalem (chs. 8–9). They should forgive and comfort the sorrowful wrongdoer (2:5-11). He exhorts the Christians to cleanse themselves from every defilement since they are the temple of God (6:14–7:1). He urges them to test themselves (13:5). He writes this rather strict letter while he is away from them, so that at his third visit he may not have to be severe in his use of authority, for the Lord gave that apostolic authority to him for building up and not for tearing down (10:8 and 13:10). Paul himself in the first place makes it his aim to please the Lord; he knows that he, too, will appear before the judgment seat of Christ (5:9-10). He hopes that God will raise him and bring him, together with the Corinthians, into the presence of the Lord Jesus (4:14).

To be sure, Paul is an apostle of Christ by the will of God (1:1) and as such unique in his vocation. In a most particular way he carries in his body the dying of Jesus and the life of Jesus is manifested in his mortal flesh (4:10-11). He has been appointed as a minister, as it were, between Christ and the people; he is God's ambassador (5:18-20). Yet it would be wrong to radically separate Paul's union with Christ from that of other Church leaders, i.e., past and present missionaries or ministers and pastors. What is more, all Christians should consider him as their authoritative guide, a model of authentic spirituality, for in all honesty he himself goes so far as to invite all of us: "Be imitators of me, as I am of Christ" (1 Cor 11:1). All Christians, with unveiled faces, are beholding as in a mirror the glory of their Lord and, through the Spirit, are being transformed into the Christ-image, from glory to glory (2 Cor 3:18).

9. *General Bibliography*

Note: Publications listed here are cited throughout this commentary by the author's name and short title only. The same procedure is followed for the bibliography for each passage.

There are separate bibliographies for some major sections of the letter:

For 2 Cor 2:14–7:4 as a whole, see p. 48.

For chs. 8–9 as a whole, see p. 143.

For chs. 10–13 as a whole, see p. 162.

Commentaries

Allo, Ernest-Bernard. *Saint Paul: Seconde épître aux Corinthiens*. EtB. 2nd ed. Paris: Gabalda, 1956.

Barnett, Paul W. *The Second Epistle to the Corinthians*. NIC. Grand Rapids: Eerdmans, 1997.

Barrett, Charles Kingsley. *A Commentary on the Second Epistle to the Corinthians.* BNTC. New York: Harper, 1973.

Belleville, Linda A. *2 Corinthians.* IVP. Downers Grove, Ill.: InterVarsity, 1996.

Bruce, Frederick F. *1 and 2 Corinthians.* NCeB. Grand Rapids: Eerdmans, 1971.

Bultmann, Rudolf. *The Second Letter to the Corinthians.* Translated by Roy A. Harrisville. Minneapolis: Augsburg, 1985.

Carrez, Maurice. *La deuxième épître aux Corinthiens.* CNT(N) Geneva: Labor et Fides, 1986.

Danker, Frederick W. *II Corinthians.* Augsburg Commentary NT. Minneapolis: Augsburg, 1989.

Fallon, Francis T. *2 Corinthians.* NTMes. Wilmington, Del.: Michael Glazier, 1980.

Furnish, Victor Paul. *II Corinthians.* AB 32A. Garden City, N.Y.: Doubleday, 1984.

Getty, Mary Ann. *First Corinthians. Second Corinthians.* CBC. Collegeville: The Liturgical Press, 1983.

Héring, Jean. *The Second Epistle of Saint Paul to the Corinthians.* Translated by A. W. Heathcote and P. J. Allcock. London: Epworth, 1967.

Hughes, Philip E. *Paul's Second Epistle to the Corinthians.* NIC. 8th ed. Grand Rapids: Eerdmans, 1980.

Klauck, Hans-Josef. *2. Korintherbrief.* Neue Echter Bibel. Würzburg: Echter Verlag, 1986.

Lietzmann, Hans. *An die Korinther II.* Edited by Werner Georg Kümmel. HNT. 5th ed. Tübingen: Mohr-Siebeck, 1969.

Martin, Ralph P. *2 Corinthians.* WBC. Waco: Word Books, 1986.

Metzger, Bruce M. *A Textual Commentary on the Greek New Testament. A Companion Volume to the United Bible Societies' Greek New Testament.* 2d ed. Stuttgart: German Bible Society, 1994.

Plummer, Alfred. *A Critical and Exegetical Commentary on the Second Epistle of St Paul the Apostle to the Corinthians.* ICC. Edinburgh: T & T Clark, 1915.

Prümm, Karl. *Diakonia Pneumatos. Der zweite Korintherbrief als Zugang zur apostolischen Botschaft. Auslegung und Theologie.* Vol. I: *Theologische Auslegung des zweiten Korintherbriefes.* Rome, Freiburg, and Vienna: Herder, 1967.

Thrall, Margaret E. *The Second Epistle to the Corinthians.* Vol. I (chs. 1–7). ICC. Edinburgh: T & T Clark, 1994.

Windisch, Hans. *Der zweite Korintherbrief.* Edited by Georg Strecker. KEK. 9th ed. Göttingen: Vandenhoeck & Ruprecht, 1970.

Witherington, Ben III. *Community and Conflict in Corinth: A Socio-Rhetorical Commentary on 1 and 2 Corinthians.* Grand Rapids: Eerdmans, 1995.

Wolff, Christian. *Der zweite Brief des Paulus an die Korinther.* ThHKNT. Berlin: Evangelische Verlagsanstalt, 1989.

Studies

Aejmelaeus, Lars. *Streit und Versöhnung: Das Problem der Zusammensetzung des 2. Korintherbriefes.* Schriften der Finnischen Gesellschaft 46. Helsinki: Kirjapaino Raamattulo, 1987.

Aletti, Jean-Noel. "Paul et la rhétorique" in Jacques Schlosser, ed., *Paul de Tarse.* LeDiv 165. Paris: Cerf, 1996, 27–50.

Bieringer, Reimund, ed. *The Corinthian Correspondence.* BEThL 125. Leuven: Leuven University Press/Peeters, 1996.

Bieringer, Reimund, and Jan Lambrecht. *Studies on 2 Corinthians.* BEThL 102. Leuven: Leuven University Press/Peeters, 1994. See especially the first study with a virtually exhaustive bibliography (pp. 3–66) and the following four studies with regard to introductory questions (pp. 67–221), all by Bieringer.

Bornkamm, Günther. "The History of the Origin of the So-Called Second Letter to the Corinthians," *NTS* 8 (1961–1962) 258–264.

Carrez, Maurice. "Le 'nous' en 2 Corinthiens. Paul parle-t-il au nom de toute la communauté, du groupe apostolique, de l'équipe ministérielle ou en son nom personnel? Contribution à l'étude de l'apostolicité dans 2 Corinthiens," *NTS* 26 (1979–1980) 474–486.

Classen, Carl J. "St. Paul's Epistles and Ancient Greek and Roman Rhetoric" in Stanley E. Porter and Thomas H. Olbricht, eds., *Rhetoric and the New Testament.* JSNT.S 90. Sheffield: Sheffield Academic Press, 1993, 265–291.

Crafton, Jeffrey A. *The Agency of the Apostle: A Dramatic Analysis of Paul's Responses to Conflict in 2 Corinthians.* JSNT.S 51. Sheffield: Sheffield Academic Press, 1991.

Fee, Gordon D. *God's Empowering Presence. The Holy Spirit in the Letters of Paul.* Peabody, Mass.: Hendrickson, 1994, 282–366.

Georgi, Dieter. *The Opponents of Paul in Second Corinthians.* Philadelphia: Fortress, 1986.

Harvey, Anthony E. *Renewal through Suffering. A Study of 2 Corinthians.* Edinburgh: T & T Clark, 1996.

Malherbe, Abraham J. *Ancient Epistolary Theorists.* SBL.SBS 19. Atlanta: Scholars, 1988.

Marshall, Peter. *Enmity in Corinth: Social Conventions in Paul's Relation with the Corinthians.* WUNT II/23. Tübingen: Mohr-Siebeck, 1987.

Murphy-O'Connor, Jerome. *Paul: A Critical Life.* Oxford: Clarendon, 1996.

_____. *Paul the Letter-Writer: His World, His Options, His Skills.* GNS 41. Collegeville: The Liturgical Press, 1995.

_____. *St Paul's Corinth. Texts and Archaeology.* Expanded ed. GNS 6. Collegeville: The Liturgical Press, 1992.

_____. *The Theology of the Second Letter to the Corinthians.* NT Theology. Cambridge: Cambridge University Press, 1991.

Pickett, Raymond. *The Cross in Corinth: The Social Significance of the Death of Jesus.* JSNT.S 143. Sheffield: Sheffield Academic Press, 1997.

Reed, J. T. "Using Rhetorical Categories to Interpret Paul's Letters: A Question of Genre" in Stanley E. Porter and Thomas H. Olbricht, eds., *Rhetoric and the New Testament.* JSNT.S 90. Sheffield: Sheffield Academic Press, 1993, 292–324.

Savage, Timothy B. *Power Through Weakness: Paul's Understanding of the Christian Ministry in 2 Corinthians.* MSSNTS 86. Cambridge: Cambridge University Press, 1996.

Sumney, Jerry L. *Identifying Paul's Opponents: The Question of Method in 2 Corinthians.* JSNT.S 40. Sheffield: Sheffield Academic Press, 1990.

Theissen, Gerd. *The Social Setting of Pauline Christianity: Essays on Corinth.* Translated by J. H. Schütz. Philadelphia: Fortress, 1982.

Vanhoye, Albert, ed. *L'apôtre Paul. Personnalité, style et conception du ministère.* BEThL 73. Leuven: Leuven University Press/Peeters, 1986.

Welborn, L. L. "Like Broken Pieces of a Ring: 2 Cor 1.2-2.13; 7.5-16 and Ancient Theories of Literary Unity," *NTS* 42 (1996) 559–583.

Young, Frances, and David F. Ford. *Meaning and Truth in 2 Corinthians.* Biblical Foundation in Theology. London: S.P.C.K., 1987.

TRANSLATION, NOTES, INTERPRETATION

1. *Greeting the Saints and Blessing God* (1:1-2 and 1:3-11)

1. Paul, apostle of Christ Jesus by the will of God, and Timothy, our brother, to the church of God that is at Corinth, with all the saints who are in the whole of Achaia: 2. Grace to you and peace from God our Father and the Lord Jesus Christ.

3. Blessed (be) the God and Father of our Lord Jesus Christ, the Father of mercies and God of all consolation, 4. who consoles us in all our distress in order that we may be able to console those who are in any distress through the consolation with which we ourselves are consoled by God. 5. For as the sufferings of Christ are beyond measure in us, so through Christ our consolation, too, is beyond measure. 6. If we are in distress, (it is) for your consolation and salvation; if we are consoled, (it is also) for your consolation which is actively present in (your) endurance of the same sufferings that we too suffer. 7. And our hope for you is firm because we know that, just as you share in the sufferings, so (you will share) in the consolation as well.

8. For we do not want you to be unaware, brothers and sisters, of our distress that came about in Asia, that is, we were utterly weighed down, beyond (our capability of) resistance, so that we despaired even of living. 9. Yes, within ourselves we had received the sentence of death, in order that we should not be relying on ourselves but on God who raises the dead; 10. (he) who has rescued us out of so great a (danger of) death will (again) rescue (us); on him we have fixed our hope that he will still rescue (us), 11. while you, too, are cooperating by your prayer for us, in order that by many persons (God) may be thanked on our behalf for the gift granted us through (the prayerful help of) many.

NOTES

1. *Paul, apostle of Christ Jesus by the will of God, and Timothy, our brother:* Paul mentions himself and Timothy as senders of the letter. However, one is allowed to

suppose that Paul alone wrote or dictated this letter, with Timothy's approval, of course. Paul is the apostle of "Christ Jesus." It would seem that he puts Christ, not Jesus, first for reasons of emphasis (otherwise in v. 2). Moreover, the titular meaning "Messiah" may be present. Paul is convinced that his apostleship is intended by God, that it originates in God (cf. the encounter with the risen Christ). Paul's co-worker Timothy, co-sender of the letter, is not an apostle in this strict sense. Timothy is called here *ho adelphos* (literally: "the brother"), i.e., the well-known brother of Paul but also of the Christians in Corinth and the whole of Achaia: our common Christian brother. He must have been a familiar figure there indeed. Together with Silvanus, Timothy was present in Corinth during the first proclamation of the gospel (see v. 19: with Paul they were preaching); later he was sent by Paul to Corinth, probably from Ephesus (see 1 Cor 4:17).

to the church of God that is at Corinth, with all the saints who are in the whole of Achaia: The addressees are the Christians of the local church at Corinth and, in addition, "all the saints who are in the whole of Achaia." God is mentioned again in v. 1b: the church "of God." Corinth is the capital of the Roman province of Achaia. Most probably Paul preached the gospel not only in the city itself but also (at times) in its surroundings. When in this commentary the Christians of Corinth are referred to, those of Achaia should be included. Yet the emphasis on "the whole of Achaia" remains somewhat unexpected (but see 9:2).

As elsewhere in Paul's letters, the Christians are called "saints," a qualification that was first applied to the Christians of Jerusalem (cf. 1 Cor 16:1; 2 Cor 8:4; 9:1, 12). The term itself here does not say anything about the quality of their moral life, although by vocation they should, of course, live morally, in a saintly manner.

2. *Grace to you and peace from God our Father and the Lord Jesus Christ:* The salutation "grace and peace" is typically Pauline (and Christian); it is no longer an ordinary Greek salutation (*chairein,* "to rejoice") nor, for that matter, the common Jewish greeting ("peace"). God is the Father of all Christians; Jesus Christ is their Lord. God and Christ stand together, Christ alongside God. There is but one preposition: "from." Paul hopes that God the Father and the Lord Jesus Christ will realize the wishes that the salutation expresses: the gift ("grace") and its result ("peace").

3. *Blessed (be) the God and Father of our Lord Jesus Christ, the Father of mercies and God of all consolation:* According to v. 2 God is our Father; here he is called "the God and Father" of Jesus Christ (cf. 11:31). This God and Father must be blessed. There is no verb in the Greek, but with "blessed" at the beginning "be" should probably be added mentally. Paul probably utters a prayer expressing a wish. An apposition, introduced by a second "Father," follows; it constitutes the start of a long qualification and thus prepares the ensuing motivation of the blessing: "the Father of mercies and God of all consolation." The chiasm in v. 3 strikes the reader: God-Father and Father-God (*a b b a*). The "Father of our Lord Jesus Christ" is the "Father of mercies"; the "God of our Lord Jesus Christ" is "the God of mercies and God of all consolation." "Consolation" (singular) appears to be one aspect of "mercies" (plural).

"Consolation" translates *paraklēsis*. This noun and its cognate verb *(parakaleō)* can signify consolation, comfort, encouragement, but also exhortation or admonition. It is by no means accidental that Paul uses this terminology no less than ten times in vv. 3-7. By employing the same noun and verb in English— in addition to the distinction of singular–plural (noun) and that of active– passive (verb)—our translation tries to preserve the intended monotony and emphasis.

4. *who consoles us in all our distress in order that we may be able to console those who are in any distress:* Paul says that God consoles him ("us"; Timothy may be included, but see vv. 8-11) over and again (with the present participle in Greek) in all his distress or affliction *(en pasē tē thlipsei).* God's action, however, is not without aim. It enables Paul to console those who are "in any distress" *(en pasē thlipsei,* no article). Distress is caused by difficulties and tribulations which Paul encounters. In vv. 5-7 a more or less equivalent term is used: *pathēmata* ("sufferings").

    through the consolation with which we ourselves are consoled by God: Paul can console them with the very consolation with which he himself is consoled by God. The comfort comes from God and reaches the apostle; it then goes from the apostle to those Christians who in their distress are in need of it.

5. *For as the sufferings of Christ are beyond measure in us, so through Christ our consolation, too, is beyond measure:* In v. 4 Christ is not mentioned; in v. 5 he is, again (see v. 3). There is a comparison between sufferings and consolation: *kathōs . . . houtōs* ("just as . . . so also"). Just as Paul has an overflowing share in Christ's sufferings *(ta pathēmata),* so also through Christ he has an overflowing share in the consolation. Paul twice employs the verb *perisseuō* (literally: "to exceed the measure") in v. 5a and v. 5b, but the symmetry of the two clauses is not complete (see "of Christ–through Christ" and "in us–our"). In this verse Paul refers to himself alone (with Timothy), not to the other Christians. He wants to indicate that he has, as it were, access to consolation, even of exceedingly great consolation. The verse is introduced by "for"; it grounds Paul's bold claim in v. 4. In v. 5a Paul spontaneously, as it were, reveals how he experiences his sufferings: they are those of Christ. His conformation to Christ enables the suffering he endures to become a participation in Christ's suffering. Such is Paul's profound conviction.

6. *If we are in distress, (it is) for your consolation and salvation; if we are consoled, (it is also) for your consolation:* The second person plural in this verse refers to the consolation and salvation of the Corinthians and to their endurance of sufferings. With regard to himself Paul distinguishes two possibilities: "if we are in distress," and "if we are consoled." What follows after the two clauses is no longer antithetical or symmetrical. Twice we have: "(it is) for your consolation." The first time, after "if we are in distress," this is rather surprising. Moreover, Paul adds the eschatological dimension by expanding and writing "and (for your) salvation."

    which is actively present in (your) endurance of the same sufferings that we too suffer: This second time, after "if we are consoled, (it is) for your consolation,"

Paul explains what that consolation "effectuates" (*energoumai,* middle with active sense). Their consolation is actively present; it shows its "energy" in their endurance of the same sufferings (*pathēmata,* cf. v. 5) that Paul also endures. The same verb is used in Gal 5:6 in the famous expression *pistis di' agapēs energoumenē,* "faith working through love." Both the suffering and the consolation of Paul are thoroughly apostolic. *Paraklēsis* in v. 6 may perhaps contain the nuance of "encouragement." The variant readings that present a shorter text of vv. 6-7 are most probably secondary.

7. *And our hope for you is firm because we know that, just as you share in the sufferings, so (you will share) in the consolation as well:* Paul further develops the idea of their sharing in sufferings and consolation. He now looks to the future. His hope regarding the Corinthians is never shaken for he knows that they will share in the consolation. Again there is a comparison *(hōs . . . houtōs):* "just as" you have a share in the sufferings, "so" will you have a share in the consolation "as well." In v. 7b one must supply the same adjective *(koinōnos,* "participant, sharing") and the same verb "to be," but in the future tense, as in v. 7a. Perhaps Paul is referring to the end time.

8. *For we do not want you to be unaware, brothers and sisters, of our distress that came about in Asia, that is, we were utterly weighed down, beyond (our capability of) resistance, so that we despaired even of living:* What Paul writes in vv. 8-11 is connected with the preceding verses by an explicative *gar* ("for"). It is the first time that he uses the vocative "brothers and sisters"; this vocative reappears on only two other occasions: the introduction to the collection (8:1) and the final exhortation (13:11). (The expansion "and sisters" better conveys in today's English Paul's intention of addressing the Corinthian community as a whole.) By means of a stereotyped introductory formula ("we do not want you to be unaware") Paul refers to a specific misfortune in Asia. Its "weight" was extremely heavy: cf. the verb *bareō* ("to weigh down") as well as the expressions "utterly" and "beyond power of resistance," and also the mention of the consequence (Paul despaired even of his life). In the Greek v. 8 is one long sentence: first the main clause, then an explicatory clause (with *hoti,* "that is") and finally a consequential clause (with *hōste,* "so that"). Notwithstanding the general indication of the place of this misfortune and the emphasis on its magnitude, it is no longer possible for us to know what Paul is referring to, exactly what happened to him, and precisely where and when it happened. It probably occurred not long before the writing of the letter. Most frequently reference is made by commentators either to 1 Cor 15:32 (Paul fought, as it were, with wild beasts at Ephesus) or Acts 19:23–40 (the narrative about the riot at Ephesus). Yet uncertainty remains. We may also refer to 2 Cor 4:9-10: "persecuted, but not abandoned; struck down, but not destroyed; always carrying the dying of Jesus in the body in order that the life of Jesus be manifested in our body."

9. *Yes, within ourselves we had received the sentence of death, in order that we should not be relying on ourselves but on God who raises the dead:* The sense of *alla* is here most likely reinforcing: "yes" or "indeed." Paul now informs the reader to what insight that dangerous tribulation has led him. The style is dense. The

translation of *to apokrima tou thanatou* by "the sentence of death" may suggest a forensic connotation that, however, is not certain. Where does the *apokrima* (literally: "answer") come from?

It would seem that Paul's reasoning can be paraphrased as follows: "Yes, my impression—the answer to my question—was that a certain death awaited me; this brought me to the insight that through that danger of death God wanted me to rely, not on myself, but only on the God who raises the dead." Paul thus detects a divine intention behind the event (in the Greek we read a *hina*, "in order that"). What is then his inner conviction? Again we must paraphrase: if God can raise the dead, God can also deliver me in this life from such a deadly peril as I encountered: see v. 10. For further evidence of Paul's acquaintance with the Jewish belief in God "who raises the dead" compare Rom 4:17. Of course Paul also has in mind the resurrection of Jesus.

10. *(he) who has rescued us out of so great a (danger of) death will (again) rescue (us); on him we have fixed our hope that he will still rescue (us):* God has delivered him from "so great a death." This brought Paul to the faith certainty that in the future God will likewise deliver him. He writes "he will rescue" twice, without, it would seem, giving that phrase a strictly eschatological meaning. Grammatically vv. 9-11 are probably one long sentence. In v. 10 we have two relative clauses: "(God), who has rescued us and will rescue us" and "(God), on whom we have fixed our hope that he will still rescue us." It should be noted that there are several, admittedly less important, variant readings.

11. *while you, too, are cooperating by your prayer for us, in order that by many persons (God) may be thanked on our behalf for the gift granted us through (the prayerful help of) many:* In vv. 8-10 Paul tells the Corinthians what happened to him (life-threatening distress and divine liberation) and also expresses his own firm hope in case of future incidents. In v. 11 his attention goes back to the Corinthians. "While you are cooperating" (cf. Rom 15:30) translates a Greek genitive absolute; it could have a causal nuance ("because"). Paul probably means cooperating with himself, not working together, i.e., cooperating with the prayers of one another in Corinth.

The request for prayer is awkwardly worded. What must be prayed for consists of a lengthy *hina* clause ("in order that"). The whole verse is overloaded and also somewhat repetitious; this, too, may mark the end of a paragraph. "The gift granted" is the translation of *charisma* ("a grace given"). "Through (the prayerful help) of many" is but one possible paraphrase of *dia pollōn*; moreover, its grammatical function is far from certain: does it go with *charisma* or with "may be thanked" (repeating then "by many persons")? It should not go unnoticed that, here at the end of the blessing, Christians are invited to thank God for Paul, while Paul more often thanks God for his Christians.

INTERPRETATION

a. *Structure and Line of Thought.* In 2 Corinthians there is after the epistolary prescript in 1:1-2 no thanksgiving in the strict sense. God has to be blessed for the consolation granted to Paul (v. 3: "Blessed be God . . ."). There is, however, no major difference between thanksgiving and blessing. One may perhaps suggest that in the first Paul thanks God for what God has done in the Church, while in the second Paul blesses and praises God for the gifts he personally experienced. This distinction, however, is not very convincing. Verses 3-7 deal with consolation in general; in vv. 8-11 Paul refers to a specific misfortune, a deadly peril out of which he has been rescued.

It is not clear where the blessing ends. Perhaps Paul did not want a formal ending: see the continuation in v. 8, as well as in v. 12, twice with *gar* ("for"). Or must we after all limit the blessing to vv. 3-7? This could be defended since in vv. 8-11, just as in 1:12–2:13, Paul deals with what took place after his departure from Corinth and in v. 8, for the first time in this letter, he writes "brothers and sisters," which could point to a new beginning. Moreover, v. 8 begins with a full disclosure formula that could be taken as signaling the opening of the letter-body. However, the arguments against this view seem to be stronger. By means of his mention of the specific danger in vv. 8-11 Paul concretizes the general considerations of vv. 3-7. In addition, in vv. 8-11 Paul still narrates what happened to him alone; from v. 12 onward he will discuss matters in connection with the Corinthians. Finally, the solemn "full" v. 11 appears to round off the passage, and the theme there present of "thanking" corresponds quite nicely with that of "blessing" in v. 3 (a sort of inclusion). All this invites us to see vv. 3-11 as a more or less consistent, self-contained pericope. It has to be conceded, however, that in vv. 12-14 "the day of our Lord Jesus" is spoken of (v. 14; cf. 1 Cor 1:8: end of the thanksgiving). Does this mention of the parousia perhaps indicate that vv. 12-14 still belong to the introductory blessing? It is well known that in the Pauline thanksgivings a reference to the (eschatological) future comes toward the end, as an appropriate conclusion.

b. *Characteristics and Problems.* The salutation proper in v. 2 is identical with that of the first letter (1 Cor 1:3). The indication of both authors and addressees differs. A brief comparison is worthwhile. In 1 Corinthians we read: "Paul, called by the will God (to be) an apostle of Christ, and Sosthenes our brother, to the church of God which is at Corinth, (to) those who are sanctified in Christ Jesus, called (to be) saints, with all those who in every place call on the name of our Lord Jesus Christ, their (Lord) and our (Lord)" (1:1-2). The co-author in 1 Corinthians, Sosthenes, is, just as in 2 Corinthians, (literally) "the brother." Paul sees himself as "called by the will of God (to be) an apostle of Christ Jesus" (compare "an apostle of Christ Jesus by the will of God" in 2 Cor 1:1). "Called" stresses God's initiative even more. Paul addresses his first letter equally in the first place to "the church of God at Corinth," yet in 1 Corinthians Paul emphasizes the vocation of Christians also: "called (to be) saints." However, the idea of a vocation "to be" should not divert the attention from what has already taken place: the Christians "are sanctified in Christ Jesus." The addressees are not only the Corinthians but also, differently from 2 Corinthians ("all the saints in the whole of Achaia"), rather surprisingly "all those who in every place call on the name of our Lord Jesus Christ, their (Lord) and our (Lord)." The formulation of this last clause is somewhat laborious and stresses universality. One cannot avoid the impression that Paul, in his second letter, does not want to repeat that all-encompassing address of the first.

It may be that in vv. 3-11 Paul deliberately christianizes (already existing?) synagogue benedictions, especially elements from the first benediction (e.g., "blessed are you, Lord our God and God of our fathers") and from the second ("blessed are you, Lord, who makes the dead alive").

c. *Theological Reflection.* In the notes we pointed to the frequent use of consolation vocabulary in vv. 3-7. One should assume influence from Isaiah (especially Deutero-Isaiah) and the psalms of confidence (see, e.g., Pss 23, 71, 86, and 74). Different words indicating distress or suffering also occur in these verses, and this applies, with a variation of theme, to vv. 8-11 as well. In these last verses Paul stresses deliverance instead of consolation. Consolation *in* distress becomes deliverance *out of* (danger of) death. Because of its vocabulary this entire pericope, especially its first half, possesses an intended monotony; consolation is its *cantus firmus* (Hofius, "'Der Gott allen Trostes'").

At the beginning of his letter Paul blesses God who consoles him in all his troubles. He is convinced that his suffering means a share in the suffering of Christ and that the consolation is granted him through Christ. It would seem that such a blessing contains a scarcely hidden appeal to the addressees: they too should bless God for all that Paul experienced.

The Christians suffer the same suffering as Paul. They must endure it; they, too, will be consoled. Paul understands what happened to him in a thoroughly apostolic way. He accepts his suffering as well as his consolation in view of their efficacy for other Christians. The deadly peril in which he found himself in Asia taught him to put his hope in God alone, for God, who raises the dead, rescued him out of that danger; this God will rescue again in the future. Does Paul, in the mention of this insight, not implicitly invite his readers to participate in such a conviction?

The Corinthian Christians should help Paul with their prayer for him. Divine preservation and deliverance are closely tied to the intercession on his behalf. The ultimate aim of that request is that God be thanked by as many persons as possible for the saving protection of Paul. In the psalms, too, the person who has experienced God's salvation (often deliverance from death) invites the others to join in blessing God and in the thanksgiving.

God and Paul are the main figures in vv. 3-11. Yet through asking the Corinthians' help Paul also stresses the reciprocity, the partnership and, therefore, their reconciliation with him.

At the end of our interpretation some uncertainties remain. It could be that in vv. 3-4 Paul is not expressing a wish but simply stating, by way of prayer, that God "is" blessed. Moreover, one may rightly hesitate to call the whole of 1:3-11 a "blessing." In vv. 4-11 Paul almost neglects that theme; all his attention is given to consolation in distress and to deliverance out of his deadly peril. Finally, it could be asked whether the consistent translation of *parakaleō* vocabulary in vv. 3-7 by "to console" is after all not too weak. Must the idea of "comfort" not be made explicit?

d. *Critical Remarks and Actualization.* In listening to this pericope today's Christians may experience two difficulties. Many may opine that Paul too easily ascribes his deliverance to God who will raise the dead at the last day. Nowadays it is rightly asked whether God enters history and works rescue from death in such a this-worldly manner.

The second and even more difficult point is Paul's manner of dealing with suffering. It is true that, for Paul also, not distress, not suffering, but consolation is the ideal condition, and salvation the final destiny of all. Yet one could fear that, with his emphasis on suffering in this pericope, Paul runs the risk of somewhat exalting suffering as such. Perhaps more than in the past Christians realize that, besides the inevitable suffering, there is in this world much misery and pain that should be avoided and be removed as much possible: hatred, disease, hunger, war.

Notwithstanding these justifiably critical remarks, Christians should continue to admire Paul's obvious union with Christ, his prayerful benediction of God and his conviction of the apostolic fruitfulness of his sufferings. In 1:3-11 Paul is most probably thinking of those sufferings that are caused by being a Christian and an apostle. Yet what about the following generalization? Can today's Christians, in imitation of Christ and Paul, make all their sufferings, senseless in themselves and so varied in origin, meaningful as well as apostolically "productive"?

We rightly long for divine (and human, cf. 7:5-7) consolation. When consolation is granted to us we should console and comfort others and thank God. When Paul is implicitly exhorting his original Corinthian readers, he exhorts all of us as well. In the same manner he also invites all of us to believe and trust in God who raises the dead.

FOR REFERENCE AND FURTHER STUDY

Belleville, Linda L. "A Letter of Apologetic Self-Commendation: 2 Cor. 1:8–7:16," *NT* 31 (1989) 142–163.

Bjerkelund, Carl J. *Parakalō. Form, Funktion und Sinn der parakalō-Sätze in den paulinischen Briefen.* Bibliotheca theologica Norvegica 1. Oslo: Universitäts- forlaget, 1967, 141–155.

Hemer, Colin J. "A Note on 2 Corinthians 1:9," *TynB* 23 (1972) 103–107.

Hofius, Otfried. "'Der Gott allen Trostes'. *Paraklēsis* und *parakalein* in 2 Kor 1,3-7," in idem, *Paulusstudien.* WUNT 51. Tübingen: Mohr-Siebeck, 1989, 244–254.

Hughes, Frank W. "The Rhetoric of Reconciliation. 2 Corinthians 1.1–2.13 and 7.5–8.24," in Duane F. Watson, ed., *Persuasive Artistry. Studies in New Testa- ment Rhetoric* (FS G. A. Kennedy). JSNT.S 50. Sheffield: Sheffield Academic Press, 1991, 246–261.

Murphy-O'Connor, Jerome. "Co-Authorship in the Corinthian Correspondence," *RB* 100 (1993) 562–579.

O'Brien, Peter T. *Introductory Thanksgivings in the Letters of Paul.* NT.S 49. Leiden: Brill, 1977, 233–258.

Wiles, Gordon P. *Paul's Intercessory Prayers. The Significance of the Intercessory Prayer Passages in the Letters of Paul.* MSSNTS 24. Cambridge: Cambridge University Press, 1974, 226–229 and 271–276.

I. PAUL'S RELIABILITY (1:12–2:13)

2. *Paul's Reliability* (1:12–2:13)

12. For our (reason for) boasting is this: the testimony of our conscience, that we have behaved ourselves in this world, and above all toward you, in simplicity and godly sincerity, not by fleshly wisdom but by the grace of God. 13. For we write to you nothing other than what you read and (can) understand as well. But I hope that you will understand fully 14.— as you have understood us in part—that we are your boast as you, too, (are) ours on the day of our Lord Jesus.

15. With that confidence (in mind), I wanted to come to you first—in order that you might have a second grace (later)—16. and pass through you to Macedonia and from Macedonia come again to you and (then) be sent on my way to Judea by you. 17. So, in planning this, was I acting with that (so-called) levity? Or what I decide, do I decide (it) according to the flesh so that there is with me that "yes, yes" and (at the same time)

that "no, no"? 18. God is reliable: our word to you is not "yes" and (at
the same time) "no." 19. For the Son of God, Jesus Christ, proclaimed
among you by us, (i.e.,) by me, Silvanus, and Timothy, did not become
"yes" and "no," but in him "yes" has become (and remains). 20. For
whatever promises of God (exist), in him (came) (their) "yes"; therefore,
through him, too, the "amen" (goes) to God for his glory, through us. 21.
(The one) who establishes us with you in Christ and has anointed us is
God, 22. who has also sealed us and given the first installment in our
hearts, the Spirit.

23. I call upon God as witness—my life for it—that it was to spare
you that I have not come to Corinth again. 24. Not that we (want to)
domineer over your faith, but as companions we work for your joy. For
you stand firm in the faith. 2:1. For I made up my mind not to come to
you again in sorrow. 2. For if I sadden you, who then (will be) the one
who makes me glad, except the one who is saddened by me? 3. I have
written this very (letter) in order that, when I come, I might not receive
sorrow from those who should have made me rejoice, since (I was) confident in you all that my joy is (that) of all of you. 4. For I have written
to you out of much distress and anxiety of heart, with many tears, not in
order that you be saddened, but in order that you may know the love
that I have for you beyond measure. 5. But if any one has caused sadness, he did not sadden me, but to some degree—not to exaggerate—all
of you. 6. The punishment by the majority (imposed) on that person is
enough, 7. so that instead you should rather forgive and console (him),
lest that person perhaps be overwhelmed by excessive sorrow. 8. Therefore, I beg you to confirm your love for him. 9. For the reason why I have
written to you (was) to test you and to know whether you are obedient
in everything. 10. The one whom you forgive I, too, (forgive). For indeed, what I have forgiven—if I have forgiven anything—I (have done
it) for your sake in the presence of Christ, 11. lest we be cheated by Satan;
for we are not unaware of his schemes.

12. When I came to Troas to preach the gospel of Christ, although a
door had been opened in the Lord, 13. I had no relief for my spirit because I did not find Titus my brother. So, having said farewell to them, I
went to Macedonia.

Notes

12. *For our (reason for) boasting is this: the testimony of our conscience, that we have
behaved ourselves in this world, and above all toward you, in simplicity and godly
sincerity, not by fleshly wisdom but by the grace of God:* Possibly the correct reading is not "simplicity" *(haplotēti)* but "holiness" *(hagiotēti,* as, e.g., in the
manuscripts 𝔓⁴⁶ and B). The first "of God," which qualifies both "simplicity"
(or "holiness") and "sincerity," may be a so-called Hebrew genitive, more or
less the equivalent of an adjective: Paul's conscience witnesses that he con-
ducted his life in "divine" simplicity (holiness) and sincerity, not in "fleshly"

wisdom but in (i.e., by, through) the grace of God. This testimony is his pride, the reason for his boasting *(kauchēsis,* the act of "boasting"). Paul adds that this correct, exemplary behavior was meant in a more than usual way *(perissoterōs)* for the Corinthians. Fleshly wisdom (cf. "the wisdom of the world" in 1 Cor 1:20 and 2:5) is opposed to the grace of God. "Fleshly," like "worldly, earthly," here probably lacks the nuance of "sinful" (cf. v. 17). The whole sentence is introduced by *gar* ("for"), but it can be asked if the particle in this verse possesses its full motivating force.

13a. *For we write to you nothing other than what you read and (can) understand as well:* With "read" and "understand" there is a play on words in the Greek: *anaginōskō* and *epiginōskō* (cf. Paul W. Barnett, *Second Epistle* 96: "'comprehend' and 'apprehend' as a partial analogy in English"). The second verb, which in v. 13a is probably employed in a "modal" way ("can" understand), is repeated twice more in vv. 13b-14.

13b-14. *But I hope that you will understand fully—as you have understood us in part—that we are your boast as you, too, (are) ours in the day of our Lord Jesus:* Whether *heōs telous* means "fully" (opposed to "in part" of v. 14a) or "until the end" (cf. "the day of our Lord Jesus" in v. 14b; see also 1 Cor 1:8) is difficult to decide. Or is there a *double entendre?* For Paul's hope of a mutual understanding compare 5:11 and 13:6.

Grammatically v. 14b must probably be connected with v. 13b: I hope that you will fully understand that we are your pride as you are ours. In this view v. 14a is an interruption. It cannot but strike the reader that the direct object of "understand" changes three times: understanding what is written in the letter (v. 13a); partly understanding what Paul really is (v. 14a); and understanding that Paul and the Corinthian church are the boast of one another (vv. 13b and 14b). In v. 14b we would rather expect a future tense: that I will be your pride and you will be mine at the parousia. By using the present tense, however, Paul suggests that he and the Corinthians already are mutual sources of pride. Or is Paul's reasoning slightly different? Perhaps he says: I hope that (in the near future) you will understand that I "am" your boast as you, too, "will be" my boast at the parousia? In this interpretation the "day of our Lord Jesus" would qualify the comparative clause alone.

The OT "day of YHWH"—of either judgment or salvation—has become for Paul "the day of our Lord Jesus," the day of his return, his parousia. The term *kauchēma* (= the object of boasting) constitutes an inclusion with *kauchēsis* of v. 12.

15-16. *With that confidence (in mind), I wanted to come to you first—in order that you might have a second grace (later)—and pass through you to Macedonia and from Macedonia come again to you and (then) be sent on my way to Judea by you:* In vv. 12-14 Paul defends himself, but he certainly also writes in a hortatory way, implicitly pleading for reciprocal confidence. At the beginning of v. 15 he mentions this confidence in order to make the alteration of his travel plans acceptable to the Corinthians. In 1 Cor 16:5 he had announced: "I will visit you after passing through Macedonia," yet the travel plan he describes in 2 Cor 1:15-16 is different: first Corinth, then Macedonia, and again Corinth. The

Christians in Corinth must have been informed of that first change, but even this altered plan has not been followed. Paul did not immediately go back from Macedonia; he went to Ephesus. The return visit ("second grace") was postponed (cf. 1:23: "not again"). "First" translates *proteron* (literally: "earlier, formerly") and appears to be opposed to "second" (v. 15b) and "again" (v. 16). Therefore it should probably not be connected with "wanted" (= a previous decision) but with "come."

Some manuscripts have *charan* ("joy"), but *charin* ("grace") is to be preferred as the more difficult reading. "A second grace" thus concretely means a second visit, i.e., Paul's planned return from Macedonia to Corinth. The term "grace" probably points to Paul's God-given kindness toward the Corinthians, a sign and proof of his good will (differently Fee, "*CHARIS*": a second gracious opportunity for the Corinthians to assist Paul along the way, see v. 16: "to be sent on my way by you"; also cf. Rom 15:23-24). "And (then) be sent on my way to Judea by you" alludes to the help he expected from the Corinthians in the final stage of the collection for the poor Christians in Judea. See the same expression in Rom 15:24, "to be sent on my way by you" (to Spain).

17. *So, in planning this, was I acting with that (so-called) levity? Or what I decide, do I decide (it) according to the flesh so that there is with me that "yes, yes" and (at the same time) that "no, no"?:* In v. 17a the verb is in the past tense: "was I acting?". Paul appears to be pointing to the first change. The article *to* ("the," rendered "that") probably refers to an accusation of levity—Paul's lack of reliability—on the part of the Corinthians.

With its verb in the present tense ("I decide"), v. 17bc is more general. It can include the second change as well, i.e., the non-execution of the altered plan, or it may refer to his conduct in general. For "according to the flesh" see "fleshly" in 1:12. The article *to* (again rendered "that") seems to indicate that the repetition "yes, yes" and "no, no" is formulaic and well known. Paul concretizes the Corinthians' complaint or charge: some say that there is with him "yes, yes" and "no, no." Probably one has to supply "at the same time" (cf. v. 18).

Verse 17c is notoriously difficult to interpret. The easier shorter, yet weakly attested reading (without the duplication, cf. Jas 5:12) is hardly original. Conjectural emendations have been proposed (e.g., Hahn, "Problem"). Is the repetition "yes, yes" and "no, no" here merely for emphasis? Is it due to a Semitic idiom (Van Unnik, "Reisepläne")? Are the formulae a substitute for the oath (recently Welborn, "Double Affirmation": I am like a man who must continually employ such strong formulae)? Or are the second "yes" and "no" predicates (yes is yes, no is no, as in James 5:12; see Young, "Note")? What is the exact nuance of *par' emoi* ("with me")? Finally, does Paul echo a traditional saying still in its oral stage (a dominical logion? Cf. Matt 5:37)?

18. *God is reliable: our word to you is not "yes" and (at the same time) "no":* Paul continues his self-defense. He now uses by way of introduction a kind of oath formula: the faithful God guarantees that his speaking to the Corinthians is not "yes" and at the same time "no." "Our word to you" is hardly still lim-

ited to the explanation of his travel plans, i.e., his going and coming to Corinth. It already also refers to the preaching of the gospel (cf. v. 19). So Paul is leaving behind him the discussion of the journeys; he broadens the horizon and brings in the sincerity of his (first) proclamation of the word (for "word" in the meaning of gospel word cf. 1 Cor 1:18; 2:4; 15:2). In vv. 19-21 he will provide us with a profound meditation on the "yes" of God in salvation history.

19. *For the Son of God, Jesus Christ, proclaimed among you by us, (i.e.,) by me, Silvanus and Timothy, did not become "yes" and "no," but in him "yes" has become (and remains):* "Our word" (v. 18) is explained as the proclamation of "the Son of God, Jesus Christ." Paul is careful to make it clear that "by us" should not be taken as an epistolary plural. Paul and his fellow workers Silvanus and Timothy, who were present at Corinth during the foundational visit, preached the same gospel (cf. 1 Cor 15:11). The Son of God was not at the same time "yes" and "no"; for in Jesus Christ the final "yes" came and "remains" (*gegonen*, "has become," has this added nuance). This needs to be clarified.

20. *For whatever promises of God (exist), in him (came) (their) "yes"; therefore, through him, too, the "amen" (goes) to God for his glory, through us:* In Christ the "yes" of all God's promises came about: the promises were fulfilled by him. Christ is the realization of what God promised in the Old Testament. Paul immediately adds that therefore *(dio),* thanks to Christ's mediation, the approving, assenting "amen" is spoken to God (by all Christians?). This happens to the glory of God. Yet there is a second mediation: "through us," that is, through the missionaries (cf. v. 19). What Paul writes in this verse also reveals that the Gentile Christians in Corinth must have been acquainted with the Old Testament promises and that they perhaps already employed the responsory "amen" in their liturgy. According to W. C. van Unnik ("Reisepläne") Paul thought in Aramaic and the whole of vv. 15-24 is thematically and logically kept together by "amen" and some cognates (cf. the Aramaic equivalents of *pistos* and *pistis, nai, gegonen, bebaioō*). Yet one might ask whether if this is the case Paul's writing would have been fully intelligible to his Greek-speaking addressees.

21-22. *(The one) who establishes us with you in Christ and has anointed us is God, who has also sealed us and given the first installment in our hearts, the Spirit:* The God who establishes Paul and his fellow missionaries ("us"), together with the Corinthians ("with you"), in Christ and has anointed them is the same God who has also sealed them and given in their hearts the Spirit. In the Greek the four verbs are participles; in all of them God is the one who acts. The first participle is in the present tense and points to an ongoing act of establishing (for the same verb see especially 1 Cor 1:8). The phrase *eis Christon* ("in Christ") is reminiscent of a baptismal formula (cf., for example, Rom 6:3).

The other three participles are in the aorist; they all recall what happened at the Christians' baptism: anointing and sealing (two metaphorical terms), as well as the gift of the Spirit as guarantee. The Greek word *christos* means "anointed"; later, in the second century, a real anointing took place at baptism. "Who has anointed" may refer to the baptismal incorporation into the community of Christ as well as to qualification of Christian life and mission received through baptism. A seal can authenticate ownership. The Jews referred to the circumcision as a sealing and a seal; for the Christians, baptism is their sign of belonging to God. In the expression that reads literally "the earnest *(arrabōn,* a legal term) of the Spirit," the genitive most probably is epexegetical and indicates what that earnest, i.e., the first payment or first installment, contains, namely the Spirit. So the Spirit functions as guarantee. The Spirit, who is given at baptism, remains in our hearts and, as a down payment, guarantees our final salvation. See 5:5 and compare Rom 8:23: the Spirit is called the "first fruits" *(aparchē,* a cultic term).

Because the first two participles are joined together by the same article— as are the last two—and because the "also" in v. 22 could point to a consecutive step, it has been suggested that "anointing" denotes a prebaptismal divine action in the candidate's hearing of and believing in the word of truth (de la Potterie, "L'onction"). This proposal, however, appears farfetched and unlikely.

The style of this fourfold affirmation is solemn and imposing in its simplicity.

23. *I call upon God as witness—my life for it—:* Paul comes back to his decisions after he left Corinth. *Egō* ("I") is the emphasized first word. Except for v. 24 Paul uses the first person singular in the whole of 1:23–2:13; this underlines his personal involvement in what he is going to discuss. Moreover, in v. 23 he calls upon God as witness literally "over his soul," that is, his life. The clause means that he is willing to give his life in case he is not telling the truth: "my life for it."

that it was to spare you that I have not come to Corinth again: In v. 23b Paul refers to the second change in his plans. He did not adhere to the already altered scheme. He has not yet come to Corinth again *(ouketi,* "not once more, not again"). The reason is added: it was "to spare you" (cf. the threat in 13:2: "when I come again I will not refrain").

24. *Not that we (want to) domineer over your faith, but as companions we work for your joy. For you stand firm in the faith:* What Paul says in v. 23 might be misunderstood as the language of a person who "lords it" *(kyrieuō)* over others. Therefore he stresses that he is working, together with Timothy (and others?), for their joy. "Joy" may point here to the full happiness of a really Christian life, yet the term also introduces the opposition between sorrow and gladness present in 2:1-7; these feelings depend on the situation and its evolution in Corinth. Paul is convinced that the Corinthians are standing firm, are steady in and by the faith. Is "faith" here the equivalent of "gospel" or does the term point to an activity: you stand firm "by believing"?

2:1. *For I made up my mind not to come to you again in sorrow:* The textual variant *de* ("but"), instead of *gar* ("for"), although also well attested, is not to be preferred in this context. Paul's intention was not to go back to Corinth "in sorrow." The last expression probably not only refers to Paul's own sadness but also to the sorrow a new visit may cause to the Corinthians. From "not . . .

again" we can conclude that such a sorrowful visit has already taken place: the so-called painful (short) visit, the second (for the third, cf. 12:14 and 13:1).

2. *For if I sadden you, who then (will be) the one who makes me glad, except the one who is saddened by me?* Paul contrasts sorrow and gladness and, through the tone of this desperate question, also emphasizes the union between himself and the Corinthian community. The apodosis of this conditional period is a question, introduced by *kai* ("then").

3. *I have written this very (letter) in order that, when I come, I might not receive sorrow from those who should have made me rejoice:* Literally this reads "I have written this very thing." Paul almost certainly refers here to the "letter of tears" which we think is lost. That letter has replaced the planned return visit mentioned in 1:15 (for the letter see also 2:9 and 7:8). As in v. 2 he thinks of the joy the Corinthians should have given him *(edei me chairein:* "I ought to have rejoiced"). This would have been utterly impossible if he had gone back immediately.

   since (I was) confident in you all (and convinced) that my joy is (that) of all of you: At the end of the verse he also has in mind the Corinthians' joy: his confidence in them brings about the conviction that his own joy is equally the joy of all of them (cf. the mutual pride in 1:14). "Confident" and "convinced" translate the same participle *pepoithōs* because it is followed by a double construction: "in" and "that."

4. *For I have written to you out of much distress and anxiety of heart, with many tears, not in order that you be saddened, but in order that you may know the love that I have for you beyond measure:* Surely this letter was a letter of tears, written in the midst of affliction and with anguish of heart. Paul knew that his writing would cause sorrow, but that was not his intention. He wanted the Corinthians to realize the excess of love that he had for them *(perissoterōs,* literally: "more than abundantly"; cf. 1:12). Not only by this adverb but also by its position in the Greek text (before "that you may know") he puts extreme emphasis on "love."

   In 2:1-4 the vocabulary of sorrow and gladness are predominant. Through it Paul emphasizes the bonds that exist between the apostle and his Christians, bonds he wants to strengthen even more. He manifests his love for them and so, at the same time, recognizes his vulnerability, i.e., his dependence on them with respect both to joy and to pain.

5. *But if any one has caused sadness, he did not sadden me, but to some degree—not to exaggerate—all of you:* His speaking of sadness brings Paul to the mention of the painful event that took place probably during his second visit to Corinth. He refers to a certain person who caused pain first of all to himself—which he denies rhetorically—but also to the Corinthians. He nuances this last statement carefully by "to some degree" *(apo merous;* see the same phrase in 1:14) and "not to exaggerate." That person and what he did was, of course, known to the Corinthians. For us, the readers of today, notwithstanding what Paul writes in 2:5-11 and also in 7:11-12, the identity of this person and his wrongdoing remain rather mysterious. (See, e.g., the recent very hypothetical

reconstruction by Thrall, "Offender": the offender is a Corinthian; the offense is his appropriation of collection money given by another member of the Christian community.)

6. *The punishment by the majority (imposed) on that person is enough:* We can suppose that the severe letter as well as Titus' visit were not without result. The majority of the Christians have distanced themselves from the wrongdoer; they even punished him. Paul now says that this is enough. Titus will have informed him about the turn for the better that this matter took after the arrival of the severe letter (cf. 7:6-7).

7. *so that instead you should rather forgive and console (him), lest that person perhaps be overwhelmed by excessive sorrow:* Cessation of punishment is only a first step. The Christians must also (*tounantion*, literally: "on the contrary"; in this context: "instead") forgive him and comfort (*parakaleō*, "console, comfort") him. Otherwise he might be crushed by too great (*perissoteros*, "excessive"; cf. v. 4) grief.

8. *Therefore, I beg you to confirm your love for him:* "I beg" is the translation of *parakaleō* (cf. the same verb in v. 7, yet with a different meaning). In this verse Paul formulates an appeal that goes still further: they must reaffirm their love for him. One remembers that a moment ago (in v. 4) Paul spoke of his own love for the Corinthians, a love "beyond measure."

9. *For the reason why I have written to you (was) to test you and to know whether you are obedient in everything:* Apparently Paul has dealt with that person as well as with the Corinthians' attitude in his severe letter: "I have written." The phrase *eis touto* ("to this very end") points to the real intention of that letter. It was, he now says, to know their true character: whether or not they would be obedient to him in all things. "To test and to know" translates *hina gnō tēn dokimēn hymōn*, literally "in order that I might know (the result of) your testing, i.e., your passing the test."

10. *The one whom you forgive I, too, (forgive):* The verb "to forgive" (*charizomai*) was also used in v. 7; in v. 10 it is repeated three more times in what could be called a typical Pauline style. Paul forgives the one the Corinthians forgive. Of course, the same person is intended.

    For indeed, what I have forgiven—if I have forgiven anything—I (have done it) for your sake in the presence of Christ: The parenthesis "if I have forgiven anything" probably means: "if I have anything to forgive." Through the rather strange wording of this verse one feels Paul's sensitiveness, but also his Christian and apostolic passion: the minimalizing of the injustice he personally experienced, his forgiving, his concern for the Corinthians (they should follow his example), and his union with Christ (cf. "in the presence of Christ").

11. *lest we be cheated by Satan; for we are not unaware of his schemes:* Satan comes to the forefront. He can take advantage of too severe a reaction on the part of the Christians. We should not allow ourselves, Paul says, to be cheated by Satan. Paul probably has in mind the salvation of that isolated, repentant and, perhaps, depressed person (cf. v. 7b). The *noēmata* (literally: "thoughts," here

"schemes") of Satan are his designs, his (hidden) intentions. "To be unaware" is the translation of *agnoeō* (compare the same verb in 1:8, yet in a formulaic disclosure clause).

12. *When I came to Troas to preach the gospel of Christ, although a door had been opened in the Lord:* The narrative proper, which was interrupted after 2:1, is taken up again in v. 12. Paul comes to Troas, a port in Asia Minor. (Does the article before Troas perhaps make clear that the region, the Troad, indicated by the same Greek term, is meant?) His departure from Ephesus is not explicitly mentioned. One is rather amazed that the primary aim of his going to Troas is the preaching of the gospel and not the fixed meeting with Titus. Paul, not without emphasis, speaks of the good possibilities for the proclamation of the gospel at Troas: "a door has been opened in (= by?) the Lord" (cf. 1 Cor 16:9). This last clause is, in the Greek text, a genitive absolute; its concessive nuance can be presumed.

13. *I had no relief for my spirit because I did not find Titus my brother. So, having said farewell to them, I went to Macedonia:* Two personal verbs express what is really going on within Paul: (1) without Titus in Troas he did not find inner serenity; and (2) after the farewell to the people there he left for Macedonia. Paul would certainly desire that the mention of his uneasiness be interpreted by the Corinthians as a token of his love for them. The cause of that lack of ease was the uncertainty of their reaction to the painful letter and to Titus's visit.

   The idea of an eventual successful preaching remains, as it were, present in his mind. So, after v. 13, he again interrupts the narrative for what is going to be a very lengthy exposé (2:14-7:4).

INTERPRETATION

a. *Structure and Line of Thought.* Within 1:12–2:13 one finds a short introduction (1:12-14) and, at the end, a brief, interrupted narrative (2:12-13). Moreover, two major parts can be distinguished: 1:15-22 and 1:23–2:11.

The introduction (1:12-14) constitutes a sort of transition wherein Paul gives a rather general consideration regarding the sincerity of his behavior and correspondence: he is the boast, the pride of the Corinthians just as the Corinthians are his pride on the day of the Lord. He expresses his hope that the Corinthians will fully understand the way he acted and acts. At the end of the passage (2:12-13) Paul tells his addressees how (after leaving Ephesus) he reaches Troas and finds there an opportunity for preaching the gospel. Although "a door was opened by the Lord," he could not stay there for a long time because Titus was not present at the agreed-upon meeting. He leaves the city and goes to Macedonia.

In the first major part (1:15-22) Paul justifies the (first) alteration of his travel plans. In the second (1:23–2:11) he explains why he does not immediately come to Corinth (second change): this coming should not be a visit "in sorrow," for such a sorrowful visit has already taken place; moreover, he has written a severe letter and also sent Titus.

Yet each major part broadens out into further considerations. In the first, Paul denies that the change of plans occurred with levity, "according to the flesh"; his "yes" is not at the same time "no" (1:17-18). This self-defense leads him to a profound meditation on God's work in Jesus Christ who is the definitive "yes" of God, the fulfillment of all God's promises (1:19-22). In the second part Paul reflects on how community and apostle are the joy and sorrow of one another (2:2-4). This reflection, then, brings him to discuss the painful incident at Corinth and to give his directives to the Corinthians: the guilty person is punished enough; he must now be given forgiveness; he should experience love on the part of his fellow Christians.

b. *Characteristics.* 2 Cor 1:12–2:13 contains some typical features of Paul's style: the repetitious use of the same terminology in certain small units (see 2:13-14; 1:17-18; 1:24–2:5; 2:7 and 10), the strange interruptions of the line of thought (in 1:18-22 and 2:2-11) and the frequent use of the epistolary plural (in 1:12-18, but also see the first person singular in 1:23 and 2:1-13).

c. *Theological Reflection.* More important than the form, however, is the content. Three items merit particular attention. First, in this long text Paul provides much information about what he has done in the time between his first foundational visit to Corinth and the writing of 2 Corinthians. He visited Corinth a second time; this visit most probably turned out to be painful for him (a failure?); a certain person saddened him personally. He wrote to Corinth a severe letter out of a greatly troubled and distressed heart and with many tears, a letter that in our opinion is most probably lost. He sent Titus to Corinth, perhaps as carrier of that letter; he waited for him at Troas for a certain length of time. Not finding Titus he traveled on to Macedonia to meet him there. Because of the adverse situation in Corinth, Paul is forced to change his plans twice. Apparently the Christians have blamed him for this and ascribed the alterations to levity and lack of reliability. The passage, above all, informs us about Paul's pastoral concern, his great desire that the Corinthians give him joy again, his inner unrest with the result that he interrupts what promised to become a successful proclamation of the word at Troas in order to see Titus as soon as possible and to learn from him how the situation at Corinth is developing.

Second, it is quite uncertain that from this passage much can be learned about the "constitution" of the Corinthian church. A reference to baptism in 1:21-22 appears evident. Yet these verses hardly depict the genesis of faith: God's specific actions, first before baptism (v. 21), then baptism (v. 22; some find here a reference to confirmation also; see notes). One could extract too much data from 2:5-11: e.g., that a "formal" excommunication took place or that with his authority Paul "officially" requires the reintegration of the sinner into the community. Yet the text does inform us about some aspects of Paul's apostolic strategy: there was the unsuccessful attempt of his own second visit; then, a new attempt was made with the changed tactic of a severe letter as well as the sending of Titus as a go-between; finally there was the apologetic, pleading writing of 2 Corinthians itself.

Third, in a totally unexpected way Paul in 1:19-22 presents his vision of salvation history and Jesus Christ. In 1:17-18 he is still dealing with the truthfulness of his own yes and no. God is his guarantee. Notwithstanding the fact that he has to change his travel plans twice, his reliability in this matter participates in the reliability of his gospel proclamation, in the faithfulness of Christ and God. "Word" in v. 18 is, of course, already more than what is said about travel changes. In v. 19 Paul explains this "word" and startlingly expands his argument. In the Son of God all promises of God are fulfilled: Jesus Christ is their "yes." The gospel is God's "yes" to the world. This is the main point, the substance of what he preached in Corinth. To this good news Christians speak their "amen" to God's glory. God firmly and continually establishes all Christians in Christ. Through baptism God anointed and sealed them; through this baptism God also gave the Spirit in their hearts as first payment. Although some connection with the context can be detected, vv. 19-21 constitute a remarkable theological digression.

It may have been without premeditation, but Paul writes here in a "trinitarian" way: the Father works through Christ and gives the Spirit. Salvation history finds its climax in Christ. Paul emphasizes the union of Christians with Christ in and through the Spirit.

d. *Actualization.* We are confronted here with a Paul who is humanly worried and anxious, as well as with an apostle who is caring for his Christians. The Corinthians cause him pain, but he loves them sincerely, exceedingly; they are his joy and pride. And the very person who saddened him must be won back, fully reintegrated.

Of course, reading this section of Paul's letter not only provides us with interesting information about the relationship between Paul and the Corinthian community. In a subtle yet undeniable way the text also very strongly insists that the Corinthians, and today's Christians as well, must agree with Paul's vision of salvation history. The passage equally invites them and all of us to follow Paul's example of apostolic loving concern.

FOR REFERENCE AND FURTHER STUDY

Barrett, Charles Kingsley. "*Ho adikēsas* (2 Cor. 7.12)," in idem, *Essays on Paul*. London: S.P.C.K., 1982, 108–117.

————. "Titus," in idem, *Essays on Paul*. London: S.P.C.K., 1982, 118–131.

Belleville, Linda L. "A Letter of Apologetic Self-Commendation: 2 Cor. 1:8–7:16," *NT* 31 (1989) 142–163.

————. "Paul's Polemic and Theology of the Spirit in Second Corinthians," *CBQ* 58 (1996) 281–304 (for 2 Cor 1:21-22 see especially pp. 283–286).

Bieringer, Reimund. "Plädoyer für die Einheitlichkeit des 2. Korintherbriefes. Literarkritische und inhaltliche Argumente," in Bieringer and Lambrecht, *Studies on 2 Corinthians*. BEThL 125. Leuven: Leuven University Press/ Peeters, 1996, 13–179, especially 161–166.

Derrett, J. Duncan M. "*Nai* (2 Cor 1:19-20)," *Filologia neotestamentaria* 4 (1991) 205–209.

Dugandzic, Ivan. *Das "Ja" Gottes in Christus. Eine Studie zur Bedeutung des Alten Testaments für das Christusverständnis des Paulus*. FzB 26. Würzburg: Echter Verlag, 1977, 20–56.

Fee, Gordon D. "*CHARIS* in II Corinthians I.15: Apostolic Parousia and Paul-Corinth Chronology," *NTS* 24 (1977–1978) 533–538.

Hahn, Ferdinand. "Ist das textkritische Problem von 2 Kor 1,17 lösbar?" in *Studien zum Text und zur Ethik des Neuen Testaments. FS for H. Greeven*. BZNW 47. Berlin: de Gruyter, 1989, 158–165.

Potterie, Ignace de la. "L'onction du chrétien par la foi," *Bib.* 40 (1959) 12–69, especially 14–30.

Thrall, Margaret E. "The Offender and the Offence: A Problem of Detection in 2 Corinthians," in B. P. Thompson, ed., *Scripture. Meaning and Method. FS A.T. Hanson*. Hull: Hull University Press, 1987, 65–78.

————. "2 Corinthians 1:12: *hagiotēti* or *haplotēti*?" in J. K. Elliott, ed., *Studies in New Testament Language and Text. FS G.D. Kilpatrick*. NT.S 44. Leiden: Brill, 1976, 366–372.

Unnik, W. C. van. "Reisepläne und Amen-Sagen. Zusammenhang und Gedankenfolge in 2. Korinther 1:15-24," in idem, *Sparsa collecta I*. NT.S 29. Leiden: Brill, 1973, 144–159.

Welborn, L. L. "The Dangerous Double Affirmation: Character and Truth in 2 Cor 1,17," *ZNW* 86 (1995) 34–52.

Wenham, David. "2 Corinthians 1:17, 18: Echo of a Dominical Logion," *NT* 28 (1986) 271–279.

Young, Frances. "Note on 2 Corinthians 1:17b," *JThS* 37 (1986) 404–415.

II. PAUL'S APOSTLESHIP (2:14–7:4)

3. *Paul's Ministry* (2:14–3:6)

14. But thanks be to God, who in Christ always celebrates his victory over us by a triumphal procession, and through us manifests the fragrance of the knowledge of him in every place. 15. For we are the aroma of Christ to God among those who are being saved and among those who are perishing, 16. to the latter a fragrance from death to death, to the former a fragrance from life to life. Who is sufficient for these things? 17. For we are not, like the majority, peddling God's word; but out of sincerity, but from God, in the sight of God, in Christ we speak.

3:1. Are we beginning again to commend ourselves? Or do we need, as some do, letters of recommendation to you or from you? 2. You are our letter, written on our hearts, known and read by all, 3. because you show that you are a letter of Christ, ministered by us, written not with ink but with the Spirit of the living God, not on stone tablets but on tablets that are hearts of flesh.

4. We have such a confidence through Christ before God. 5. Not that we are sufficient of ourselves to claim anything as coming from ourselves. But our sufficiency comes from God, 6. who also made us sufficient to be ministers of a new covenant, not of the letter but of the Spirit; for the letter kills, but the Spirit gives life.

NOTES

14. *But thanks be to God:* Every authentic Pauline letter, except 2 Corinthians and Galatians, begins with a thanksgiving using the verb *eucharisteō*. Those thanksgivings are called "epistolary" thanksgivings and are sometimes quite developed and lengthy. Here we have a short non-epistolary formula, with *charis* ("grace, gift, thanks"), not infrequent in Paul's letters (e.g., Rom 6:17; 7:25; 2 Cor 8:16; 9:15). Thanks to the placement of *theǭ* at the beginning, before *charis*, the emphasis falls on "God," not on the "thanks." Similarly, *Christou* occurs at the very beginning of v. 15 for the purpose of emphasis.

who in Christ always celebrates his victory over us by a triumphal procession: In the Greek text God is determined by two participial phrases that are similar in structure: the two active verbs are in the present tense *(thriambeuonti* and *phanerounti).* God is the subject; the verbs describe the action of God; in each case Paul has a functional role in that action. It follows, one would assume, that the two phrases can hardly differ greatly in content. "Who . . . celebrates his victory over us by a triumphal procession" is the translation of *thriambeuonti hēmas.* What does the verb *thriambeuō* mean? At first sight one would guess: God makes us triumph, causes us to triumph, or God makes us participate in his triumph. Yet this causative, factitive sense is not attested at the time of Paul. *Thriambeuō,* a loanword from Latin, means "to celebrate a victory with a parade, a triumphal procession."

Three main proposals must be discussed. (1) Followed by a direct object the nuance could be "to lead someone (as a captive, a defeated enemy) in a triumphal procession": see Lamar Williamson, "Led." Scott J. Hafemann, *Suffering,* would add the nuance "led to death and rescued from it." Peter Marshall, "Metaphor," refers to the metaphorical use of "to lead captives in triumph" in Latin and wants to discern in Paul's use also a metaphor of social shame. (In view of the uncertainty of chronologically relevant evidence one hesitates to subscribe to R. B. Egan's translation ["Lexical Evidence"] "to publicize, divulge," with no hint of a triumphal procession, more or less the equivalent of the verb *phanerounti* in v. 14c.) Paul would be presenting the wonderful spread of the gospel everywhere as an ongoing (present tense, *pantote*) triumphal procession; God thus celebrates the victory won in and through Christ. Yet Paul also reflects on his apostolic function. For a moment he thinks of his concrete situation (persecuted, attacked, calumniated, suffering, poor). Whether the idea of "defeated and captive" should be pressed is uncertain, but a reference to "social shame" could be on his mind. In paradoxical language God's victory and the apostle's shameful existence are put forward by means of the same expression. In v. 14 Paul's vivid mind combines and, very quickly, seems to move from God's manifest victory (the spread of the gospel) to his own miserable condition and back to the victorious apostolic manifestation.

(2) According to Paul Duff, "Metaphor," for whom 2:14 is the beginning of an independent letter fragment, Paul must have had a rhetorical strategy with the image "led in triumph." The Corinthian community suspects Paul of less than sincere motives. The opponents have succeeded in raising doubts about the legitimacy of his apostleship. "Paul, in keeping with the rhetoricians' advice on the construction of the *insinuatio* [= a subtle opening], begins his defense by taking up the theme of his opponents, his 'weakness' and suffering, and describing it metaphorically with the image of himself 'led in triumph.' . . . but throughout the course of the letter fragment he subtly redefines it . . ." (p. 91). A triumphal procession is metaphorically not strictly limited to the military parade. In the Greco-Roman world it was also used for the epiphany procession of a deity. Paul's own use of *thriambeuō* takes this broadening of sense into account. Thus on the one hand *thriambeuō* "immediately calls to mind the comparison of the apostle with prisoners of war led to their execution in the triumphant processions of the Roman empire—an image that would, no doubt, be quickly embraced by Paul's opponents. On the other hand, the metaphor also leaves open the possibility that Paul is referring to something else, . . . an epiphany procession" (p. 92).

(3) Cilliers Breytenbach, "Paul's Proclamation," however, prefers a different metaphorical understanding. The verb *thriambeuō* with a person as direct object can also mean "to celebrate a victory over that person by means of a triumphal procession." Through Paul's conversion on the way to Damascus

God won in Christ a victory over Paul. God celebrates that victory over him by a triumphal procession that does not take place once (in Rome), but always, i.e., during and through Paul's missionary journeys. According to Breytenbach, in v. 14b Paul is presenting himself not as a captured prisoner led in that procession but as a conquered missionary apostolically driven by God.

The preference of this commentary goes to the third proposal.

and through us manifests the fragrance of the knowledge of him in every place: Verse 14c, as well as vv. 15-16, teaches us that the aspect of "making known" is present already in the triumph metaphor of v. 14b. The expression "of the knowledge of him" is as a whole an epexegetical genitive; the fragrance is the knowledge. The genitive "of him" probably refers to God (not to Christ; cf. 4:6).

Where does the image of fragrance *(osmē)* come from? There are three possibilities that are not necessarily mutually exclusive. (1) Incense was burned along the route of a triumphal procession. Thus it is possible that *osmē* continues the imagery of God's triumphal march. Breytenbach may be right in highlighting this first background. (2) The term could, perhaps, also possess a liturgical connotation; the expression *osmē euōdias* ("a good smell, a pleasing odor") is frequent in the Old Testament and *euōdia* is used in v. 15a. Paul then would interpret his apostolic life as a sacrifice pleasing to God. (3) A third possible background is to be found in the Wisdom literature where, as in Sir 24:15, wisdom is referred to as a perfume: "I (= Wisdom) have exhaled a perfume . . . I have breathed out a scent. . . ." In v. 14c God is manifesting the knowledge of God (which is wisdom) through the missionaries.

It is the first time in this letter that Paul uses the verb *phaneroō* ("to manifest"; eight more times in 2 Corinthians). The verb determines the function of the fragrance motif: it is a "spreading and manifesting" odor.

15. *For we are the aroma of Christ to God:* In this motivating clause Paul forces the imagery: we ourselves are the aroma. It is difficult to know which kind of genitive *Christou* is: subjective, objective, or of origin. Perhaps the last is the correct one: "the aroma that comes from Christ." Or is Paul suggesting that his sufferings constitute a continuation of Christ's sufferings (see 4:10-11) and are, therefore, a sacrifice with which God is well pleased?

among those who are being saved and among those who are perishing: We have present participles here. Although "to save" and "to perish" are eschatological terms, Paul is convinced that salvation and perdition are already being achieved in this life. The relation between "aroma" (a positive term) and "those who are perishing" is somewhat strained. For the combination of the verbs we can refer to 1 Cor 1:18: "For the message about the cross is foolishness to those *who are perishing,* but to us *who are being saved* it is the power of God" (cf. the nouns in Phil 1:28).

16. *to the latter a fragrance from death to death, to the former a fragrance from life to life:* In view of "death" the neutral "fragrance" reappears. We might note the chiastic progression that unites vv. 15 and 16: salvation-perdition; death-life. No literal meaning is to be given to "from death" or "from life." The expres-

sions "from death to death" and "from life to life" are rhetorical, employed more for reasons of style, the sole purpose being to emphasize death or life by means of an intensification (cf. Rom 1:17: "from faith to faith"). Although vv. 14-16 constitute one lengthy sentence it would seem that from the end of v. 15 Paul is no longer paying attention to his thanksgiving in v. 14a.

Who is sufficient for these things? Although it is God who is leading and directing all things, Paul has noted that the ministers are not completely passive: "and *through us* manifests . . ." (v. 14c). In v. 17 Paul will again stress what we might term his active receptivity or capability of being an apostle, of manifesting the knowledge of God, yet it would seem that the question in v. 16c is properly a question of resignation. The implied answer is: Of course, nobody is adequate from and by him- or herself (cf. 3:5). This appears to be Paul's first reaction.

17. *For we are not, like the majority, peddling God's word:* Verse 17 does not provide a direct answer to the question of v. 16c; it rather continues vv. 15-16ab. "Like the majority" (i.e., the more numerous rival missionaries) is the rendering of *hōs hoi polloi.* The variant reading *hōs hoi loipoi* ("like the others") appears to be of Western origin and, also because of its rather offensive character, secondary (cf. Metzger, *Textual Commentary* 508). The tone of this clause is outspokenly apologetic and indirectly polemic. The term *kapēleuō* ("to peddle for profit, to hawk in return for money"; note the periphrastic construction) is a *hapax legomenon* in the NT. From the time of Plato on it was used to describe the activity of pseudo-philosophers who gave popularized, falsified, or superficial lectures, very often for financial gain. Is any reference to mercenary motives intended by Paul in his accusation? "To peddle" stands in opposition to "sincerity" (v. 17b); Paul accuses his many opponents of being insincere. They dilute or adulterate (cf. 4:2: *doloō,* "tamper with") God's word, i.e., the gospel. "Peddling" contains this idea, but the nuance of "money-grubbing" is present as well.

but out of sincerity, but from God, in the sight of God, in Christ we speak: The twofold *all' hōs* ("but as") and the repetition of God, followed by "in Christ," betray emphasis and emotion on Paul's part. He provides a biting comparison of his "sincerity" with the way his own opponents act. The grammatical construction with the double *all' hōs* is unclear. We must perhaps admit an elliptical text and reckon with an ascensive second *alla* ("indeed"): "but as (those who speak) out of sincerity, indeed as (those who speak words coming) from God, we speak in the sight of God in Christ" (cf. 12:19). Yet the last three formulae present themselves, it would seem, as a further explanation of "out of sincerity."

It is important to note that Paul's behavior is regulated not by subjective preferences but by the objective reality of God. God is always present and witnesses to what is spoken (or on the final day God will be the judge). In Hellenistic Greek *laleō* was used to qualify "loose speaking" or "speaking too much," but in the LXX and here the verb is employed in conjunction with prophetic or inspired speech. Elsewhere in the New Testament the term has a similar meaning (cf., for example, Mark 13:11).

3:1. *Are we beginning again to commend ourselves?* 2 Cor 2:17 could be taken as a self-commendation. Hence Paul's question in 3:1. The expected answer is negative. There is a slight problem here in determining to what previous self-commendation Paul is referring by "again." Is he thinking of charges previously leveled against him by the community of Corinth or his opponents (cf. 4:2; 5:12)? Or is Paul referring to self-commendations in an earlier letter to the Corinthians (cf. 1 Cor 3:10; 4:1-4, 15-17; 9:1-3)? Since Paul has no letters of recommendation he is forced to recommend himself.

Or do we need, as some do, letters or recommendation to you or from you? The answer to this second question, introduced by *mē*, is again "no." "As some do" is another polemic statement *vis-à-vis* his opponents (cf. 2:17 and 10:12-13). Letters of introduction were used in the early Church as a means of establishing the credentials of itinerant preachers. They were used throughout the profane world as well. There are, moreover, several examples of such "letters" in other Pauline writings (Rom 16:1-2; 1 Cor 16:10-11; Philemon; cf. Acts 15:22-31 and 18:27). Since in 2 Cor 3:1 Paul reacts against some such letters, there must have been something in them that Paul considered to be false and reprehensible. Paul is now speaking not only of letters to the Corinthians but also of letters written by them to be sent somewhere else. He is amalgamating and generalizing. One should also note that "to you and from you" functions as an introduction to v. 2.

2. *You are our letter, written on our hearts, known and read by all:* The variant reading "on your hearts" is but weakly attested (yet present in Sinaiticus) and seems to be introduced for the sake of an easier sense. For "on our hearts" cf. 7:3 and 1 Cor 9:2. It would seem that the phrase "written on our hearts" may be influenced by Jer 31:33 (LXX 38:33; see also below). The heart is to be understood as the very core of the person where God's Spirit is active (v. 3). Normally one reads and then knows. Paul has reversed this order. We should, however, not force Paul into a too rigorously logical sequence. "Read by all" is perhaps a flattering allusion to the prestige and importance of Corinth as an international city. This statement also appeals to the responsibility of the Corinthians. Paul must have spoken to others of this letter (the Corinthian church). Verse 3 further explains the public character of the letter.

3. *because you show that you are a letter of Christ, ministered by us:* "because you show" renders the participle *phaneroumenoi* which stands in apposition to the subject of v. 2: "you are. . . ." At first sight it looks strange that Paul uses the expression "a letter of Christ" so shortly after "our letter" in v. 2. "Christ," however, is clearly intended here as a correction or, at least, a specification. Paul is just a helper (cf. 4:5); the real "author" is Christ. This reference at the same time demonstrates Paul's belief that Christ was present in his missionary action. "Ministered" is an aorist participle pointing back to Paul's foundational visit to Corinth. Paul sees himself here as a scribe (secretary), not as a deliverer (carrier).

written not with ink but with the Spirit of the living God: Paul continues the letter imagery by contrasting "ink" to "the Spirit of the living God." This last expression occurs nowhere else in the Bible. The founding of a church is

God's life-giving work, a new creation. God works "with" (= by means of) the Spirit.

not on stone tablets but on tablets that are hearts of flesh: There is a definite shift in the imagery. "Stone tablets" clearly contains a reference to the Law (cf., for example, Exod 24:12; 31:18; 34:1; Deut 9:10-11). "Ink" and "stone tablets" are negative qualifications over against the "Spirit of the living God" and "tablets that are hearts of flesh." In the Greek text "fleshly hearts" is in apposition to "tablets." Paul may mean "our hearts" as in v. 2 or, more likely, the hearts of the Corinthians. Verse 3 shows Paul's use of Exod 31:18 ("tablets of stone") as well as of Ezek 11:19 and/or 36:26-27 ("Spirit," "of stone," and "hearts of flesh"). It is quite probable that in 3:3 (or already 3:2) the "old covenant" text (Exodus 34; cf. 2 Cor 3:7-18) and the famous "new covenant" text of Jer 38:31-34 (LXX; cf. 2 Cor 3:6) are also present in Paul's mind.

4. *We have such a confidence through Christ before God:* The construction *pepoithēsis pros* ("confidence before") is a *hapax legomenon* in the whole Bible. The confidence Paul has is probably not to be understood as confidence "in" God. "Such" refers back to what precedes. It is Paul's confidence that the Corinthians are a letter written by the Spirit and "ministered" by him (vv. 2-3). As in 2:17 Christ and God are mentioned. The objective basis for Paul's confidence is twofold: first, Christ is actively present in what Paul confidently feels; second, even God is witness to all this.

5. *Not that we are sufficient of ourselves to claim anything as coming from ourselves:* In this translation the infinitive "to claim" is taken as the complement of "we are sufficient." Paul does not attribute his confidence (v. 4) to his own merits. "Sufficient," however, is a repetition of the same term in 2:16c. Therefore we should perhaps interpret v. 5 as follows: Paul is of himself not sufficient, i.e., not qualified for his ministry, so that he cannot claim (= infinitive of result) anything of this ministry as coming from himself. Although what follows in vv. 5b-6 seems to confirm this understanding we hesitate to accept it since an infinitive of result is grammatically not very likely here.

But our sufficiency comes from God: This positive statement is brief and clear. The expression "from God" is the opposite of "from ourselves" (see v. 5a) and reminds us of 2:17 where the expression "from God" (without article, however) is also present.

6. *who also made us sufficient to be ministers of a new covenant:* After the adjective *hikanos* ("sufficient," see 2:16c and 3:5a) and the substantive *hikanotēs* ("sufficiency," see 3:5b) Paul here employs the verb *hikanoō* ("to make sufficient"). With the past tense he most probably refers to his conversion, which at the same time was his apostolic vocation. The *kai* in the Greek text is here translated "also." Not only does his competence in general come from God, but God made him "also" competent for a specific task, i.e., the ministry of the new covenant. Paul is but a minister of the new covenant. The term "minister" introduces (yet see "ministered" in v. 2) a theme that will become very important in the following passages of the letter. The counterpart of "new covenant" *(kainē diathēkē)* is mentioned in 3:14, albeit with a different nuance:

"old covenant = the written Torah" *(palaia diathēkē)*. Although the expression "new covenant" is certainly known to Paul from the institution narrative of the Eucharist (see 1 Cor 11:25), influence from Jer 38:31-34 (LXX) should in no way be excluded. By "new covenant" Paul means God's eschatologically new initiative in Christ. What follows in v. 6 is intended as an elucidation.

not of the letter but of the Spirit: These genitives are genitives of qualification: thus a covenant of the Spirit, not the one of the letter, of the written Torah. Paul's use of *grammatos* instead of *graphēs* is partly due to considerations of style. It makes a better parallel with *pneumatos*. Also *graphē* as a word for Scripture has a positive sense; the connotation of "letter" here is negative: Torah as written. The new covenant has nothing to do with the letter, i.e., the Law written on stone tablets (cf. v. 7); it is the covenant of the Spirit of the living God (cf. v. 3). For the opposition "letter-Spirit," see Rom 2:27-29 and, together with "old-new," Rom 7:6. In our passage the opposition is not between legalistic and true or spiritual observance of the Law, nor between a literal, superficial and a deep, inner, spiritual sense of the Law, but between the written, not executed, hence powerless Law and God's new covenant wherein the Spirit (cf. Ezekiel 11 and/or 36) is active. The contrast thus is salvation-historical, not hermeneutical.

for the letter kills, but the Spirit gives life: The explication continues ("for"). Two soteriological notions, killing and giving life, are introduced. "To kill" refers to sin and to the death it produces. "To give life" ultimately refers to final salvation. See "death" and "life" in 2:16.

INTERPRETATION

a. *Structure and Line of Thought.* 2 Cor 2:14–7:4, situated as it is between the autobiographical sections 1:8–2:13 and 7:5-16, is rightly considered a relatively independent part of this Pauline letter and is often more specifically called Paul's Apologia, a defense of his ministry (see Introduction, pp. 9–11). Within this substantial unit it would seem that 2:14–4:6 forms a first major division. While 2:14–3:6 and 4:1-6 contain apologetic and polemic elements indicating an opposition between Paul and other (false) missionaries, intruders, the opposition in 3:7-18 is between Moses' ministry and that of the new covenant, between Moses and Paul, between the sons of Israel and Christians. Unlike the surrounding sections, the entire pericope 3:7-18 seems to refer to the same Old Testament text, Exod 34:27-35. Yet this is but a first impression. The scriptural background of Jeremiah 38 (LXX), Ezekiel 11 and/or 36 and Exodus 34, as well as the contrast between old and new covenants (ministries) are very much present in all three sections.

A closer inspection of the text reveals that the threefold division 2:14–3:6; 3:7-18; and 4:1-6 is better explained according to a concentric *A-B-A'* pattern. The first and third sections correspond to each other. Readers will agree that in 2:14–3:6 Paul speaks of himself (and his co-workers) and of his apostolic existence. The tone of the pericope is at the same time apologetic (an apology directed toward the Corinthian Christians) and polemic (an indirect counterattack against the intruders and opponents). All this does not apply to the middle section. From 4:1 onwards, however, Paul is again talking very clearly about the minister and his way of life. A survey of all identical or similar words that occur in each of the two framing passages could confirm this view in a rather convincing way (see Lambrecht, "Structure," 348–349), demonstrating the identity or similarity of both vocabulary and thematic content.

The pericope 2:14-17 opens with a thanksgiving to God and dwells on the reasons why Paul should thank God: Paul and his co-workers are the aroma of Christ, spreading in every place the knowledge of God (2:14-16b). In 2:16c Paul poses the question: Who could be qualified for work like this? There is no immediate direct answer given to this question in 2:17, but the answer can be deduced from 3:5-6: only the one who is qualified by God. The root of the key word *hikanos* in 2:16c reappears three times in 3:5-6: *hikanoi, hikanotēs, hikanōsen*. We noted that the connection of 2:17 with 2:16c is not very smooth. In v. 17 Paul seems to defend himself against an accusation of corruption or insincerity. Of course both such sins would disqualify an apostle. The whole of 2:14-17 clearly deals with Paul's own apostolic status, his ministry.

Does this also apply to 3:1-3? The question about self-commendation in v. 1a (do we commend ourselves?) refers back to what Paul had just said in 2:17, and that of v. 1b (do we need letters of recommendation?) also speaks of Paul himself. But the main focus of the following verses is on the status of the Corinthian community, their being a letter. The reader here is confronted with a series of antitheses. The first occurs in 3:1 where Paul distinguishes between what could be seen as his own self-commendation (cf. 2:17) and the letters of recommendation that others use. This leads to a second antithesis: the written credentials (cf. 3:1) are now opposed to the Corinthians who themselves are Paul's living letter, written in his heart (3:2). We read a third (and twofold) antithesis in 3:3 where Paul puts ink and stone tablets over against the Spirit of the living God and tablets that are hearts of flesh. Noteworthy also is Paul's specification: "our letter" of 3:2 becomes in 3:3 "Christ's letter ministered by us." The third antithesis appears to oppose the old written Law (Exodus 34) and the new law written by the Spirit in the hearts (Jeremiah 38 [LXX] and Ezekiel 11 and 36).

With 3:4-6 Paul returns to the ideas present in 2:14-17. To be sure, the opening clause of 3:4 (such is the confidence we have) points back to the insight into the status of the Corinthians as described in 3:2-3, but the same clause probably also takes up Paul's own conviction that he really is Christ's minister (2:14-16b) and, moreover, a sincere minister (2:17). In 3:5-6a, as in 2:16c, there is the terminology of sufficiency. Here Paul clearly states that his sufficiency is not from himself but from God (cf. his sincerity plea in 2:17). God has qualified him to be a minister of a new dispensation. This statement reminds us of what he had said about his position in 2:14-16b. Moreover, the life-death antithesis in 2:16ab and 3:6b works as one of the numerous inclusion indicators.

Thus there can scarcely remain any doubt with regard to the concentric structure and line of thought in 2:14–3:6: *a* Paul (2:14-17); *b* the Corinthian Christians (3:1-3); *a'* again Paul (3:4-6). The *b* section is framed by *a* and *a'*, which correspond to one another. Of course, *a'* is not a literal repetition of *a*. In composing 3:4-6 Paul is influenced by what he has just written in 3:1-3. Not only does "such a confidence" in 3:4 refer back to the previous verses, but 3:6 depends heavily on 3:3 for both motifs and vocabulary. The idea of the "new covenant" was present in Paul's mind already during the composition of 3:2-3; *diakonous* ("ministers") in 3:6 recalls *diakonētheisa* ("ministered") in 3:2; and the double opposition of "letter-spirit" and "killing-life giving" explains the antitheses of "ink-Spirit of the living God" and "stone-hearts of flesh" in 3:3.

Section *a* is more missionary, dynamic and universal. Section *b*, with its attention fixed on the Corinthian addressees, is more local (but see the end of v. 2: known and read by all). Section *a'* appears to be more theoretical, abstract, and static. However, these differences, nuances, and particular emphases should not cause us to forget the basic unity of 2:14–3:6. In all its sections Paul reflects on his ministry: its origin, qualification and qualities.

b. *A Characteristic Feature.* In 2:14–3:6 (and even in the whole of 2:14–4:6) many shifts in Paul's reasoning are present. Joseph A. Fitzmyer comments on this strange feature: "What is operative here, and what is perhaps not noted often enough, is the free association of ideas that runs through the entire passage. The association is caused by catchword bonding, in which one sense of a term suggests another, and so the argument proceeds. . . . In any case, his [= Paul's] mode of argumentation cannot be subjected to syllogistic analysis" ("Glory," 68–69). Fitzmyer mentions six sets of associations that are at work in 3:1-18. The first two, letters *(epistolai)* and letter *(gramma)*, are found in vv. 1-6.

c. *Theological Reflection.* The presence of such associations, however, hardly pleads against the presence of theological reasoning in 2:14–3:6. Notwithstanding his unrest in Troas and his departure to Macedonia (2:12-13) Paul is convinced of the marvelous spread of the gospel. He thanks God for this victorious celebration, always and everywhere. The apostle himself is a conquered person in Christ and as such led in this triumphal procession, but God uses him in the manifestation of knowledge. Paul is Christ's irresistible aroma and fragrance. He realizes the critical importance of his function for those he approaches: life or death, salvation or doom. And then—quite matter-of-factly, one would say—he exclaims: Who is competent for those things? The expected answer is: no human being. Paul does not provide an explicit answer. At this point some element in his reasoning is missing: yet, although not sufficient by myself, I am an honest apostle and servant. Paul then stresses his sincerity: it is from God, in the sight of God and in Christ that he speaks. He is not a peddler of God's word as others are. This last remark betrays a polemical bent.

One cannot be surprised that, after this daring and self-confident utterance, Paul asks his addressees: are we beginning to commend ourselves again? This brings him to the second question: do we need letters of recommendation to you or from you? Paul adds, again polemically: some others do. Paul's very recommendation is the existence and quality of the Corinthian church: they are his letter, written on his heart, known and read by all. Paul softens what he had just said: as a matter of fact you are Christ's letter, just ministered by me. He now describes by means of contrasts the qualities of Christian life in Corinth: the activity of the Spirit of the living God (not written with ink), the presence of hearts of flesh (not written on tablets of stone). Paul applies the newness of covenant and the heart quality (as prophesied by Jeremiah and Ezekiel) to the results of his ministry and opposes all of this to the lawgiving depicted in Exodus 34.

Paul then resumes the main point of his exposition: the existence and authenticity of the church in Corinth is the confidence he possesses through Christ toward God. He repeats: there is nothing he can claim as coming from himself; his whole sufficiency has its origin in God. Therefore it is God who made him also competent to be a minister of the new covenant. As in 3:3 Paul uses antitheses to further qualify the newness of that covenant: not a covenant of letter, i.e., a written code, but of Spirit, not a letter that kills, but the Spirit who makes alive. On the one hand the old covenant is pointed to (cf. Exodus 34, which will be explicitly used in vv. 7-18); on the other hand the new covenant of Jer 38:31-34 (LXX) and the life-giving Spirit of Ezek 11:19-20 and/or 36:25-26 are referred to. The Christian church which through Paul's ministry came into existence is no less than the realization of the eschatological renewal announced by the prophets.

d. *Final Remarks.* Three final remarks may conclude our interpretation. (1) We are given a glimpse of Paul's opponents as people who are peddlers of God's word (2:17) and use, in a wrong way, letters of recommendation (3:1b). In contrast with them Paul emphasizes his sincerity as minister and recognizes God as the sole source of his competence; his recommendation is the Corinthian church.

(2) A most impressive factor in this pericope is Paul's conviction regarding God's work in Christ, his own ministry, and the identity of Christian life: all of it is the fulfillment of the spiritual newness of the covenant prophesied by Jeremiah and Ezekiel. The highly astonishing but inevitable consequence is that what Moses brought is no longer relevant.

(3) The denigrating way in which Paul refers to the old covenant and its Law in 3:3 and 6 cannot but surprise the reader. Many commentators attempt to soften the radicality of Paul's statements (see notes). To be sure, the negative characterization functions as background for the positive qualification of the new covenant. Yet to understand what Paul really means by this brief labeling one has to go to his lengthy treatments in Galatians and Romans. However, even if one grants that the Law must condemn its transgressors and, in this sense, causes "death," uneasy questions linger. What was God's original intention in giving the Law to Israel? Why is transgression in the old covenant so hopelessly "deadly" and why is atonement not mentioned? It should be noted: for Paul, the letter that kills points to a covenant where the Spirit is absent because Christ has not been recognized or admitted. In 3:7-18, the passage that immediately follows the radical statement of 3:6a, Paul will emphasize the antithesis "old-new" by sharply contrasting the two ministries.

For Reference and Further Study

2 Corinthians 2:14–7:4 as a whole

Collange, Jean-François. *Enigmes de la deuxième épître de Paul aux Corinthiens: étude exégétique de 2 Cor. 2:14–7:4*. MSSNTS 18. Cambridge: Cambridge University Press, 1972.

Lorenzi, Lorenzo De, ed. *The Diakonia of the Spirit (2 Co 4:7–7:4)*. Benedictina 10. Rome: Abbazia di San Paolo fuori le mura, 1989.

_____, ed. *Paolo. Ministro del Nuovo Testamento (2 Co 2,14–4,6)*. Benedictina 9. Rome: Abbazia di San Paolo fuori le mura, 1987.

Oliveira, Anacleto de. *Die Diakonie der Gerechtigkeit und der Versöhnung in der Apologie des 2. Korintherbriefes. Analyse und Auslegung von 2 Kor 2,14–4,6; 5,11–6,10*. NTA n. s. 21. Münster: Aschendorff, 1990.

Schröter, Jens. *Der versöhnte Versöhner. Paulus als unentbehrlicher Mittler im Heilsvorgang zwischen Gott und Gemeinde nach 2 Kor 2,14–7,14*. TANZ 10. Tübingen and Basel: Francke Verlag, 1993.

2 Corinthians 2:14–4:6

Barth, Gerhard. "Die Eignung des Verkündigers in 2 Kor 2,14–3,6" in Dieter Lührmann and Georg Strecker, eds., *Kirche. FS G. Bornkamm*. Tübingen: Mohr-Siebeck, 1980, 257–270.

Belleville, Linda L. *Reflections of Glory: Paul's Polemical Use of the Moses-Doxa Tradition in 2 Corinthians 3.1-18.* JSNT.S 52. Sheffield: Sheffield Academic Press, 1991.

Breytenbach, Cilliers. "Paul's Proclamation and God's 'THRIAMBOS'. Notes on 2 Corinthians 2:14-16b," *Neotest.* 24/2 (1990) 257–271.

Duff, Paul B. "Metaphor, Motif, and Meaning: The Rhetorical Strategy behind the Image 'Led in Triumph' in 2 Corinthians 2:14," *CBQ* 53 (1991) 79–92.

Egan, R. B. "Lexical Evidence on Two Pauline Passages," *NT* 19 (1977) 34–62.

Fitzmyer, Joseph A. "Glory Reflected on the Face of Christ (2 Cor 3:7–4:6)," in idem, *According to Paul: Studies in the Theology of the Apostle.* New York: Paulist, 1993, 64–79.

Hafemann, Scott J. *Suffering and the Spirit. An Exegetical Study of II Co. 2:14–3:3 within the Context of the Corinthian Correspondence.* WUNT II/19. Tübingen: Mohr-Siebeck, 1986.

Hickling, Colin J. A. "The Sequence of Thought in II Corinthians, Chapter Three," *NTS* 21 (1974–1975) 380–395.

Hofius, Otfried. "Gesetz und Evangelium nach 2. Korinther 3," in idem, *Paulusstudien.* WUNT 51. Tübingen: Mohr-Siebeck, 1989, 75–120.

Hooker, Morna D. "Beyond the things that are written? St Paul's use of scripture," in eadem, *From Adam to Christ. Essays on Paul.* Cambridge: Cambridge University Press, 1990, 139–154.

Koperski, Veronica. "Knowledge of Christ and Knowledge of God in the Corinthian Correspondence," in Reimund Bieringer, ed., *The Corinthian Correspondence.* BEThL 125. Leuven: Leuven University Press/Peeters, 1996, 377–396.

Kreitzer, L. Joseph. *Striking New Images: Roman Imperial Coinage and the New Testament World.* JSNT.S 134. Sheffield: Sheffield Academic Press, 1996.

Lambrecht, Jan. "Structure and Line of Thought in 2 Cor 2,14–4,6," in Bieringer and Lambrecht, *Studies on 2 Corinthians.* BEThL 102. Leuven: Leuven University Press/Peeters, 1994, 257–294.

McDonald, James I. H. "Paul and the Preaching Ministry. A Reconsideration of 2 Cor. 2:14-17 in Its Context," *JSNT* 17 (1983) 35–50.

Marshall, Peter. "A Metaphor of Social Shame: *thriambeuein* in 2 Cor. 2:14," *NT* 25 (1983) 302–317.

Murphy-O'Connor, Jerome. "A Ministry Beyond the Letter (2 Cor 3:1-6)," in L. De Lorenzi, ed., *Paolo. Ministro del Nuovo Testamento,* 105–129.

_____. "*Pneumatikoi* and Judaizers in 2 Cor 2:14–4:6," *ABR* 34 (1986) 42–58.

Oliveira, Anacleto de. "'Ihr seid ein Brief Christi' (2 Kor 3,3). Ein paulinischer Beitrag zur Ekklesiologie des Wortes Gottes," in Rainer Kampling and Thomas Söding, eds., *Ekklesiologie des Neuen Testaments FS K. Kertelge.* Freiburg, Basel, and Vienna: Herder, 1966, 356–377.

Provence, Thomas E. "'Who Is Sufficient for These Things?' An Exegesis of 2 Corinthians ii 15-iii 18," *NT* 24 (1982) 54–81.

Richard, Earl. "Polemics, Old Testament, and Theology. A Study of II Cor. III,1–IV,6," *RB* 88 (1981) 340–367.

Sloan, Robert B. "2 Corinthians 2:14–4:6 and 'New Covenant Hermeneutics'—A Response to Richard Hays," *BBR* 5 (1995) 129–154.

Stimpfle, Alois. "Buchstabe und Geist. Zur Geschichte eines Missverständnisses von 2 Kor 3,6," *BZ* 39 (1995) 181–202.

Stockhausen, Carol Kern. *Moses' Veil and the Glory of the New Covenant: The Exegetical Substructure of II Cor. 3,1–4,6.* AnBib 116. Rome: Pontificio Istituto Biblico, 1989.

Theissen, Gerd. *Psychological Aspects of Pauline Theology.* Translated by John P. Galvin. Edinburgh: T & T Clark, 1987.

Thrall, Margaret E. "A Second Thanksgiving Period in II Corinthians," *JSNT* 16 (1982) 101–124.

Williamson, Lamar. "Led in Triumph. Paul's Use of *Thriambeuō*," *Interp.* 22 (1968) 317–332.

4. *The New Covenant* (3:7-18)

7. Yet if the ministry of death, engraved in letters upon stones, came into being with glory, so that the Israelites could not gaze at Moses' face because of the glory of his face which was vanishing, 8. how more (surely) will not the ministry of the Spirit be with glory? 9. For if glory (belongs) to the ministry of condemnation, much more (surely) the ministry of righteousness abounds with glory. 10. For in fact, what has been glorified has in this case not been glorified because of the surpassing glory. 11. For if what was vanishing (was) with glory, much more (surely) what endures (is) with glory.

12. Therefore, since we have such a hope, we act with great boldness 13. and not as Moses (did): he used to put a veil over his face, so that the Israelites might not gaze at the end of what was vanishing. 14. Their minds, however, were hardened. For until this very day during the reading of the Old Testament the same veil remains unlifted, because (only) in Christ is it abolished. 15. Indeed, until today, whenever Moses is read, a veil lies on their heart. 16. However, when one turns to the Lord the veil is taken away. 17. Now the Lord is the Spirit; and where the Lord's Spirit is, there is freedom. 18. But all of us, with uncovered face beholding the glory of the Lord as in a mirror, are being transformed into the same image from glory to glory, as this comes from the Spirit of the Lord.

NOTES

7. *Yet if the ministry of death, engraved in letters upon stones, came into being with glory:* Verses 7-8 constitute a long conditional period employing an *a fortiori* reasoning (in fact *a minori ad maius.* Cf. two more such sentences in vv. 9 and 11. Jews call this technique of argumentation *qal waḥomer,* "light and heavy").

The conditional period is a *realis*, a simple condition. The logical connection between two pieces of data is expressed: if this is true, then that is also true. In such reasoning the protasis is presumed to be accepted.

The genitive "of death," resuming the idea present in v. 6 (the letter "kills"), characterizes the type of service or ministration: that ministry leads to death. Instead of "engraved in letters on stones" one expects simply "written on stone." By the explicit mention of "stones" and "letters" and by "engraved" as well, Paul refers back to 3:3, 6 and to Exod 34:1-4, 27-28. "Engraved" translates a perfect participle, thus a past action the consequences of which remain. The finite verb *egenēthē* ("came into being") points to the Sinai event, the coming into existence of the Mosaic Covenant. In this pericope a new term is introduced: *doxa* ("glory, splendor"). In 3:7-18 the noun *doxa* will be used no less than eleven times (as well as the verb *doxazō*, "to glorify" twice). Glory or splendor is the manifestation of God's presence, which consists of both light and power. The foundation of the Sinai covenant was accompanied by visible divine glory.

so that the Israelites could not gaze at Moses' face because of the glory of his face which was vanishing: "Israelites" is the translation of *huioi tou Israēl* (literally "the sons of Israel"). Verse 7b employs Exod 34:30 somewhat freely. This added consecutive clause makes the protasis too long and somewhat out of balance. Just as Paul and his co-workers are the ministers of the new covenant (v. 6), so was Moses the minister of the Sinai covenant. The verb *atenizō* ("to gaze" or "to look intently") will appear again in the purpose clause of v. 13. In vv. 7-14 the verb *katargeō* (literally: "render inactive," and further also "abolish") is used four times. It would seem that here (and in vv. 11 and 13) the form is either a deponent passive or middle with the meaning of "fading out, passing away, vanishing." The present participle *katargoumenēn* is in the attributive position with "glory": the transient glory, a glory in the process of passing away and vanishing. The way in which the active form of this verb is used with reference to the Law in Rom 3:31 might surprise us (do we then "abolish" the Law by faith?) since the answer there is negative.

8. *how more (surely) will not the ministry of the Spirit be with glory?* The second member of the conditional period is not a plain apodosis. The apodosis is contained in a question. The literal rendering of *pōs ouchi mallon* is "how not more." The expected answer to this question is: of course, yes. For a question introduced by *pōs ouchi* see Rom 8:32: "He (= God) who did not spare his own Son but gave him up for us all, will he not also (*pōs ouchi kai*) give us all things with him?" In v. 8 the certainty is emphasized by *mallon* ("more surely"; cf. "much more surely" in v. 9 as well as in v. 11), but perhaps also the quantity and quality of glory.

Over against "ministry of death" we expect "ministry of life," but Paul writes "of the Spirit." As in v. 7a we have a qualifying genitive: the Spirit is the characteristic feature of this new ministration. The future "will be," as opposed to the past tense "came into being" (v. 7a), is probably not a logical future. Yet it is not purely eschatological either. Since the coming of Christ this event no longer lies completely in the future. In v. 11 Paul speaks of the glory as a permanent, already existing reality. However, one is tempted to ask what this present glory of Paul's ministry means in terms of visibility (but see v. 18).

9. *For if glory (belongs) to the ministry of condemnation:* a variant reading in v. 9a (present in B among others) has "ministry" as subject and "glory" as predicate. The text that is preferred in this commentary, with "ministry" in the dative and "glory" as subject, provides a chiastic pattern over against v. 9b: dative and nominative (subject) in v. 9a, nominative (subject) and dative in v. 9b. The qualifying genitive "of condemnation" points to a ministry characterized by God's condemnation. The protasis repeats the content of the protasis in v. 7a, but with a slightly different vocabulary and in a shorter, more balanced form.

much more (surely) the ministry of righteousness abounds with glory: Elements of this wording, construction, and type of reasoning are also present in Rom 5:15-20. The emphasis intended by Paul in this *a fortiori* reasoning interrupts the purity of the grammatical balance; there is nothing in the protasis that corresponds to "abounds" in v. 9b. There is not only a more certain presence of glory in the new ministry; this glory is also "abounding," greater, more intense than the former one. The use of *dikaiosynē* ("righteousness") in the sense of justification is typically Pauline. The genitive is again best seen as qualifying: a ministry characterized by God's justifying activity.

10. *For in fact, what has been glorified has in this case not been glorified because of the surpassing glory:* "For in fact" translates *kai gar*. The neuter expression "what has been glorified" points to the "glorious" ministry of Moses. In Greek *ou dedoxastai to dedoxasmenon* is a paradoxical statement in which, through the negation (*ou*, "not"), the two perfect passive forms (personal verb and participle of the same verb; cf. Exod 34:29, 30, 35) clash: what has been glorified has not been glorified. "In this case" and "because of the surpassing glory" soften and explain the paradox. *En toutǭ tǭ merei* (literally: "in this part") is a simple enough phrase in appearance, yet several explanations have been proposed. We mention three of them. (1) Translated as "in this case" it means in comparison with the abundant splendor of the ministry of righteousness (cf. v. 9). (2) Translated as "on this occasion" it refers to the Sinai event. (3) Translated as "as far as this is concerned" or "in this respect" it may refer to death and condemnation in vv. 7 and 9. Common to all is the affirmation that on account of the superabundance of the glory of the new ministry the glory of the old is of no value at all. The preference of this commentary goes to the first proposal. The very emphatic statement of v. 10 is undoubtedly a rhetorical exaggeration.

11. *For if what was vanishing (was) with glory:* As in vv. 7-8 and v. 9, we again have a conditional period. The neuter *to katargoumenon* (an articular present participle passive or middle) no longer refers to the glory itself but to the ministry of death and condemnation (cf. "what has been glorified" in v. 10) and therefore indirectly also to the Sinai covenant. Since *dia* with the genitive ("through") can indicate attendant circumstances and since in v. 7a Paul uti-

lizes *en* with the dative ("in, with") without visible difference, it is doubtful that *dia* in v. 11a points to the transitory character of the old glory while *en* in v. 11b would stress the permanency of the new glory. The variation is probably stylistic.

much more (surely) what endures (is) with glory: Again we encounter an apodosis and, at the same time, *a fortiori* reasoning (cf. vv. 8 and 9b), and again the phrase "much more" (cf. v. 9b). In the whole of v. 11 there is no personal verb. In v. 11a a past tense ("was") and in v. 11b a present tense ("is") are most likely to be supplied.

12. *Therefore, since we have such a hope, we act with great boldness:* With "therefore" and the clause (literally) "having such a hope" Paul resumes the result of his reasoning. "Such a hope" refers to the eschatological and already present "glorious" reality depicted in vv. 7-11 (cf. especially "what endures" in v. 11b). *Parrēsia* ("boldness") was in the Greek world the privilege of a free man, free and bold especially in speech. Because of the immediate context (Paul as a minister), most probably boldness with the people, boldness in proclamation is meant (cf. 7:4: *parrēsia pros hymas*, "toward you"; see also Rom 1:16). However, one wonders whether boldness with God is totally excluded (see v. 13: Moses).

13. *and not as Moses (did): he used to put a veil over his face:* For the "veil" motif and the whole verse see Exod 34:33-35. *Kalymma* ("veil") is the key word for vv. 12-18 (four times in vv. 13, 14, 15 and 16; cf. the verb *anakalyptō*, "to uncover," in vv. 14 and 18). It would seem that Paul begins a comparison with Moses but never finishes it. One should assume the presence of an incomplete construction that can be supplied as follows: "and (we do) not (do) as Moses (did who) put. . . ." According to W. C. van Unnik, while v. 12 contains a specific Greek term (*parrēsia*, "boldness"), v. 13 has a Semitic background; as to content, however, the expression "with unveiled face" is the equivalent of "boldness." The imperfect *etithei* ("he put") expresses repetition and frequency.

so that the Israelites might not gaze at the end of what was vanishing: The second half of v. 13 is reminiscent of v. 7b and is equally dependent on Exod 34:30. Should one, therefore, assume also a consecutive meaning for v. 13b? If the differences between the two verses are taken into account (in v. 13b *pros to* instead of *hōste*, no *dynasthai*) and if it is recognized that v. 14 appears to correct what is said in v. 13b, then the full original force of *pros to* ("in order that") can be retained. Paul writes a purpose clause. *Telos* here is not "goal" or "fulfillment" but "end." For the neuter "what was vanishing" see v. 11. Again not the glory or splendor is meant but Moses' (glorious) ministry and, through it, the Mosaic covenant. Paul describes the action of Moses in a negative way, yet it is perhaps too strained to make him suppose that Moses intentionally wanted to deceive his people. To be sure, in v. 13 Paul is harsh in his treatment of Moses; however, he must have noticed it and in v. 14 he begins to put the blame not on Moses but on "the Israelites."

14. *Their minds, however, were hardened:* The attention shifts to the culpability of the Israelites, away from Moses. Paul thus softens his statements in v. 13. For

the theme of "hardening" and Old Testament background cf. Rom 11:7-8 (and Isa 6:9-10; 29:10). Normally one would take "were hardened" as a divine passive and God as agent. Yet from 2 Cor 4:4 ("the god of the present age has blinded the minds of the unbelievers") we may perhaps assume that the agent of the passive verb is Satan. The noun *noēmata* (literally: "thoughts") refers to the faculty of thinking, "the minds."

For until this very day during the reading of the Old Testament the same veil remains unlifted, because (only) in Christ is it abolished: In vv. 7, 11, 13 and 14a Paul refers back to the time of Moses; from v. 14b onward he reflects on Israel's situation in his own time. "The same veil" means a veil similar to that of Moses (v. 13), i.e., a veil with the same effect. Of course "veil" is now used metaphorically; it has become an internal veil. The preposition *epi* (plus dative) is better not taken in a local sense and not connected with the verb "remains" (the veil remains "over" the reading . . .); its meaning here appears to be temporal: "during." The expression *palaia diathēkē* ("old covenant") is a *hapax legomenon* in the New Testament, most likely coined by Paul himself as the antithesis of the *kainē diathēkē* ("new covenant") of v. 6 (see, however, Heb 8:13). Yet the meaning of *diathēkē* is different: otherwise than in v. 6, the expression of v. 14 points to Scriptures that are read in the synagogues.

The phrase *mē anakalyptomenon hoti* could be understood as an absolute construction: "the revelation not having been made that." The meaning of the verb would be the same as that of *apokalyptō* ("to reveal"). Preference, however, is given to the view that the participle stands in a predicate position and must be linked with *kalymma:* the cover remains not uncovered because . . . that is, the veil remains unlifted because. . . . This is an easier reading of the text and, moreover, in it the verb *anakalyptō* ("to uncover") has the sense present also in v. 18. In Hellenistic Greek the negation *mē* ("not") is regularly used with a participle.

The subject of "is abolished" is the veil, not the Old Testament. Grammatically speaking—especially when one accepts the absolute construction mentioned above—the translation "the old covenant is being abolished" is possible, yet because of the immediate context improbable; moreover, *diathēkē* would mean covenant, not Scriptures as in v. 14b. *Katargeitai* is here certainly a passive. The present tense is somewhat surprising, but although Christ has abolished that veil in the past, it must still be done away with in Paul's time (cf. the present verbs in vv. 15b and 16b) as well.

15. *Indeed, until today, whenever Moses is read, a veil lies on their heart:* This verse repeats and renders more explicit what is said in v. 14b: we now know where the veil lies. The *alla* does not introduce an opposition; it is rather intensive: "indeed." Of course not the person of Moses but the Torah, the Scripture is indicated. The verb "is read" is a present subjunctive passive. While in v. 14b "the same veil" refers to Moses' veil, here "veil" has no article so that the metaphor can even more easily point to a non-material, an internal veil. Differently from v. 14b *epi* (here plus accusative) is local; it depends on "lies." "Heart" refers to the same thinking faculty as is indicated in v. 14a by *noēmata* ("thoughts," hence "minds"; cf. 4:4).

16. *However, when one turns to the Lord the veil is taken away:* The grammatical structure of this sentence is similar to that of v. 15, yet there are major differences: besides the different content, in v. 16a a personal subject is to be supplied (most likely not Moses but "one") and the verb, an aorist subjunctive active, points to a specific eventuality in the future ("when," as it were: "as soon as"; not "whenever"). A comparison with Exod 34:34, Paul's source text here, is instructive. The Septuagint reads: "And whenever Moses went in before the Lord to speak to him, he took off the veil, till he went out" (translation by L.C.L. Brenton). (1) The Pauline text is much shorter (without "to speak with him" and "until he came out"). (2) In v. 16a there is no "whenever" and no repeated "went in before the Lord" but the possible "turning to the Lord" of a contemporaneous Israelite, not of Moses. (3) The verb in v. 16b is present passive, not imperfect deponent, and the agent is God (or Christ, see v. 14c), not Moses. (4) "To turn to" (instead of "go in, enter") is the equivalent of conversion.

If it can be assumed that for the reader v. 16, notwithstanding the differences, remains a real quotation, then "Lord" points to God, to the Father. If not, the reader will almost spontaneously think of v. 14c and identify the Lord with Christ as one often does in other Pauline passages. See further discussion of this point in the comment on v. 17.

17. *Now the Lord is the Spirit:* There can be no doubt that in this specific context the particle *de* ("but") introduces an explanatory clause. The definite article *ho* before "Lord" in v. 17a is anaphoric. Paul intends to say: I mean by the Lord of v. 16 the Spirit (for a similar exegetical addition see, for example, 1 Cor 10:4c: the rock just mentioned was in fact Christ; cf. also Gal 4:25 and 1 Cor 15:55b-56a). The reason why Paul in v. 17 and v. 18 explicitly brings in the Spirit is his characterization of the new covenant as a covenant of the Spirit (see vv. 3, 6 and 8) over against the old, that of the letter (v. 6).

Who is the Lord of v. 16, before the identification with the Spirit takes place? There are three possibilities. (1) According to the *christological* interpretation Paul refers to Christ: when people turn to the Lord Jesus Christ, then . . . (v. 16). For Jews who already believe in God, this Lord can scarcely be Yнwн. It must be Christ. In v. 17a Paul then explains that by Christ he concretely means the Spirit (cf. 1 Cor 15:45). This approach makes it possible to see Christ in all the occurrences of *kyrios* ("Lord") in vv. 16-18. Christ is experienced in the new covenant through the Spirit, i.e., through what the Spirit of Christ realizes in Christians. The identification of Christ and Spirit is functional, dynamic. See the emphatic presence of Christ in the last clause of v. 14. (2) The *theological* interpretation maintains that in v. 16 Paul intends to "quote" Exodus, albeit in a free way. In v. 17a he then explains that the OT *kyrios,* God, must be considered as the Spirit. The midrashic character of this passage, it is said, pleads for such an understanding. Moreover, there is no explicit mention of Christ in vv. 16-17. (3) One could wonder whether what Paul intends to say is not situated somewhere between the two above interpretations. Is he not writing in a *pneumatological* way (cf. Emily Wong, "The Lord is the Spirit")? Paul perhaps means the Spirit already in v. 16. The function of

v. 17a then is one of concretizing a still open concept, "Lord," or also preventing a less correct understanding of v. 16 (i.e., God or Christ). Verse 17a then would not provide an identification, but only an explanation, a filling of a still undetermined "Lord," or, if needed, a correction of what should not have been thought. The preference of this commentary, however, goes to the christological understanding.

Two notes should be added. First, in a conjecture, old (Johannes M. S. Baljon, *De tekst der brieven van Paulus aan de Romeinen, de Corinthiërs en de Galatiërs als voorwerp van de conjecturaalkritiek beschouwd* [Utrecht: J. Van Boekhoven, 1884]) but proposed again (e.g., by Jean Héring, *The Second Epistle* [1967]), a *hou de* is substituted for *ho de* in v. 17. The result of this correction is an excellent progressive parallelism in v. 17: "Where the Lord is, there is the Spirit; where the Lord's Spirit is, there is freedom." Yet a better style and smoother argument are hardly valid reasons for accepting the conjecture. Second, there is no serious ground for considering v. 17 a Gnostic gloss, as one or two commentators still do today.

and where the Lord's Spirit is, there is freedom: "Lord" in v. 17b almost certainly means Christ: where the Spirit of Christ is. "Freedom" must certainly be understood as freedom from the negative features of the old covenant (= the abolition of the veil). Yet freedom is positively filled with what characterizes the new covenant: justification, life, boldness, and, according to v. 18, transformation. For "freedom" see 1 Cor 10:29; Gal 2:4; 5:1, 13; for the Spirit who brings about freedom and glorification cf. Rom 8:14-16.

18. *But all of us, with uncovered face beholding the glory of the Lord as in a mirror:* The addition of "all" to "us" implies that Paul has in mind all (Corinthian) Christians, not himself (and his fellow missionaries) alone. The Christians are opposed not only to Moses, but also to the Israelites in the desert who were not able to see (v. 13) and whose minds were hardened (v. 14a), and more particularly to the later Israelites on whose hearts a veil still lies (vv. 14b-15) and who are not turning to the Lord (cf. v. 16). The expression "with uncovered face" (not "heart" as v. 15 could suggest) refers back to the covered face of Moses (v. 13) but is obviously employed here in a metaphorical sense: there is no "veil" in the new covenant; there is freedom. The perfect of this participle (*anakekalummenō*) points to a realized, permanent condition. The action in the past, i.e., the "uncovering," which brought about that situation, is God's justification of the Christian.

The verb *katoptrizomai* is a *hapax legomenon* in the New Testament; it is not found in the Greek versions of the Old Testament or in Greek writers before the Christian era (cf., however, Philo, *Leg. all.* 3.101). The deponent middle sense is most probably transitive: to behold the glory as in a mirror. Some exegetes prefer "to reflect" because of the supposed context. The weakened sense of "seeing," (attested in Latin versions or comments) is unlikely; the verb in v. 18 appears to retain its original force, i.e., the mirror notion. Paul wants to suggest that Christ's glory is seen as in a mirror. The vision itself thus is not direct (cf. 1 Cor 13:12). Christians see the "glorious" Christ but indirectly, as in a mirror. What is this mirror? One may think here of Christ's visibility as "mirrored" in the gospel proclamation and in the specific Christian way of life that the gospel inspires. This seeing is, of course, also an interior experience. What kind of change does such a vision bring about?

are being transformed into the same image from glory to glory: Joseph A. Fitzmyer ("Glory") points out that one should not exaggerate the general Hellenistic impact that the use of *metamorphoumai* ("to be transformed") betrays. Passages from the Qumran documents witness to the fact that illumination (transformation by vision?) is a Palestinian Jewish motif as well. Together with others, Fitzmyer also emphasizes that Paul is not thinking of a mystical union or complete identification with Christ. It would seem to us that Paul detected the idea of "transformation by vision" in his reading of Exodus 34. The glorious transformation that happened to Moses becomes a possibility for every Christian. The expression "into the same image" warns us that Paul means real *trans*formation, more than *con*formation (so, e.g., in Rom 8:29). He envisages a profound idea of unity with Christ (without loss of separate identity). According to 4:4 Christ is the image of God (cf. Col 1:15). To be God's image is to manifest God's glory. With the expression "the same image" Paul refers to the image implicitly given in the preceding expression, "beholding as in a mirror." Together with mirror, the idea of mirror-image is present. Therefore "image" in v. 18 probably possesses a double reference: Christ as image of God, and the Christ-image seen by the Christians as in a mirror. Thus all of us, beholding the glory of Christ, are being changed (present tense) into the image, into Christ. That image is "the same" as what we are beholding as in a mirror; that image is the glorious Christ. "From glory to glory" indicates a process: from one degree of glory to another. It is better not to distinguish two sorts of glory, e.g., temporal and eschatological, or God's glory as source and that of the Christians as result.

as this comes from the Spirit of the Lord: Is the particle *kathaper* ("as") purely comparative? It probably possesses a motivating or causal nuance. The final expression *apo kyriou pneumatos* is not clear. The genitive *pneumatos* could be an apposition: "from the Lord who is the Spirit." The translations "from the Lord of the Spirit" or, rather, "from the Spirit of the Lord" are also possible. Again "Lord" probably refers to Christ. This last clause looks like a corrective addition by which Paul wants to dispel a possible misunderstanding: the change is the work of Christ's Spirit, not so much ours!

INTERPRETATION

a. *Structure and Line of Thought.* Within 2:14–4:6 the pericope 3:7-18 constitutes the middle section. It deals, directly at least, with the relation between the ministry of the old covenant and that of the new, between Judaism and Christianity. The statements in 3:6 occasioned this central passage, a much needed clarification: the antithesis present in v. 6 has to be worked out. The new beginning at 3:12 indicates that a twofold division is present: vv. 7-11 and vv. 12-18.

It is immediately evident that the key word in 3:7-11 is *doxa* ("glory"). The glory of the ministry of the new covenant is compared with that of the ministry of the old. There is gradation and opposition. In this section it seems that opposition is more important than gradation; see the antitheses death/stone/letter/condemnation/vanishing and life/heart/Spirit/righteousness/enduring. The two glories and ministries become polarized, and more so with each verse. The first glory, that on the face of Moses, which is perishable and transitory, is spoken of in a denigrating fashion, while the second glory becomes, as it were, more and more brilliant and is permanent. One must not fail to recognize that Paul is not free to deny the glory of Moses, for Exodus 34 is quite clear on that point and Paul cannot but accept it. Yet Paul manages to convey his attitude regarding that glory by a thoroughly unfavorable comparison with the new glory. This attitude is crystallized in the negation of v. 10: compared with the glory of the ministry of righteousness there is no glory at all in the ministry of condemnation; what is glorified there is not glorified. Thus the poles of opposition are, as it were, irreconcilable.

What is the inner structure of 3:7-11? The first sentence of the subunit is a long question running through two verses. Actually, v. 7a is the condition for the question that comes in v. 8. Verse 7b, a brief excursus, depicts how seemingly great and fantastic the splendor of the old dispensation was. Nevertheless, the ministry of death is confronted with the ministry of the Spirit. Within the conditional sentence an *a minori ad maius* argumentation appears: the question in v. 8 is introduced by "how more (surely)." The second sentence (v. 9) is very concise. It serves as a continuation and an explanation (see *gar*, for) of the first period. The opposition now is constituted by the ministry of condemnation and the ministry of righteousness, which is more or less the parallel of the first opposition. Again we have a conditional period combined with an *a minori ad maius* reasoning ("much more"). This apodosis, however, is not phrased in terms of a question; it is an affirmative statement. This feature, together with the verb "abounds," provides the passage with a rising tone. The crescendo movement reaches a climax in v. 10, although the oxymoron within this verse is presented as an incidental motivating clause *(gar)*. In effect Paul asserts that when compared with the overwhelming new glory, the glory of the old covenant is no longer real glory. Paul may rhetorically exaggerate here, but his readers understand all the better what he wants to convey about the newness of his ministry and the covenant. Verse 10 formulates the conclusion of the whole argumentation. It is a rather daring affirmation for Paul to make. Verse 11, once more introduced by *gar*, is again a conditional period and presents us with a third *a minori ad maius* progression ("much more"). The content is very similar to that of the first two (vv. 7-8 and 9): "What is vanishing" and "what endures" point directly to the ministries, indirectly to their respective glory. With v. 11 Paul has come full circle, returning to where he began. This last verse, then, together with vv. 7-8 and 9, frames the central verse 10 (cf. also the including elements at the beginning and at the end: *katargoumenēn* in v. 7 and *katargoumenon* in v. 11). Verses 7-9 represent a crescendo that reaches its climax in v. 10 and is resolved in v. 11. No doubt—notwithstanding the *gar* connections—the structure of 3:7-11 is concentric: *a* (vv. 7-9: *a fortiori*), *b* (v. 10: paradox) and *a'* (v. 11: *a fortiori*). We thus rightly assume that v. 10 not only motivates *(gar)* but also grounds the surrounding argumentation.

While vv. 7-11 provide a rather rational and static meditation, a comparison of two opposite splendors, vv. 12-18 are more what could be called "existential" and dynamic. Paul is personally involved: see v. 12 (since we have such a hope) and v. 18 (all of us are being changed; the "we" of v. 18, however, is broadened and includes all Christians). If the key word in vv. 7-11 was *doxa* ("glory"), that for vv. 12-18 is *kalymma* ("veil"). The use of this terminology conveys a rather sad and pained attitude on Paul's part toward unconverted Jews, which contrasts sharply with his boastful, self-confident, and hopeful view of himself and other Christians. This confrontation between the "we" and the "they" determines the equally concentric structure of this subunit: *a* (vv. 12-13, we), *b* (vv. 14-17, they) and *a'* (v. 18, we).

Verses 14-17 contain an indirect attack as well as an indirect appeal with regard to the Israelites. Actually Paul begins speaking of the Israelites already in v. 13b. Taken by itself this clause could leave us with the impression that Moses himself is responsible for the fact that the Israelites do not see the transitoriness of the old glory. That is why Moses covers his face: to deceive the sons of Israel. However, from vv. 14-15 it is obvious that Paul does not want his readers to believe this. In these verses Paul stresses the guilt and culpability of the Israelites, not of Moses. His charge of obduracy is leveled in v. 14a. Verses 14b and 15, by means of parallelism, go on to enforce the notion of the hardening of the minds of the Israelites both past and present. Between them, however, falls verse 14c: in Christ the veil is abolished. This positive datum, sandwiched between two negative verses, is taken up in vv. 16-17 which speak of the possibility of the removal of the veil, i.e., the conversion of the people of Israel.

After this analysis of structure and line of thought in separate subunits one must underline the unity of vv. 7-18, the whole pericope. Verse 12 resumes what precedes ("hope") and links *(oun,* "therefore") the two subdivisions. Verse 13 is connected with v. 7b in vocabulary as well as content. Verse 14 (old *diathēkē*) refers back to v. 6 (new *diathēkē*) of which vv. 7-11 are but the exposition. Verses 17-18 again take up the Spirit qualification of the new ministry (v. 9; cf. vv. 3 and 6). Furthermore, there are a number of words and phrases common to both sections: *katargoumai, hoi huioi Israēl, Mōÿsēs, prosōpon,* and *doxa.* Moreover, one must not forget the numerous internal links and, of course, the common Exodus 34 background.

b. *A Particular Problem.* It is clear that in 2 Cor 3:7, 10, 13, and 16 there are irrefutable references to Exod 34:1, 4, and 27-35. Although 2 Cor 3:3 and 6 share elements with Exodus 34, by far the most obvious dependence on Exodus is in 2 Cor 3:7-18. Yet there are remarkable differences between the Old Testament source text and the Pauline text. According to Exod 34:1 and 4 Moses cut two new tablets of stone and went up to Mount Sinai, and according to 34:27-35 Moses wrote the words of the covenant on the tablets. When Moses came down, the appearance of the skin of his face was glorified. Aaron and the elders of Israel feared to approach him and Moses had to call them. Afterward all the people of Israel came to him and he handed on to them all that the Lord had commanded him on the mountain. "And when he ceased speaking to them, he put a veil on his face. And whenever Moses went in (the tabernacle) before the LORD to speak to him, he took off the veil till he went out" (vv. 33-34; translation of the LXX by L.C.L. Brenton).

In 2 Cor 3:7b Paul accentuates the idea that the Israelites could not look at Moses' face because of its brightness; he emphasizes several times that Moses' glory is vanishing; in v. 13 he states that Moses covered his face in order that the Israelites might not see the end of the vanishing splendor. Such data cannot be found in the Septuagint version of Exodus 34. In his text Paul made an extensive and at the same time a very free use of Exodus 34. We are left with the impression that it was the author's intention to look for some illustrative, if not familiar, material so as to better explain his own ideas. In that way a remarkable actualization came into existence. The fact that his ideas are at times different from, and even contrary to, the literal sense of the Exodus passage does not seem to bother Paul, if indeed he was much aware of the discrepancy.

It has been claimed that the passage is unlike the framing sections. One could extract it from its context, some say, with almost no resultant lack of continuity between 2:14–3:6 and 4:1-6. Paul's reading of Exod 34:27-35 is a reinterpretation, a "Christian midrash." The new text is controlled by Paul's presuppositions. Paul is polemically commenting on a text that his opponents were using (so Hans Windisch, *Der zweite Korintherbrief,* ad loc). The passage 2 Cor 3:7-18 was conceived by Paul earlier than the letter proper and written outside that letter context (so Hans Lietzmann, *An die Korinther,* ad loc). The numerous *hapax legomena* (words and phrases) must be mentioned: *diakonia tou thanatou, atenizō* and *entypoō*

(v. 7), *kalymma* (vv. 13, 14, 15, and 16), *achri tēs sēmeron hēmeras* and *palaia diathēkē* (v. 14), *anakalyptō* (vv. 14 and 18); *hēnika an* (v. 15), *hēnika ean* and *epistrephō pros kyrion* (v. 16), *katoptrizomai* (v. 18). On the basis of so many *hapax legomena* in so short a text, as well as in view of the other elements that seem to separate vv. 7-18 from the surrounding texts, Siegfried Schulz ("Die Decke") and others after him conclude that Paul made use of a source text that he commented on and interpolated in such a way as to change its original sense. The pre-Pauline midrash was, it is said, a Jewish-Christian document from the Diaspora; its most significant feature is the positive appreciation of Moses.

Dieter Georgi *(Opponents)* goes further in attempting to reconstruct this source text in more detail and in claiming that the midrash was composed by Paul's opponents. Two points are stressed. First, since the opponents called themselves *diakonoi Christou* (see 2 Cor 11:23), their reflection on Moses' ministry is anything but accidental. Like Moses, the Jewish and Jewish-Christian missionaries are ministers. As Moses was glorified—and is therefore a *theios anēr* ("divine man")—so are they. The fact that Moses is seen as a minister means that his glory is for the people: what happened to him is possible for others (viz., the actual ministers). Second, the motif of the veil, explained by Paul in a negative sense, was positive in the midrash. After his speaking to the people, Moses put a veil on his face so that the Israelites might not see the end, i.e., the aim, the completion of Moses' transforming experience of God. This gesture is an incentive for others to long for the same experience. When Israel turns to the Spirit, the spiritual sense of Scripture is grasped and the transformation process commences. Paul's opponents thus defend the continuity between their old Jewish tradition and the new Christian Spirit experience. Other authors, mostly depending on Georgi, explain the origin of 3:7-18 in a similar way.

It should be recognized that if such hypotheses could be accepted exegetes would be able to compare the original midrash with Paul's critical re-editing of it. The intentions of Paul would become more evident and the position of his opponents more apparent. The majority of commentators, however, maintain serious reservations regarding the so-called source text and, it would seem, rightly so. The whole operation is too hypothetical: the indication of pre-Pauline elements, the exact wording and content of the document and, by means of this, the reconstruction of the opponents' theology. In accepting the existence of a source one has, moreover, to make a number of supplementary suppositions: Paul would have had access to this text; he would then have, so to speak, attacked his opponents with their own weapons; he would have managed to twist the source text, making it say the exact opposite of its original affirmations.

Why should one postulate the existence of an intermediate text between Exodus 34 and 2 Cor 3:7-18? It would seem that Paul himself could have created this midrash and for this purpose made direct use of the Exodus passage. The sharp antitheses of 3:3 and 3:6, which in their compactness are rather mysterious, compelled Paul, as it were, to compose this elucidation. The *hapax legomena* find a sufficient explanation in the presence of traditional subject matter and its dependence on Exodus 34. It is not to be excluded that Paul employed and/or criticized elements from contemporary midrashic Exodus traditions (e.g., the increase of Moses' glory). Reference can here be made to the Pauline "midrash" 1 Cor 10:1-13, more particularly with regard to the Rock which in Jewish exegesis was identified with the Law.

c. *Theological Reflection.* Two summarizing and more theological considerations seem appropriate. (1) The first section of the pericope deals with *glory:* this concept is taken from Exodus 34. Moses' glory is a symbol of the old covenant. Later Judaism was of the opinion that the glory of Moses was lasting, but Paul's conviction is just the opposite. That glory is vanishing. The old covenant is the ministration of death and condemnation; because of the absence of the Spirit it is only engraved on tablets of stone. No Jew who was not a Christian would speak in this way. It is a Jewish Christian who looks back on his non-Christian Jewish past. Paul gained this insight through his experience with the new covenant (Christ and justification, the Spirit and real life already given and present but at the same time still hoped for), through his conviction that the prophetic announcements in Jer 38:31-34 (LXX) and Ezek 11:19-20 and/or 36:25-26 have become a reality. Paul's comment, then, is a challenging, daring, and uncommonly free reinterpretation of Exodus 34. An Old Testament text is used to prove the inferiority and end of the old covenant and its ministry!

(2) The whole of the second section treats the motif of the *veil*, which also comes directly from Exodus 34. In vv. 12-13 Paul deals with the "we" of the apostles. As an apostle he is a servant of the new covenant. His apostolic boldness is based on the hope for a lasting, imperishable splendor. Paul acts differently from Moses, without a veil. In vv. 14-17 the theme of the veil is still present, but we are confronted with an actualizing transposition. In v. 13 the expression "the Israelites" refers to the generation of the desert. From v. 14b onwards Paul's attention turns especially to his non-Christian Jewish contemporaries. "Moses" is read to this very day. The veil has become a symbol of Jewish obdurateness; it is this factor that makes the understanding of Scripture impossible for them and prevents their recognition that Christ abolished the veil (vv. 14-15). With vv. 16-17 a more positive approach comes to the fore: we are dealing here with the removal of that same veil. The expression "with uncovered face" (v. 18) is

for a Semite the same as "with boldness" (v. 12) and "in freedom" (v. 17).
A process of interior yet also visible transformation into Christ, the image
of God, is for all Christians the result of their beholding Christ's glory as
in a mirror, i.e., of their seeing Christ and listening to Christ in the gospel
and their following him in daily life.

d. *Critical Questions.* Before leaving this mysterious text we must ask why
Paul here contrasts old and new, unbelieving Jews and believing (Jewish
and non-Jewish) Christians, and why he writes in such a negative way
about Moses' ministry. First, what is worked out in vv. 7-18 is in harmony
with Paul's teaching in Galatians and Romans: the Torah functions as a
transitory reality; the Law cannot justify; the Law cannot bring life; the
Law condemns the sinner to death; the Law is only provisional. The Law
is no longer a valid way to salvation; as a matter of fact, it never was. So
the content of 2 Cor 3:7-18, however strange it might look through its use
of Exodus 34, is profoundly Pauline. The passage gives expression to the
very core of Paul's conviction; it is certainly meant for the instruction of
the Corinthian addressees.

Nevertheless, something has to be added. In this unit Paul does not
seem to be attacking his Christian rivals (as he did in 2:17–3:1, at least
indirectly). Must we therefore postulate the existence of a non-Christian
Jewish opposition in Corinth? Paul could here be responding to criticisms
from his fellow Jews who are not Christians. However, he could also be
answering Jewish Christian intruders who reproach him for his failure to
convert more than a very few Jews; or did these intruders and their sym-
pathizers in Corinth perhaps defend the salvific function of the old covenant Law? It would seem that the teaching presented in 3:7-18 must also
have been occasioned by critical utterances in Corinth. According to
some scholars the intruders are Paul's missionary rivals who defend the
enduring validity of the old covenant. In 3:3, 6, 7-18 Paul is arguing
against such a view. It must be added, however, that such qualifications
of Paul's enemies remain inevitably hypothetical.

In 3:7-18 Paul writes both polemically and apologetically. This passage
is allusively autobiographical. However, what is said about the splendor
and freedom of the new covenant, as well as about the transformation
from glory to glory, applies to Christians of all times and places.

FOR REFERENCE AND FURTHER STUDY

See also the bibliography following 2:14–3:6.

Belleville, Linda L. "Tradition or Creation? Paul's Use of the Exodus 34 Tradition
in 2 Corinthians 3.7-18," in Craig A. Evans and James A. Sanders, eds., *Paul*

and the Scriptures of Israel. JSNT.S 83. Sheffield: Sheffield Academic Press, 1993, 165–186.

Dumbrell, William J. "Paul's Use of Exodus 34 in 2 Corinthians 3," in P. T. O'Brien and D. G. Peterson, eds., *God Who is Rich in Mercy. FS D.B. Knox.* Sydney: Anzea Publishers, 1986, 179–194.

Dunn, James D. G. "2 Corinthians III.17—'The Lord is the Spirit,'" *JThS* 21 (1970) 309–320.

Dupont, Jacques. "Le chrétien, miroir de la gloire divine, d'après II Cor. III,18," *RB* 56 (1949) 382–411.

Fitzmyer, Joseph A. "Glory Reflected on the Face of Christ (2 Cor 3:7–4:6)," in idem, *According to Paul: Studies in the Theology of the Apostle.* New York: Paulist, 1993, 64–79.

Georgi, Dieter. *The Opponents of Paul in Second Corinthians.* Philadelphia: Fortress, 1986.

Hafemann, Scott J. *Paul, Moses and the History of Israel. The Letter/Spirit Contrast and the Argument from Scripture in 2 Corinthians 3.* WUNT 81. Tübingen: Mohr-Siebeck, 1995.

Hickling, Colin J. A. "Paul's Use of Exodus in the Corinthian Correspondence," in Reimund Bieringer, ed., *The Corinthian Correspondence.* BEThL 125. Leuven: Leuven University Press/Peeters, 1996, 367–376.

Koch, Dietrich-Alex. "Abraham und Mose im Streit der Meinungen. Beobachtungen und Hypothesen zur Debatte zwischen Paulus und seinen Gegnern in 2 Kor 11,22-23 und 3,7-18," in Bieringer, ed., *The Corinthian Correspondence,* 305–324.

Lambrecht, Jan. "Transformation in 2 Cor 3:18," in Bieringer and Lambrecht, *Studies on 2 Corinthian.* BEThL 102. Leuven: Leuven University Press/Peeters, 1994, 295–307.

Schulz, Siegfried. "Die Decke des Moses. Untersuchungen zu einer vorpaulinischen Überlieferung in II Cor. 3.7-18," *ZNW* 49 (1958) 1–30.

Thrall, Margaret E. "Conversion to the Lord. The Interpretation of Exodus 34 in II Cor. 3:14b-18," in Lorenzo De Lorenzi, ed., *Paolo. Ministro del Nuovo Testamento (2 Co 2,14–4,6).* Benedictina 9. Rome: Abbazia di San Paolo fuori le mura, 1987, 197–232.

Unnik, W. C. van. "'With Unveiled Face'. An Exegesis of 2 Corinthians iii 12-18," in idem, *Sparsa Collecta I.* NT.S 29. Leiden: Brill, 1973, 194–210.

Vanhoye, Albert. "L'interprétation d'Ex 34 en 2 Co 3,7-14," in De Lorenzi, ed., *Paolo. Ministro del Nuovo Testamento,* 159–180.

Wong, Emily. "The Lord is the Spirit (2 Cor 3:17a)," *EThL* 61 (1985) 48–72.

5. *The Minister and His Gospel* (4:1-6)

1. Therefore, having this ministry by God's mercy, we do not lose heart. 2. On the contrary, we have renounced the deeds one hides for shame; we do not practice cunning nor do we falsify the word of God, but through the open preaching of the truth we commend ourselves to anyone's conscience in the sight of God.

3. But if our gospel is veiled all the same, it is veiled only to those who are perishing, 4. in whose case the god of the present age has blinded the minds of the unbelievers so that they do not see the light of the gospel of the glory of Christ, who is the image of God.

5. For we are not proclaiming ourselves but Jesus Christ as Lord, ourselves, however, as your servants for Jesus' sake. 6. For (it is) the (same) God who said, "Let light shine out of darkness," who has caused his light to shine in our hearts to spread the light of the knowledge of God's glory in the face of Jesus Christ.

NOTES

1. *Therefore, having this ministry by God's mercy:* The connective "therefore" is very much stressed at the beginning of this pericope and most likely refers to what precedes (not to what follows). "By God's mercy" renders the comparative clause (literally: "as we have been shown mercy [by God]") which should be seen as depending on "having," not on the main verb. This results in paraphrase: having obtained this ministry by the mercy of God. The past tense probably refers to Paul's conversion and call to apostleship.

   we do not lose heart: The same statement reappears in 4:16 (with *dio*, the equivalent of *dia touto*, "therefore"). Margaret E. Thrall, *Second Epistle* 298–299, prefers: we do not grow lax, reluctant, remiss (in our duty), a sense attested in extrabiblical sources.

2. *On the contrary, we have renounced the deeds one hides for shame:* The aorist indicative of the verb points to a past and complete renunciation that results in an ongoing behavior (see most other verbs in vv. 1-2). The phrase "the deeds one hides for shame" renders the genitive construction *ta krypta tēs aischynēs* ("the hidden things of shame") and takes the genitive as subjective: shame makes a person conceal these things. Or should we perhaps assume a Hebrew qualifying genitive and translate "shameful hidden things?"

   we do not practice cunning nor do we falsify the word of God: Alfred Plummer, *Commentary* 111, comments on *panourgia* ("cunning"): "unscrupulous readiness to adopt any means in order to gain one's ends." From 12:16 it would seem that Paul has been accused of "cunning" in financial matters. Is this the point here also? At any rate 4:2 might evidence not only an apologetic but also a polemic tone. For "we do not falsify the word of God," compare 2:17: "we are not peddling God's word."

but through the open preaching of the truth we commend ourselves to anyone's con-science in the sight of God: "Open preaching" is the rendering of *phanerōsis* ("manifestation"). "The truth" here is another term for "the word of God." In vv. 3-6 we will also meet "gospel," "Jesus Christ as Lord," "the knowledge of God's glory in the face of Christ": all these terms and phrases indicate the same reality. For "in the sight of God" cf. 2:17: "before God"; for "we commend ourselves" see 3:1. People judge the content of Paul's preaching with their conscience. There seems to be some tension with what Paul says in 1 Cor 4:3-5.

3. *But if our gospel is veiled all the same:* The order of the words in Greek *(ei de kai,* "but if all the same") betrays emphasis (with *estin,* "is," which may signify "remains"). Paul can be reacting against an accusation of obscurity or absence of eloquence. His preaching, his gospel lacks "evident" glory. If so, this verse, like the previous one, is polemical. The use of the verb *kalyptō* ("to veil") twice in this verse reminds the reader of "the veil" and "uncovering" in 3:12-18.

it is veiled only to those who are perishing: for comment on the expression "those who are perishing" see 2:15.

4. *in whose case the god of the present age has blinded the minds of the unbelievers:* The grammatical structure of this clause is contorted. The genitive "of the unbe-lievers" further determines "those who are perishing" of v. 3. The two ex-pressions most probably point to the non-Christian Jews (cf. 3:14-15), not to the Gentiles. "The god of the present age"—a *hapax legomenon* in the New Tes-tament—is Satan. "Here we have an example of the kind of dualism inherent in Paul's own thought. The present age is under the domination of evil cos-mic powers, the devil and his angels, who are in conflict with Christ. . . . What makes 2 Cor 4:4 distinctive is the very strong and virtually unparalleled expression used to describe Satan: he is the *god* of this world" (MacRae, "Polemic," 422). Although the devil is the cause of blindness, the addition at the end of "unbelievers" may contain a connotation of human culpability. For "minds" see the note on 3:14.

so that they do not see the light of the gospel of the glory of Christ, who is the image of God: "so that" suggests a consecutive sense. However, one may question whether the original purpose character of the *eis to* construction is totally ab-sent. With his blinding, Satan has a definite aim. The verb *augasai* here is tran-sitive and most probably means "to see sharply" (not "to shine"; cf. the more or less equivalent verb in 3:7 and 13). The subject has to be supplied from what immediately precedes: "the unbelievers"; *phōtismos* is the direct object. This last term can mean "light" or "illumination" (the action of giving light). It would seem that the first sense is present in v. 4, the second in v. 6. The light comes from "the gospel" (genitive of origin) and the gospel spreads "the glory of Christ" (glory: objective genitive). C. K. Barrett comments on this string of genitives: "This heaping up of genitives is Jewish Greek" (*Commen-tary* 131), a note which equally applies to the end of v. 6. Both 4:4 and 3:18 em-ploy the term "image" and the parallel expressions "the glory of Christ" or "the glory of the Lord" respectively. Furthermore, 3:18 speaks of "beholding as in a mirror," an action of all believers, whereas in 4:4 the expression "so that they do not see the light" points to the blindness of the unbelievers.

Transformation in 3:18 is ascribed to the Spirit; obduration in 4:4 to Satan. There is, then, a fourfold parallelism and/or opposition between 3:18 and 4:4: (1) "glory" (of Christ), (2) verbs of seeing, (3) divine/satanic causality, and (4) "image." For the probable background of Christ as the image of God see Wis 7:25-26 (wisdom is an image of God's goodness) and/or Gen 1:26-27 (humankind created in the image of God).

5. *For we are not proclaiming ourselves but Jesus Christ as Lord, ourselves, however, as your servants for Jesus' sake:* "Christ" traditionally refers to Jesus who died and is risen, and "Lord" to Jesus as the exalted one, actually living and reigning. Both "Lord" and "your servants" are in the predicative position (hence the translation "as"). However, one has to weaken the force of the verb as far as the second term is concerned: of course, Paul does not proclaim or preach himself as a servant. The mention of "Jesus" again at the end probably betrays that Paul here envisages Jesus as the one who suffered and died on the cross and who, as such, is the example for the apostle (cf. also the frequent use of "Jesus" in 4:10-11). A well-attested text variant has "through Jesus" (*dia* + genitive) instead of "for Jesus' sake" (*dia* + accusative).

6. *For (it is) the (same) God who said, "Let light shine out of darkness," who has caused his light to shine in our hearts:* The *hoti* ("for, because") at the beginning is strongly motivating. The grammatical construction in the Greek text is not smooth: an *estin* ("is") seems to be lacking. The quotation is not literal. Two Old Testament texts suggest themselves: Gen 1:3 and/or Isa 9:2 (LXX). The verb *lampō* means "to shine." In the Pauline text *phōs* ("light") is the grammatical subject. With God as subject in the second use of the verb *(elampsen)* it presumably carries the causative nuance of a Hebrew *hiphil*: "caused (light) to shine." The alternative rendering would be "who has shone." In both cases the indicative aorist probably refers back to Paul's conversion and call, i.e., to his Christophany (cf. 4:1). For the expression "in our hearts" see Gal 1:16 (God revealed his Son "in me").

to spread the light of the knowledge of God's glory in the face of Jesus Christ: On *phōtismos* (here "illumination") and on the presence of three genitives see the note on v. 4. The translation given here, "to spread the light," can be misleading. We take "knowledge" as a subjective, not an objective genitive. Moreover, it is probably not God, but the apostle who causes the knowledge to illuminate (missionary interpretation; cf. 2:14-16 and see also Gal 1:15-16). A paraphrase of this compact construction runs, then: "in order that we (Paul) may make the knowledge illuminate (the Gentiles)." It is the knowledge of God's glory that is on the face of Jesus Christ. The glory of God became visible in Jesus Christ (cf. v. 4: Christ is the image of God). Besides the opposition between "the god of the present age" in v. 4 and "God" in v. 6, there is a striking similarity of both vocabulary and structure between the following clauses:

v. 4: *eis to mē augasai ton phōtismon tou euangeliou tēs doxēs tou Christou*

v. 6: *pros phōtismon tēs gnōseōs tēs doxēs tou theou en prosōpǭ Christou.*

Of course v. 4 is negative but v. 6 positive. Moreover, we assume for *phōtismos* the sense of "illumination" in v. 6 and that of "light" in v. 4.

INTERPRETATION

a. *Structure and Line of Thought.* With "therefore, having this ministry . . ." in 4:1 Paul draws his conclusion. The beginning of this conclusion is clearly marked by "therefore"; yet at the same time, precisely by means of the term "ministry," an obvious connection is made with 3:7-18 (and 3:3 and 3:6). Ideas present in 3:7-18 (= B), but also in 2:14–3:6 (= A), are taken up. Paul again speaks of his ministry and the possible reaction to it; he commends himself and emphasizes his openness and sincerity as a minister; he points to the origin of that ministry and to the source of its splendor. One will easily agree on the inclusion function of 4:1-6 (= A') (see pp. 43–44).

From 4:1 onward Paul is again talking very clearly about the apostle and his way of life. At the time of his conversion Paul was given a ministry (4:1; cf. 3:6); he does not lose heart. In v. 2 Paul deals with his honest attitude, with the fact that he is not tampering with God's word and with the way in which he commends himself: these are all themes that occur also in 2:14–3:6, especially in 2:17 (sincerity) and 3:1-5 (recommendation, appointment). The tone is decisively apologetic, but polemics do not seem absent either. Perhaps Paul has been accused of guile (cf. v. 2; here also the matter of recommendation) and of obscurity or lack of eloquence (cf. v. 3). Verse 5 takes up an obvious apologetic-polemic idea: we proclaim not ourselves but Jesus Christ as Lord (cf. 3:3); we are but your servants for Jesus' sake (cf. 3:5-6). These observations should sufficiently corroborate the conception that the two outer pericopes (A and A') correspond with each other and, indeed, do include or frame the central pericope (B).

In an A–B–A' structure the A' part is rarely a pure repetition of the A part, no matter how closely they are attuned. The author has to harmonize the A' part with the content of the immediately preceding B part. Between B and A' there are many corresponding elements. A thematic and vocabulary analysis of 4:1-6 proves that 3:7-18 can in no case be a later insertion: the author has utilized the previous pericope in composing 4:1-6. (1) "Therefore, having this ministry by God's mercy" (v. 1) summarizes the result of the description of the two dispensations in 3:7-18; "we do not lose heart" evidently refers back to the apostolic "boldness" of 3:12-13 and perhaps also to the "freedom" of Christians mentioned in 3:17. (2) In 4:2-4 there is, notwithstanding the difference of context, the opposition between manifestation and hiddenness that was presumably suggested to the author by the veil-motif of 3:14-16. (3) With "has blinded the minds of the unbelievers" v. 4 resumes the clause of 3:14a: "their minds were hardened." Although in 4:4 Satan is mentioned as the agent, the specification of "unbelievers" reveals that here also, just as in 3:14-15, the author does not want to deny the culpability of those "who are perishing" (4:3). In both passages most probably the non-Christian Jews (cf. "the sons of Israel," 3:13) are referred to. (4) Together with v. 6, v. 4 also has the term "glory," the very theme that is woven throughout the whole of the middle section. (5) Finally, numerous connections exist between v. 4 and v. 6 on the one hand and 3:18 on the other, as has been indicated in the Notes.

Sharp divisions are not to be expected within the short pericope 4:1-6, yet a close reading of the passage detects here also a somewhat concentric movement of the line of thought. In v. 1 Paul states that he does not lose heart. Paul employs the first person plural ("we"), but means primarily himself. Verse 2 then explains the opposite of not losing heart. Paul defends himself against the accusation of secrecy: I have renounced the deeds one hides for shame. In the Greek text three present participles explain the implications of this honest apostolic attitude: no cunning, no falsification of God's word, and complete openness to anyone's conscience.

This brings Paul to deal with the fact that his gospel remained veiled to some people: it is not recognized or accepted by all (v. 3). If there is, notwithstanding his openness, still a veiled gospel, then it is only in the case of those who are perishing, the unbelieving Israelites ("they"). In v. 4 Paul adds that their blindness, i.e., their inability to see the light of the gospel, is caused by the god of this world. But this, it would seem, does not take away the culpability of these Jews: they are "unbelievers."

In 4:5-6 Paul comes back to his apostolic existence (first person plural: "we"). Verse 5 is introduced by a *gar* ("for") as if Paul were saying: I am not to be blamed for that state of blindness because I do not proclaim myself, but Jesus Christ as Lord. What Paul adds is meant for his Corinthians: I am only your servant. In v. 6 God's initiative is underlined once more (cf. v. 1). This is the true explanation (*hoti*, "for, because") of why Paul is (only) a servant of the Corinthians for Jesus' sake. It is God who caused light to shine in Paul's heart so that he could make this light shine for others, especially the Gentiles. In an impressive way vv. 5-6 round off the passage (4:1-6), which itself is the conclusion of 2:14–4:6.

The cyclic character within the pericope has become apparent. There is an *a b a'* movement: from "we" (*a*: vv. 1-2) to "they" (*b*: vv. 3-4) and back to "we" (*a'*: vv. 5-6).

b. *A Characteristic Feature*. In 3:2-3 Paul corrects his statement. "You are our letter" becomes "you are the letter of Christ, ministered by us." In 4:5 a similar concern is present. Paul's self-understanding comes to the fore. What is his position in the economy of salvation? Paul is not proclaiming himself but Jesus Christ as the Lord. He himself is but a servant (see the Notes regarding the literal sense: Paul can hardly "proclaim" that he is a servant). "Servant" *(doulos)*, not "minister" *(diakonos)*, is employed here because of the preceding "Lord" *(kyrios)*. Yet the last part of v. 5 is more than a correction. Paul reflects on his apostolic function. As a servant he is proclaiming that Jesus Christ is the reigning Lord. For Jesus' sake he is a servant of the Corinthians. Christology and ecclesiology are intimately connected.

c. *Theological Reflection*. Gen 1:3 ("And God said, 'Let there be light'"; the term "darkness" is present in vv. 2 and 4) should be compared with 4:6: "It is the (same) God who said, "Let light shine out of darkness." Strictly speaking, Paul does not cite Genesis. Those who think, rightly in our opinion, that there is an intended reference see Paul paralleling the God-Creator of Genesis with God again taking the initiative and causing light to shine in the heart of the minister. Paul is once more affirming that he himself is not the origin of his ministry; his ministry is, as it were, "created" by God.

Many scholars take the clause in 4:6 to be (also) an allusion to Isa 9:2 (LXX): "O people walking in darkness, behold a great light: ye that dwell in the region and shadow of death, a light shall shine upon you" (translation by L.C.L. Brenton). For them Paul's enlightenment is the fulfillment of the long-promised messianic light. In Isa 9:1, however, it is the prophet who speaks, while in Gen 1:3 and 2 Cor 4:6 it is God.

In his own references to his conversion Paul indicates a connection with the faculty of sight: see Gal 1:16 (revelation); 1 Cor 9:1 (seeing); and 1 Cor 15:8 (appearance). Does "in the hearts" of 2 Cor 4:6 suggest that the conversion was merely an internal event? Most probably not. It would seem that Paul twice in this verse employs the verb *lampō* ("to shine") in order to present the Damascus experience as an experience of splendor full of light. In his interpretation G. W. MacRae links the conversion of Christians in general and Paul's specific vocation: ". . . it seems difficult to exclude from 2 Cor 4:6 an allusion to Paul's conversion, but the language of the verse is so unspecific that he seems to have wished to generalize to the level of the Christian experience of conversion. That both a specific echo and a generalization are intended is certainly not impossible" ("Polemic," 423).

d. *Actualization*. 2 Cor 3:18 deals with all Christians, with their vision and their transformation, and not just with Paul's own reflection on his ministry. Yet in view of 2:14–4:6 as a whole and especially 4:6 (according to our interpretation), it would not be wise to exclude the idea of active apostolate. The brightness that first is seen and personally adopted and that transforms the Christians "into the same image" (the glorious Christ) is afterward communicated to others by "illumination": transformation and apostolic activity are interrelated. Both take their origin in God, both are christologically conditioned, both are essentially pneumatic and ecclesial. Even if in 4:6 Paul is considering himself in the first place, the illumination of his own "heart" (according to a different interpretation), in view of the context and more particularly v. 5 with its verb "to proclaim" as well as the qualification of Paul as "servant" of the Corinthians, the apostolic implications are certainly not absent. "The revelation of light in Paul's conversion was for the dissemination, through Paul's apostolic work, of knowledge" (Barrett, *Commentary* 135).

Paul will deal with the apostolic sufferings more extensively in 4:7-18 and further in his letter. One should, however, not lose sight of the paradoxical nature of the "glory" of apostle and Christians alike. Actual transformation "from glory to glory" and manifestation of that glory, considered from outside and humanly speaking, seem to be the opposite of brightness and splendor: our nature is wasting away. This precisely is the dialectical element in Christian existence; it recalls the striking discontinuity between the present life and the eschaton. Yet what is strong already manifests itself in what is weak; the future, as it were, already erupts into the present; what is lasting breaks through what is perishable; what is eternal already enlightens what is temporary and transitory.

Major sections of 2 Corinthians have an apologetic tone. The letter is written to people who were Christians and (still?) friends of Paul, but in danger of being influenced by those he considered his opponents. In trying to understand as fully as possible what Paul was saying to his friends (apologetic aspect) we must take into account what he is attacking (polemic aspect). Paul's argument is probably pitted against the rather triumphalistic propaganda of the opponents. It is in all his trials, and not just in future life, that Paul sees the presence of glory. It is not in those who work showy deeds, but in those who undergo a radical transformation—in those who lead a humble and honest life—that one finds the true "servant of Jesus Christ" and, analogously, the true Christian.

For Reference and Further Study

See also the bibliography following 2:14–3:6.

Garrett, Susan R. "The God of This World and the Affliction of Paul: 2 Cor 4:1-12" in David L. Balch, Everett Ferguson, and Wayne A. Meeks, eds., *Greeks, Romans, and Christians. FS for A.J. Malherbe.* Minneapolis: Fortress, 1990, 99–117.

Kertelge, Karl. "Jesus Christus verkündigen als den Herrn (2 Kor 4,5)" in Karl Kertelge, Traugott Holtz, and Claus-Peter März, eds., *Christus bezeugen. FS W. Trilling.* Erfürter theologische Studien 59. Leipzig: St. Benno-Verlag, 1989, 227–236.

Klauck, Hans-Josef. "Erleuchtung und Verkündigung. Auslegungsskizze 2 Cor 4,1-6" in Lorenzo De Lorenzi, ed., *Paolo. Ministro del Nuovo Testamento*. Benedictina 9. Rome: Abbazia di San Paolo fuori le mura, 1987, 267–297.

MacRae, George W. "Anti-Dualist Polemic in 2 Cor. 4,6?" *StEv* 1 (TU 102). Berlin: Akademie-Verlag, 1968, 420–431.

6. *The Treasure in Clay Jars* (4:7-15)

7. We have this treasure, however, in clay jars in order that the excess of power be God's and not from us. 8. In every way we are hard pressed, but not confined; at a loss, but not in despair; 9. persecuted, but not abandoned; struck down, but not destroyed; 10. always carrying the putting to death of Jesus in the body in order that the life of Jesus be also manifested in our body. 11. For we who live are always given up to death because of Jesus in order that the life of Jesus be also manifested in our mortal flesh. 12. So death is at work in us, but life in you.

13. However, since we have the same spirit of faith according to what is written, "I believed, therefore I spoke out" (Ps 115:1 LXX), we too believe; therefore we also speak out, 14. for we know that the one who raised the Lord Jesus will raise us also with Jesus and place us together with you (in his presence).

15. For (it) all (occurs) for your sake in order that grace, having increased thanksgiving through many, may abound to the glory of God.

NOTES

7. *We have this treasure, however, in clay jars:* With "this treasure" Paul presumably points back to his ministry (cf. 4:1). He seems to correct himself: "however." Through his preaching he reveals "the light of the gospel of the glory of Christ" (4:4); he spreads "the light of the knowledge of God's glory" that is on the face of Christ (4:6). Yet this glorious ministry is, as it were, contained and hidden in clay jars, in fragile vessels; it is surrounded by much affliction.

The image "in clay jars" appears to be taken up further in the text by "in our body" (v. 10), "in our mortal flesh" (v. 11), and "in us" (v. 12). A strictly dualistic interpretation that would oppose body and soul is therefore to be excluded. Apostolic life is lived by the whole person and its tribulations are not undergone by the body alone, but also by the "inside" of the person. It should be recognized, however, that with the terms "jar," "body," and "flesh" Paul stresses the visible "outside" of the apostle. In the image "clay jar" it is probably the nuances of fragility and weakness that prevail over that of total dependency (cf. Rom 9:19-24: clay, jar, and artisan) or that of instrumentality (cf. Acts 9:15: a "chosen vessel").

in order that the excess of power be God's and not from us: This is the first of four
purpose clauses in this passage, all introduced by *hina* ("in order that," see
also vv. 10, 11b, and 15b). All these clauses point to an aim but also to something of a conclusion, a consequence. "The excess (or: surplus) of power" indicates the exceeding power inherent in the apostolic preaching and
operative in the adverse circumstances surrounding that preaching. In Rom
1:16 and 1 Cor 1:18 the gospel and the word of the cross are referred to as "the
power of God." Therefore the use of the term "power" may carry a more or
less technical nuance here. The construction "God's" and "from us" is asym-
metrical (we do not read: "from God"). Finally, we might perhaps supplement: in order that it "be evident that. . . ." Regarding the content of v. 7b,
cf. 1:9b: "in order that we should not be relying on ourselves but on God, who
raises the dead."

8. *In every way: En panti* presumably applies to the four antitheses of vv. 8-9 and
not only to the first; later in the passage the expression is reinforced by *pantote* (v. 10, "always") and *aei* (v. 11, "always"), both terms also at the beginning
of a clause. Verses 8-10 form a cluster of participles grammatically, it would
seem, in apposition to the subject "we" in *echomen* ("we have") at the beginning of v. 7, or they may be absolute participles that stand in place of independent personal verbs (cf. our translation). In vv. 8-9 we find the first,
admittedly brief list of hardships in this letter (cf. 6:4-10; 11:23-29; 12:10; see
Interpretation after 6:4-10).

we are hard pressed, but not confined; at a loss, but not in despair: The first member of each antithesis in vv. 8-9 indicates an apostolic hardship; the second is
introduced each time by "but not" and refers, it would seem, to the presence
of God's power. Strictly speaking the rhetorical figure is a *correctio*. By itself
the grammar does not require strict simultaneity: hard-pressed, but (at the
same time) not confined. Posteriority of the second member is also possible.
In all eight members we have a present participle in the nominative plural
ending in-*menoi*. In the second antithesis there is a play on words: *aporoumenoi
all' ouk exaporoumenoi,* in a literal translation "at a loss, but not utterly at a
loss." Commentators refer to Paul's concession in 1:8c ("so that we despaired
even of living"); one should not interpret the two verses 1:8c and 4:8b as contradictory, since in the latter verse Paul's attention moves to the effect of
God's power.

Some maintain that the clauses that in vv. 8-9 follow *alla ouk* ("but not") do
not indicate God's intervention but point to the very limit of suffering ("but
not yet"): utterly miserable, almost dead. In the whole of vv. 8-9 Paul depicts
his hardships and vulnerability. Only in vv. 7b, 10b, and 11b is there reference
to God's power or Jesus' life. This interpretation, however, fails to account for
the antithetical force of *ouk alla* (cf. also 4:16).

9. *persecuted, but not abandoned; struck down, but not destroyed:* The verb *enkatalei-
pomenoi* ("abandoned") is a *hapax legomenon* in Paul, recurring only once more
in the whole New Testament: "My God, my God, why have you abandoned
me" (Mark 15:34). Some claim that Paul refers to the passion narrative. This,
however, seems very unlikely since he would be contradicting Jesus. The lat-

ter member of the fourth antithesis stresses that there is no total loss of life, no actual death or complete destruction, yet in what follows Paul will deal with his continual process of being put to death.

10. *always carrying the putting to death of Jesus in the body:* In Paul (and the New Testament) the Greek term *nekrōsis* occurs only twice and means either the dead condition, the deadness (Rom 4:19) or, here, the process of "mortification," of putting to death. It is not the Christian's burial into death by baptism (cf. Rom 6:3-10), but what causes death during the entire life of the apostle. Verse 10a summarizes and qualifies in a christological way what is expressed in vv. 8-9, as well as in v. 7a: apostolic suffering and fragility are not just human pain caused by opposition and persecution. No, the putting to death of Jesus himself is present in it, visible in the body of the apostle. In vv. 10, 11, and 14 Paul, contrary to his habit, refers to Christ simply as "Jesus" (see already in 4:5). By so referring to his Lord he may want to parallel his own suffering with that endured by the earthly Jesus and thus to present his own suffering as a continuation of that of Jesus. However, the expression "the life of Jesus" in vv. 10b and 11b indicates that for Paul the earthly Jesus is not separated from the risen, glorified Christ. It may be going too far to assume that the phrase "another Jesus" in 11:4 suggests that with "Jesus" in 4:10-14 Paul criticizes the opponents' christology that—it is claimed—neglects the suffering of Christ and his sacrificial death.

in order that the life of Jesus be also manifested in our body: This purpose clause continues the christological characterization present already in v. 10a. Its formulation, contrary to that of the second member in the antitheses ("but not"), is positive. Together with the purpose clause of v. 7b it frames the whole of vv. 7-10. The content of both vv. 10b and 7b is similar: "the life of Jesus" corresponds to "the power of God." The aim of the apostle's dying is the visible, bodily manifestation of Jesus' life (i.e., God's power).

11. *For we who live are always given up to death because of Jesus:* Paul must have sensed that the *nekrōsis* language of v. 10 is not that easy to grasp. He now clarifies his ideas ("for"). At first sight v. 10 and v. 11 look like parallels in both structure and vocabulary as well as in content. Verse 11, however, is grammatically speaking an independent sentence. In v. 11a "in the body" is missing, but "we who live" (literally: "we the living ones") is added. In place of the genitive "of Jesus" we have the motivating "because of Jesus." The passive construction "we are given up to death" replaces the active "carrying the putting to death." The identification of Paul's suffering with Jesus' dying (v. 10a) disappears, yet the choice of the specific verb "we are given up" to death may be motivated by Paul's interpretation of his suffering in close relationship to Jesus' "having been given up" to death (probably a term already present in the tradition; cf. Mark 9:31; 10:33: 14:18, 21).

in order that the life of Jesus be also manifested in our mortal flesh: Notwithstanding its symmetry with v. 10b, the purpose clause in v. 11b presents the following deviations: the place of the verb in the middle of the clause, "flesh" instead of "body," and the addition of "mortal."

The changes in both v. 11a and v. 11b thus modify the structure when compared with that of v. 10. Three particular features should be noted. (1) We can detect in v. 11 a chiastic structure: the verbs in v. 11a and v. 11b stand in the middle; at the beginning of v. 11a we have "we who live" and at the end of v. 11b "in our mortal flesh"; at the end of v. 11a we find "for Jesus' sake" and at the beginning of v. 11b "the life of Jesus." (2) The opposition between death and life is made explicit in *both* clauses of v. 11 (compare death in v. 10a and life in v. 10b). (3) Whereas in v. 10 the being-put-to-death of Jesus stands over against his life, in v. 11 the opposition is between "*we*, the living ones" who are always being given up to death (v. 11a) and "the life of *Jesus*" which is manifested in our mortal flesh (v. 11b).

12. *So death is at work in us, but life in you:* While in vv. 7-11 Paul speaks only of himself (we, the apostles), in v. 12 the addressees are mentioned. The apostolic significance of the suffering is emphasized; it is put forward as a consequence: *hōste* ("so"). The particle *hōste* appears to be used here to introduce an independent sentence. It would seem that the idea of substitution or, better, representation (vicarious suffering) is present. No polemical note, however, should be supposed. The "you" is not to be taken here as pointing to the self-confident, satisfied Corinthians of 1 Cor 4:8-10.

13. *However, since we have the same spirit of faith:* The logical connection with what precedes is not evident. It could be the idea that suffering is not all that is required of the apostle. Faith leads to proclamation. Not the "same spirit" as that of the Christian Corinthians is meant; rather, Paul points to the spirit (the Holy Spirit?) of the one who speaks (David?) in the psalm quotation that follows. Since in v. 14 the resurrection is mentioned, one could ask whether Paul already has in mind faith in this resurrection. This is unlikely not only because in v. 13a it is still Old Testament faith but also because v. 14 appears to be giving an additional reason for Paul's bold preaching, which reason is introduced not by "we believe," but by "we know."

according to what is written, "I believe, therefore I spoke out": The quotation is from Ps 116:10 (= LXX 115:1). The Septuagint, upon which Paul's comparison and application are based, is different from the Hebrew text ("I kept my faith, even when I said").

we too believe; therefore we also speak out: Paul means his Christian believing conviction, i.e., more his state as believer than the content of his faith. The "speaking out" points to his apostolic preaching, his missionary proclamation of the gospel. Since in the psalm the "speaking out" addresses God it is rather unlikely that Paul, who changes that speaking into preaching to people, intends to refer to the broader context of that psalm (situation of need).

14. *for we know that the one who raised the Lord Jesus:* Paul probably integrates here (part of) an old traditional credal formula (cf. 1 Cor 6:14 and Rom 8:11). God is the subject of the verb "raised." In view of its rather strong attestation (e.g., 𝔓⁴⁶ and B) the shorter variant reading "Jesus" is perhaps to be preferred to "the Lord Jesus." This would, then, be a sixth use of "Jesus" (without "Lord"

or "Christ") in chapter 4: see vv. 5, 10a, 10b, 11a, 11b and 14a; one more such use follows in v. 14b.

will raise us also with Jesus: The phrase "with Jesus," of course, cannot be understood as if Jesus would rise once more in the future. Paul means something like "just as Jesus in the past" or, better, "owing to our union with him." One should not admit a non-eschatological, present-life sense of the verb "raise." The meaning is not: God will raise us, over and over again, to a full Christian life before death (against Norbert Baumert, "Täglich sterben," and Jerome Murphy-O'Connor, "Faith").

and place us together with you (in his presence): The place where Paul and the other Christians will be found is not indicated. The phrase could refer to a "tribunal," meaning that they are to account for their deeds on the last day (cf. 5:10). It seems, however, more likely that Paul has in view here a future state of being "in the presence" of Jesus or God (cf. 1 Cor 1:9; 1 Thess 4:17; 5:10). Again, a present-life understanding of this clause is to be rejected: Paul does not say that within the course of ongoing history on earth God will present Paul, together with the Corinthian believers, to the public forum, i.e., the world (so Baumert and Murphy-O'Connor).

15. *For (it) all (occurs) for your sake:* The Greek text has no main verb in the sentence. With "for your sake" Paul returns to the apostolic idea expressed in v. 12; it may, again, imply substitution, representation.

in order that grace, having increased thanksgiving through the many, may abound to the glory of God: There are various possibilities for reading this purpose clause. Is the verb *pleonazō* ("to increase") transitive or intransitive? The same question can be asked regarding *perisseuō* ("to abound"). Furthermore, what is the grammatical function of the accusative "thanksgiving"? We take the first verb to be transitive (with "thanksgiving" as direct object), the second intransitive. In his commentary Alfred Plummer appropriately notes "the play of words between *charis* and *eucharistia,* and the alliteration, *pleonasasa . . . pleionōn . . .*, and the climax from *pleonasasa* to *perisseusē*" (*Commentary* 134). Regarding the vocabulary and the redundant, overloaded character of this clause, cf. 2 Cor 8:7; 9:8a; 9:12; Rom 5:15; 5:20; 6:1; 1 Thess 3:12. One has the impression that this text unit comes to a close at this point.

INTERPRETATION

a. *Structure and Line of Thought.* 2 Cor 4:7–5:10 contains a second section of Paul's so-called (first) apology. A characteristic reflection comes clearly to the fore, a reflection that concerns the outward appearance and inward condition of Christian ministry. Paul meditates on the paradox of a process of death that bears within itself, and already manifests, life, and that ultimately, through the resurrection, will culminate in an eternally lasting and glorious existence. What is mortal will, finally, be swallowed up by what is life (cf. 5:4). Because Paul reflects here on the relationship between his suffering and eventual glory, we can to some extent separate this section from what precedes (2:14–4:6) and what follows (5:11–7:4). From 4:7 onward there is no longer the opposition between the old covenant (and Moses as its minister) and the new covenant (and Paul as its minister). In 5:11–6:10 Paul will again defend himself and reflect on his ministry of reconciliation.

Two subdivisions should be distinguished in 4:7–5:10. In the first, 4:7-15, Paul pays more attention to the suffering of the "present time"; in the second, 4:16–5:10, he points to what ministers and Christians may expect of the "future." This is one reason for a differentiation within this section. There is a second factor as well. In 4:7-15 Paul is more explicitly occupied with the addressees, the people for whom he lives, to whom he preaches. In 4:16–5:10 he considers rather the destiny of all Christians. The opposition "we-you" of the first unit seems to disappear in the second. One may assume that the "you" of the first unit is included in the use of "we" in that second. These are two separate units, to be sure, but between them there are many connecting links as far as the vocabulary and content are concerned. The subject matter of the second unit is already announced in the first (see 4:14: the final outcome), and Paul in the second unit (see 4:16-18) treats further the theme of suffering which is dealt with in the first.

A division of 4:7-15 into three (unequal) parts appears to be justified: vv. 7-12, 13-14, and 15. In vv. 7-12 Paul begins with the statement that the apostle has the treasure of his ministry in clay vessels. This must be so in order that it be clear that the extraordinary apostolic power belongs to God and does not come from the apostle himself (v. 7). Paul formulates the antitheses of vv. 8-9 out of his own experience and thus illustrates what he intends to say by the opening opposition in v. 7 between fragile and powerful. In vv. 10 and 11, by means of subtle variations, Paul basically depicts the same antithesis of dying and remaining alive, yet he now reflects upon the christological dimension of his apostolic existence. Both the death and life of the apostle are connected with the death and life of Jesus. Verse 12 marks a conclusion, but it strikes the reader that Paul brings about a shift. He now restricts death to the apostle and life to the Corinthian Christians.

In v. 13 we have a new beginning indicated by the particle *de* ("but, however"). Paul no longer insists that, notwithstanding his dying, there is life, already now here on earth. In the complex sentence construction of vv. 13-14 he explains that his apostolic activity of proclamation is grounded in his faith conviction; it is also grounded in his certainty of a final outcome, his resurrection after death—firmly based on Christ's past resurrection—and what can be called a gathering forever of all Christians in the presence of Jesus or God.

With v. 15 Paul both summarizes and motivates the main ideas of the first two parts. Suffering and preaching occur for the sake of the Corinthians. Then, by means of abundant terms and phrases, the last purpose clause points out the ultimate aim of all apostolic activity, namely the glory of God. People are to be persuaded to be thankful. God's free gift of the ministry should lead to giving thanks to God. Having thus increased the thanksgiving by many people, the gift itself overflows to the glory of God.

b. *A Specific Problem.* It may be noted that as far as the origin of the list of hardships (the antitheses of vv. 8-9) is concerned, some have suggested war or fighting terminology (cf. 10:3-5). Moreover, similar catalogues or lists occur in Stoic literature. Nor should one forget to refer to a possible Old Testament background of some of the participles Paul uses: the suffering of the righteous and the expected hardships and tribulations of the end of this age. Above all, however, Paul is presumably pointing, albeit in a general way, to his own suffering and weakness, to real dangers and difficulties he actually endured. To a certain extent vv. 8-9 are autobiographical. Furthermore, the lyrical and rhetorical tone, the play on words, and the antitheses are typical of Paul.

c. *Theological Reflection.* The proclaimer must reflect the proclaimed. What are the inspiring factors in an apostolic (and Christian) existence?

Paul repeatedly stresses that his misery is not all-encompassing. He distinguishes between suffering and liberation. Death is not total; life triumphs. One may perhaps think here of a distinction in time: over and over again there is tribulation, but this does not lead to complete despair or final destruction. One could say: there is first apostolic suffering and then divine liberation (cf. 1:8-10). Yet Paul also speaks of simultaneous dying and renewal. Is that process by which the "inner self is being renewed day by day" (4:16) invisible? The answer cannot be a simple yes. Paul's apostolic endeavor is not an ordinary lifestyle. Paul's behavior is unique; people cannot but see him, and they like him or hate him. The life of Jesus is manifested in Paul's mortal body. In the midst of labor and affliction, suffering and being put to death, in the midst thus of hardships and utter weakness God's power is paradoxically revealed. Paul over and again experiences his deliverance out of what must often have appeared to be a hopeless situation. Living with such experiences will have provided him with a first source of inspiration and courage.

On an even deeper level there was Paul's intimate knowledge of his union with Christ. In view of parallel texts such as 2 Cor 1:5; 13:4; Gal 6:17; Phil 3:10-11 we have to interpret Paul's carrying in his body the putting to death of Jesus and the twofold mention of Jesus' life manifested in the apostle in terms of participation, the natural result or effect of his union with Christ. However difficult it may be to specify that union, a kind of ontological oneness with Christ is postulated by Paul and referred to frequently in his writings. That union with Christ can be considered in different ways. It was realized through the historical salvation of Jesus on the cross; it is given to believers *sola fide;* it is sacramentally appropriated in baptism; it is developed in Christian life, more specifically in that of the apostle; and the Christian also looks forward to it in eschatological hope. Thus at its deepest roots apostolic suffering goes back to that participation. Hence also the consequence of that union: in Paul's suffering Christ manifests himself. No opposition between epiphany and participation or union can be detected.

A third conviction inspires Paul's dedication and makes the affliction bearable. Paul sees his efforts in an apostolic perspective; he knows that they bear fruit. In v. 12 he concludes the first part of this pericope as follows: "So death is at work in us, but life in you," and in v. 15 he states with even more clarity that everything in his apostolic existence occurs for the sake of the Corinthians.

The experience of God's power in weakness, the fundamental union with Jesus, and the presence of life in others through the apostle's being given up to death: these three reassuring aspects do not yet procure a complete picture of Paul's apostolic existence. There is a fourth factor. The present glory, i.e., the experience of anticipated resurrection life in apostle and Christians alike, awaits a final breakthrough. Suffering is still a daily reality, a wasting away. Yet Paul knows for certain that God who raised Christ from the dead will raise him with Christ and bring him, together with the other risen Christians, into Christ's and God's presence. For Paul this inner, indestructible faith certainty is perhaps the most important basis for encouragement and strength. That God has raised Jesus and will raise those Christians who remain faithful to the end is the source *par excellence* of Paul's apostolic boldness.

God's power is operative in the midst of weakness; Paul is united with Jesus in such a manner that his dying manifests Jesus' life; apostolic suffering brings about life in one's brothers and sisters; through the resurrection both apostle and Christians will live forever with Christ in God's presence. With these four fortifying insights the apostolic existence, as well as every genuine Christian life, does make sense. All these still somewhat anthropological considerations, however, are embedded in the ultimate theological perspective. Grace must extend to more and more people; grace must increase thanksgiving, to the glory of God (v. 15).

d. *Actualization.* What kind of life, then, do the Corinthian Christians possess thanks to Paul's work and suffering? Is it glory without distress? At the beginning of his letter Paul explains how apostle and Christians endure the same sufferings (see 1:6-7). The "we" of 4:16-17, like that of 3:18, is broader than the apostolic or personal "we" that is frequently encountered elsewhere in the letter. Both the wasting away of the outer self and the renewal of the inner self apply to all Christians. There is no reason for considering the already present and increasing glory of the Corinthian Christians to be different from that of the apostle. For the Christians, too, the ongoing transformation, from one degree of glory to another, is not yet a final, complete, and manifest glorification. Yet through their authentic Christian existence the Corinthians are a letter of Christ, known and read by all (3:2-3). For them, and for Christians of all times, there will thus be that paradoxical combination of death and life, of suffering, maybe persecution, but not ultimate destruction.

For Reference and Further Study

Baumert, Norbert. *Täglich sterben und auferstehen. Der Literalsinn von 2 Kor 4,12–5,10.* StANT 34. Munich: Kösel, 1973.

Bouttier, Michel. "La souffrance de l'apôtre. 2 Co 4,7-18," in Lorenzo De Lorenzi, ed., *The Diakonia of the Spirit (2 Co 4:7–7:4).* Benedictina 10. Rome: Abbazia di San Paolo fuori le mura, 1989, 29–49.

Duff, Paul. "Apostolic Suffering and the Language of Processions in 2 Corinthians 4:7-10," *BTB* 21 (1991) 158–165.

Ebner, Martin. *Leidenslisten und Apostelbrief. Untersuchungen zu Form, Motivik und Funktion der Peristasenkataloge bei Paulus.* FzB 66. Würzburg: Echter Verlag, 1991, 196–242.

Fitzgerald, John T. *Cracks in an Earthen Vessel: An Examination of the Catalogues of Hardships in the Corinthian Correspondence.* SBL.DS 99. Atlanta: Scholars, 1988.

Hodgson, Robert. "Paul the Apostle and First Century Tribulation Lists," *ZNW* 74 (1983) 59–80.

Lambrecht, Jan. "The *'nekrōsis'* of Jesus: Ministry and Suffering in 2 Cor 4,7-15" in Bieringer and Lambrecht, *Studies on 2 Corinthians.* BEThL 102. Leuven: Leuven University Press/Peeters, 1994, 309–333.

_____. "The Eschatological Outlook in 2 Corinthians 4, 7-15" in idem, 335–349.

Murphy-O'Connor, Jerome. "Faith and Resurrection in 2 Cor 4:13-14," *RB* 95 (1988) 543–550.

Schrage, Wolfgang. "Leid, Kreuz und Eschaton: Die Peristasenkataloge als Merkmale paulinischer *theologia crucis* und Eschatologie," *EvTh* 34 (1974) 141–175.

Wolff, Christian. "Niedrigkeit und Verzicht in Wort und Weg Jesu und in der apostolischen Existenz des Paulus," *NTS* 34 (1988) 183–196.

7. The Future Destiny (4:16–5:10)

16. Therefore we do not lose heart; on the contrary. . . . Even though our outer self is wasting away, our inner self is being renewed day by day. 17. For the momentary light (weight) of our tribulation is producing a more and more exceeding and eternal weight of glory for us 18. who are not looking to what is seen but to what is unseen; for what is seen is transitory, but what is unseen (is) eternal.

5:1. For we know that if our earthly house or tent should be destroyed we have a building from God, a house not made with hands, eternal, in the heavens. 2. For indeed in this (tent) we groan, longing to put our dwelling from heaven on over (it) 3.—if (it is) really (true that) by having in fact put on we will not be found naked—. . . 4. For indeed we who are in this tent groan, being weighed down, because we do not wish to take off, but to put on over, in order that what is mortal may be swallowed up by life.

5. Now the one who shaped us for this very thing (is) God, who has given us the guarantee, namely, the Spirit.

6. Since we are, therefore, always of good courage and since we know that being at home in the body we are away from the Lord 7.—for we walk by faith, not by sight— . . . 8. Yes, we are of good courage and would rather go away from the body and get home to the Lord.

9. Therefore we also aspire, whether at home or away from home, to be pleasing to him. 10. For we must all be manifested before the tribunal of Christ so that each one may receive what (he [or she] deserves) according to what he [or she] did through the body, whether good or evil.

NOTES

16. *Therefore we do not lose heart; on the contrary . . . :* With "we" Paul means himself or the apostles. Also compare the same verb in 4:1-2 where Paul writes: "Therefore . . . we do not lose heart. On the contrary *(alla,* but), we have renounced. . . ." After (the first) *alla* in v. 16 we expect a similar verb or something like "but (= on the contrary) we are fully involved." This *alla* reply is not present. Hence, there is no smooth flow of thought. In what immediately follows Paul does not point to a positive, courageous attitude but simply expresses a faith conviction. One should assume an anacoluthon in v. 16.

Even though our outer self is wasting away, our inner self is being renewed day by day: Before "our inner self" Paul writes a second *alla;* its sense is: "yet" (= notwithstanding the fact of wasting away). In this clause there is a double contrast: our outer self/our inner self *(ho exō hēmōn anthrōpos/ho esō hēmōn)* and wasting away/being renewed. The expression "day by day," a *hapax legomenon* in the New Testament, justifies the English present continuous translation of the two verbs.

In Rom 6:6 Paul speaks of *ho palaios hēmōn anthrōpos* ("our old self") and in Rom 7:22 of *ho esō anthrōpos.* The opposition in Romans 7 between the "inner self," i.e., the mind that delights in the law of God on the one hand, and the self sold under sin on the other, is not the same antithesis as that in 2 Corinthians. In 4:16 "the outer self," as it were Paul's mortal frame, corresponds to the clay jars, the body, and the mortal flesh of vv. 7, 10, and 11. Thus the "wasting away" of "the outer self" in v. 16 resumes the hardships that are depicted in vv. 7-12; it has nothing to do with sin. "The inner self" that "is being renewed" is equally different from the unregenerate self in Romans 7 who (still) wants to live according to the Law. The renewal in 2 Cor 4:16 is the equivalent of the transformation mentioned in 3:18. The phrases "outer self" and "inner self" may have a Hellenistic origin, yet they are not to be understood in a strictly dualistic fashion (separable body and soul). Both phrases point to the whole person, although from a different angle: outward-visible and inward-hidden.

17. *For the momentary light (weight) of our tribulation is producing a more and more exceeding and eternal weight of glory for us:* Several data in this verse render the translation difficult. The adjective "momentary" is in Greek an adverb (*parautika*, a *hapax legomenon* in the NT). The idea of weight may be present in the adjective *elaphron* ("light") used as a noun: the light (weight) of the (heavy) tribulation. In our translation we kept the "of" construction because of its parallelism with "weight of glory." The phrase *kath' hyperbolēn eis hyperbolēn* is perhaps a contraction of two originally separate expressions; as a whole it indicates a continually growing abundance. The Hebrew root *kbd*, from which the substantive *kabôd* (= *doxa* in Greek) is derived, means "to be heavy"; hence probably the term *baros* ("weight"). The continual inward renewal of v. 16, as well as the actual process of transformation into glory of 3:18, suggest an already present participation in that future glory.

The sentence introduced by "for" motivates v. 16a (why we do not lose heart), as well as explaining v. 16b (what the renewal achieves). There is, however, a development of the thought as well as the presence of a new element ("eternal"), that will be explained further in v. 18. Alfred Plummer appropriately comments: "We are accustomed to think of glory as transient and affliction as lasting. But the Apostle reverses that. In comparison with the glory, affliction is short-lived, and permanence is on the other side. Still more are we accustomed to attribute weight to affliction rather than to glory. The Apostle reverses that also" (*Commentary* 137–138).

Affliction produces glory: does Paul store up "merits" by his suffering? This verse has been claimed in support of this idea. It would seem that the Council of Trent, with reference to our passage, gives the right answer to this question in emphasizing that we should not boast of ourselves but of the Lord *cuius tanta est erga omnes homines bonitas, ut eorum velit esse merita, quae sunt ipsius dona* (*Decretum de iustificatione*, ch. 16: "whose goodness toward all is so great that he desires his own gifts to be their merits." Translation by N. P. Tanner.).

18. *who are not looking to what is seen but to what is unseen:* "Who are not looking" translates a Greek genitive absolute that continues the sentence of v. 17. The verb stresses that the attention is fixed upon the future invisible realities that,

however, by way of anticipation are already present in the inner self. "What is seen" refers back to all that surrounds the outer self, that which is transitory and will disappear.

for what is seen is transitory, but what is unseen (is) eternal: The motivating clause resumes the antithesis "seen-unseen" and qualifies its terms. "Transitory" points to "momentary" in v. 17a and "eternal" is taken up from v. 17b.

5:1. *For we know that if our earthly house or tent should be destroyed:* As "for" indicates, Paul is continuing his reflection. It is not clear whether all Christians are included in "we know." A reference to previous teaching does not seem to be present. Different images or metaphors are employed for the body; the first relates to "house" (cf. "building" in v. 1b and "dwelling" in v. 2). We may take *tou skēnous* ("of the tent") as an epexegetical, appositive genitive: house, i.e., tent (*skēnos* is a *hapax legomenon* in the New Testament). The earthly house, our present body, is but a tent. Literary dependency on Wis 9:15 can be postulated: "For a perishable body 'weighs down' (*barynei;* cf. *baros* in 4:17 and *baroumenoi* in 5:4) the soul, and 'the earthly tent' (*to geōdes skēnos*) burdens the thoughtful mind." It is difficult to know to what extent Paul thinks of the body as "house" of the soul (or, better, of the inmost self, 4:16). The destruction of Paul's body is his death (cf. Isa 38:12: same verb and image). "If . . . 'should be' destroyed" translates the condition (*ean* + subjunctive: an *eventualis*) and may suggest that Paul still hopes not to die before the Parousia, although he no longer excludes this possibility.

we have a building from God, a house not made with hands, eternal, in the heavens: In v. 1a Paul speaks of dying; in v. 1b the metaphorical language points to the resurrection of the body. Paul, however, is probably not suggesting that this resurrection occurs immediately after death (before the Parousia), since what is depicted at the end of v. 4 will according to 1 Cor 15:23 and 54 occur at the Parousia. "We have" is a present with a future sense and expresses the certainty of ultimately acquiring the new house. The phrase "in the heavens" goes with "a house," not with "we have." The variation in the *oik*-vocabulary, perhaps with slightly differing nuances, is worth noting: in v. 1 *oikia* and *oikodomē* and in v. 2 *oikētērion* (house, building and dwelling). This house is the resurrection body, the "spiritual body" (cf. 1 Cor 15:44). It is rather unlikely that, in writing this clause, Paul has been influenced by Jesus' prophecy of the destruction of the Temple (and of himself?), but for identical or related terms see Mark 14:58: "to destroy," "not made with hands," and the verb "to build."

2. *For indeed in this (tent) we groan, longing to put our dwelling from heaven on over (it):* The explanation goes on ("for"); the "groaning" is, as it were, a proof of the knowledge about the future (v. 1). Yet there is also a development in the reasoning, even a certain shift. In v. 1 Paul recalls the certainty of the bodily resurrection of the dead; in v. 2, however, he mentions groaning that is painful because of the present sufferings but also because of his desire to put the heavenly dwelling (as a garment) over the earthly one (= the tent), i.e., without first taking off the earthly garment, thus without first dying. Two images are connected here in a very uncommon fashion: that of "building" and that

of "clothing." The preposition *epi* in *ependysasthai* (as it were "to super-clothe") adds the nuance of putting (an outer garment) over (the undergarment). This verb with its double preposition is a *hapax legomenon* in the whole Bible and retains here and in v. 4 its full force. Actually, the figurative "super-clothing" is a transformation (cf. Phil 3:21: Christ "will change our lowly body to be like his glorious body"). At the Parousia, besides the resurrection of the dead there will be the transformation of those still living (cf. 1 Cor 15:51-52).

One could be inclined to give *en toutǭ* (lit. "in this") a retrospective sense that points back to the knowledge presented in v. 1: in this knowledge. However, because of "we who are in this tent (= body)" in v. 4, we prefer an implicit resumption of *skēnos* of v. 1a and consider the expression in v. 2 as its parallel: "(being) in this (tent)."

3. —*if (it is) really (true that) by having in fact put on we will not be found naked*— . . . : This brief verse, which can rightly be called an afterthought, is difficult (see, e.g., Thrall, "'Putting On'"). Our explanation cannot but remain somewhat hypothetical. There are two variant readings. (1) 𝔓⁴⁶, B, D, and several other witnesses have *eiper* ("if indeed, since") at the beginning of the verse, yet this is most likely a secondary clarification. The particle *ei* ("if") with a corroborating *ge* ("really") is to be preferred; the sense of *ei ge* is restrictive, "if it is really true that," or "at least if." It seems better not to connect *kai* with *ei ge* and thus to reject a concessive sense; *kai* emphasizes what follows: "in fact." (2) Some recent text editions (e.g., N/A²⁶, ²⁷) and commentators prefer the Western variant *ekdysamenoi* ("having taken off") to *endysamenoi* ("having put on"). In a personal comment, however, Bruce M. Metzger writes: "In view of its superior external support the reading ἐνδυσάμενοι should be adopted, the reading ἐκδυσάμενοι being an early alteration to avoid apparent tautology" (*Textual Commentary* 511). It would seem that Metzger's position is the correct one.

The aorist participle *endysamenoi* is not coordinated with "not naked" and therefore is not part of the predicate; it refers to an action anterior to that of the main verb. In Greek the preposition in a compound verb is sometimes left out if it would constitute a repetition. Moreover, *endysamenoi* seems to postulate the same direct object as in v. 2. Finally, the *kai* after *ei ge* is probably adverbial and emphasizes (= "in fact") the participle "having put on" that follows; it recalls an idea present in the preceding sentence in order to underline it. For all these reasons *endysamenoi* in v. 3 most probably has the same meaning as *ependysasthai* of vv. 2 and 4. "We will not be found" refers to the moment of the Parousia. In its figurative sense "naked" points to the anthropological situation of being without a body (not to the absence of merits or virtues, which would be the soteriological or moral interpretation). "Naked" indicates the intermediate state of not yet being clothed with the glorious body (cf. 1 Cor 15:37).

A statement in restrictive form does not necessarily express a real doubt, but can, on the contrary, be a figure of speech for a subjective certainty, for assurance. One might paraphrase v. 3 as follows: "if at least we may believe

that after having put on the glorious garment we will not be found naked."
Although the grammatical construction is conditional and restrictive, Paul's
faith conviction is nonetheless as firm as possible (compare for real doubt Gal
3:4, the only other passage in Paul where *ei ge kai* occurs).

4. *For indeed we who are in this tent groan, being weighed down:* After the interruption of v. 3 Paul takes up the idea of v. 2, partly with the same words, but also
with more explicitness and clarity. Verses 2 and 4 are thus parallel to a certain
extent. The reason for groaning is first of all the suffering: *baroumenoi* ("being
weighed down," cf. Wis 9:15 and see our explanation of v. 2).

because we do not wish to take off but to put on over: "Because" renders the not so
clear Greek phrase *eph' hō* (cf. the difficult clause in Rom 5:12). Verse 4b presents a second reason for his groaning. Paul once more expresses his hope not
to die before the Parousia. But there is more than the instinctive fear of death;
it is the "nakedness" that follows death, the disembodied state that Paul
wants to avoid.

in order that what is mortal may be swallowed up by life: The purpose force of this
clause should not be explained away. In 1 Cor 15:54cd Paul gives a quotation
from Isa 25:8a: "then the saying that is written will be fulfilled: 'Death has
been swallowed up in victory'" (a pre-Theodotion translation is cited; the LXX
has the active verb: "The death, being strong, swallowed up"). In 2 Cor 5:4c
Paul refers back to the same Isaiah text but does not mention the prophet.
Notwithstanding the differences between v. 4c and 1 Cor 15:54d, the basic
idea remains the same: death will be destroyed, life will engulf what is mortal.

Why does Paul write here *to thnēton* ("what is mortal") instead of "death,"
and why is "life" as the agent of the passive verb added (and "in victory"
omitted)? The adjective "what is mortal" is an abstract term. This is no longer
the language of "death" taken as a personification (as in 1 Corinthians 15).
However, one should not mentally add "body" to "mortal." Only what is
mortal will be destroyed, not the body as such; the transformed body will
become immortal. The agent "life" is presented as a person, not natural life,
of course, but resurrection life. The expression "by life" replaces, as it were,
"in victory." After all, resurrection life is victorious. To be sure, v. 5 will indicate the real agent: God through the Spirit.

5. *Now the one who shaped us for this very thing (is) God, who has given us the guarantee, namely, the Spirit:* The articular participle *ho katergasamenos* is translated
by "the one who shaped" (us). The verb also occurs in 4:17: "is producing."
The particle *de* ("now") may have a corrective nuance: not we, but God has
prepared us for that event by giving the Spirit. "For this very thing" is the
ultimate investiture and, at the same time, precisely the annihilation of what
is mortal (v. 4c). The verb "is" has to be supplied. The Spirit (an epexegetical
genitive) is given as guarantee, as deposit (see 1:22). The Spirit is the pledge,
the assurance that God will fulfill the promise to provide the resurrection
body. For the mention of "Spirit" in the preceding context, see 3:3, 6, 8, 17-18
(and 4:13?). According to 1 Cor 15:57 God gives us the final victory over death
"through our Lord Jesus Christ" (cf. 15:22; in 15:45 it is, however, stated that
Christ "became a life-giving Spirit").

6. *Since we are, therefore, always of good courage and since we know that being at home in the body we are away from the Lord:* This verse, too, is an anacoluthon: no main verb is present; v. 7 is an interruptive clause (cf. 4:16 and 5:3). It would seem that Paul initially wanted to write something like "we look forward to death" (cf. v. 8) as a main clause. Moreover, the flow of thought is not easy to follow: one does not see how the content of vv. 6-8 ("therefore") suits vv. 1-5. Paul's preference for "putting on over" and not dying before the Parousia is, as it were, forgotten. Attention is given now to another aspect of life on earth: being in the body is being away from the Lord. Furthermore, just as in 4:16, there is also here a shift from attitude ("being of good courage") to reflection ("knowing"). The coordination of the participles is also somewhat strained in relation to the content: how and why do courage to confront hardships and knowledge concerning life in exile go together?

   In the New Testament the paired verbs *endēmeō/ekdēmeō* ("to be at home/ to be away from home") occur only in 2 Cor 5:6, 8-9. The "body" of v. 6 corresponds to "our earthly house or tent" of v. 1.

7. *—for we walk by faith, not by sight— . . . :* This explicative (*gar*, "for") interruption is somewhat reminiscent of 1 Cor 13:12a: "For now we see in a mirror, dimly, but then we will see face to face." The noun *eidos* means "visible form." Margaret E. Thrall translates: "For we live our lives in the sphere of faith, not in the presence of his visible form" (*Second Epistle* 357). This form is that of the glorious risen Lord. Notwithstanding the linguistic difficulty, in view of *dia* + genitive ("by means of") and because of the opposing term "faith" (active: believing, trusting), the usual active rendering by "vision, sight" is perhaps to be preferred. Paul would then contrast Christian believing and Christian (future) seeing. As soon as we stop walking by faith we start seeing God face to face.

8. *Yes, we are of good courage and would rather go away from the body and get home to the Lord:* In v. 8 we have a new start that returns to v. 6 with a resumptive *de* ("yes"). What was a participle in v. 6 becomes a personal main verb in v. 8: "we are of good courage." It is not to be excluded that within the context of the whole passage the added *eudokoumen mallon* ("we would rather, we prefer") gives way to a less ideal solution, i.e., the necessity of dying before the Parousia. Paul would posit that the situation after death is already one step closer to the Lord (cf. Phil 1:21-24). The verb *eudokeō*, together with *mallon*, may be less strong and less positive than *epipotheō* of v. 2. The translation "go away" and "get home" points to the ingressive character of the aorist tense of the verbs *ekdēmeō* and *endēmeō*.

9. *Therefore, we also aspire, whether at home or away from home, to be pleasing to him:* Paul continues with something that is more than the preference of going away from the body and getting home to the Lord. He now speaks of the aspiration to lead a life that pleases the Lord, "whether at home or away from home." The meaning of the last expression is: in or out of the body, living or dead; the expression (two participles in Greek) qualifies "aspire to please" as a whole. But, one may ask, how can a person still act after death? Alfred Plummer comments on this difficulty and then proposes the following (rather

far-fetched) interpretation: "We aim at winning the Lord's approval, whether at his coming he finds us in the body or already out of it" (*Commentary* 155). Perhaps a better solution is to assume less careful writing on the part of Paul or a free rhetorical language that should not be pressed.

10. *For we must all be manifested before the tribunal of Christ:* In 4:16a, Paul is still speaking without doubt about his own apostolic attitude; yet by the time he gets to 5:10 ("we . . . all") he most probably points to all Christians. It would be rather unwise to hold that this change took place no earlier than v. 10. One has the impression that Paul has been broadening his horizon, perhaps beginning already in 4:16b. This is due partly to the density or importance of the reflection. Considerations about the eschatological future concern all Christians. There should, however, be no misunderstanding: in v. 10 a general, universal judgment (cf. Rom 2:6-11) is not meant, only that of Christians.

The verb *phanerōthēnai* ("to be manifested"; cf. v. 11: "to be open") is stronger than *phainesthai* ("to appear"): we shall all be seen for what we are (cf. 1 Cor 4:5). Christ will function as judge (in Rom 2:16 God judges "through Christ Jesus").

so that each one may receive what (he or she deserves) according to what he or she did through the body, whether good or evil: The expression "through (*dia* + genitive) the body" is the equivalent of "by means of the body," more than "in the body." The last words "whether good or evil" specify either *pros ha* ("according to what he or she did") or the more removed *ta* ("what [he or she deserves]"). In the first and more plausible case Paul means good or evil deeds, in the second he points to the reward or punishment. Be this as it may, it is unlikely that Paul here speaks of a proportional reward. *Phaulos* is more than "of lesser worth"; it means "bad, evil," as in 1 Cor 3:12-15. The variant *kakos* ("bad"), although well attested, is almost certainly secondary.

INTERPRETATION

a. *Structure and Line of Thought.* For the place of 4:16–5:10 in 2:14–7:4 and, more particularly, in 4:7–5:10, see pp. 75–76. In this pericope one can distinguish, it would seem, five small subdivisions: 4:16-18; 5:1-4; 5:5; 5:6-8; and 5:9-10. The first subdivision starts with an affirmation: "We do not lose heart." The motive behind this attitude is present in what precedes ("therefore"), but also given in the same v. 16: the renovation of the inner self, already in this life, day by day. In v. 17, however, this last motivation changes; the slight momentary affliction is opposed to the (future) eternal transcendent weight of glory. The consideration of v. 18 brings to light yet another element of the opposition: the transient visible and the eternal invisible. Then, in 5:1-4, Paul reflects on that desirable future. We know, he says, that after the destruction of our earthly body (after our death) we will possess a new heavenly body. Paul, however, does not want to die: he groans and longs to put on his heavenly body over the earthly one, on the assumption, of course, that through this further clothing he will not have to die or have to take off his earthly body and will not be found disembodied, i.e., naked. Thus, he repeats in v. 4, while we are in the body we sigh with anxiety, we groan, for we do not want to strip—no, we wish to "super-clothe" in order that what is mortal may be swallowed up by what is real life. In 5:5 Paul states in all clarity: It is God's work; it is God who through the presence of the Spirit as a guarantee has prepared us for this eschatological reality. In 5:6-8 a new kind of reflection suddenly appears: the knowledge that being in the body is being separated from the Lord, and that walking in faith is not yet vision. Therefore Paul is full of confidence and would prefer to leave the body and get to the Lord. The attentive reader gets the impression that fear about the disembodied (naked) state after death has, as it were, vanished. In 5:9-10 Paul draws the conclusion with regard to Christian moral life. The fact that "all of us" (i.e., all Christians) must appear before the judgment seat of Christ and each will receive a reward according to deeds strongly motivates our aim to please him.

One is tempted, with John Gillman, "Comparison," to detect a concentric structure in these five subdivisions: *a* (4:16-18), *b* (5:1-4), *c* (5:5), *b'* (5:6-8) and *a'* (5:9-10). Although the idea of judgment in *a'* is not present in *a*, and the sharp antitheses of *a* are missing in *a'*, the two small units are both introduced by *dio* ("therefore") and both deal with an attitude that they motivate through reflection; the present time is contrasted with the future. Parts *a* and *a'* to some extent frame the pericope. Subdivisions *b* and *b'* are similar because of the imagery of "house" *(b)* and the verbs "be at home" and "be away" *(b')*—the tent (v. 1) is the body (v. 6)—as well as the verbs "to long" (v. 2) and "to prefer" (v. 8). Both *b* and *b'* have parentheses (v. 3 and v. 7) and, just as v. 4 resumes v. 2, so does v. 8 take up v. 6. Yet while in *b* Paul does not want to die but to "put on" the celestial body "over" the earthly one, in *b'* he prefers to leave the earthly body and "get to the Lord." It should be conceded that these nuances do not fully coincide. Subunit *c*, finally, can be considered as the theological center of the pericope: the presence in us of the Spirit is the guarantee that God has prepared us for that complete annihilation of what is mortal. The results of this analysis are attractive and impressive. However, it has to be admitted that neither content nor vocabulary sufficiently reveal a clear Pauline intention to work out such a concentric structure.

b. *Particular Problems*. It would seem that in this passage there are three unfinished sentences (indicated by ". . ."): see 4:16; 5:3 and 7.

Paul's use of Wis 9:15 (cf. 4:16) and of expressions such as "outer self, inner self" (4:16), "naked" (5:3), "to be at home in the body" and "to go away out of the body" (5:6 and 8) points to Hellenistic influence, to the presence of "foreign," admittedly popularized, categories of thought. Yet no radical hellenization or Greek dualism should be assumed. In the eschaton there is ultimately no existence without the body (see the explanation of 5:4c), no purely spiritual soul freed from the prison of the material body. The everlasting glorious life comes not from the soul's immortality, but is achieved by God (cf. 5:5).

Some exegetes are of the opinion that the house imagery of 5:1b should not be understood with relation to the individual Paul (or the Christian). Different and quite divergent proposals have been put forward. In v. 1b Paul would allude to Jesus' prediction of the rebuilding of the Temple. That heavenly temple is the collective body of Christ, the messianic community. Some interpret "our earthly house" of v. 1a in a collective sense as well: the whole Adamic human race whose corporeality carries death in itself (according to another proposal the expression points not to the body itself, but to our earthly way of life). Yet the added genitive "tent" in v. 1a, the clothing metaphor in vv. 2-4 (which in 1 Cor 15 certainly refers to the individual glorified bodies), the term "body" itself in vv. 6 and 8, and finally the whole content of the pericope, as well as its context: all these data make unacceptable any interpretation that does not consider the two sorts of houses as the earthly and glorified body of Paul (and/or Christians). Also unconvincing is the attempt of Norbert Baumert and others to explain 4:7–5:10 in an exclusively non-eschatological sense, i.e., as referring to the experience of the salvation Paul possesses here and now, a continual putting on of Christ between baptism and death.

c. *Theological Reflection.* The destruction of the earthly house or tent in 5:1 points to death. Already in v. 1 Paul may be thinking of an event he would like to avoid because of the "naked," disembodied state that follows. If so, he would be giving himself courage: even if I have to die, I know that there will be a bodily resurrection. Just as in 1 Cor 15:51-55, so also in 2 Corinthians 5, along with the resurrection of the dead, Paul has in mind the transformation of the living. In vv. 2-4, then, he expresses his personal wish not to die before the Parousia so that he can put on the glorious body over the earthly one. That dislike of the intermediate state and the desire of "putting on over" are no longer at the forefront in vv. 6-8. Death is better than life; living in the body is walking in faith, without vision; one is still away from the Lord (vv. 6-7). In v. 8 Paul even says in a quite general fashion: I would like to put down what hinders the vision; I prefer to leave the body and get home to the Lord. There appears to be a tension between Paul's longing for transformation (at the imminent Parousia) and his longing to be with the Lord (immediately after death, before the Parousia). Does Paul perhaps argue against somewhat gnosticizing opponents who preach the ideal of "nakedness," i.e., the eternal disembodied existence of the soul? One hesitates to answer this question with a simple yes.

A question that can hardly be avoided is whether or not Paul has changed his eschatological expectations during the course of his apostolic life, or even from letter to letter. The main texts that are brought into the discussion are 1 Thess 4:13-18 (and 5:10); 1 Cor 15:50-58; 2 Cor 5:1-10; Phil 1:21-24 and 3:20-21. This order may indicate their exact sequence in time. Those who defend an evolution in Paul mention the following arguments. In 1 Thessalonians and 1 Corinthians Paul sees the time period after death still as a state of "sleeping"; in Philippians and presumably in 2 Corinthians as well this situation is depicted as "being with Christ." There is in Paul an ongoing process of spiritualization to the point that in 1 Corinthians and later he claims a radical discontinuity between earthly corporeality and the heavenly body. In 2 Corinthians Paul tends to use more Hellenistic concepts and terms. The expectation of the imminent Parousia appears to diminish. From 2 Corinthians onwards, death before the Parousia belongs to the normal course of events and Paul himself reckons with his own death. In 2 Corinthians he is still somewhat afraid of death; in Philippians he is longing for it.

Those who hesitate to accept a drastic evolution in Paul's eschatological outlook appropriately remark that much argumentation remains highly hypothetical and that the relatively short period of time between his first letter (1 Thessalonians) and the last (Romans) makes a radical Pauline development rather improbable. This applies especially to the short time between 1 and 2 Corinthians. If Paul changed his mind after the important chapter on the resurrection, 1 Corinthians 15, it is strange that he did not more clearly indicate this when writing 2 Corinthians 5 to the very same community. Yet some development has to be assumed. Paul employs more Hellenistic vocabulary and categories of thought in 2 Corinthians 5 than in 1 Corinthians 15. Moreover, an experience such as depicted in 2 Cor 1:8-10 may have revealed to him the possibility of dying before the Parousia. Above all, an increasing union with Christ in his life of faith already on earth must have brought about the conviction that even death cannot destroy that union, and that dying brings the Christian closer to the full, immediate presence and the face to face vision.

d. *Actualization.* Whether or not an evolution has to be assumed in Paul's thinking on resurrection, the grandiose prospect of the future beyond death remains evident in this letter, as elsewhere in his writings: the bodily resurrection, the being at home with the Lord for ever. Because of this faith conviction we, too, should always be of good courage, even in the midst of hardships, and it should be our aim to be pleasing to God in all circumstances. We know that our union with Christ cannot be broken by death. God's Spirit, already present in us, will take care of the future, engulfing what is mortal in resurrection life.

FOR REFERENCE AND FURTHER STUDY

Baumert, Norbert. *Täglich sterben und auferstehen*. StANT 34. Munich: Kösel, 1973.
Berry, Ronald. "Death and Life in Christ: The Meaning of 2 Corinthians 5.1-10," *SJTh* 14 (1961) 60–76.
Craig, William L. "Paul's Dilemma in 2 Corinthians 5.1-10: A 'Catch-22,'" *NTS* 34 (1988) 145–147.
Ellis, E. Earle. "II Corinthians V.1-10 in Pauline Eschatology," *NTS* 6 (1959–1960) 211–224.
Erlemann, Kurt. "Der Geist als *arrabōn* (2 Kor 5,5) im Kontext der paulinischen Eschatologie," *ZNW* 83 (1992) 202–223.
Gillman, John. "A Thematic Comparison: 1 Cor 15:50-57 and 2 Cor 5:1-5," *JBL* 107 (1988) 439–454.
Glasson, Thomas F. "2 Corinthians v. 1-10 versus Platonism," *SJTh* 43 (1990) 145–155.
Lambrecht, Jan. "La vie engloutit ce qui est mortel. Commentaire de 2 Corinthiens 5,4c" in Bieringer and Lambrecht, *Studies on 2 Corinthians*. BEThL 102. Leuven: Leuven University Press/Peeters, 1994, 351–361.
Lincoln, Andrew T. *Paradise Now and Not Yet. Studies in the Role of the Heavenly Dimension in Paul's Thought with Special Reference to his Eschatology*. Cambridge: Cambridge University Press, 1981, 59–71.
Murphy-O'Connor, Jerome. "'Being at home in the body we are in exile from the Lord' (2 Cor 5:6c)," *RB* 93 (1986) 214–221.
Osei-Bonsu, Joseph. "The Intermediate State in the New Testament," *SJTh* 44 (1991) 169–194.
Schnelle, Udo. *Wandlungen im paulinischen Denken*. SBS 137. Stuttgart: Katholisches Bibelwerk, 1989, 42–45.
Thrall, Margaret E. "'Putting on' or 'Stripping off' in 2 Corinthians 5:3" in Eldon Jay Epp and Gordon D. Fee, eds., *New Testament Textual Criticism. Its Significance for Exegesis. FS for B.M. Metzger*. Oxford: Clarendon, 1981, 221–237.
Walter, Nikolaus. "Hellenistische Eschatologie bei Paulus? Zu 2 Kor 5,1-10," *ThQ* 176 (1996) 53–64.

8. The Ministry of Reconciliation (5:11-21)

11. Therefore, since we know the fear of the Lord, we try to convince people, but we are open to God. I hope, however, to be also open to your consciences. 12. We do not again commend ourselves (to you), but

we (are) giving you an occasion for boasting about us, in order that you might have (something to say) to those who are boasting about appearances and not about (the qualities of) the heart. 13. For if we have been beside ourselves, (it was) for God; if we are sober-minded, (it is) for you.

14. For the love of Christ holds us in its grip, since we have reached the conclusion that one has died for all; therefore, all have died, 15. and he died for all in order that those who live might live no longer for themselves but for him who died and was raised for them. 16. So that henceforth we know no one according to the flesh; but even if we (once) knew Christ according to the flesh, now we no longer know (him so). 17. So that, if anyone (is) in Christ, (that one is) a new creation; the old passed away, behold the new has come.

18. All (this), however, (comes) from God who reconciled us to himself through Christ and gave us the ministry of reconciliation, 19. as (it is well known) that in Christ God was reconciling the world to himself, not counting their trespasses against them, and that God entrusted the word of reconciliation to us. 20. Therefore, we are ambassadors on behalf of Christ, as if God is making his appeal through us. We beseech you on behalf of Christ: "Reconcile yourselves to God." 21. Him who knew no sin, he made (him to be) sin for us, in order that by him we might become the righteousness of God.

NOTES

11. *Therefore, since we know the fear of the Lord, we try to convince people, but we are open to God:* The beginning of this verse is clearly related to the preceding one. The particle *oun* ("therefore") announces a conclusion. The "fear of the Lord (= Christ)," which Paul experiences and possesses, is present in him precisely because he realizes that he will have to account for his conduct (cf. 5:10). The verb *phaneroumai* ("to be made clear, open"), which occurs twice in this verse, is already employed in v. 10, so it too serves as a connecting link between 5:11 and the foregoing passage.

Verse 11b has an opposing *de* ("but"). One may assume that the particle *men* must be supplied in v. 11a. This points to the presence of the distinction "on the one hand . . . on the other hand." It is well known that in such a construction the first clause is often concessive so that the main emphasis lies on the second. We could paraphrase v. 11ab as follows: "it is true that we try to convince people, but in doing this we are open to God." It would seem that here Paul is answering the accusation that he employs an unscrupulous, insincere method in his efforts to convince people.

The basic meaning of *peithō* in v. 11a is "(to try) to persuade, (to try) to convince." Many exegetes state that the verb here is conative. But is this correct? A *praesens de conatu* denotes an attempt which is not carried into effect. The action has no result (cf., for example, the conative imperfect in Luke 1:59: "they tried to call"). In v. 11a, however, the action is being carried out: Paul is doing something; he is trying to persuade. To be sure, in the present the only action is the attempt to convince. Whether the result is positive or negative is not indicated, yet the nuance of "trying" belongs to the verb as such and cannot be taken as "conative" in the grammatical sense. The aspect of the present tense points solely to the duration, to the action in progress: "We are persuading people."

What does Paul persuade people of? Some commentators understand that Paul is convincing them of the honesty and unselfishness of his way of life. The context seems to support such an understanding, for in v. 11bc Paul speaks of his "openness" to God and the Corinthians, and in v. 12 sound, good boasting is opposed to false, dishonest pride. However, a closer consideration of the context militates against this interpretation. In v. 11a Paul mentions an activity that he then qualifies in v. 11b as open. The emphasis lies on the sincerity of that activity; his real apology is to be found in v. 11bc, not so much in v. 11a. So we are brought to the missionary sense. Paul tries to win over people by preaching the message, to persuade them by means of the proclamation of the gospel. In this apostolic activity he has been and still is completely open to God, and he hopes that his openness is acknowledged by the Corinthians as well (v. 11bc).

Due attention should be given to the perfect tense of the verb in v. 11b: *pephanerōmetha.* In v. 10 the aorist pointed to the future appearance before the judgment seat. Here, in v. 11b, Paul's openness, because of past facts, is already an enduring situation as far as God is concerned. When did those acts take place? We may assume that Paul, by means of this perfect, refers to the whole of his bold apostolic dealings with people (cf. 3:12). It was always his intention to be honest with God.

I hope, however, to be also open to your consciences: Verse 11c, beginning with *de* ("but, however"), functions as a sort of afterthought. In it Paul immediately adds—he does not want his readers to forget this—that he hopes he is known also to them. Yet v. 11c is equally a transition to what follows. Verses 12-13 will continue the theme present in v. 11c. One should also notice that in the whole of vv. 11b-13 Paul (first person singular and plural) addresses the Corinthians (second person plural). It is Paul's firm hope to be already open also to the consciences of the Corinthians. The verb "to be open" is again in the perfect. Of course we can assume that Paul hoped that the Corinthians always found him "an open book" in his dealing with them, but here in the specific context of his apology and plea, his hope is also that this very letter, i.e., its sincere and honest argument up to this passage, has not been without result.

12. *We do not again commend ourselves (to you):* This clause is similar to 3:1a: "Are we beginning to commend ourselves again?" In both verses Paul requires that his openness and honesty should not be considered "again" as a wrong self-centered recommendation. This hardly points back to commendations present in the letter alone. Most probably Paul mainly refers to his apologetic behavior and perhaps exaggeratedly defensive actions that preceded this letter and could easily have been interpreted as less than appropriate. Yet in 3:1

and 5:12 Paul also fears that the explicit assertions of his sincerity in 2:17 and 5:11 might be misunderstood "again" as ill-suited recommendations.

but we (are) giving you an occasion for boasting about us: In v. 12 Paul is reflecting on what he is doing. We have before us an *ou . . . alla* ("not . . . but") construction, but in the *alla* clause (v. 12b) a finite verb is missing. However, the participle *didontes* ("giving") can probably be considered as its equivalent, since with remarkable frequency in 2 Corinthians Paul continues with a co-ordinate participle after a finite verb. The term *aphormē* means both (objective) "occasion" and (subjective) "incentive," thus a suitable basis and motivation. The nuance of *kauchēma* ("boast") seems to be active here (therefore one rather expects *kauchēsis,* "boasting"): occasion for boasting, or incentive to boast and take pride in. In v. 12b "boasting" has a positive, legitimate sense. Three important manuscripts ($\mathfrak{P}^{46}$, ℵ, and B) have *hyper hymōn* ("about you"). According to this variant Paul would be giving the Corinthians the chance to show boldness about themselves. They (in contrast to the other people of whom the verse goes on to speak) can rightly pride themselves "on their heart." This variant does, no doubt, represent the more difficult reading. Nevertheless, most commentators prefer *hyper hēmōn* (*hymōn,* then, caused by itacism) in light of the line of thought in this passage, and rightly so, it would seem.

in order that you might have (something to say) to those who are boasting about appearances and not about (the qualities of) the heart: The purpose nuance of *hina* ("in order that") is to be retained. The direct object of "might have" is not expressed. One must probably supply "something to say." The Corinthians are able to answer those who boast about appearances by pointing to the inner quality of their apostle Paul. In the Greek text *en prosōpǭ* ("about the face") is opposed to *en kardiǡ* ("about the heart"). Reference is often made to 1 Sam 16:7: "a person sees what is outward *(eis prosōpon),* but God sees what is within *(eis kardian)."* In view of 2:17 and 4:2 (and the preceding 5:11?) the contrast of insincerity with honesty may also be present. The "appearances" are, for example, letters of recommendation, eloquence, success, perhaps also marvelous works and ecstasies. Paul's opponents visibly boast of the wrong things.

13. *For if we have been beside ourselves, (it was) for God; if we are sober-minded, (it is) for you:* The *eite . . . eite* ("if . . . if") construction opposes in the conditional clauses (the protases) the verbs *existēmi* ("to be beside oneself"; in Paul a *hapax legomenon)* and *sōphroneō* ("to be sober-minded"), and in the main clauses (the apodoses) "God" and "you." Moreover, we have an aorist indicative in v. 13a contrasting with a present indicative in v. 13b. Probably the same verb "to be" has to be supplied in the two elliptic main clauses.

What does "we have been beside ourselves" mean? One thinks here of Mark 3:21 (people are saying that Jesus "is beside himself"). This meaning, however, cannot be accepted in 2 Cor 5:13. Most commentators refer to ecstatic experiences. It is possible that such experiences are part of the "appearances" mentioned in v. 12c. Moreover, in 12:1-7 Paul speaks of his personal "ecstasies." The distinction between "for God" and "for you" is also present in 1 Cor 14:2 (and 28) with regard to the spiritual gifts (speaking in tongues and prophecy). In 2 Cor 5:13 Paul most probably refers to past ecstatic experiences (aorist) that were for God; now he asserts that he is in his right mind (present tense) for the Corinthians. So in the apodosis of v. 13a "was" must be supplied, in that of v. 13b "is." With "for God" Paul seems to defend himself against the charge that in his apostolic life there were no religious ecstasies or that they were not visible.

In view of the fact that elsewhere Paul never uses *existēmi* (or *ekstasis*) for ecstatic phenomena one may ask whether in 5:13 he does not point to his vehement, exaggerated reactions, a behavior that was easily (mis)interpreted as self-commendation. For God, however, this behavior was completely transparent. His normal and actual state of mind is sober, sane, reasonable, and thus entirely open to the Corinthians. However, this interpretation seems somewhat forced.

14. *For the love of Christ holds us in its grip, since we have reached the conclusion that one has died for all:* Verse 14ab provides the motivation or explanation for Paul's openness to God and the Corinthians (cf. vv. 11-13). Verse 14a is the main clause; in v. 14b the participle *krinantas* (literally: "judging") is grammatically added to "us" and may have a causal nuance (in a rather free translation: "since we once reached the conclusion"). The words *touto hoti* ("this [conclusion] that") announce the content of the conclusion. Most probably v. 14c, introduced by *ara* ("therefore, so"), is an independent clause.

"The love of Christ" can be compared with "the fear of the Lord" of v. 11a; "of Christ" is a subjective genitive and "of the Lord" an objective one. Christ proved and manifested his love in the past through his death on the cross, while we fear Christ as our future judge. Christ's love holds Paul fast, i.e., that love is the all-determining factor in his life. The verb *synechō* has three possible meanings: "to hold together," "to enclose," and "to hold fast, to hold in one's grip, to constrain." It is the third sense that, we think, is to be preferred (cf. Phil 1:23). The idea of being compelled by Christ to apostolic service or the notion of Christ leading Paul to a selfless existence, although not necessarily absent, are probably not directly envisaged. It can be asked whether the epistolary "us" is not vaguely referring to all Christians as well, thus whether Paul is not presenting himself as an example for his fellow Christians.

In view of "therefore, all have died" in v. 14c one should presume that "for all" in v. 14b takes on the nuance of "instead of all" as well; the preposition *hyper* can mean both. The inclusive representative sense is present. In v. 14b some late manuscripts write *ei* ("if") instead of *eis* ("one"). This scribal correction presumably wants to avoid the fact that the verb "he has died" depends directly on *krinantas touto*. According to this variant reading *ei* introduces a conditional protasis, while the preceding *hoti* would, above all, command v. 14c: "that, if . . . therefore. . . ."

therefore, all have died: Verse 14c does not belong to the conclusion Paul reached in the past (see v. 14b); it rather formulates a deduction from it. Paul uses the same verb and the same tense as in v. 14b, but here "to die" has a metaphorical sense: death to sin. Just as in Rom 5:15 through Adam's sin "the many" died (in sin), so in 2 Cor 5:14 in the death of the new Adam, Christ, all died because of their sins and died (to sin); cf. v. 15b: they live. Paul is pointing here to what happened in the cross event, not to death in baptism as in Rom 6:3-11.

15. *and he died for all in order that those who live might live no longer for themselves but for him who died and was raised for them:* Paul's reasoning continues. The main clause is again, just as in v. 14, situated at the beginning (v. 15a) and now a long purpose clause follows (v. 15b: *hina,* "in order that").

Verse 15a resumes v. 14b, but "one" is omitted. There are, moreover, several shifts in v. 15. The opposition is not "one/all," but "death/life"; "all" is no longer emphasized. While v. 14bc looks to the past (the cross event and its result), v. 15b clearly envisages the future (the Christian life); v. 14bc reflects on the gift, v. 15 on the task.

The expression "those who live" probably no longer includes the whole of humankind that is, in a real sense, represented on the cross. What the death of Christ brings about is not yet the final salvation; those who have died with Christ must respond and live for Christ. Precisely this is expressed by the purpose clause. It would seem, therefore, that with "those who live" Paul has the Christians concretely in mind.

"And was raised" looks like an addition, somewhat surprising after the emphasis on Christ's death in vv. 14b and 15a. This addition, however, proves that for Paul Christ's death and resurrection are inseparable ("for them" qualifies both). In a similar manner dying (to sin) is called "living" in v. 15b. Although that life, if lived "for him who died for them," is an anticipation of our future resurrection, Paul probably would not yet call it "resurrection" (cf. Rom 6:5: the resurrection of Christians lies in the future).

16. *So that henceforth we know no one according to the flesh; but even if we (once) knew Christ according to the flesh, now we no longer know (him so):* With "so that" *(hōste)* Paul draws a conclusion from what he said in vv. 14-15. He concretizes for himself what he depicted in v. 15b regarding all. The "so that" of v. 16a, however, seems more specifically linked with v. 14a: both clauses have the epistolary first person plural. The initial "we" *(hēmeis)* is emphatic. Because Paul is controlled by Christ's love there is for him a new type of knowledge.

In v. 16 two sentences must be distinguished: first the more or less independent consecutive clause (v. 16a); then the conditional period with a (concessive) protasis (v. 16b) and an apodosis (v. 16c), somewhat strangely introduced by *alla* ("yet"; not translated). Verse 16a is anthropological, v. 16bc christological. Verse 16a is the main statement; v. 16bc constitutes its confirmation and extreme illustration.

The best manuscripts witness to the reading *ei kai* in v. 16b; this reading is generally regarded as original with the concessive meaning "even though." Paul concedes that in his pre-conversion life he regarded Christ in a "fleshly" way. The phrase *kata sarka* ("according to the flesh") is to be taken with the verb, not with "no one" or "Christ" (so, e.g., Bultmann, *Second Letter,* ad loc). The following variants may be noted: *ei de kai* ("but even if"): the sense remains practically the same; *ei de* ("but if"): the concessive nuance disappears;

kai ei ("and if"; cf. the Vulgate that reads *et si*): here also the concessive nuance is no longer present.

The verbs *oida* and *ginōskō* are synonymous in v. 16. Paul's "knowledge" is, of course, not just theoretical but also experiential, existential, moral. Twice a clear caesura in time is indicated: "henceforth" and "no longer." He refers to the time before his conversion. The expression *kata sarka* means a "fleshly," here more specifically a wrong, sinful approach: Paul persecuted Christ (in the Christians, v. 16b). Paul's vision of Christ (and humankind) has since radically changed.

17. *So that, if anyone (is) in Christ, (that one is) a new creation:* This verse has two parts. First there is once more a somewhat independent consecutive sentence, again with "so that" *(hōste)* (v. 17a). It is a conditional period, consisting of a *protasis* and *apodosis*. Its style is staccato-like; in both clauses the verbs are missing. The other part (v. 17b) has two short parallel clauses. Whereas the content of v. 16 is connected with v. 14a, v. 17 seems to be more closely linked with v. 14bc and v. 15. In their conclusions both v. 16 and v. 17 concretize the universal statements of vv. 14-15. In v. 16 Paul speaks of himself; in v. 17 he specifically refers to Christians. The Vulgate translates: *Si qua ergo in Christo nova creatura, vetera transierunt: ecce facta sunt omnia nova.* In this version the protasis runs up to *"creatura"*: "If (there is) in Christ a new creature, (then) the old (things) have passed away: behold all (things) have been made new." *Omnia* ("all things") comes from a variant reading. But this punctuation can hardly be accepted because of the rather strange reasoning it supposes. Moreover "in Christ" is no longer the predicate and the parallelism in v. 17b is broken.

Twice, in the *apodosis* as well as in the *protasis* of v. 17a, the same verb "to be" must be supplied. Almost certainly "new creation" is the predicate of the apodosis: that person is a new creation, a newly-created person. Paul employs the phrase "a new creation" *(kainē ktisis)* once more, namely in Gal 6:16: in his opinion "neither circumcision counts for anything, nor uncircumcision, but a new creation." The terminology could be Pauline. Alternatively Paul may have borrowed it from early Christian tradition or from Judaism or directly from the Old Testament. More particularly, both Deutero- and Trito-Isaiah speak of eschatological newness brought about, created by God (see 48:5: "Now I show you new things"; cf. 65:17 and 66:22: new heaven, new earth). Since in 2 Cor 6:2 Paul quotes Isa 49:8, Old Testament influence is very likely to be present also in 5:17.

Although *ei* ("if") certainly underlines the condition, in Hellenistic Greek *ei tis* ("if anyone") is often more or less the equivalent of the *hostis* introducing a general relative clause: "every one who, all who." Verse 17a should thus not be interpreted in an individualistic way. All who are in Christ are a new creation.

The typically Pauline formula *en Christǭ* ("in Christ") expresses participation: cf. v. 14bc with its implicit Adam/Christ opposition. However, most probably v. 17a is different from v. 14 in the sense that it no longer envisages the whole of humankind but only the Christians. "To be in Christ" is certainly a gift, but it also supposes human acceptance, appropriation, and response. Verse 17a is not in the first place an informative statement; it contains a hidden appeal in its protasis. One could paraphrase: "If you want to become a new creature, you must be in Christ, since only Christians are a new creation." The "newness" is ultimate and definitive.

the old passed away, behold the new has come: In the Greek text v. 17b has a chiastic structure: subject and verb, verb and subject. The second clause of v. 17b is introduced by *idou* ("behold"). For Paul, "old" points to the past pre-Christian realities (e.g., knowing according to the flesh, v. 16) and "new" represents Christ's eschatological achievement. In Isa 43:18-19 the terms "old," "behold," and "new" are also present. Although content and context differ greatly, Paul may have been influenced by the vocabulary and the "old-new" contrast in that passage.

The function of the two clauses is explanation. Verse 17b shows what "new creation" really means. Because of v. 17a, notwithstanding the neuter plural of the subjects, the sense is primarily anthropological. Verse 17b, however, is also a proclamatory celebration. This is clear from "behold," the chiastic form, the antithetical style, and the cosmological broadening. Yet by omitting the article before *kaina* ("new") Paul makes clear that he regards the "new" not as those (or all) new things (i.e., persons); he rather pays attention to the nature of newness. We can perhaps also admit here an implicit imperative nuance. "New things" come into existence only *if* there is human acceptance. The replacement of the old does not occur automatically.

Due attention should be given to the difference between *parēlthen* (aorist: "passed by") and *gegonen* (perfect: "has come"). The contrast of the verbs seems to point to discontinuity, but one must reckon here with stylistic exaggeration and ask precisely what disappears and what continues to exist, though, of course, in a transformed way.

Some commentators—less correctly, it would seem—take "the old" as the subject of the "behold"-clause as well and "new" as its predicate: "the old things have become new."

18. *All (this), however, (comes) from God who reconciled us to himself through Christ and gave us the ministry of reconciliation:* Verse 18a is the main clause, without a verb; "to be" or "to come" should be supplied. Two participles, *katallaxantos* ("having reconciled," v. 18b) and *dontos* ("having given," v. 18c), are added to "God" and have only one article for their attributive position.

The phrase *ta panta,* "all (this)," must not be understood in a cosmological sense nor is it particularly connected with "new creature" of v. 17a. "All this" refers to what Paul has written in the whole of vv. 14-17, more specifically to the soteriological statements in vv. 14-15. In v. 18a (cf. the adversative *de,* "but, however") Paul introduces a new idea. While vv. 14-17 were christocentric, from v. 18 onward Paul emphasizes his theocentric view. Ultimately in "all this" God has had the initiative.

The first participle (v. 18b) expresses God's reconciliation of humankind to himself. In the New Testament humans do not reconcile God to themselves. The aorist indicates the action as such, with beginning and end; the phrase "through Christ" and, moreover, the whole context puts that action in the past. The cross event is envisaged. In light of the epistolary plural in vv. 14 and 16 and, more specifically, in v. 18c, with "us" in v. 18b Paul points to himself (and fellow workers); yet it could also include all Christians (and humankind?). As elsewhere in vv. 14-21 Christ is the eschatological agent in his total career. In this verse, however, "through Christ" may refer in a special way to Christ's death and resurrection (cf. end of v. 15).

The second participle (v. 18c) indicates the appointment by God, God's "giving of the ministry" in the past, yet it is uncertain whether Paul is thinking more concretely here of a specific moment, e.g., the cross event or his conversion. The dative "us" here clearly means Paul himself (and the fellow workers; cf. "us" in v. 18b? Cf. also v. 19c). Verse 18 is thus not only theocentric (and christological), but also ecclesial; it introduces the theme of ministry. God's initiative and Christ's death must be brought to people by the apostles. "Of reconciliation" is an objective genitive, indicating also the content of Paul's ministry. It is possible that *diakonia* ("ministry") referred to an office in the Pauline churches (cf. Philippians 1:1), but what kind of office? It is equally possible that Paul's opponents called themselves "ministers of Christ" (cf. 11:23). Paul here adopts this term for identifying his apostolic function.

According to Seyoon Kim, "2 Cor. 5:11-21," with the first person plural in v. 18 (and v. 19c; also in vv. 13-14, 16) Paul refers to the Damascus event, to his own reconciliation with God and apostolic vocation (cf. Gal 1:12-16).

19. *as (it is well known) that in Christ God was reconciling the world to himself:* Grammatically v. 19 continues the sentence of v. 18. The meaning of the introductory particles *hōs hoti* in this verse is highly debated. The clause in 19a, probably a periphrastic construction (*ēn . . . katallassōn,* "he was reconciling"), depends on them. Again two participles follow: *logizomenos* ("counting," v. 19b) and *themenos* ("having placed," v. 19c). The first is certainly in a predicative position (no article); it is attached to the subject of the preceding clause. Does this apply to the second participle "having placed"? Most likely it does not, since this participle may be the equivalent of a finite verb.

Verse 19a basically repeats v. 18b, yet in both structure and content there are differences. The parallelism may strike the reader (twice: God reconciles to himself); however, the tenses are different: aorist in v. 18b and a periphrastic imperfect in v. 19a. The position (in Greek) of "us . . . through Christ" (v. 18b) and "in Christ . . . the world" (v. 19a) is chiastic to some extent.

The phrase *hōs hoti* also occurs in 11:21 and 2 Thess 2:2. In both passages it points to something that is not true ("as though"). In v. 19a, however, one cannot detect such a nuance. The comparative meaning of the particle *hōs* ("as") does not always suggest something subjective and/or false. It can also mean "as (it is well known)," or, with a motivating nuance, "because (it is well known)." We assume that in v. 19a *hōs* has something of both these meanings, comparative and causal. The phrase *hōs hoti* is thus most probably elliptic. The verb on which *hoti* ("that," introducing the object clause) depends has to be supplied, e.g., "it is well known" (or: "it is said"). What Paul states in v. 18b is repeated in v. 19a, but that repetition functions as an explanation and even, because of its more general character, as a kind of foundation. One may paraphrase it as follows: "because the fact is well known that in Christ God was reconciling the world to himself."

In v. 19a the attention is not so much on God as on God's activity. Whereas v. 18b was narrative (aorist), v. 19a is descriptive (imperfect). Verse 19a depicts what was occurring on the cross. The parallelism of *en Christō* (v. 19a) with *dia Christou* (v. 18b) suggests an instrumental sense for *en*. Yet the nuance of God's presence in Christ should not be overlooked. A cosmological understanding of the term *kosmos* ("world") must be avoided because of the context and, more particularly, because of "against them" in v. 19b. "World" here means (sinful) humankind. "World," however, is undoubtedly broader, more objective and universal than "us" in v. 18b.

not counting their trespasses against them: Verse 19b is an explanatory clause that has no counterpart in v. 18. Both vocabulary and content are thoroughly Pauline. The present participle "counting," in apposition to the subject "God" of v. 19a, functions as an adverbial clause: God reconciles in that (or: because) God does not count their trespasses against them. The originally financial metaphor expresses God's forgiving activity.

and that God entrusted the word of reconciliation to us: The parallelism of v. 19c with v. 18c is eye-catching. It could well be that the second participle, *themenos* ("having placed"), an aorist, is not coordinated with the first ("counting," present) but constitutes the equivalent of the finite form "he placed," i.e., "he entrusted." If so, v. 19c continues on the same level as v. 19a (compare this same connection in v. 18bc). "God placed in us (= Paul)" is more distanced and objective language than the "God gave us" of v. 18c. The Greek construction, however, remains strange; there may be an allusion to Ps 103:27 (LXX) where the same construction is used to refer to what Moses and Aaron have to do. "The word of reconciliation" also betrays a more objective style than "ministry" in v. 18c. Instead of "word" 𝔓[46] and a few other, less important manuscripts write "gospel." The "reconciliation" occurs through the message the minister proclaims by word and no less by his whole existence (cf., for example, the lists of hardships of 6:3-10 and 11:23-29 and Paul's dying with Christ mentioned in 4:10-11). It would seem that v. 19c already prepares the appeal of v. 20 (cf. *oun*, "therefore").

20. *Therefore we are ambassadors on behalf of Christ, as if God is making his appeal through us:* Verse 20 goes a step further. The ministry given to the apostles according to v. 18c and v. 19c is now carried out. Paul and his fellow workers "are ambassadors." The originally political verb is used in a transposed sense. The preposition *hyper* ("for, in favor of") in v. 20a (and v. 20c) probably contains the nuance "instead of."

The particle *hōs* ("as"), here followed by a participial absolute (v. 20b: "God appealing"), seems to mean "as if," which, however, is to be taken in a real sense; it explains and concretizes the expression "on behalf of Christ" in v. 20a: "as if God makes his appeal through us." Through the fact of God making this appeal the apostle takes a position similar to that of Christ. What

Jesus wrought on the cross, once for all, the apostle (and through him God) proclaims in the present. Like Christ, he is God's mediator. One must realize that ambassadorship means more than just proclamation in words; the whole apostolic existence with all its trials is involved (cf., for example, 6:3-10).

We beseech you on behalf of Christ: "Reconcile yourselves to God": Verse 20b ("as if God is making his appeal through us") must be taken together with v. 20a and not, as is sometimes said, with v. 20cd. To be sure, the whole of v. 20ab already introduces the appeal of v. 20d; at the same time, however, v. 20ab still looks back to and develops vv. 18c and 19c. Therefore the repetition of v. 20c ("we beseech you on behalf of Christ"), concretely leading up to the appeal itself, is appropriate.

Many exegetes maintain that *katallagēte* in v. 20d is a divine passive; the agent "God," then, must be supplied: "be reconciled to God (by God)." According to vv. 18-20a and 21a God is the subject indeed: God was and is reconciling us to himself. The following arguments, however, militate against a passive understanding. (1) In that hypothesis the dative "to God" is rather awkward ("God" twice in the same clause, but with different functions). (2) The imperative here would seem to expect a response through which the addressees are more "active" than a strict passive could suggest. (3) In 1 Cor 7:11 as well as Matt 5:24 the passive forms are most probably deponent and have an active (reflexive) meaning: "Let her reconcile herself *(katallagētō)* to her husband" and "Reconcile yourself *(diallagēthi)* to your brother." A deponent is possibly also present in 2 Macc 7:33 and 8:29 with God as subject. Therefore it would seem that in 2 Cor 5:20d Paul beseeches the Corinthians as follows: "Reconcile yourselves to God." Human cooperation is required (cf. 6:1-2).

The aorist tense forbids one to speak here of an action that is to be repeated every day. Paul asks for a concrete decision, as soon as possible. Some interpreters therefore take unconverted people as the addressees of this appeal. Yet this can hardly be correct. Of course the Corinthians are already converted; they are already reconciled to God, yet there is the opponents' influence in Corinth, the distrust toward Paul; in the community there are inner tensions and moral imperfections, past and present. Paul points to the root of all this and requires a renewed reconciliation with God. Verse 20 can rightly be called the center, the focus of vv. 14-21. The whole reflection leads up to this appeal.

21. *Him who knew no sin, he made (him to be) sin for us:* This verse could belong to the appeal of v. 20d as its motivation. If so, it is part of the appeal proper. Yet Paul appears to abandon his appeal and continue his reflection. Moreover, the first person plural in v. 21 differs from that in v. 20. Together with vv. 14-15, v. 21 constitutes an inclusion of the passage.

The grammatical subject "God," not mentioned in v. 21a, is easily supplied from v. 20b. God has the initiative as in vv. 18-19 (cf. also v. 20b). Since the verb "to know" again possesses (cf. v. 16) its Semitic sense, the expression "him who knew no sin" means "the one who has not committed sin." "Sin" here points to the whole reality of sinning. The preposition *hyper* means "instead of," rather than its original "on behalf of." Christ takes our place and represents us. "For us" could be all-inclusive: the whole of humankind. However, Paul probably refers in the first place to the Corinthians and himself.

The second *hamartia* is most probably not "sin-sacrifice." It is claimed (rightly?) that *hamartia* is found with this meaning in Leviticus 4 (LXX). Several interpreters defend this understanding in Paul as well (here and in Rom 8:3 with *peri hamartias*). However, the term at the end of v. 21a probably retains the same meaning as in the first half of the clause. In light of the corresponding antithetical expression "the righteousness of God" in v. 21b we must presume that the sin that is meant in v. 21a is human sin. To be made sin is, as it were, to be made a sinner. Christ thus represents all sinners. Of course Paul's language is paradoxical. Both the metonymy and the phrase "for us" subtly safeguard the sinlessness of Christ. The soteriological v. 21a explains what happened in Christ's death (vv. 14-15) and how the not counting of trespasses came about (v. 19b). Christ was made sin for us and so took away our sins. The time reference of the verb "made" is to the cross event.

in order that by him we might become the righteousness of God: Verse 21b is a purpose clause dependent on v. 21a. In the Greek text of v. 21a Christ ("[he] who . . .") is referred to at the beginning of the clause; the expression "by him" in v. 21b points to him chiastically at the very end of the clause. In v. 21a the verb "he made" (with God the subject) is in the Greek text at the end; "in order that we might become" (with "we" the subject) is at the beginning of v. 21b, again chiastically. In v. 21 there is also the antithesis of sin and righteousness, as well as of Christ and Christians.

The purpose clause of v. 21b indicates God's intention that, in a certain sense, is already effected by God. A hidden imperative, however, is inherent in it: we must "become" righteous (cf. the *hina* clause of v. 15b); "we" (*hēmeis*, in an emphatic position) have to accept God's gift and thus collaborate with God. If this view is correct, the forensic term righteousness possesses here a moral connotation as well. Like the second "sin" in v. 21a, "righteousness" in v. 21b is an *abstractum pro concreto*. We must become righteous people, i.e., righteous with God's righteousness. Of course, in v. 21b also Paul's language is stretched to the extreme. The *en* in *en autǭ* is probably instrumental: "by him" (cf. "through Christ" in v. 18b), yet the local, inclusive sense may also be present: we are righteous through Christ and through our being in him.

In the whole of v. 21 there is much more than a simple exchange between God and humankind. On God's part there is, through the representative action of Christ, forgiveness of our sins; on our side there is justification as a result, yet as a way of life as well. In Gal 3:13 Paul uses similarly paradoxical language: "Christ redeemed us from the curse of the law, having become a curse for us." Here, too, a (double) purpose clause follows (see v. 14).

INTERPRETATION

a. *Structure and Line of Thought.* In 4:16–5:10 most of the attention was centered on the future: the resurrection or the future of Christians. In 5:9-10 the motif of final judgment stands out. All of us must appear before the judgment seat of Christ and will be judged according to our deeds. The beginning of 5:11 is clearly related to the preceding verse. The particle "therefore" announces a conclusion. We realize that we shall have to account for our conduct and, therefore, there is "the fear of the Lord" in us. The verb *phaneroumai* ("to be made manifest," twice in v. 11), since it was already employed in 5:10, serves as a connecting link between 5:11 and the foregoing passage. Yet in spite of these connections with what precedes, a different line of thought breaks through in 5:11. In this verse Paul returns to his self-defense and plea. No longer the future common destination of all Christians, but the actual situation—his strained relations with the Corinthians—will be treated. With 5:11 the more abstract, speculative speaking about a faith reality is concluded for the time being. Paul is again addressing himself directly to the Corinthians. His opponents are mentioned as well.

Within 2 Cor 2:14–7:4 (the so-called "major insertion") 5:11–6:10 forms a rather self-contained unit. We find in it a somewhat concentric structure: *a* (5:11-13), *b* (5:14-21) and *a'* (6:1-10). One can compare the first person plural of 5:11 ("we try to convince people") with that of 6:1 ("working together [with God] we entreat you"). More striking still is the fact that both *a* and *a'* contain, among other things, a self-defense and that in both Paul depicts his attitude toward God and his fellow Christians; again, in the two passages he uses the pronoun "you" several times. The *b* unit, although duly connected with *a* by "for" in v. 14a, is much more theological; 5:14-21 provides reflection, meditation, exposition, but also appeal. Here Paul situates his apostleship within the whole of God's salvific plan, i.e., in connection with the Christ event. This reflection leads up to its climax in the appeal of v. 20. Hereafter v. 21, which corresponds to vv. 14-15, rounds off the unit.

In the *a* unit (5:11-13) Paul begins by affirming that he is already known to God. He is full of hope that he may be known to the consciences of the Corinthians as well. He refers to a knowledge that should enable them to answer the opponents. Paul's behavior is radically different from that of his opponents. They are boasting about outward appearances, perhaps also about ecstatic experiences. For Paul, however, such experiences are a matter between himself and God only, not a matter for public display.

In the *b* unit (5:14-21) Paul presents his profound reflection that should provide the Corinthians with insight into his apostolic status, but must also ground the appeal to reconciliation. In this central passage two sections can be distinguished, 5:14-17 and 5:18-21. Both of them may further be divided, the first into vv. 14-15 and 16-17, the second into vv. 18-19 and 20-21. (1) In 5:14-17 Paul starts by explaining what the basic event,

Christ's death and resurrection, brought about for humankind: death to sin and life for Christ (vv. 14-15). Two consequences follow from this event, the first concerning the way of "knowing," the second with regard to the ontological change effected by Christ (vv. 16-17). (2) Within 5:18-21 Paul first specifies, in compact formulae, what God has done in Christ: the reconciliation of the world to himself and the inauguration of the ministry of reconciliation (vv. 18-19). In accordance with the reference to ministry Paul then exhorts the Corinthians that they should reconcile themselves with God; he motivates that appeal by referring once more to God's action in Christ (vv. 20-21).

In the *a'* unit (6:1-10) Paul repeats the appeal of 5:20. The participle "working together," as well as the phrase "the grace of God" in 6:1, points back to what is said in 5:18-21. In 6:1-2 the urgent call comes to the fore (note the double "behold" in v. 2). The two verses constitute both exhortation and warning. With 6:3-4a Paul stresses the commendable honesty of his ministry. No doubt this apology must serve to reinforce his plea. In 6:4b-10 we meet one of Paul's famous "catalogues of trials." Paul thus concretely depicts his actual apostolic existence. Because of its length, the *a'* unit will be dealt with in the following section of this commentary.

b. *A Particular Problem.* In 5:14-15 Paul has most likely been using a traditional formula; however, he does not quote it literally. In this connection the technical term *Sterbensformel* ("death-formula") is often mentioned. The fixed and possibly more original long formula states that "Christ has died for (the removal of) sins" (cf. 1 Cor 15:3b; see also, e.g., the eucharistic words in Mark 14:24: "my blood . . . which is poured out for many"). Quite often in his letters Paul employs the soteriological *hyper* ("for") phrase (three times in 2 Cor 5:14-15 and once in 5:21; see also Rom 5:6, 8; 8:32; 14:14; 1 Cor 11:24; 15:3; Gal 1:4; 2:20; 3:13).

In v. 14b we read: "One died for all." When v. 14 and v. 15 are taken together it appears that Paul not only rewrites the traditional formula but also provides a brief comment on it. His editorial work is remarkable indeed. (1) "One" replaces "Christ"; "for our sins" (or, according to the short formula, maybe "for us") is replaced by "for all." Paul thus underscores the universal significance of Jesus' death. He brings in one of his favorite oppositions, namely, "one/all." In adding this antithesis Paul must have been thinking of Christ as the new Adam. Christ, like Adam, is an inclusive figure. In v. 14b the presence of that antithesis seems to alter the original meaning of *hyper* ("for") into "instead of." (2) In v. 14c, which again is clearly universalist, the "one/all" opposition is no longer explicit. With "so all have died" Paul draws the conclusion from v. 14b. In Jesus' death the death of all took place. The typically Pauline inclusion of all in Christ is worked out. We must not, of course, overlook how human death (to sin) is different from Jesus' (physical) death. (3) In v. 15 there is a shift from past to future, from gift to task. That connection of "indicative" (past) and "imperative" (future) is equally characteristic of Paul. (4) Paul adds the resurrection idea at the end of v. 15b. By doing this he emphasizes the unity of dying and rising in Christ's salvific work. (5) Finally, by means of the preceding v. 14a Paul already provides an explanation of the statement that follows in v. 14b. He considers Jesus' death a manifestation of his love (cf. Gal 2:20). Moreover, he regards Christ's love as the determining factor in his own life from the time of his conversion onwards.

One must not try to find a formal quotation in v. 14b. Nonetheless, it contains a traditional kernel. Paul agrees with that tradition; he receives it. But in taking it up, he makes changes that betray his own emphasis. In his use of the tradition Paul explains it; he enriches it with his own universalistic and corporate, inclusive perspectives. That he nonetheless remained conscious of the traditional character of v. 14b clearly appears in the fact that he comments on it (vv. 14a, 14c, and 15b) as well as repeats it (v. 15a).

c. *Theological Reflection.* In his letters Paul infrequently uses the "interpersonal" category of reconciliation. Therefore some exegetes (especially Ernst Käsemann, "Some Thoughts") have looked for tradition in vv. 18-19 as well. Yet one may presume that Paul himself is at work here. For the first time in his writings he employs the idea of "reconciliation" (between humans) to describe what took place between God and humans. Already in Hellenistic-Jewish writing a horizontal category was applied vertically: God is reconciled (cf., for example, 2 Macc 5:20; 7:32-33; 8:29). But Paul is breaking new theological ground. He "deliberately makes a fundamental correction . . . it is not God who needs to be reconciled to human beings, but it is human beings who need to be reconciled to God" (Kim, "2 Cor. 5:11-21," 362).

We can assume that Paul himself composed the whole of these two verses. In v. 19 he repeats the preceding verse, but not without variation of style and progression of thought: through Christ God reconciled us with himself and gave us the ministry of reconciliation, because it was in fact God who in Christ was reconciling the (estranged) world to himself. The stylistically rather heavy repetition in v. 19 functions as a broadening of the content of v. 18; it simultaneously grounds that verse.

What is the main point of vv. 18-21 as far as the content is concerned? Rather than fixing on one single idea, one should take into account the possibility of a double shift and hence recognize a threefold accent. First, in vv. 18-19 Paul accentuates God's initiative of reconciling humankind with himself in Christ, as well as the institution of the ministry of reconciliation. Then in v. 20 Paul, as appointed ambassador of Christ, cannot refrain from exercising that ministry at once by means of an appeal: "reconcile yourselves to God." This appeal, too, is not without emphasis. Finally, at this juncture Paul seems to notice that although in vv. 18-20 Christ is mentioned in each verse, his salvific work as such is not explained or reflected upon. That is why—it would seem—Paul, in v. 21, again (cf. vv. 14-15) formulates what God did in Christ, this time by means of forceful, paradoxical language. Yet, notwithstanding these shifts, it would seem that the appeal to reconciliation in v. 20 can be called the focus, the center of vv. 14-21 (see Notes above).

d. *Reconciliation, "Atonement," Justification.* A brief critical investigation cannot be omitted. It concerns the relation between reconciliation and representation (in the past often and in some circles still called "substitution" and "vicarious atonement") on the one hand and justification on the other.

With regard to the first relation, two sets of terms present themselves in the New Testament: (1) *katallassō* ("to reconcile") and derivatives, cf. Matt 5:24 *(dia-)*; 1 Cor 7:11; 2 Cor 5:18-20; Rom 5:10-11; 11:15; Col 1:20, 22 *(apo-)*, and (2) *hilaskomai* ("to expiate, to propitiate") and derivatives, cf. Rom 3:25 *(hilastērion)*; Heb 2:17; 8:12; 9:5; 1 John 2:2; 4:10. The first category, "reconciliation" (German *Versöhnung*), has its origin in the interpersonal social sphere (according to C. Breytenbach, *Versöhnung*, a Hellenistic military-diplomatic background). Reconciliation is the end of hostility and brings about peace between two opposing parties. As such the category is not cultic. The other concept, "expiation" (German *Sühne*), on the contrary, refers in the New Testament to cultic practice, either in the literal or metaphoric sense: expiatory sacrifices, means of propitiation. This second category deals with reconciliation between God and humankind. A strict distinction between "reconciliation" and "expiation" seems to be to the point. This is confirmed—it is often claimed—by the fact that Paul does not mix the two concepts or use them in the same context. Nevertheless in 2 Cor 5:14-21 one finds, along with the terminology of reconciliation, the *hyper* phrases (vv. 14-15 and 21) and other statements that together point to inclusive substitution, i.e., representation. Therefore it can be maintained that for Paul the two thought-complexes are not as disparate and mutually exclusive as some authors seem to assume. After all, one must also understand Rom 5:10 ("we were reconciled to God by the death of his Son") as pointing to Jesus' sacrificial and representative action on the cross alluded to in 5:9 ("we are now justified 'by his blood'").

In Paul's letters to the Galatians and Romans the notion of "justification" is evidently central, yet it would seem that the less frequent "reconciliation" is not therefore to be called a secondary, less important category. Paul himself creatively applied horizontal reconciliation to God's vertical action of making peace between God and hostile human-kind. Ernst Käsemann, "Some Thoughts," stresses that by speaking of reconciliation Paul intensifies, as it were, the idea of justification into a "justification of enemies." Moreover, both concepts, justification and rec-onciliation, refer to what God did in Christ: we have been justified; we have been reconciled. Yet in 2 Cor 5:20 Paul also uses "to reconcile" for what still must be done ("reconcile yourselves to God"), and we also saw that in 5:21b ("in order that we might become the righteousness of God") an imperative nuance is probably present. Seyoon Kim emphasizes that "'reconciliation' . . . originated from Paul's personal experience of God's reconciliation of him to himself on the Damascus road" ("2 Cor. 5:11-21," 360). Whether the Servant Song of Isaiah 53 directly influenced Paul in composing the reconciliation passage of vv. 18–21 (so Hofius and others) is uncertain but not to be excluded. One might perhaps also assume that Paul introduced the reconciliation concept to describe the soteriological aspect of Jesus' death on the cross because of the tensions in Corinth, i.e., the absence of interpersonal reconciliation.

For Reference and Further Study

Bieringer, Reimund. "Paul's Understanding of Diakonia in 2 Corinthians 5,18" in Bieringer and Lambrecht, *Studies on 2 Corinthians.* BEThL 102. Leuven: Leuven University Press/Peeters, 1994, 413–428.

_____. "2 Kor 5,19a und die Versöhnung der Welt" in idem, 429–459.

_____. "Sünde und Gerechtigkeit Gottes in 2 Korinther 5,21" in idem, 461–513.

_____. "Traditionsgeschichtlicher Ursprung und theologische Bedeutung der HYPER-Aussagen im Neuen Testament" in Frans Van Segbroeck et al, eds., *The Four Gospels 1992. FS F. Neirynck I.* BEThL 100A. Leuven: Leuven University Press/Peeters, 1991, 219–248.

Breytenbach, Cilliers. *Versöhnung. Eine Studie zur paulinischen Soteriologie.* WMANT 60. Neukirchen-Vluyn: Neukirchener Verlag, 1989, 107–143.

Hahn, Ferdinand. "'Siehe, jetzt ist der Tag des Heils'. Neuschöpfung und Versöhnung nach 2. Korinther 5,14-6,2," *EvTh* 33 (1973) 244–253.

Hengel, Martin. "Der Kreuzestod Jesu Christi als Gottes souveräne Erlösungstat. Exegese über 2. Korinther 5,11-21" in *Theologie und Kirche. Reichenau-Gespräch der Evangelischen Landessynode Württemberg.* Stuttgart, 1967, 60–89.

Hofius, Otfried. "Erwägungen zur Gestalt und Herkunft des paulinischen Versöhnungsgedankens" in idem, *Paulusstudien.* WUNT 51. Tübingen: Mohr-Siebeck, 1989, 1–14.

_____. "'Gott hat unter uns aufgerichtet das Wort von der Versöhnung' (2 Kor 5,19)" in idem, 15–32.

Hooker, Morna D. "Interchange in Christ" in eadem, *From Adam to Christ. Essays on Paul.* Cambridge: Cambridge University Press, 1990, 13–21.

Käsemann, Ernst. "Some Thoughts on the Theme 'The Doctrine of Reconciliation in the New Testament'" in James M. Robinson, ed., *The Future of Our Religious Past. FS R. Bultmann.* Translated by Charles E. Carlston and Robert P. Scharlemann. London: S.C.M., and New York: Harper, 1971, 49–64.

Kim, Seyoon. "2 Cor. 5:11-21 and the Origin of Paul's Concept of 'Reconciliation,'" *NT* 39 (1997) 360–384.

Koperski, Veronica. "Knowledge of Christ and Knowledge of God in the Corinthian Correspondence" in Reimund Bieringer, ed., *The Corinthian Correspondence.* BEThL 125. Leuven: Leuven University Press/Peeters, 1996, 377–396.

Lambrecht, Jan. "'Reconcile yourselves . . .': A Reading of 2 Corinthians 5,11-21" in Bieringer and Lambrecht, *Studies on 2 Corinthians,* 363–412.

Martin, Ralph P. *Reconciliation: A Study of Paul's Theology.* Atlanta: John Knox, 1981.

Mell, Ulrich. *Neue Schöpfung. Eine traditionsgeschichtliche und exegetische Studie zu einem soteriologischen Grundsatz paulinischer Theologie.* BZNW 56. Berlin and New York: Walter de Gruyter, 1989, 327–388.

Stuhlmacher, Peter. "Erwägungen zum ontologischen Charakter der *kainē ktisis* bei Paulus," *EvTh* 27 (1967) 1–35.

Wolff, Christian. "True Apostolic Knowledge of Christ. Exegetical Reflections on 2 Corinthians 5.14ff" in A. J. M. Wedderburn, ed., *Paul and Jesus. Collected Essays.* JSNT.S 37. Sheffield: Sheffield Academic Press, 1989, 81–98.

9. *As Ministers of God* (6:1-10)

1. Working together (with God), then, we also entreat you not to receive the grace of God in vain. 2. For he says: "In a favorable time I listened to you; on the day of salvation I helped you" (Isa 49:8 LXX). Behold, now (it is) a favorable time; behold, now (is) the day of salvation.

3. We give no offense in anything lest our ministry be blamed, 4. but as ministers of God we commend ourselves in all things: with great endurance, in afflictions, hardships, (and) constraints, 5. in beatings, imprisonments, (and) riots, in labors, sleepless nights, (and) fastings, 6. by purity (and) knowledge, patience (and) kindness, the Holy Spirit (and) genuine love, 7. by the word of truth (and) in the power of God, by means of weapons of righteousness for attack and defense, 8. in honor and dishonor, in ill-repute and good repute, as deceivers yet truthful, 9. as unknown yet well-known, as dying and behold we live, as punished yet not put to death, 10. as saddened but always rejoicing, as poor but enriching many, as having nothing yet possessing everything.

NOTES

1. *Working together (with God), then, we also entreat you not to receive the grace of God in vain:* Some authors understand *synergountes* in the sense of "all of us working together." However, the preceding context leaves no doubt that "to collaborate" here means "to work together with God": see 5:20 (cf. also 1 Cor 3:9: *theou . . . esmen synergoi,* "we are God's fellow workers"). "God's grace" is a comprehensive phrase and refers to God's salvation: reconciliation and justification.

The *kai* (here adverbial: "also") qualifies not only the subsequent verb but all of what follows in v. 1. "Not to receive the grace of God in vain" is not just a repetition of "reconcile yourselves" (5:20) but its specification. Because of the expression "in vain" and the past tenses in v. 2a the verb *dexasthai* is often thought to refer to a past act: that God's grace (which has been given in the past, at the time of the conversion) might not "have been received" in vain. But just as in 5:20, here also an actual invitation to accept the grace of God is meant. This explanation is strongly confirmed by the double "behold, now" in v. 2b. One should recognize, however, that the appeal to reconcile now when addressed to people who are already Christians could appear somewhat strange. The expression must be interpreted as a renewal and deepening of the reconciliation already received. However, the tense of the verb, an aorist, does not allow the sense of a repeated or continuing "receiving." Paul thus calls for a decision. He warns his readers; they should decide—to put it negatively—not to fail to live as "reconciled" people. The tensions and difficulties in the Corinthian community necessitate this call.

The subject of the infinitive *hymas* ("you," in our translation the direct object of "we entreat") stands at the end for the sake of emphasis, but one should not therefore assume that in 5:20 the second person is universal (the whole of humankind) and that Paul addresses the Corinthians only in 6:1. With regard to the vocabulary, it is perhaps the adjective *dektos* ("favorable") in the quotation in v. 2a that suggested to Paul the use of the verb *dexasthai* in v. 1. One should note the sequence of *dexasthai* (v. 1), *dektō* (v. 2a), and *euprosdektos* ("favorable," v. 2b).

2. *For he says: "In a favorable time I listened to you; on the day of salvation I helped you"* (Isa 49:8): The exhortation in v. 1 is motivated (*gar,* "for") by a quotation from Deutero-Isaiah. Paul considers Scripture as relevant to his own day. The Septuagint text is cited by Paul without any modification. "God" is almost certainly the subject of "says."

Paul does not seem to take into account the rich theological ideas present in the Isaian context, 49:1-13. A fourfold new reading of the Old Testament verse itself occurs. (1) Eschatological: the time indications point to the extreme importance of the present moment (cf. the double "behold, now" in v. 2b). (2) Christological: Both the acceptable time and the day of salvation refer to the saving event of Jesus' death and resurrection, by which God brought about the reconciliation of the world (cf. 5:14-21). The verbs, augmented aorists, envisage that action as having occurred in the past (= the Christ event). (3) Ecclesiological: the second person singular no longer refers to the Servant of the Lord (as in Isaiah), nor does it indicate Paul (alone). In line with the immediate context and especially because of *hymas* ("you") at the end of v. 1, the pronouns *sou* and *soi*, though singular in form, must be understood here first of all as designating the Corinthians. (4) Theological: *kairǭ dektǭ* signifies, as in Isaiah, "a time acceptable (to God)": God is the grammatical subject of the clause. It is a time when God mercifully listened to the Corinthians. According to Paul this time was the apex of salvation history; it is the time of the Christ event.

Behold, now (it is) a favorable time; behold, now (is) the day of salvation: Paul further comments on the quotation, actualizing it. It is not certain that the double compound *eu-pros-dektos* reinforces the *dektos* of v. 2a very much. The two verbs for v. 2a are missing; both "time" and "day" are now in the nominative and each of them is preceded by the urgent exhortative "behold, now." As in v. 1, Paul addresses the Corinthians. Most probably "favorable" in v. 2b no longer means acceptable to God (so *dektos* in v. 2a) but welcome, acceptable to the Corinthians. This is a remarkable shift. There is still a second shift, connected with the first: from past (v. 2a) to present (v. 2b). In v. 2b Paul emphasizes the extreme significance of the eschatological "now." In contrast to God's gift (v. 2a) he underlines the human task (v. 2b), not without urgency: the opportunity can be lost.

3-4a. *We give no offense in anything lest our ministry be blamed, but as ministers of God we commend ourselves in all things:* In vv. 1-2, notwithstanding the qualification of his ministry by "working together (with God)," Paul's main attention is directed toward his addressees. From v. 3 to v. 10 he will describe the "circumstances" of his own apostolic existence and thus defend his ministry before the Corinthians. The participles *didontes* ("giving," v. 3a) and *synistantes* (or the variant *synistanontes,* "commending," v. 4a) are, like "working together" in v. 1, grammatically in apposition to the subject of *parakaloumen* ("we entreat"). The whole of vv. 3-10 thus constitutes a participial continuation of v. 1, v. 2 being a parenthesis. However, Paul is fond of writing coordinate participles after a finite verb; these participles may be more or less the equivalent of independent sentences. Hence the new start in the translation.

The noun *proskopē* ("offense") is a *hapax legomenon* in the New Testament. The phrases *en mēdeni* (v. 3a) and *en panti* (v. 4a) seem to be neuter: "not in anything" and "in all things." The verb *mōmaomai* ("to be blamed") of v. 3b is used once more by Paul in 2 Corinthians (see 8:20). Paul wants to avoid human blame. Verse 4a repeats positively what is stated negatively in v. 3a. "As ministers of God" is a nominative and qualifies the subject: "as (= as it becomes) ministers of God we commend ourselves" (for self-recommendation, cf. 3:1; 4:2; 5:2; 7:11; 12:12, 18). Paul commends himself to his fellow men and women.

4b-5. *with great endurance, in afflictions, hardships, (and) constraints, in beatings, imprisonments, (and) riots, in labors, sleepless nights, (and) fastings:* Here begins the second (cf. 4:8-9) list of "hardships" (compare the German term *Peristasenkatalog,* catalogue of "circumstances"). The length of "with great endurance" and the meaning of the first *en* ("with") as well as "endurance" itself, differing in sense from the following terms, suggest that this first expression of the catalogue is more strictly introductory. It applies, as it were, to all that follows. In the rest of vv. 4b-5 Paul first lists three times three "circumstances" in the plural, preceded by *en* ("in"). These are all external difficulties. While the terms of the first triad appear to be synonymous, those of the second point to different hardships. In the third triad Paul refers to his own courageous apostolic conduct. For most of the terms in v. 5, cf. 11:23, 27.

6-7a. *by purity (and) knowledge, patience (and) kindness, the Holy Spirit (and) genuine love, by the word of truth (and) in the power of God:* Paul now uses four pairs of singular nouns, each preceded by *en* (rendered "by"). They indicate "virtues" or moral and spiritual qualities. "Knowledge" here probably means insight that is sensitive to God's will. It is not clear whether *en pneumati hagiǭ* also points to a virtue ("a holy spirit") or, more likely, to "the Holy Spirit" (see Gal 5:22 where kindness and love are parts of "the fruit of the Spirit"). In the phrase "the word of truth" it would seem that "truth" is an objective genitive: the word that speaks truth (not a truthful word or truthful speech).

7b. *by means of weapons of righteousness for attack and defense:* This rendering is rather a paraphrase. Verse 7b is the first of three double *dia* qualifications. It would seem that the term "righteousness" is not used in the typically Pauline sense, but in its moral meaning. The genitive is probably objective: the weapons with which one fights for righteousness. Weapons for attack (literally: "of the right hand," e.g., a sword) and weapons for defense ("of the left hand," e.g., a shield) may be indicated. Yet alternatively "right hand" and "left hand" could simply designate all the spiritual weapons that are needed.

8a. *in honor and dishonor, in ill-repute and good repute:* With the second and third *dia* phrases Paul points to the circumstances "in" which he works. From here to the end the catalogue employs antithetical expressions. We note the chiasm in v. 8a: honor and dishonor, ill-repute and good repute.

8b-10. *as deceivers yet truthful, as unknown yet well-known, as dying and behold we live, as punished yet not put to death, as saddened but always rejoicing, as poor but enriching many, as having nothing yet possessing everything:* Paul concludes the list with seven antithetical pairs each introduced by *hōs* ("as"), which applies to the first term only. Both terms in the pairs can be said to be true, except for the first one in v. 8b: "deceivers." The language thus becomes paradoxical. In the first, second, fourth, and last oppositions the terms are linked by an adversative *kai* ("yet"), in the fifth and sixth by *de* ("but"). In the third antithesis Paul writes a *kai idou* ("and behold"). Thus within the basically identical structure there is some amount of variation. The second term in the seven pairs generally refers to a paradoxical manifestation of God's power (cf. 4:8-9) and must in the last two cases ("enriching many," "possessing everything") be understood in a metaphorical, spiritual sense.

INTERPRETATION

a. *Structure and Line of Thought.* The majority of the commentaries understandably devote most attention to the long list of trials in 6:3b-10, yet one should not lose sight of the fact that the whole of 6:1-10, the *a'* section, corresponds to 5:11-13, the *a* unit (see pp. 102–103). Within 6:1-10, moreover, the Greek grammar makes clear that v. 1 contains the main clause and the rest is subordinated to it. Yet is there a real subordination of thought?

With regard to the content, the exhortation not to receive the grace of God in vain (vv. 1-2) clearly stands out, at least at first sight. In vv. 3-4a Paul then underscores his correct behavior, and vv. 4b-10 have to prove this circumstantially. As pointed out in the Notes, the participles of vv. 3a and 4a could be the equivalent of finite verbs; if so, they are coordinated with the main verb of v. 1 and mark, after the interruption of v. 2, a continuation or, better, a new beginning. The division of 6:1-10, therefore, is: vv. 1-2 (exhortation), vv. 3-4a (sincerity of the apostle), vv. 4b-10 (illustration of that sincerity). Paul's evidently irreproachable apostolic conduct reinforces his urgent appeal. However, one will easily admit that when writing vv. 4b-10 Paul no longer has in mind the grammatical connection with vv. 1-2.

Verse 1 takes up the appeal of 5:20. By means of the expression "the grace of God" the verse refers back to what is explained in vv. 14-19 and 21. But in 6:1-2 it is Paul himself who speaks, as it were, in his own name, no longer God through Paul as has been the case in 5:20. He is entitled to do this in full confidence since he is a fellow worker of God (v. 1), but also because no fault can be found with his apostolic existence (vv. 3-10). Within 6:1-10 Paul first directs his attention to the exhortation of the Corinthians and its urgency and, then, with a list of his trials and with great emphasis, to the moral quality of his apostolic ministry. As is becoming to a minister of God, he can commend himself in complete honesty.

b. *Isaiah Quotation and Catalogue of Trials.* In v. 2a Paul motivates his appeal by means of a quotation from Isaiah: "In a favorable time I listened to you; on the day of salvation I helped you" (Isa 49:8). In Gal 1:15 he applies Isa 49:1 to his own vocation and mission. The phrase "in vain" in 2 Cor 6:1 and Phil 2:16 possibly alludes to Isa 49:4, so Paul must have been acquainted with the context. In 49:1-13 the prophet deals with the sending of the Servant of the Lord to the survivors of Israel and to the Gentiles. Yet in 2 Cor 6:1-2 there is no clear indication that this context is referred to or that with "you" (singular) Paul is referring to himself. Without modifying the Septuagint text—but with the help of his own vv. 1 and 2b—he thoroughly interprets the citation within the new context. The emphasis is now on the eschatological moment: a favorable time, the day of salvation. Paul understands the salvation mentioned in the quotation to be the saving work done by Christ. In Christ God helped us. What the prophet announced has been fulfilled. Paul sees in the "you" (second person singular) the collectivity of his addressees, the Christians of Corinth (cf. the plural "you" at the end of v. 1). For Paul, as the introductory formula appears to suggest, the speaker of the quotation most probably is God; God is also the subject of both verbs in the scriptural citation.

Verses 1 and 2b further interpret and actualize the quotation (v. 2a). It is possible that Paul in v. 1 has employed the verb *dexastai* ("to receive") under the influence of *dektos* ("favorable") in the chosen text from Scripture. However, in v. 1 Paul looks forward to the future, while within v. 2a attention is given to what Christ has done in the past. A similar shift, from past to present (or near future), takes place in v. 2b: "Behold, now it is a favorable time; behold, now is the day of salvation." While in the quotation "acceptable" probably means favorable to God's grace, i.e., to God's merciful work, in v. 2 *euprosdektos* ("favorable") refers to the time favorable to the Corinthians, that is, a time well adapted to what they must do. There is thus a shift also from God to humankind, from gift to task.

Although the participle in v. 3a can be taken as the equivalent of a finite verb, the connection with v. 1 is obvious from the content of vv. 3-4a. Paul reflects on his active apostolic behavior. He sees that his ministry cannot be blamed; his lifestyle as minister (cf. vv. 4b-10) constitutes a self-commendation. Here in v. 4a, just as in 4:2 and in contrast to 3:1 and 5:12, self-commendation is legitimate. For a more thorough discussion of this matter, see 10:12-18.

The extensive list of "hardships" in vv. 4b-10 is most probably a free composition by Paul. Its structure is impressive. After the introductory title phrase "with great endurance" one should distinguish four strophes:

	4b	with great endurance,
(1)		in afflictions, hardships, (and) constraints,
	5	in beatings, imprisonments, (and) riots,
		in labors, sleepless nights, (and) fastings,
(2)	6	by purity (and) knowledge,
		patience (and) kindness,
		the Holy Spirit (and) genuine love,
	7	by the word of truth (and) in the power of God,
(3)		by means of weapons of righteousness for attack and defense,
	8	in honor and dishonor,
		in ill-repute and good repute,
(4)		as deceivers yet truthful,
	9	as unknown yet well-known,
		as dying and behold we live,
		as punished yet not put to death,
	10	as saddened but always rejoicing,
		as poor but enriching many,
		as having nothing yet possessing everything.

(1) In the first strophe (vv. 4c-5) Paul illustrates his endurance by pointing to the outward "circumstances." We can detect in it three sets of three hardships. In Greek all the nouns are in the plural and are introduced by *en* ("in").

(2) In the second strophe (vv. 6-7a) there is a shift to the characterization of his ministry. Four sets of two qualities are listed. The nouns are in the singular; again, all of them are preceded by *en*. The last two sets are somewhat longer.

(3) The third strophe (vv. 7b-8b) contains the indication of Paul's ministerial means and circumstances. The enumeration becomes antithetical. There are three sets of two nouns and each set is preceded by a single *dia:* "by means of" in the first set; attending circumstances in the second and third sets.

(4) The fourth and last strophe (vv. 8c-10) further characterizes Paul's ministry. It contains seven antithetical and paradoxical phrases, all introduced by *hōs* ("as"). The symmetry of these phrases is not complete; slight variations break the monotony. The seventh and last pair is rightly termed "an oratorical climax" by David L. Mealand.

c. *Theological Reflection.* The passage 6:4b-10 contains the second of the four catalogues of trials *(Peristasenkataloge)* in 2 Corinthians: see also 4:8-9; 11:23-29 and 12:10 (cf. also 1 Cor 4:10-13a; Phil 4:12; Rom 8:35b, 38-39). Those lists are (mainly) autobiographical: the sufferings, persecutions, and difficulties Paul himself experienced, and the attitudes he himself developed and fostered. How did Paul regard these sufferings?

Stoic authors, more or less contemporaries of Paul, sometimes illustrate their philosophy by means of such "listed" antithetical descriptions (cf., e.g., Bultmann, *Stil*). These kinds of Stoic catalogues may have been known to Paul: the same or similar motifs, images, and vocabulary. In such lists the authors express the ideal of stalwartness and impassibility. The wise Stoic remains unmoved by sufferings such as bodily pain and needs, catastrophes, illness, war, loss of friends, even the death of beloved relatives. Inwardly the Stoic is an island of rest and silence, possessing imperturbable happiness. The Stoic attains this ideal by his or her own power, through asceticism and persistent exercise. A comparison shows that Paul is not a cold, hard Stoic. Paul is completely cast down by the hardships: both body and soul have a share in the sufferings. He is not at all impassive. Liberation comes not through his own work but from God alone.

Besides the writings of the Greco-Roman Stoa a second, perhaps equally important background has also been suggested: Jewish apocalyptic literature (cf. Schrage, "Leid"). Although the apocalyptic lists do not contain antitheses (which are sometimes present in Paul), they offer not only hardships but also "virtues" (as Paul also does). Moreover, they are characterized by an eschatological horizon that, through the Christ event, is also visible in the Pauline catalogues. The major difference, however, is that in the apocalyptic writings the typical Christian tension between "already" and "not yet" is missing. Furthermore, the apocalyptic, messianic woes are determined according to a divinely fixed timetable. To Paul, however, the future is unknown; "circumstances" depend on the uncertainties and insecurities of his apostolic existence.

However, there existed not only in Stoic philosophy or Jewish apocalypticism, but more widely also within Hellenistic Judaism, Pharisaic Judaism (see the Mishnah), and incipient Gnosticism catalogues that can be compared with those of Paul (cf. Hodgson, "Tribulation Lists"). Evidently the genre of the tribulation list existed and was available to him. Paul may have borrowed rhetorical commonplaces, yet he builds them into his personal compositions and incorporates them into his new faith. Moreover, the lists are, as it were, his personal, autobiographical documents.

Paul's great endurance, i.e., his enduring "afflictions, hardships, (and) constraints . . . beatings, imprisonments, (and) riots . . . labors, sleepless nights, (and) fastings" (vv. 4c-5) is not a purely passive matter. Suffering is not sought after; it overcomes him. He confronts it because he wants to be a faithful apostle. The so-called virtues of "purity (and) knowledge, patience (and) kindness, the Holy Spirit (and) genuine love" (v. 6) point to an inner activity that transforms the suffering, yet suffering and trial remain what they are: suffering and trial. Where, then, does one find Paul's hidden, God-given power? And what is his theological vision of suffering?

In 4:10-11 Paul characterizes the trials he has just mentioned as follows: "Always carrying the putting to death of Jesus in the body in order that the life of Jesus be manifested in our body. For we who live are always given up to death for Jesus' sake in order that also the life of Jesus be manifested in our mortal flesh." In Rom 8:17 he states that the Christians are God's children and fellow heirs with Christ because they "suffer with him in order that (they) may also be glorified with him." In Rom 6:3-4 burial with Christ by baptism into death is mentioned, and in 6:6 being crucified with him. In 2 Cor 5:14 Paul affirms that all have died since one has died for all. Paul thus sees his suffering in connection with the death of Christ. To be united with Christ means that the minister will have to suffer as Christ did. Through all his trials he really participates in the suffering of Christ. He hopes to "know him and the power of his resurrection"; he hopes to share in his sufferings, "becoming like him in his death, that if possible (he) may attain the resurrection from the dead" (Phil 3:10-11). From all this it would seem that Paul's profound christological conviction offers him the ultimate explanation for his suffering, as well as a source of inspiration.

The antitheses in the catalogues (e.g., 2 Cor 6:8-10) elucidate that, in the midst of dying, life is present in a paradoxical way. Notwithstanding utmost misery and oppression, Paul is at the same time full of joy; notwithstanding poverty he possesses everything; in spite of his dying he is alive (cf. 4:16: "Even though our outer self is wasting away, our inner self is being renewed day by day"). But this togetherness will at some point have to give way; the paradoxical situation of "dying and behold we live" must end. Paul is convinced that "the momentary light (weight) of our tribulation is producing a more and more exceeding and eternal weight of glory for us" (4:17). What is seen is transitory; what is unseen is eternal (cf. 4:18). Suffering and death belong to this passing eon.

One more characteristic of the catalogues should be mentioned. Most, if not all of these lists depict Paul in his apostolic existence. The hardships he undergoes appear to be connected with his missionary life.

d. *Suffering.* It has been claimed that Paul regarded his own trials as being strictly bound up with his apostleship. However, his suffering is certainly also linked with that of the (Corinthian) Christians: "If we are in distress, (it is) for your consolation and salvation; if we are consoled, (it is also) for your consolation which is actively present in (your) endurance of the same sufferings that we too suffer" (2 Cor 1:6). He appeals to the Corinthians in 1 Cor 11:1: "Be imitators of me, as I am of Christ," and in 1 Thess 1:6, with explicit reference to suffering: "You became imitators of us and of the Lord, for you received the word in much affliction, with joy inspired by the Holy Spirit."

Paul's apostolic suffering is not detached from the trials any Christian meets in following the Lord in everyday life, with its joys and worries. It would seem that for a Christian all misfortunes, even senseless setbacks, can be upgraded into fruitful, apostolically productive suffering.

FOR REFERENCE AND FURTHER STUDY

Bultmann, Rudolf. *Der Stil der paulinischen Predigt und die kynisch-stoische Diatribe.* FRLANT. Göttingen: Vandenhoeck & Ruprecht, 1910.

Ebner, Martin. *Leidenslisten und Apostelbrief. Untersuchungen zu Form, Motivik und Funktion der Peristasenkataloge bei Paulus.* FzB 66. Würzburg: Echter Verlag, 1991, 243–330.

Fitzgerald, John T. *Cracks in an Earthen Vessel: An Examination of the Catalogues of Hardships in the Corinthian Correspondence.* SBL.DS 99. Atlanta: Scholars, 1988.

Hahn, Ferdinand. "'Siehe, jetzt is der Tag des Heils'. Neuschöpfung und Versöh-
nung nach 2. Korinther 5,14–6,2," *EvTh* 33 (1973) 244–253.
Hodgson, Robert. "Paul the Apostle and First Century Tribulation Lists," *ZNW* 74
(1983) 59–80.
Hoïstad, Ragnar. "Eine hellenistische Parallele zu 2. Kor 6,3ff," *CNT* 9 (1944) 222–
227.
Lambrecht, Jan. "The Favorable Time: A Study of 2 Cor 6,2a in Its Context" in
Bieringer and Lambrecht, *Studies on 2 Corinthians*. BEThL 102. Leuven: Leuven University Press/Peeters, 1994, 515–529.
Manus, C. U. "Apostolic Suffering (2 Cor 6:4-10): The Sign of Christian Existence
and Identity," *Asia Journal of Theology* 1 (1987) 41–54.
Mealand, David L. "'As having nothing and yet possessing everything', 2 Cor
6:10c," *ZNW* 67 (1976) 277–279.
Schrage, Wolfgang. "Leid, Kreuz und Eschaton: Die Peristasenkataloge als Merkmale paulinischer *theologia crucis* und Eschatologie," *EvTh* 34 (1974) 141–
175.

10. *Apostolic Appeal and Exhortation* (6:11–7:4)

11. Our mouth stands open to you, Corinthians; our heart is made wide.
12. You are not cramped in us, but you are cramped in your (own) affections. 13. As a recompense in kind—I speak as to (my) children—you,
too, be wide open (to us).

14. Do not be yoked unevenly with unbelievers. For what partnership (is there) between righteousness and iniquity, or what fellowship (is
there) for light with darkness? 15. What (is) the accord of Christ with
Beliar, or what part (is there) for a believer with an unbeliever? 16. What
agreement (is there) between the temple of God and idols? For we are
the temple of the living God, as God has said: "I will dwell in them and
move about (among them), and I will be their God and they will be my
people" (Lev 26:12). 17. Therefore, "Come out from their midst and be
separate (from them)," says the Lord, "do not touch anything unclean"
(Isa 52:11), "and I will receive you, 18. and I will be a father to you, and
you will be sons and daughters to me" (2 Sam 7:14), says the Lord
almighty. 7:1. Since we have these promises, beloved, let us therefore
cleanse ourselves from every stain of the flesh and the spirit, while we
are making perfect (our) holiness in the fear of God.

2. Make room for us; we have done wrong to no one, we have corrupted no one, we have defrauded no one. 3. I do not condemn (you).
For I have (already) said that you are in our hearts to die together and to
live together. 4. I (have) great frankness in (dealing with) you; I (have)
great pride in you; I am filled with consolation; I overflow with joy in the
midst of all our distress.

NOTES

11. *Our mouth stands open to you, Corinthians; our heart is made wide:* Because of the parallelism between "mouth" and "heart" and between the two verbs (*aneō-gen*, "is made open" and *peplatyntai*, "is made wide"), one could be inclined to take the two clauses as expressing the same idea. But between them there is a shift. In v. 11a Paul says that he has spoken openly to the Corinthians, with frankness; this probably is an allusion to his words in the preceding vv. 3-10. In v. 11b, however, Paul emphasizes his sincere affection for the Christians of Corinth: my heart is enlarged by the warmth of my love; it is made wide open to you.

    From the insistence present in v. 11, as well as from the address "Corinthians"—Paul rather rarely uses such addresses (cf. Gal 3:1 and Phil 4:15)—the reader gets the impression that the lengthy section 2:14–7:4 is nearing its end.

12. *You are not cramped in us, but you are cramped in your (own) affections:* The first clause (v. 12a) repeats the idea of v. 11b, but in different words and in a negative way; the second clause (v. 12b) contains a severe reproach. Paul contrasts his loving attitude to the meager feelings of the Corinthians. For Jews the term *splagchna* ("bowels," also in Hebrew) refers to "emotions." For "to be cramped" the Greek text twice uses the verb *stenochōreomai* (literally: "to be confined, to be short of space)."

13. *As a recompense in kind—I speak as to (my) children—you, too, be wide open (to us):* The Greek text commences with a stereotypical expression that can be rendered roughly as "give the same recompense to me" or "in fair exchange." The meaning of the interruption that follows is either "I speak as to children," i.e., in a way adapted to children, or, more likely (cf. 1 Cor 4:14), "I speak as a father to his children." The imperative "be wide" takes up the verb (*platyno-mai*) of v. 11b. After the reproach of v. 12b, v. 13 expresses an appeal.

14a. *Do not be yoked unevenly with unbelievers:* Although the text proceeds with a second imperative, the transition is very abrupt. A radical separation is required from the Christians. They must keep apart from the Gentile unbelievers. Within this context the term *apistoi* retains its normal meaning (cf. v. 15; in 4:4 it also means non-Christians, but Jews). The verb *heterozygeō* is employed metaphorically. It contains the vivid image of two kinds of animals (e.g., ox and ass) who together form an uneven (and uneasy, if not impossible) team or yoke: they are unevenly yoked. The prohibition sounds general and may include worship, marriage, business and social contact (but cf. 1 Cor 5:9-11).

14b-16a. *For what partnership (is there) between righteousness and iniquity, or what fellowship (is there) for light with darkness? What (is) the accord of Christ with Beliar, or what part (is there) for a believer with an unbeliever? What agreement (is there) between the temple of God and idols?* These verses consist of five short, somewhat symmetrically composed rhetorical questions, all of which motivate (cf. *gar*, "for," in v. 14b) the prohibition of v. 14a. Each time it is asked whether two opposing realities or persons can go together: righteousness and iniquity, light and darkness, Christ and Beliar, believer and unbeliever, the temple of God and idols. Each question is introduced by the interrogative pronoun *tis* ("what?" cf. Sir 13:2, 17-18). Each time, of course, a negative answer is expected. As in 6:7, "righteousness" possesses a moral nuance; it is not used in the typically Pauline sense. "Beliar" is a distortion of "Belial," a common Jewish name for Satan, "the god of the present age" (4:4). "Believer" is, as it were, the technical term for "Christian." Together the Christians are "the temple of God" (in 1 Cor 6:19a the body of the individual Christian is called a "temple of the holy Spirit").

16b-f. *For we are the temple of the living God, as God has said: "I will dwell in them and move about (among them), and I will be their God and they will be my people":* The rest of v. 16 contains a further explanation (again a motivating *gar*, "for") and an Old Testament quotation, Lev 26:12, which is introduced by "as God has said." The LXX text is as follows: "And I will walk (= move about) among you, and be your God, and you shall be my people" (Translation by L.C.L. Brenton). The quotation is expanded at the beginning by "I will dwell in them" (cf. Ezek 37:27a). No doubt the expansion occurs because the "temple of God" is spoken of in v. 16a: the <u>Christians are that temple</u> (v. 16b). The quotation offers the well-known covenant formula. The future verbs originally point to a promise on the part of God. The Christians, however, must consider this promise as fulfilled. They already are the people of God. Translations often mark a difference between God's sovereign "I will be" and the more imperatival "they shall be." This is hardly correct here. In Lev 26:12 the addressees are mentioned in the second person plural. Paul alters this into the third person plural, perhaps under the influence of the covenant formula in Ezek 37:27bc.

17a-c. *Therefore, "Come out from their midst and be separate (from them)," says the Lord, "do not touch anything unclean":* Because the Christians are God's people ("therefore") they must avoid the contacts with the Gentiles and strive for purity. This verse contains a second quotation, Isa 52:11. The formula "says the Lord," which usually introduces a cited text, stands in the middle here. In Isaiah, Israel is summoned to leave Babylon; for the sake of cultic purity the Israelites (or their Levites?) should not touch what is unclean. In v. 17 the Old Testament text is abbreviated, ordered in a slightly different way, and to a certain extent rewritten. This adaptation results in the double command of separation and the ban on a (figuratively understood) uncleanness. It is no longer Babylon that has to be left; the Christians must "come out of the midst" of the unbelievers and keep their distance from them; they should keep away from the moral impurity of Gentile unbelievers.

17d-18. *"and I will receive you, and I will be a father to you, and you will be sons and daughters to me," says the Lord almighty:* What follows the orders of v. 17abc is a third quotation, again a promise, 2 Sam 7:14: "I will be to him a father, and he shall be to me a son" (LXX, translation by Brenton). It contains part of the divine promise that the prophet Nathan spoke to David. According to the Old Testament text God will be a father to David's son, and he (Solomon) a son to

God. That promise, the adoption formula, is somewhat rewritten in 2 Corinthians. Just as v. 16b was an addition to the first citation, so also v. 17d expands the third quotation, again at its beginning: "and I *(kagō,* emphatic) will receive you" (possible influence from Ezek 20:34a). God's promise will be kept, already now in history, on the condition that the Christians will do what is required of them in v. 17abc. The adaptation to the new context manifests itself in the second person plural, "sons," as well as by (some will feel) Paul's surprising addition of "and daughters." The so-called introductory formula now stands at the very end: "says the Lord almighty." "Almighty" *(pantokratōr)* is the Septuagint translation of "the Lord of hosts" (cf., for example, 2 Sam 7:8).

7:1. *Since we have these promises, beloved, let us, therefore, cleanse ourselves from every stain of the flesh and the spirit, while we are making perfect (our) holiness in the fear of God:* The presence of "therefore" and the vocative "beloved" mark this verse as a conclusion. It consists of one lengthy sentence; the main verb is "let (us) cleanse ourselves" which repeats the injunction of the second quotation (see 6:17a and c). The Greek participle *echontes* ("having") possesses causal nuance: since we have these promises. The phrase "these promises" refers to the first and third quotations (see 6:16def and 6:17d-18ab). For Christians the content of the promises does not lie totally in the future. A complete cleansing affects both the body and the spirit. Yet "cleansing" is but the negative part of the Christian vocation, which in positive terms is called "holiness" (cf. Rom 6:19). At the end of the verse the expression *en phobǭ theou* ("in the fear of God") implicitly refers to the judgment and thus adds an eschatological connotation (see 2 Cor 5:10 and cf. 5:11: "the fear of the Lord").

2. *Make room for us; we have done wrong to no one, we have corrupted no one, we have defrauded no one:* The first clause of this verse is to be connected with 6:13. Paul repeats its command. In 7:2a, the verb *chōrēsate* ("make room") has the same root as the verb of 6:12 *(stenochōreomai,* "to be cramped"). After this appeal Paul defends himself against three insinuations: unspecified wrongdoing, religious or moral corruption, and financial fraud (cf. 12:17). Three times his emotional defense commences with *oudena* ("no one") in the Greek text; the brief clauses have no connecting "and." While in 6:13 the motivation of the appeal was Paul's love, to which the Christians must respond, that in 7:2bcd is his innocence. Paul vindicates himself.

3. *I do not condemn (you). For I have (already) said that you are in our hearts to die together and to live together:* Paul seems to fear that his apology might be experienced by the addressees as a reproach. Therefore he explicitly states that he does not want to condemn the Corinthians (v. 3a). Then, in v. 3b, he once more (cf. 6:12a) emphasizes his profound union with them, so as "to die together and to live together." The sequence of the last two verbs is probably not accidental: first physical death and, after that, life forever (see Interpretation). If so, the expression is no longer referring to the common motif of lasting loyalty or the usual declaration of the bond of human friendship ("together in life and death").

4. *I (have) great frankness in (dealing with) you; I (have) great pride in you; I am filled with consolation; I overflow with joy in the midst of all our distress:* The style continues to be very emotional. We notice the shift to the first person singular. There are four brief clauses, again without any connective "and." As to content the first and second clauses belong together; so do the third and fourth. All four clauses explain what that unity produces in Paul: frankness in speech toward them (cf. 6:11a), boasting about them, abundance of consolation, and overwhelming joy in the midst of all the troubles. The last expression, *epi pasę tę thlipsei hēmōn* (literally: "at all our distress") no doubt refers back to the description in 6:3-10.

INTERPRETATION

a. *Structure and Line of Thought.* 2 Corinthians 6:11–7:4 constitutes the last section of 2:14–7:4. Without any difficulty the passage can be divided into three small units: 6:11-13; 6:14–7:1; and 7:2-4. Both style and content are very similar in the first and third units; the second unit is scarcely connected to these framing texts. One may be permitted, therefore, to speak of an *a b a'* structure. In *a* and *a'* we detect the presence of allusions to 6:1-10. In the list of trials in 6:3b-10 Paul has spoken to the Corinthians with great frankness (see 6:11a and 7:4a). The "listed" hardships and virtues prove that the Corinthians are not in the least "cramped" in him (see 6:12b), and this catalogue also shows how they are present in his heart (see 7:3b). Just as in 6:3-4a (and 6:4b-10), in 7:2bcd Paul defends his apostolic conduct. With the final expression in 7:4 ("in the midst of all our distress") he once more refers to the hardships of 6:3b-10.

The subtle shifts within the train of thought of 6:11-13 *(a)* and 7:2-4 *(a')* were already mentioned in the Notes. Initially one has the impression that 6:11a and 11b are perfect parallels. However, v. 11b must be read together with v. 12a which explains and completes its sense: our heart is wide open for you; there is in us no lack of space for you. Thus vv. 11b-12a represent the first shift; Paul moves from the statement of his openness or frankness in speech (v. 11a) to an affirmation of his loving relation and affection *vis-à-vis* the Corinthians. Then in v. 12b Paul rebukes his addressees, a second shift: there is no space in them for Paul. The third shift in thought occurs in v. 13; after the rebuke Paul formulates an appeal: you also, be wide open to me.

Verse 7:2a repeats and reinforces the appeal of 6:13. In 7:2b Paul then gives the motive: the Corinthians should make room for him "since" he has wronged none of them. This motivation differs from that suggested in 6:12-13 where the reason was that the Corinthians should act toward Paul just as he acted toward them. In 7:3a he expresses his fear that his self-defense might seem offensive to his readers; Paul does not want to condemn them. On the contrary, he says in 7:3b, they should realize the union that exists between him and them so as to die together and live together. In 7:4 Paul explicates what this union concretely means for him: it enables him to be frank with the Corinthians and to boast about them and, further, to be full of consolation and overflowing with joy in the midst of all the affliction. Once again, also in 7:2-4, there are subtle changes in the line of thought: from appeal to motivation (self-defense) to excuse (loving union with the Corinthians) to a depiction of his way of acting and feeling.

Notwithstanding these many shifts, 6:11-13 *(a)* and 7:2-4 *(a')* are both characterized by a strikingly emotional and personal appeal. There are many asyndeta, i.e., clauses not connected by a conjunction. Not only are tone and style similar; ideas and, to some extent, wording are equally parallel.

Compare:	with:
6:11a: openness, frankness	7:4a: openness, frankness
6:11b-12a: loving union	7:3b: loving union
6:12b: rebuke	7:2bcd: rebuke
6:13a: softening	7:3a: softening
6:13b: appeal	7:2a: appeal

Units *a* and *a'* contain the emotional appeal that concludes Paul's lengthy so-called apology in 2:14–7:4. Together they also frame 6:14–7:1, the *b* unit; they thus form an inclusion. In *a* and *a'* Paul asks for the reciprocal love of the Corinthians. He underscores his openness, his innocence and, above all, his genuine love of them.

Unit *b*, 6:14–7:1, seems to stand almost completely isolated between *a* and *a'*. In the self-contained *b* unit the readers listen to a severe warning against contact with unbelievers. As light shares nothing with darkness, so believers have nothing in common with unbelievers. Three times this passage cites the Old Testament in order to motivate the injunction or to repeat it. By cleansing themselves from every defilement the Corinthian Christians will perfect their holiness.

b. *The "Fragment."* A specific question regarding the passage 6:14–7:1 must be considered. A majority of exegetes are of the opinion that 6:14–7:1 is a fragment, an insertion and, moreover, an un-Pauline text. Several factors are brought forward to dispute the authenticity of this central passage: (1) the interruption of the final appeal (one can easily read 7:2-4 immediately after 6:11-13); (2) words that occur only in this passage *(hapax legomena;* also words that Paul elsewhere employs in a different sense); (3) the particular way in which the Old Testament is quoted; (4) ideas and

Second Corinthians

phrases that are also present in the Essene writings (Qumran); and (5) the so-called un-Pauline content, e.g., the strict separation, the call to holiness. The number as well as the convergence of these data are impressive indeed. One has certainly to concede that the content (see point 5) must have been fairly strange to the Corinthians themselves. How can Paul, after having written 1 Cor 5:9-11 (Christians cannot leave the world), so insist on physical separation from unbelievers, or is his language here purely metaphorical?

Nevertheless, more and more exegetes (recently, for example, Reimund Bieringer, James M. Scott, Gerhard Sass) nowadays defend the Pauline authenticity and integrity of this passage. No manuscript suggests that an insertion has been made. It is well known that Paul interrupts himself quite often. One cannot exclude the possibility that in 6:14–7:1 Paul is employing and editing material that at first sight seems rather strange. Besides the *hapax legomena* there are also Pauline terms and constructions in the text. In the other letters there are more instances of Paul joining together citations from the Old Testament (cf., for example, Rom 3:10-18; 9–11).

Is the content of this passage as isolated from its narrow context and from the entire letter as many commentators take for granted? The answer is no. First, attention must be given to four details in text and context. (1) Both 6:13 and 6:14a have verbs in the second person plural imperative: the transition between them is not so abrupt after all. (2) 7:2-4 is not only the continuation, but also the resumption of 6:11-13. This seems to indicate that there was always an interruption after 6:13. (3) If we admit that it was Paul himself who was responsible for the interruption in 6:14–7:1, then the clause "I have (already) said" (7:3), which refers back to 6:11-12, becomes perfectly understandable. (4) An author, not always consciously, may take up (sometimes with a different meaning) words and phrases used not long before. What has been employed remains, as it were, at the writer's disposition. Hence the use of the terms *sarx* and *phobos* in 7:5 may suggest that Paul was influenced by what he himself had just written in 7:1. We see also the presence of *dikaiosynē* (moral meaning!) in both 6:7 and 6:14 and can compare *phobos kyriou* in 5:11 with *phobos theou* in 7:1c. These literary data suggest that 6:14–7:1 can hardly be separated from its preceding and ensuing context.

Second, a logical connection between 6:14–7:1 and its context is not completely absent. One may refer to the exhortation in 5:20 and 6:1-2 and conclude that the appearance of paraenesis in 6:14–7:1 is not so unexpected after all (cf. the verb *parakaleō* in 5:20 and 6:1). One could perhaps also discern some logical link with 6:11-13: open wide your hearts to us in return (6:13) and, therefore, do what we ask (6:14–7:1).

Third, as far as the whole letter is concerned it would seem that the injunction to separate from the (Gentile) unbelievers must not be understood literally. Paul insists on moral purity and proper behavior. A comparison with 12:20-21 may prove enlightening. Quite suddenly, just as in 6:14–7:1, Paul refers here to "many who sinned before and have not repented of the impurity, fornication, and debauchery they have practiced" (12:21). In both passages there is concern for the believers' ethical conduct. In addition to Paul's polemics against the opponents and his plea to the Corinthians for a better relationship, there is in 2 Corinthians also a warning against sin, i.e., against a present or possible sinful, immoral way of life. As in 12:20-21 and 13:2 Paul squarely addresses that third problem in 6:14–7:1. Michael Goulder, moreover—albeit in a somewhat strained way—detects a similar sequence of thought in 2 Corinthians 5–7 and 1 Corinthians 4–6. In his commentary Paul Barnett defends a more literal interpretation. The passage appears in its position "as the climax of the entire apologia for Paul's new covenant ministry" (*Second Epistle,* 341). Barnett continues: Paul's "call for separation from the temple cults of Corinth and probable associated sexual activities was not new. It dominated the center section of the First Letter (1 Cor 6:12-20; 8:1–11:1) and was probably the occasion of his emergency second visit and followup 'Severe letter'" (Ibid.).

Whatever the Pauline authenticity of the unit may be, its remarkable composition merits a more detailed discussion. Four unequal parts (A B C D) can be distinguished.

A	14a	Do not be yoked unevenly with unbelievers.
B *a*	14b	*For* what partnership (is there)
		between righteousness and iniquity,
b	14c	or what fellowship (is there)
		for light with darkness?
a'	15a	What (is) the accord
		of Christ with Beliar,
b'	15b	or what part (is there)
		for a believer with an unbeliever?
–	16a	What agreement (is there)
		between the temple of God and idols?
C –	16b	*For* we are the temple of the living God,
	16c	as God has said:
a	16d	"I will dwell in them and move about (among them),
	16e	and I will be their God
	16f	and they will be my people"
		(Lev 26:12).

b	17a	Therefore, "Come out from their midst
		and be separate (from them),"
	17b	says the Lord,
	17c	"do not touch anything unclean"
		(Isa 52:11),
a'	17d	"and I will receive you,
	18a	and I will be a father to you,
	18b	and you will be sons and daughters to me"
		(2 Sam 7:14),
	18c	says the Lord almighty.
D	1a	Since we have these promises, beloved,
	1b	let us *therefore* cleanse ourselves from every
		stain of the flesh and the spirit,
	1c	while we are making perfect (our) holiness in the
		fear of God.

It would seem that part B and, even more so, part C are composed with great literary skill. The first four oppositional clauses of part B are constructed as *a–b* (vv. 14b and 14c) and *a'–b'* (vv. 15a and 15b): in Greek twice *tis* and *ē tis* ("what" and "or what"). The fifth clause (v. 16a) functions as a conclusion and, at the same time, as a transition to v. 16b.

It is generally claimed that, notwithstanding the presence of only three introductory formulae, more than three quotations are linked and fused together in order to form a concatenation. The following quotations or references have been proposed:

Lev 26:12 and Ezek 37:27	for 6:16def
Isa 52:11	for 6:17ac
Ezek 20:34 (or 11:17,	
or Zeph 3:20)	for 6:17d
2 Sam 7:14	for 7:18ab
Isa 43:6	for 6:18b ("and daughters")
2 Sam 7:8	for 6:18c ("the Lord almighty").

We admitted possible influence from Ezek 37:27 (at the beginning of the first quotation and within it) and from Ezek 20:34 (at the beginning of the third quotation). The other added references are not very likely, nor are they really needed (with the exception of 2 Sam 7:8: "the Lord almighty"). But in any case those possible influences do not multiply the explicit quotations.

Part C stresses that the believers are the temple of the living God, the phrase "temple of God" being an element of the final opposition in B. This affirmation is verified by citations from the Old Testament. First, by means of Lev 26:12, the covenant formula, it is pointed out that the promise of God's presence with God's people is, in spite of the future tense, realized already now for believers. From this state of affairs it follows (cf. "therefore" in v. 17a) that, according to the second quotation taken from Isa 52:11, the believers should leave the Gentile unbelievers, be separated from them, and stop touching unclean things. If this is done, God will receive them; God will be a father to them and they will be God's sons and daughters. This is the third quotation, the well-known promise to David, from 2 Sam 7:14: the adoption formula.

The structure of this *catena* of citations is striking. Note should be taken of the placing of the quotation formulae: at the beginning and end respectively of the first and third quotations *(a* and *a'),* and in the middle of the second *(b).* The central position of this second citation is by no means accidental: between the covenant formula, which depicts an already existing reality (the basis of a new ethical life), and the promise to David that refers to God's future gift (depending on the believer's moral attitude). Attention should also be given to the structural symmetry (each time three clauses) and to the similarity in content of both promises, i.e., the covenant formula *(a)* and adoption formula *(a').*

By now the chain of thought in 6:14–7:1 should be apparent. The author motivates his exhortation in A by reminding the believers of what they are (part B). By means of five terms he explains their identity and by opposing these terms to their contraries draws out the implications of that identity. The accord of Christ with Beliar is impossible. In C the identity referred to by the expression "temple of the living God" is once more stressed and now proved by Old Testament quotations depicting the relation between God and God's people or family. In the middle of this part there is again an exhortation: come out, be separated, no longer touch. The lengthy sentence of D resumes the entire admonition for the last time.

c. *Theological Reflection.* The end of the section offers us an unexpected item for reflection. In 7:3 Paul speaks in a softened manner: I do not say this to condemn you; I have said before that you are present in my heart "to die together and to live together" *(eis to synapothanein kai syzēn).* Five questions can be raised with regard to this last phrase. (1) Is the grammatical subject of the two verbs "you" or "I," or both together? (2) Is the dying and living together a "together with one another" or a "together with Christ"? (3) How should we explain the strange sequence "to die/to live"? (4) Why is there a change in the tenses of the verbs in the original Greek, from aorist (punctual aspect) to present (duration)? (5) Finally, what kind of death and what kind of life are referred to?

An answer to these questions should be attempted. (1) The grammatical subject of the two verbs is the inclusive "we": Paul and the Corin-

thians. Paul intends: I carry you in my heart, and this means that we together will die and live; we are together, we are united so as to die together and to live together. Of course this saying should not be
understood literally as if Paul were thinking of a simultaneous death. (2)
The second question (together with whom?) can easily be answered.
There is no third category or person. The dying and living will occur together, i.e., with one another, I with you and you with me. This means
that dying and living with Christ are not (directly) dealt with here. (3)
The inversion, first dying and then living, is not accidental; it is intended
by Paul. He does not point here to present life on earth, but to life after
death. He refers to the death all will die in Christ and to the future life
after death, eternal life in Christ. (4) The shift from aorist to present is also
anything but accidental. Death is but a transition, a moment, a fact without duration, while the life that follows will last forever. These nuances
are expressed by the choice of aorist and present in Greek. (5) The answer
to the last question (the type of death and life) is implied in all that precedes. Paul does not refer to daily dying (as, for example, in 4:10-11), but
to death at the end of life; he does not mean Christian moral life before
death, but life eternal.

It could be asked whether Paul is not influenced by 2 Sam 15:21 in
which the same order is found: "As the LORD lives, and as my lord the
king lives, wherever my lord the king may be, 'whether for death or for
life' *(kai ean eis thanaton kai ean eis zōēn)*, there also your servant will be."
It is quite understandable that Ittai first mentions death. David is fleeing
from Absalom. At that moment death is for him a very concrete possibility. However, to postulate direct influence from this Old Testament passage on 2 Cor 7:3 is rather far-fetched. Except for the sequence death/life
there is nothing in the context or in the vocabulary that could point to a
literary contact of v. 3 with 2 Sam 15:21. A striking difference between the
two texts must not go unnoticed. Ittai refers to two mutually exclusive
eventualities: either death or life. Paul speaks of two consecutive states of
affairs in both of which the reciprocal union is stressed.

Although the phrase "to die together and to live together" ultimately
comes from the profane language that employs it to illustrate faithfulness, friendship, and love in this world, in 7:3 the phrase contains much
more than the simple "in life and death." The new formulation in 7:3 is
the product of Paul's rewriting. He changes the sequence: first dying,
then living. He opposes the two tenses, aorist and present, with one another. The two infinitives are integrated in an *eis to* construction that indicates a purpose (or, at least, a consequence).

While the *syn-* elements do not require "Christ" as an implicit complement, Paul certainly envisages the destiny "in Christ" that both he and
the Corinthians expect. Through Paul's rewriting the profane expression

is transposed in a Christian sense and thus filled with a new meaning. Within the context of 1 Thess 4:13–5:11 Paul mentions the Christians who have died and are asleep; he deals with their future rising through Christ and their "being always with the Lord" (4:17). In 2 Cor 7:3 Paul equally emphasizes life more than death, the future life of all Christians together, eternal life in Christ. Elsewhere in his letters Paul frequently considers the quality of Christian life before death. Here in 2 Cor 7:3, by means of the *eis to* construction, he points to the future life of which the actual Christian life already is an anticipation, but not yet its marvelous fullness. Through his faith in Christ Paul's vision of the future is immensely widened and deepened; its horizon transcends even death.

d. *Actualization.* It would seem that three items for actualization are present in 6:11–7:4. First, in this passage we meet a not overly self-certain Paul surrounded by tensions. He defends himself; he emphasizes the genuineness of his love; he begs for the reciprocal affection of his Corinthians. Paul's integrity as apostle and his passionate plea are exemplary. Second, the believers are called the temple of God and the people of God; they will be and already are sons and daughters of God. Because of that extraordinary identity Paul can exhort them to a life of high moral standing. Third, for the apostle and the Corinthians the eschatological future is one of "living together" after death, in Christ. One should ask whether such a transcendent hope still inspires Christians in their daily struggle.

FOR REFERENCE AND FURTHER STUDY

Beale, G. K. "The Old Testament Background of Reconciliation in 2 Corinthians 5–7 and Its Bearing on the Literary Problem of 2 Corinthians 6.14–7.1," *NTS* 35 (1989) 1–25.

Betz, Hans Dieter. "An Anti-Pauline Fragment?" *JBL* 92 (1973) 88–108.

Bieringer, Reimund. "2 Korinther 6,14–7,1 im Kontext des 2. Korintherbriefes. Forschungsüberblick und Versuch eines eigenen Zugangs" in Bieringer and Lambrecht, *Studies on 2 Corinthians.* BEThL 102. Leuven: Leuven University Press/Peeters, 1994, 551–570.

Dahl, Nils A. "A Fragment and Its Context. 2 Corinthians 6:14-7:1" in idem, *Studies in Paul. Theology for the Early Christian Mission.* Minneapolis: Augsburg, 1977, 62–69.

Derrett, J. Duncan M. "2 Cor 6,14ff. A Midrash on Dt 22,10," *Bib.* 59 (1978) 231–250.

Duff, Paul. "The Mind of the Redactor. 2 Cor 6:14-7:1 in its Secondary Context," *NT* 35 (1993) 160–180.

Fee, Gordon D. "II Corinthians vi.14–vii.1 and Food Offered to Idols," *NTS* 23 (1976–1977) 140–161.

Fitzmyer, Joseph A. "Qumran and the Interpolated Paragraph in 2 Cor 6:14–7:1" in idem, *Essays on the Semitic Background of the New Testament*. London: Chapman, 1971, 205–217.

Gärtner, Bertil. *The Temple and the Community in Qumran and the New Testament*. MSSNTS 1. Cambridge: Cambridge University Press, 1965, 49–56.

Goulder, Michael. "2 Cor. 6:14–7:1 as an Integral Part of 2 Corinthians," *NT* 36 (1994) 47–57.

Lambrecht, Jan. "The Fragment of 2 Corinthians 6:14–7:1: A Plea for Its Authenticity" in Bieringer and Lambrecht, *Studies on 2 Corinthians*, 531–549.

_____. "To Die Together and to Live Together: A Study of 2 Corinthians 7,3" in Bieringer and Lambrecht, *Studies on 2 Corinthians*, 571–587.

Murphy-O'Connor, Jerome. "Relating 2 Corinthians 6.14–7.1 to Its Context," *NTS* 33 (1987) 272–275.

_____. "Philo and 2 Cor 6:14–7:1," *RB* 95 (1988) 55–69.

Olley, John W. "A Precursor of the NRSV? 'Sons and Daughters' in 2 Cor 6.18," *NTS* 44 (1998) 204–212.

Sass, Gerhard. "Noch einmal: 2 Kor 6,14–7,1. Literarkritische Waffen gegen einen 'unpaulinischen' Paulus?" *ZNW* 84 (1993) 36–64.

Scott, James M. *Adoption as Sons of God. An Exegetical Investigation into the Background of HUIOTHESIA in the Pauline Corpus*. WUNT II/48. Tübingen: Mohr-Siebeck, 1992, 187–220.

_____. "The Use of Scripture in 2 Corinthians 6.16c-18 and Paul's Restoration Theology," *JSNT* 56 (1994) 73–99.

Stählin, Gustav. "'Um mitzusterben und mitzuleben'. Bemerkungen 2 Cor 7.3" in Otto Betz and Luise Schottroff, eds., *Neues Testament und christliche Existenz. FS H. Braun*. Tübingen: Mohr-Siebeck, 1973, 503–521.

Thrall, Margaret E. "The Problem of II Cor. vi.14–vii.1 in Some Recent Discussions," *NTS* 24 (1977–1978) 132–148.

Walker, William O. "The Burden of Proof in Identifying Interpolations in the Pauline Letters," *NTS* 33 (1987) 610–618.

Webb, William J. *Returning Home. New Covenant and Second Exodus as the Context for 2 Corinthians 6.14–7.1*. JSNT.S 85. Sheffield: JSOT Press, 1993.

Zeilinger, Franz. "Die Echtheit von 2 Cor 6:14–7:1," *JBL* 112 (1993) 71–80.

III. TITUS'S RETURN (7:5-16)

11. *Titus's Return* (7:5-16)

5. For in fact when we came to Macedonia our flesh had no relief, but (we were) afflicted in every way: from outside strife, from within fears. 6. However, the one who consoles the downcast, God, consoled us by the arrival of Titus 7.—not only by his arrival but also by the consolation

with which he has been consoled about you—as he told us of your long-ing, your grieving, your zeal for me, so that I rejoiced (even) more.

8. For even if I saddened you by my letter, I do not regret (it). Even if I regretted (it)—for I see that that letter saddened you, though only for a time—9. now I rejoice, not because you were saddened but because you were saddened so as to repent. For you were saddened according to God so that in no way did you suffer damage from us. 10. For a sadness ac-cording to God produces repentance without regrets, (leading up) to sal-vation; the sadness of the world, however, produces death. 11. For behold, what eagerness that very (experience of) being saddened ac-cording to God produced for you, but (also what) defense, (what) indig-nation, (what) fear, (what) longing, (what) zeal, (what) punishment! In every way you proved yourselves innocent in that matter. 12. Therefore, even though I wrote to you, (it was) not for the wrongdoer, nor for the one who was wronged, but in order that your eagerness for us might be-come evident to you in the sight of God. 13. That is why we have been consoled.

Yet, in addition to our consolation, we rejoiced even more at the joy of Titus because his spirit has been set at rest by all of you. 14. For if I have boasted to him about anything regarding you I was not put to shame, but just as we have spoken all things to you in truth, so our boasting before Titus has proved to be the truth as well. 15. His affection for you (is growing) even stronger, as he recalls the obedience of all of you: how you received him with fear and trembling. 16. I rejoice because I can be sure of you in every way.

NOTES

5. *For in fact when we came to Macedonia our flesh had no relief, but (we were) afflicted in every way: from outside strife, from within fears:* This verse, together with vv. 6-7, concretize what comfort and joy in distress (see 7:4) means: *kai gar* ("for in fact"). The verse, however, clearly continues the narrative that was sud-denly interrupted after 2:13. In 7:5, as well as in 2:13, the coming to Macedo-nia is mentioned; the expression "to have no relief," too, is present in both verses, but instead of "my spirit" (2:13) Paul writes in 7:5 the more or less equivalent "our flesh," the human person in his/her vulnerability. In light of the resumptions our translation has preserved that expression. In the two verses Paul means: we found no rest either in Troas or in Macedonia.

In v. 5b a personal verb is lacking. The exaggerated expression "in every way" renders the rhetorically exaggerated *en panti* (literally: "in everything"; the context suggests: "from all sides"). Paul explains his troubles and distin-guishes between external and internal concerns. The "fights" (*machai,* strife) must be located in Macedonia. With "fears within" Paul most probably refers to his persistent anxiety regarding the situation in Corinth. Note the paral-lelism at the end: *exōthen machai, esōthen phoboi,* which the translation renders with a change of the word order: "from outside strife, from within fears."

6. *However, the one who consoles the downcast, God, consoled us by the arrival of Titus:* In 1:3-4 we read: "Blessed be the . . . God of all consolation, who consoles us in all our distress." In 7:6 Paul takes up that qualification of God (but see also Ps 49:1). God has consoled Paul by the return, i.e., the arrival (Parousia) of Titus.

7. *—not only by his arrival but also by the consolation with which he has been consoled about you—:* This further specification interrupts the flow of thought as well as the grammar of the one sentence of vv. 6-7. The consolation Titus experienced in Corinth consoles Paul. Compare the mutuality also present in 1:4: Paul is able to console the Corinthians with the consolation with which he himself is consoled by God.

as he told us of your longing, your grieving, your zeal for me, so that I rejoiced (even) more: God consoles Paul while Titus is speaking of the Corinthians' attitude, i.e., through Titus's report of their longing, sorrow, and zeal. It is this threefold content of the report that really consoles Paul. The Corinthians are longing for Paul; they are grieving about what has happened to him in Corinth; they have manifested their zeal for him, not least in punishing the wrongdoer. All this increases Paul's joy (cf. v. 4). For *mallon* (here: "[even] more"), see v. 13 *(perissoterōs mallon,* "much more"). In this instance consolation and joy appear to be very close to each other in meaning.

8. *For even if I saddened you by my letter, I do not regret (it):* Through the present joy Paul is brought back to the sorrow of the past. Within vv. 8-10 he repeatedly uses the same terms as those in 2:1-5: *lupeomai* ("to sadden") and *lupē* ("sadness"). The "letter of tears," the painful letter (cf. 2:3-4 and 9), also is recalled in vv. 8-13. At first sight "I do not regret (it)" appears to be a decisive final statement.

Even if I regretted (it)—for I see that that letter saddened you, though only for a time—: The grammatical construction in vv. 8-9 is not completely clear (and there are variant readings as well). Within v. 8b Paul seems to interrupt himself. The protasis "even if I regretted (it)" is probably to be connected with the beginning of v. 9, which then functions as an apodosis: "now I rejoice." So in v. 8b Paul corrects himself; he has to concede that there was a (limited) period of time when he felt sorry about his writing. Within what we consider to be an interruption (v. 8c) some important manuscripts (e.g., 𝔓⁴⁶ and B) do not have *gar* ("for").

9. *now I rejoice, not because you were saddened but because you were saddened so as to repent:* Paul has to clarify his ideas and make clear the reason for his actual joy. Of course he does not rejoice because of the Corinthians' sadness itself, but he now rejoices because it was a sadness that led them to repentance. The term *metanoia* ("repentance") is employed, here and in v. 10, not to indicate the initial conversion (i.e., becoming a Christian) but to point to the change of the Corinthians' inimical attitude toward Paul, as well as to a change in their whole mentality.

For you were saddened according to God so that in no way did you suffer damage from us: A further clarification says that this repentance was brought about by a sadness "according to (the will of) God." The quite common translation that takes *kata theon* as if it were a qualifying genitive ("godly" sadness) is probably too weak. Paul emphasizes that he wanted in no way to cause spiritual harm to the Corinthians.

10. *For a sadness according to God produces repentance without regrets, (leading up) to salvation; the sadness of the world, however, produces death:* Paul suddenly broadens his argument. He now formulates a theological insight. Sorrow that pleases God brings about repentance that leads to salvation: *metanoian eis sōterian.* Of course no regret can be felt about such a repentance. The adjective *ametamelēton* can be connected either with "repentance" (then we have an oxymoron: "a repentance without regrets") or with the whole expression "repentance (leading up) to salvation." The wrong repentance, that of the "world," causes death, i.e., eschatological ruin. In this verse God is contrasted to the world, and salvation to death. It would seem that two radically opposed sorrows are possible.

11. *For behold, what eagerness that very (experience of) being saddened according to God produced for you, but (also what) defense, (what) indignation, (what) fear, (what) longing, (what) zeal, (what) punishment!* Already within this life the appropriate sadness has wonderful effects in the Corinthians. In seven terms, introduced by "behold" at the beginning of the sentence, Paul enumerates their reaction in a very emotional manner. The first term is qualified by *posos* (literally "how much, how great"), while the other six are introduced staccato-wise by *alla* (= not only that, "but" also). The Corinthians will have understood what Paul meant by each element of this enumeration. Of course Paul at this point is praising them in a rhetorically overstated (and hence equally exhortative) manner. For "longing" and "zeal" see v. 7.

In every way you proved yourselves innocent in that matter: Paul draws the conclusion (in the same exaggerated way): the Corinthians were completely *(en panti,* "in every thing") innocent *(hagnos,* "pure") with regard to that matter. As will become evident through the following verse, "that matter" refers to the incident that was already dealt with in 2:5-11.

12. *Therefore, even though I wrote to you, (it was) not for the wrongdoer, nor for the one who was wronged, but in order that your eagerness for us might become evident to you in the sight of God:* Again in rhetorical fashion Paul now speaks of what he really aimed at with his other letter. He asserts, not without somewhat forcing the truth, that the letter was not written on behalf of the one who did the wrong (the offender) or on behalf of the one who was wronged (most likely Paul himself), but on behalf of the Corinthians, for the letter's real intention was to bring about the conditions in which the Corinthians' zeal for Paul might be revealed to them in the sight of God.

13. *That is why we have been consoled:* Two uses of the verb "console" in vv. 7 and 13a frame the lengthy explanation in vv. 8-12. Verse 13a draws the conclusion: *dia toutou* (literally "because of that," referring to what precedes). One has the impression that the relations between Paul and the Corinthian church are good again.

Yet, in addition to our consolation, we rejoiced even more at the joy of Titus because his spirit has been set at rest by all of you: There is still something more than the consolation just mentioned. Paul now refers to the positive reception of Titus by the Corinthians. Paul calls this—again, it would seem, in a rhetorical over-statement—a still greater joy for him. "Even more" translates *perissoterōs mallon* ("much more"). In popular Greek the first term often replaces the sec-ond; here the first reinforces the second. Titus's rejoicing at the experience of relief at Corinth causes the rejoicing of Paul. Again it must strike the readers that consolation and joy are more or less the same thing (cf. v. 7).

14. *For if I have boasted to him about anything regarding you I was not put to shame, but just as we have spoken all things to you in truth, so our boasting before Titus has proved to be the truth as well:* Paul gives more details. He has been boasting about the Corinthians to Titus. He is glad that he has afterward not been put to shame because of this. By the theme of Paul's boasting *(kauchaomai,* "to boast" and *kauchēsis,* "boasting"), as well as by that of his truthfulness, the ad-dressees are reminded of what they have read in 1:12-14 (see also 7:4).

15. *His affection for you (is growing) even stronger, as he recalls the obedience of all of you: how you received him with fear and trembling:* Titus's love *(splagchna,* liter-ally "bowels," a Hebraism, meaning "mercy, affection, love") of the Corin-thians is becoming even greater, stronger *(perissoterōs,* literally "more abundant"), when he remembers their obedience to him. Paul adds the con-cretization: how you received him "with fear and trembling." This last ex-pression, used in the Old Testament for the way in which humans approach God, strangely tempers the praise of the preceding verses. The situation at Corinth must have been very critical.

16. *I rejoice because I can be sure of you in every way:* For the theme of joy and re-joicing in this passage see vv. 7, 9, and 13 (cf. v. 4). Paul gives the motivation for his joy once more. He can now have complete *(en panti,* "in anything," cf. vv. 5 and 11) confidence in the Corinthians. This is, of course, another rhe-torical overstatement. The verb *tharreō* (here with *en:* "to have confidence in," "to be sure of"; in 10:1 with *eis:* "to be bold toward") is probably used in a "modal" way: "I 'can' be sure of. . . ."

INTERPRETATION

a. *Structure and Line of Thought.* After the lengthy interruption (the second major part, 2:14–7:4) Paul continues the narrative of the first part (1:12–2:13). In 1:15-22 he defended the first change in his travel plans and in 1:23–2:11 he explained why—despite this change—he did not come di-rectly to Corinth. In 2:12-13 he briefly mentioned his arrival at Troas and the apostolic work there, as well as his departure to Macedonia in order to meet Titus. In 7:5-16 he now tells his addressees of the joy caused by fi-nally meeting Titus.

Some exegetes claim that this last text originally followed 1:1–2:13 and that both texts may have constituted a separate letter: the letter of reconciliation. On the one hand it is remarkable indeed that within 7:5-16 Paul so frequently uses the vocabulary of the first two chapters (consolation, sadness, pride) and that he deals again, as in 2:3-11, with the painful letter and the Corinthian incident. On the other hand, in 7:5-16 Paul employs the epistolary plural while in 1:23 and 1:25–2:13 he had written in the first person singular. Moreover, the change of tone (joy) and the repetitions in 7:5 rather suggest that there has been an interruption after 2:13. Some terminology from 7:5-16, it should be added, also occurs in 6:12 (affection), 7:2 (to do wrong) and 7:4 (boasting, consolation, joy, distress): this, too, makes one wonder whether Paul composed 7:5-16 under the influence of 6:11–7:4 and immediately after it.

With regard to the line of thought within 7:5-16, three small units can be distinguished: vv. 5-7 (Titus), vv. 8-13a (the letter) and vv. 13b-16 (Titus again). In vv. 5-7 Paul describes his consolation at meeting Titus and more particularly his joy at the consolation Titus himself experienced in Corinth. In vv. 8-13a Paul recalls his painful letter to the Corinthians. Far from causing an enduring grief, that letter has brought about in them sorrow leading to repentance, a sorrow "according to God" that produces salvation. Such repentance becomes manifest in the Corinthians' eagerness to see Paul, their punishment of the offender, and their longing for Paul. Because of all this Paul is consoled; he greatly rejoices. In vv. 13b-16 Paul speaks again of Titus and the generous way the Corinthians received him. When Titus recalls that reception his love of the Corinthians grows stronger; this, too, causes real joy for Paul.

b. *Characteristics.* Just as in the first two chapters, Paul here also often employs the same vocabulary within a small group of verses: see especially the vocabulary of consolation in vv. 5-7, of sadness in vv. 8-11, of boasting in vv. 14-15, and of joy in vv. 7, 11, 13, and 16. Several rhetorical exaggerations have been mentioned in the Notes. It has also been pointed out that Paul had to correct himself more than once in order to nuance too bold a statement. The style of this pericope is clearly more emotional than that of chs. 1 and 2 (see the heaping up of terms in v. 7 and, above all, in v. 11).

c. *Theological Reflection.* No doubt we have before us a Paul who is consoled and who rejoices, but also a Paul who is thoroughly human. He repeatedly emphasizes his joy caused by the good news brought by Titus. The reconciliation between Paul and the Corinthians appears to be a fact, yet the very exuberance of Paul's language may betray a certain fear. In the manner of writing there also is an undercurrent of plea and exhortation. Apparently the reconciliation is still fragile, perhaps somewhat uncertain.

Titus has clearly done a good job in Corinth. From v. 7 and vv. 13b-16 one can see that Paul considered this fellow worker a real deputy, a substitute invested with Paul's authority. In her study "New Testament Envoys" Margaret M. Mitchell pays special attention to Timothy (1 Thessalonians 3) and Titus (2 Corinthians 7). Sending delegates and envoys was quite common in the Greco-Roman world. Mitchell concludes: "we find Paul working within some established conventions about envoys and their role in maintaining and reaffirming relationships between separated partners" (pp. 661–662). The second and more important conclusion is: "hardly mere substitutes for the universally preferable Pauline presence, these envoys were consciously sent by Paul to play a complex and crucial intermediary role that he could not play, even if present himself" (p. 662).

Titus's comfort is the comfort of Paul; Titus's success is for Paul a source of genuine joy. Some exegetes are of the opinion—probably correctly—that Paul speaks of Titus again at the end of this narrative (vv. 13b-16) because according to chs. 8 and 9 the same Titus will have to play an important role in completing the collection in Corinth (see 8:6, 16-19, 23; cf. also 9:3-5). The presence of Titus in 2 Corinthians 8–9 is thus well prepared for in the double reference to him in ch. 7.

d. *Actualization.* Modern readers, for the most part themselves apostolically-minded Christians, cannot but admire Paul's tactfulness and thoroughly positive approach, but also his rhetorical strategy consisting in encouragement, commendation, and praise of the addressees. They would surely like to follow Paul in the spontaneous, natural way he relates all events to God, and in his rejoicing.

FOR REFERENCE AND FURTHER STUDY

See also the bibliography following 1:12–2:13.
Mitchell, Margaret Mary. "New Testament Envoys in the Context of Greco–Roman Diplomatic and Epistolary Conventions: The Example of Timothy and Titus," *JBL* 111 (1992) 641–662.

IV. THE COLLECTION (8:1–9:15)

12. *The Collection for Jerusalem* (8:1-24)

1. We must let you know, brothers and sisters, about the grace of God that has been given in the churches of Macedonia, 2. for in the midst of much critical affliction the abundance of their joy and the depth of their poverty overflowed in the riches of their generosity. 3. For (they gave) according to their means, I can testify, and (even) beyond their means, of their own accord, 4. begging us most earnestly for the grace of sharing in this service for the saints, 5. and (they did) not just as we expected, but they gave themselves first to the Lord and (then also) to us by the will of God, 6. so that we urged Titus that, as he had (already) begun, he should also complete that grace among you.

7. However, just as you abound in every respect—in faith, speech, knowledge, as well as in general concern and in your love for us—may you abound also in this grace. 8. I do not want to speak by way of command but as testing the genuineness of your love also by (pointing to) the zeal of others. 9. For you know the grace of our Lord Jesus Christ: though he was rich he became poor for your sake, so that you might become rich by his poverty. 10. I want to give (only) an opinion in this matter. For what (I am going to say) is good for you who were the kind of people who last year began not only to do (it) but also (to do it) willingly. 11. Now then, also complete that work, in order that, like the desire of (doing it) willingly, the completion, too, might come from what you (actually) have. 12. For if that desire is present, (the gift) will be acceptable according to what one may have, not according to what one has not. 13. For (the aim is) not that others (have) relief (while) you (have) hardship, but (that it occurs) in terms of equality. 14. At the present time your abundance supplies the need of those people, in order that (one day) their abundance might supply your need, so that there be equality, 15. as it is written: "The one (who gathered) much had no excess, and the one (who gathered) little had no lack" (Exod 16:18).

16. Thanks (be) to God who gave the same zeal for you in the heart of Titus. 17. For, although he had received our appeal, he left for you of his own accord, more zealous than ever. 18. With him we sent the brother who is praised in all churches for (his service to) the gospel. 19. Not only (that), but he has also been appointed by the churches as our traveling companion (to help) with this grace that is administered by us for the glory of God and (also to prove) our eagerness. 20. This we want to avoid: that one might blame us over this generous gift administered by us, 21. for we care for what is good not only in the sight of the Lord but also in the sight of men and women. 22. With them we also sent our brother whom we have tested many times in many ways (and found him) to be zealous, now even more zealous because of his great confidence

in you. 23. Whether as to Titus, (he is) my partner and fellow worker for you, or whether (as to) our brothers, (they are) apostles of the churches, the glory of Christ. 24. Therefore show before the churches the proof of your love and of our boasting to them about you.

NOTES

1. *We must let you know, brothers and sisters, about the grace of God that has been given in the churches of Macedonia:* By employing the quite stereotypical introductory verb *gnōrizō* ("to make known") Paul means to say: "we want you to know about," or: "we must let you know about." Note should be taken of the vocative "brothers (and sisters)," which marks a new beginning. Our translation in this chapter consistently renders *charis* as "grace." In vv. 1, 6, 7, and 19 this term concretely indicates the collection for Jerusalem. The difficult and delicate task of bringing together and sending that money is termed by Paul a "grace of God," a grace given by God. The churches in Macedonia are, as far as we know, Thessalonica and perhaps more particularly, Philippi (for the gifts Paul received from that church cf. Phil 4:10, 15 and 2 Cor 11:8-9).

2. *for in the midst of much critical affliction the abundance of their joy and the depth of their poverty overflowed in the riches of their generosity:* The lengthy Greek sentence that began with v. 1 continues through to v. 6. Its grammatical construction is heavy and somewhat confused; moreover, in places, and certainly in this verse, the style is inflated. "In the midst of much critical affliction" is the free rendering of "in a great test of affliction" (apparently the test consists of affliction). "The depth of their poverty" is in Greek "their poverty according to depth." The term *haplotēs* ("simplicity, single-mindedness, sincerity") here presumably takes on the meaning of "generosity" (cf. 9:11, 13 and Rom 12:8).

3. *For (they gave) according to their means, I can testify, and (even) beyond their means, of their own accord:* One is probably right in supplying the verb "they gave" from v. 5. The first part of this second motivating clause, then, includes v. 4 with its participial construction; its second part contains the whole of vv. 5-6. The expression "I can testify" seems to qualify "according to their means" as well as "beyond their means."

4. *begging us most earnestly for the grace of sharing in this service for the saints:* "Most earnestly" renders *meta paraklēseōs* ("with an urgent appeal"). The term "grace" here means "favor." The text has (literally): "begging the favor and the sharing *(koinōnia)* of the service *(diakonia)* to the saints." The last two Greek terms are well known. The Philippians asked for the privilege of participating in that caritative undertaking. The "saints" *(hagioi)* are the poor Christians of the Jerusalem church.

5. *and (they did) not just as we expected, but they gave themselves first to the Lord and (then also) to us by the will of God:* The Philippians did more than Paul could have expected. It would seem—though this is not certain—that "first" applies

to their devotion to God (hence our addition "then also" after "and") and that the phrase "by the will of God" qualifies the giving of themselves to Paul. Yet the bringing together of "to God" and "to us" remains somewhat bold on the part of Paul (see also the end of v. 19).

6. *so that we urged Titus that, as he had (already) begun, he should also complete that grace among you:* The construction "so that" in Greek indicates a purpose (or a result). The fervor of the Philippians pushes Paul to continue, i.e., to renew his efforts with Corinth. Titus must remain the driving agent: what he began, he should also *(kai)* complete. When did he begin? Probably "last year" (cf. v. 10: the same verb although the subject is different). One should take note of the verb *parakaleō* (here "to urge," cf. v. 4) and, again, of *charis*, meaning the collection. The tortuous style may reveal that the collection at Corinth had not advanced much beyond its beginning.

7. *However, just as you abound in every respect—in faith, speech, knowledge, as well as in general concern and in your love for us—may you abound also in this grace:* Paul now gives a direct exhortation to the Corinthians. The verb *perisseuō* ("to overflow," cf. v. 2; here "to abound") is used twice in this verse. "In every respect" *(en panti)* is concretized by five terms, all of which in this context point to positive qualities in the Corinthians (cf. 1 Cor 1:5 and 7). Instead of "your love in (= for?) us" a more difficult and well attested (e.g., $\mathfrak{P}^{46}$ and B) reading presents itself: "our love in (= for?) you," (or: the love we have inspired in you?). For "this grace" see v. 6. The *hina* construction at the end of v. 7 could be the equivalent of an imperative or more likely a wish: "may you . . ." ("I wish that you . . .").

8. *I do not want to speak by way of command but as testing the genuineness of your love also by (pointing to) the zeal of others:* Although Paul states that he does not say this as a command (v. 8a; cf. 1 Cor 7:6 and especially 7:25 where we find *gnōmē*, "opinion," present in 2 Cor 8:10), his mention of the testing of the genuineness of the Corinthians' love against the zeal of the others, the Philippians, is strong language.

9. *For you know the grace of our Lord Jesus Christ: though he was rich he became poor for your sake, so that you might become rich by his poverty:* Rather unexpectedly Paul motivates his exhortation with the most impressive example, that of "our Lord Jesus Christ" (elevated style). The term "grace" here refers to the gracious gift of the incarnation. The language of the text that follows may, to a certain extent, be traditional. The verb is an ingressive aorist: "became poor" or "began to be poor." This verb *ptōcheuō* and the noun *ptōcheia* point to the destitution of a beggar rather than to the less severe poverty of a *penēs* ("poor person"). In reading v. 9 one spontaneously thinks of the more elaborated christological text in Phil 2:6-11, which many rightly or wrongly think is a pre-Pauline hymn. In both texts Paul recalls the incarnation of the pre-existent Son of God, not (so much) of Jesus' poor life on earth. By becoming "poor," however, Jesus fully participated in the limitations and weaknesses as well as the finitude of human life; for him this concretely meant death on a cross (cf. Phil 2:8). See Interpretation d.

10-11. *I want to give (only) an opinion in this matter. For what (I am going to say) is good for you who were the kind of people who last year began not only to do (it) but also (to do it) willingly. Now then, also complete that work, in order that, like the desire of (doing it) willingly, the completion, too, might come from what you (actually) have:* Verse 10a corresponds to v. 8a: only opinion, no command. The Greek of the two lengthy sentences that follow is again very tortuous. There is the basic contrast between "last year" (rest of v. 10) and "now" (v. 11), but there is also the contrast between simple doing *(poiein,* "to do") and doing willingly *(thelein,* "to have the will"). The phrase "who were the kind of people" attempts to render the force of *hoitines.* In these verses Paul underscores that it is in the Corinthians' interest to complete "the doing" (of course, willingly), but then, at the end of v. 11, a new idea appears (oddly in the form of a purpose clause): one should only give from what one possesses. This shift will be taken up and elaborated in vv. 12-15. For the beginning "last year," cf. v. 6 and also see 1 Cor 16:1-4.

12. *For if that desire is present, (the gift) will be acceptable according to what one may have, not according to what one has not:* The unexpected addition at the end of v. 11 nuances the giving. The possessions differ from person to person. Here, in v. 12, Paul explicitly states that one should (only) give in accordance with his or her means. Yet the condition for the acceptability of the gift remains the readiness, the willingness, the desire to give (cf. vv. 10-11).

13-14. *For (the aim is) not that others (have) relief (while) you (have) hardship, but (that it occurs) in terms of equality. At the present time your abundance supplies the need of those people, in order that (one day) their abundance might supply your need, so that there be equality:* Once more a new idea emerges, that of "equality" *(isotēs).* In Greek v. 13 is very brief: no main verb, no verbs in the dependent clauses. Some are of the opinion that the clause that begins with the expression "(but) in terms of equality" (at the end of v. 13) continues in v. 14: "but from the point of view of equality your abundance at the present time should supply . . . in order that (later) their abundance might supply. . . ." Yet at the end of v. 14 Paul speaks again of equality; that double mention of "equality" pleads against this proposal.

It is clear what Paul has in mind. Whereas in Rom 15:27 he will emphasize that the Gentile Christians (from Macedonia and Achaia) are giving, and must give, material help to the Jewish Christians (of Jerusalem) because they received spiritual blessings from them, here in 2 Cor 8:13-14 he deals only with reciprocal material help, stressing the contrast between "at the present time" and, not expressed, "later, one day."

Paul hardly postulates a strict equality in goods. A spiritualization of Paul's statement might run the risk of neglecting its evident material focus. Some commentators refer to Romans 11 and claim that the future abundance of Jerusalem is strictly eschatological; it is therefore a spiritual fullness, they say: Israel will be a blessing for the nations. However, this is scarcely a correct interpretation of 2 Cor 8:14.

15. *as it is written: "The one (who gathered) much had no excess, and the one (who gathered) little had no lack":* Paul cites part of Exod 16:18, a verse from the passage that gives the rules for the gathering of manna. This quotation closes Paul's first appeal.

16-17. *Thanks (be) to God who gave the same zeal for you in the heart of Titus. For, although he had received our appeal, he left for you of his own accord, more zealous than ever:* In vv. 16-24 Paul speaks of the three persons who had already left to complete the matter of the collection at Corinth. Titus is the first. For the thanksgiving in v. 16a, cf. 2:14. A less important variant reading has "who is giving" instead of "who gave." In writing "the same zeal" (cf. also "more zealous than ever") Paul probably intends to compare Titus with the Macedonians, or perhaps with himself. For Titus, see v. 6 and cf. 7:6-7 and 13-15. For *authairetos* ("of his own accord") see also v. 3. In v. 17 Paul employs a *men . . . de* construction ("on the one hand . . . on the other hand"); we consider the first clause to be concessive: "although."

The three verbs in vv. 17 ("Titus left"), 18 ("we sent"), and 22 ("we also sent") are in the past tense (aorist). It is possible, however, (but far from certain) that Paul is employing "epistolary" aorists. If so, Paul is sending them, and they are leaving, while the letter is being written (or as bearers of the letter); when the Corinthians receive the letter Paul will already have sent these persons and they will already have left.

18-19. *With him we sent the brother who is praised in all churches for (his service to) the gospel. Not only (that), but he has also been appointed by the churches as our traveling companion (to help) with this grace that is administered by us for the glory of God and (also to prove) our eagerness:* The name of the second person is not given, but he is very much commended by Paul for his work for the gospel. That person has also been officially appointed by the churches of Macedonia (cf. v. 1) as Paul's companion. Must we think here more specifically of the transfer of the collection money from Corinth to Jerusalem (cf. 1 Cor 16:3; Rom 15:25-28)? As to the concrete meaning of "this grace," see vv. 1 and 6-7. At the end of v. 19 Paul writes: (literally) "for the glory of God and our desire." The term "desire" (*prothymia*, "eagerness") is already used twice (see vv. 11 and 12; cf. 9:2). For connecting God and "us" cf. v. 5. Still, the placing of "God's glory" and "our desire" under a single preposition (*pros*) and one article (*tēn*) must surprise the reader.

20-21. *This we want to avoid: that one might blame us over this generous gift administered by us, for we care for what is good not only in the sight of the Lord but also in the sight of men and women:* In the Greek text the whole of the two verses is grammatically added to what precedes. "(This) we want to avoid" is the free translation of *stellomenoi (touto)*, a participle that commands the negative purpose clause that follows in v. 20 and is further motivated by v. 21. For the verb "to blame" (*mōmaomai*), cf. 6:3. From 12:16-18 we learn that insinuations have been made against Paul in Corinth. In v. 21 Paul makes his reflection more general: we must aim at being regarded by the people as blameless in such financial matters. "Men and women" renders the inclusive term *anthrōpoi*.

22. *With them we also sent our brother whom we have tested many times in many ways (and found him) to be zealous, now even more zealous because of his great confidence* *in you:* The other brother is not named either. He does not appear to be an official representative of the churches, but because of his apostolic eagerness and zeal he is a respected person. The same terminology and, to a certain extent, the same grammatical constructions are used as in vv. 16-17 in reference to Titus.

23. *Whether as to Titus: (he is) my partner and fellow worker for you; or whether (as to) our brothers: (they are) apostles of the churches, the glory of Christ:* Paul summarizes his recommendations. Titus is Paul's partner *(koinōnos);* he is his fellow worker *(synergos)* in Corinth. The last two brothers are called *apostoloi* ("apostles") of the churches. Paul employs this term here in a broader non-technical sense that is rather unusual for him. The added qualification "the glory of Christ" is highly laudatory. It should be noted that in 12:17-18 only one person ("the brother") is mentioned in addition to Titus.

24. *Therefore show before the churches the proof of your love and of our boasting to them about you:* This is a final exhortation. The imperative "show" translates the Greek participle *(endeiknymenoi)* according to its probable meaning in this context. A variant reading replaces this participle by an imperative aorist but is most likely a correction by a copyist. "Before the churches" depends on the verb "show"; the churches (cf. v. 23) are in the first place those of Macedonia (see v. 1). Receiving the delegates in a correct way will provide the Corinthians with a double proof, of their own genuine love and of the veracity of Paul's boasting about them. Boasting is a theme that suddenly reappears here (cf. 1:14; 7:4, 14) and requires a further treatment: see 9:1-4. With "to them" Paul refers to the brothers (and perhaps Titus; see 7:14).

INTERPRETATION

a. *Structure and Line of Thought.* The fourth major part of 2 Corinthians, the section dealing with the collection for Jerusalem, consists of chs. 8 and 9 (see Introduction, pp. 9–11). A formal conclusion at the end of the third part is lacking (see 7:16). It is not unusual for practical matters to be dealt with toward the end of a letter (cf. 1 Cor 16:1-4 as far as the collection is concerned). This pleads against those who want to separate 2 Corinthians 8–9 from chs. 1–7. Chapter 9, however, will not be the end of this letter.

Hans Dieter Betz *(2 Corinthians 8 and 9)* calls 2 Corinthians 8 a letter fragment (= the letter-body) of the so-called mixed type; it belongs to the administrative type of Paul's correspondence. The rhetoric in its first part is deliberative: *exordium* (vv. 1-5), *narratio* (v. 6); *propositio* (vv. 7-8); three-fold *probatio* ("the honorable," "the expedient," "equality," vv. 9-15). In its second part the rhetoric is juridical: commendation of the delegates (vv. 16-22); authorization of the delegates (v. 23). Verse 24 is the *peroratio.* It would seem that serious reservations must be voiced not only regarding the independent letter theory, but also as far as the delineation and identification of the sections in the first part (and the subsections in vv. 6-15) are concerned.

Within ch. 8 one can best distinguish three text units: vv. 1-6 (the example of the churches in Macedonia); vv. 7-15 (the appeal proper); and vv. 16-24 (the recommendation of Titus and two other persons). In vv. 1-6 Paul is stressing that the great fervor of the Macedonian churches with regard to the collection spurred him on to send Titus to Corinth in order to complete the collection there. His praise of the Macedonians is quite impressive and, of course, also tactical. In vv. 7-15, Paul urges the Corinthians to bring the collection, which had already been begun last year, to a successful conclusion. He cannot give a strict command, only an opinion. But he can point out what Jesus' incarnation means; he can remind the Corinthians of their former readiness; he can explain that one should only give according to what one possesses. Furthermore, he emphasizes that equality should be the aim, which means that the Corinthians must now help Jerusalem, but also—should the poor people there later have plenty—that Jerusalem will have to help the Corinthians in case they are in material need. In vv. 16-24, then, Paul finishes with a heartfelt recommendation of his partner Titus and of two other Christians, one appointed by the churches, the other chosen by Paul himself. Paul has sent them to Corinth also because he wants to avoid any complaints regarding the handling of the collection.

b. *Characteristics.* Paul's style in this chapter presents the typical characteristics we find in the other chapters as well, e.g., the repetitious use of the same words in close context. We may also mention the frequent occurrence of *charis* in its varying nuances of a gracious work done either by Christ or by Christians, as well as the presence of the "fervor" terminology. Moreover, twice, in vv. 3-6 and vv. 10-11, the grammatical construction is complicated and constrained. One can still understand what Paul intends to say, but a literal translation is hardly feasible. The tortuous character of these sentences is probably caused, at least partly, by the delicate content to be expressed.

c. *Theological Reflection.* From what Paul writes in this chapter and the following (and from 1 Cor 16:1-4 and Rom 15:25-27) one senses how the collection preoccupies him. He appears to be greatly concerned about it. After all, the collection must have been a sensitive matter in Corinth. How does Paul proceed in 2 Corinthians 8? He begins with Macedonia's example, depicted rhetorically in a somewhat hyperbolic way. In the second section, the appeal itself, he is very prudent. He does not want to command, yet he gives advice: it is better for you to finish what you began last year. The collection is presented as a test of the genuineness of their love. Then, having mentioned at the beginning the exemplary conduct of the Macedonian Christians, Paul in one solemn sentence also refers to the example ("the grace") of Jesus Christ: rich as he was, he made himself poor for your sake, in order to make you rich by means of his poverty. Then, in a rather surprising way, while insisting on a completion that should be qualified by the Corinthians' free will—a first shift—he suddenly brings in two more shifts within his argument. He states that one has only to give according to one's means, and he also deals with the idea of equality. The conclusion of the appeal is formed by a quotation from Exod 16:18, a saying about the gathering of the manna: the person who gathered much did not have too much; the one who gathered little did not have too little. Paul then goes on to recommend Titus and two highly respected Christians. The addressees are also told that by sending those persons to Corinth Paul is showing his intention to be careful with regard to financial matters, for the collection could easily stir up insinuations.

For Paul that collection is not only the implementation of the agreement with the "three pillars" (cf. Gal 2:10), nor will it only be a concrete material help to needy fellow Christians. The collection must, above all, have been seen by him as a sign of unity between Gentile Christians and the Jewish Christians of Jerusalem; in its way, the collection even achieves that unity. According to Paul the material gesture is not without spiritual dimensions, that of genuine love and of a communion that for Paul is the very stamp of a Christian enterprise.

Within the context of 2 Corinthians the collection appeal immediately follows the passage where Paul appears to emphasize the Corinthians' reconciliation with him (7:5-16). One must ask, therefore, whether Paul does not intend Corinth's collection for Jerusalem as both the demonstration and further consolidation of what surely must have been a reconciliation-in-progress.

d. *Actualization.* With actualization in view one comes back to 2 Cor 8:9. We know "the grace of our Lord Jesus Christ: though he was rich he became poor" for our sake, so that we might become "rich by his poverty." As the comments from the second to the sixth centuries witness (see Angstenberger, *Der reiche und der arme Christus*), 2 Cor 8:9 was a highly significant text for early Christian doctrine and life. The typical structure—with a participle pointing to Jesus' pre-existence and a verb in the aorist referring to the incarnation—is also present in Phil 2:6-8 ("being in the form of God . . . he emptied himself"). The *hina* clause at the end reminds us of similar clauses in 2 Cor 5:21 and Gal 3:13. As to the content, more New Testament texts could be mentioned (cf., for example, John 1:14; 1 Tim 3:16). What 2 Cor 8:9 speaks of ("rich" becoming "poor") has traditionally been termed a "wonderful change." The significance of this verse has been manifold.

Church reflection upon this and similar texts finally led to the christological definition of two natures in one person. The discussion of Phil 2:6-8 sometimes asks whether Christ "emptied" himself of his divine prerogatives. Is Jesus after the incarnation perhaps no longer God? It would seem that the wording of 2 Cor 8:9 "being rich he became poor" avoids this kind of inopportune question.

One could claim that in Phil 2:6-11 the soteriological aspect is implicit; in 2 Cor 8:9, however, it is made explicit by the expression "for your sake" and even more so by the purpose clause "so that you might become rich by his poverty." The term "poor" certainly does not exclude material poverty, yet "becoming poor" means essentially becoming a human being (cf. Phil 2:6-8). This is confirmed by the opposite term "rich." The meaning of "rich" at the beginning of the sentence (Jesus) as well as at its end (the Corinthians) evidently has nothing to do with material and earthly riches.

However, the fact remains that Paul uses this text as a motivation for the collection. Through it he exhorts the Corinthians: what Jesus did by his incarnation you should analogously do by helping the poor saints of Jerusalem; you should become (more) poor so that they may become (more) rich. The sense here is clearly limited to the material, financial aspect. It cannot but strike us that the Philippian "hymn" is used in an ethical context as well: "Let the same mind be in you . . ." (Phil 2:5a).

Within Church history—and no less today—2 Cor 8:9 contains the appeal to fellowship with the poor Christ. How can a true Christian, how can the Church be rich or wealthy while the Lord became poor? A number of Christians have willingly become poor because of the poverty of Jesus and that of his poor brothers and sisters (cf. Matt 25:31-46). The preferential option for the poor is greatly stimulated by 2 Cor 8:9. However, the Christians' continuous struggle against all kinds of human misery and destitution shows that we must never exalt or idealize poverty as such.

FOR REFERENCE AND FURTHER STUDY

2 Corinthians 8–9 as a whole:

Berger, Klaus. "Almosen für Israel. Zum historischen Kontext der paulinischen Kollekte," *NTS* 23 (1976–1977) 180–204.

Betz, Hans Dieter. *2 Corinthians 8 and 9. A Commentary on Two Administrative Letters of the Apostle Paul.* Hermeneia. Philadelphia: Fortress, 1985.

Bieringer, Reimund. "Teilungshypothesen zum 2. Korintherbrief. Ein Forschungsüberblick" in Bieringer and Lambrecht, *Studies on 2 Corinthians.* BEThL 102. Leuven: Leuven University Press/Peeters, 1994, 98–104.

Georgi, Dieter. *Remembering the Poor: The History of Paul's Collection for Jerusalem.* Nashville: Abingdon, 1992.

Hainz, Josef. *KOINONIA. "Kirche" als Gemeinschaft bei Paulus.* BU 16. Regensburg: Pustet, 1982, 134–144.

Lambrecht, Jan. "Paul's Boasting About the Corinthians: A Study of 2 Cor. 8:24–9:5," *NT* 40 (1998) 352–368.

Lodge, John G. "The Apostle's Appeal and Readers' Response: 2 Corinthians 8 and 9," *ChiSt* 30 (1991) 59–75.

Nickle, Keith F. *The Collection. A Study in Paul's Strategy.* SBT 48. London: SMC, 1966.

Stowers, Stanley K. "*PERI MEN GAR* and the Integrity of 2 Cor. 8 and 9," *NT* 32 (1990) 340–348.

Verbrugge, Verlyn D. *Paul's Style of Church Leadership Illustrated by His Instructions to the Corinthians on the Collection.* San Francisco: Mellen Research University Press, 1992.

8:1-24:

Ascough, R. S. "The Completion of a Religious Duty: The Background of 2 Cor 8.1-15," *NTS* 42 (1996) 584–599.

Angstenberger, Pius. *Der reiche und der arme Christus. Die Rezeptionsgeschichte von 2 Kor 8,9 zwischen dem zweiten und dem sechsten Jahrhundert.* Hereditas 12. Bonn: Borengässer, 1997.

Joubert, S. J. "Behind the Mask of Rhetoric. 2 Corinthians 8 and the Intra-Textual Relation between Paul and the Corinthians," *Neotest.* 26 (1992) 101–112.

13. *The Collection (Continuation)* (9:1-15)

1. For to be sure it is superfluous for me to write further to you about the service for the saints. 2. For I know your eagerness about which I boast to the Macedonians: "Achaia has been ready since last year," and your fervor stimulated most of them. 3. Yet I sent the brothers lest my boast about you may prove empty in this matter, in order that, as I said, you might be prepared, 4. lest somehow, in case (some) Macedonians come with me and find you unprepared, we—not to say you—may be put to shame in this undertaking. 5. Therefore I thought it necessary to urge the brothers to go to you ahead (of me) and arrange beforehand the already promised generous gift, so that it would be ready, namely as a generous gift and not as a stingy donation.

     6. Now this (you should keep in mind): the one who sows sparingly will also reap sparingly, but the one who sows liberally will also reap liberally. 7. (Let) each (give) according to (what) has been decided in his or

her heart, not reluctantly or under constraint, for "God loves a cheerful giver" (Prov 22:8a LXX). 8. Now God has the power to cause every gift to abound in you, in order that you, having self-sufficiency in every way (and) at all times, may abound in every good work, 9. as it is written: "He scattered abroad, he gave to the poor, his righteousness remains for ever" (Ps 111:9 LXX).

10. The one who supplies seed to the sower and bread to eat will supply and multiply your seed and will increase the fruits of your righteousness. 11. You will be enriched in every kind of generosity, which through us produces thanksgiving to God. 12. For the service of this public help is not only filling up the needs of the saints, but also abounds through many thanksgivings to God. 13. Through the evidence of this service you will glorify God by obedience to your confession of Christ's gospel and by the generosity of your contribution to them and to all, 14. and in their prayer for you they are longing for you because of the surpassing grace of God (given) to you. 15. Thanks (be) to God for his indescribable gift.

NOTES

1. *For to be sure it is superfluous for me to write further to you about the service for the saints:* Paul continues his appeal by means of a figure of style, a *praeteritio:* "there is no need for me to write." "To write further," i.e., to continue the writing, renders the present infinitive *graphein* and also the anaphoric article *to* ("this" writing in progress). The collection is now called *diakonia* (literally: "service" (see also vv. 12 and 13). The repetition of the full phrase "the service for the saints" (cf. 8:4) presumably occurs for the sake of emphasis. The particle *men* (rendered "to be sure"), the second word of this verse, will be discussed in connection with *de* ("yet") in v. 3 (see Interpretation a). "To you" supposes the same Corinthian addressees in ch. 9 as in ch. 8 (cf. "brothers and sisters" in 8:1).

2. *For I know your eagerness about which I boast to the Macedonians: "Achaia has been ready since last year," and your fervor stimulated most of them:* Verse 2 is grammatically one sentence. Main verb and main clause stand at the beginning; subordinated clauses follow. Paul is well acquainted, he says, with the Corinthians' eagerness and zeal; he is boasting of it to the Macedonians. It is likely (not certain, however) that "Achaia has been ready since last year" is direct speech. While in ch. 8 the example of the churches in Macedonia was used to encourage the Corinthians, here Paul stresses the opposite: the readiness and zeal of Achaia stirred up the Macedonians. "Achaia," the name of the Roman province of which Corinth is the capital, is probably mentioned because of the reference to the "Macedonians," Macedonia being another Roman province (cf. 11:9-10; Rom 15:25; 1 Thess 1:7, 8). For the somewhat hyperbolic statement "has been ready (or: has been prepared) since last year" see 8:10-12 and cf. also 1 Cor 16:1-4.

3-4. *Yet I sent the brothers lest my boast about you may prove empty in this matter, in order that, as I said, you might be prepared, lest somehow, in case (some) Macedonians come with me and find you unprepared, we—not to say you—may be put to shame in this undertaking:* Notwithstanding that preparedness, Paul has sent the (two or, with Titus, three?) brothers: see 8:16-23. For this past tense, see the comment on 8:16-17: possibly an "epistolary" aorist. Verses 3-4 form one lengthy sentence. The beautiful certainty about the Corinthians disappears. The main verb and main clause are, again, at the beginning. Three asyndetic purpose clauses follow: *hina mē* ("lest": literally, "lest our boast be emptied [kenoomai])," *hina* ("in order that") and *mē pōs* ("lest somehow"). Within the second and third clauses other subordinated remarks interrupt the construction. This makes the grammar rather awkward, so that the translations have to be somewhat free. Moreover, the use of the first persons singular and plural is mixed, but could be more deliberate than one might be inclined to suppose. We follow Victor P. Furnish (*II Corinthians* 427) when he claims that "undertaking" is the correct translation of *hypostasis*, not "confidence."

5. *Therefore I thought it necessary to urge the brothers to go to you ahead (of me) and arrange beforehand the already promised generous gift, so that it would be ready, namely as a generous gift and not as a stingy donation:* From the content of vv. 3-4 the necessity not only of sending but also of sending ahead has become evident. That is why Paul writes an *oun* ("therefore"). Still, v. 5a ("I thought it necessary to urge") is somewhat strange after v. 1a ("it is superfluous for me to write further"). In v. 5bc the task of the brothers is explained. Paul employs three compound verbs, each with *pro*: to go "ahead," to put in order "in advance," and promised "beforehand." Paul seemingly wants the collection to be ready so that at his arrival he and his Macedonian companions have only to transfer the money to Jerusalem. The collection receives yet another name, *eulogia* (literally "blessing," in this context "generous gift"). Besides preparedness, generosity is underscored by Paul at the end of the verse. "Avarice" is an abstract noun that here indicates, in contrast to the generous gift, a meager and stingy donation. "Namely as" paraphrases *houtōs . . . hōs* ("so . . . as"), which typifies the gift that must be ready.

6. *Now this (you should keep in mind): the one who sows sparingly will also reap sparingly, but the one who sows liberally will also reap liberally:* The demonstrative pronoun *touto* ("this") announces what is going to follow. An imperative verb should probably be added. Before Paul makes his appeal in v. 7 he asks that the Corinthians reflect on what Scripture considers to be wise advice for the farmer: see, e.g., Prov 11:24-26. Yet v. 6 is not a quotation; it is Paul's own composition. Reaping is contrasted to sowing. Paul understands the image, of course, in a metaphorical way. It would seem that the idea of a proportionate reward is discreetly present. The contrast between "sparingly" and "liberally" (*ep' eulogiais*, literally "in the hope of blessings") is the same as that at the end of v. 5. "Will reap" here is not primarily eschatological.

7. *(Let) each (give) according to (what) has been decided in his or her heart, not reluctantly or under constraint, for "God loves a cheerful giver":* The exhortative verb "give" must be supplied. "Has decided" translates another compound verb

with *pro* (cf. v. 5): to decide "beforehand." The additional qualification "not reluctantly or under constraint" (cf. 1 Cor 16:2: "whatever one can afford") is motivated by a citation from Prov 22:8a (LXX), which, however, is not introduced by a quotation formula.

8. *Now God has the power to cause every gift to abound in you, in order that you, having self-sufficiency in every way (and) at all times, may abound in every good work:* This translation is kept as literal as possible. The verb *perisseuō* is assumed to be transitive in v. 8a ("to cause to abound,") and intransitive in v. 8b ("to abound, to overflow"). The content of the verse differs somewhat from that in v. 6, where the harvest (the reward) occurs after the sowing (the giving) and attention is focused on human action. (God is not mentioned.) Here in v. 8 God comes very much into prominence: God creates the very possibility of giving, not only causing the gift to abound in the Christians but doing so in an "exceeding" way. The Corinthians will have enough, which becomes an incentive for doing more good works. Besides the verb *perisseuō*, the word *pas* ("all, each") appears four times and *pantote* ("always") once. Without any doubt, the *p*-alliteration is intended; cf. especially *en panti pantote pasan*. Paul's speaking of God here is solemn and impressive indeed.

One is somewhat surprised to come across the typically Stoic term *autarkeia* (literally "self-government," hence "independence, self-sufficiency"): God will take care that there is in the Corinthian community always enough of everything.

9. *as it is written: "He scattered abroad, he gave to the poor, his righteousness remains for ever":* A quotation from Ps 111:9 (LXX), introduced by "as it is written," concludes the solemn statement about God. Just as in the psalm, so also for Paul—somewhat strangely after v. 8—the subject "he" here is most likely not God but a human person. In Judaism *dikaiosynē* ("righteousness") sometimes signifies "generous almsgiving." The expression "remains forever" can be understood to mean that the liberality of that person will always be remembered in the future.

10. *The one who supplies seed to the sower and bread to eat will supply and multiply your seed and will increase the fruits of your righteousness:* In this verse the idea of v. 8 is resumed by means of the seed imagery (cf. v. 6). Verse 10a contains the comparison, v. 10b the application. God is again (cf. v. 8, notwithstanding v. 9) the grammatical subject of the verbs. The text is written under the influence of Isa 55:10-11 and Hos 10:12. In the Isaiah passage the word of God is compared with the rain and snow that come down from heaven and do not return until they give "seed to the sower and bread to the eater." The expression "fruits of righteousness" is present at the end of the verse in Hosea. For the sense of "righteousness" see v. 9.

11. *You will be enriched in every kind of generosity, which through us produces thanksgiving to God:* In the Greek text "you will be enriched" is a participle present absolute, probably indicating the result of God's action (v. 10) in the Corinthians. "Generosity" translates *haplotēs* ("simplicity, single-mindedness, sincerity," but here and in v. 13 its meaning is "generosity"; cf. also 8:2). The

generous liberality produces thanksgiving. This is a new theme that will be developed in the remaining verses of the chapter. The phrase "through us" points to Paul's mediation, concretely the transfer of the collection to Jerusalem, since it is the Jerusalem poor who will give thanks to God.

12. *For the service of this public help is not only filling up the needs of the saints, but also abounds through many thanksgivings to God:* The Greek text is again heavy. Paul stresses the fact that the collection will bring about much thanksgiving. That service not only meets the needs of the saints, but will also be accompanied by an outpouring of their gratitude. "Public help" is the translation of *leitourgia* (originally "secular or religious public service").

13. *Through the evidence of this service you will glorify God by obedience to your confession of Christ's gospel and by the generosity of your contribution to them and to all:* In vv. 13-14 the Greek remains tortuous and difficult. As in v. 11 we have in v. 13 a present participle *(doxazontes,* "glorifying"), again most likely indicating a kind of result. Instead of "you" many commentators take the saints (of v. 12) as the logical subject of v. 13 ("they will glorify"), which also gives a good sense but seems to force the grammar. (See, however, Interpretation c.)

"Evidence" translates *dokimē* ("test, proof"). The exact sense of the phrase *epi tē hypotagē tēs homologias hymōn eis to euangelion* (literally: "on the basis of the submission of your profession toward the gospel") remains difficult to grasp. "Profession" most likely is an objective genitive (submission to the profession) and "gospel" must be the content of that profession. Furthermore, one could be a little surprised that the Corinthians' glorification of God will occur in the first place through their obedience and only in the second place through their generous contribution. Finally, it should be noted that Paul's horizon is suddenly broadening: "and to all."

14. *and in their prayer for you they are longing for you because of the surpassing grace of God (given) to you:* The genitive absolute of v. 14 (literally "they" and "longing for") introduces another new idea. Paul says that the Jewish Christians of Jerusalem, "the saints" (8:4; 9:1, 12), will (even) long for the Gentile Christians; that longing is expressed in their prayer for the Corinthians. This really is a bold statement on the part of Paul; one may think that it is rather a hope and a dream than a certainty. For the phrase "the grace of God" cf. 8:1; this use of the expression in 9:14 as well as in 8:1 constitutes, as it were, an inclusion of both chapters.

15. *Thanks (be) to God for his indescribable gift:* For "thanks be to God" cf. 8:16. Paul himself thanks God and invites the addressees to join in. "Gift" is the translation of *dōrea,* which here most probably encompasses the whole salvation event. Within this greatest and priceless gift the gracious work of the collection (a *charis*) finds its place.

INTERPRETATION

a. *Structure and Line of Thought.* The relation between chs. 8 and 9 has been explained in different ways. Are these chapters originally part of a

Pauline letter? Did they belong together from the start? If not, which of the two is the first? Some exegetes think that ch. 9 constituted a (later) separate fragment or letter. To be sure, this chapter appears to be, to a certain extent, a repetition of what is found in ch. 8. Moreover, in 9:2 Paul mentions "Achaia"; one could ask whether the addressees are still the same as those in ch. 8, the Corinthians. Finally, in 8:1-6 Paul praises the Macedonians to the Corinthians, while according to 9:1-4 he is boasting to the Macedonians about "Achaia." This also seems rather strange.

In Hans Dieter Betz's view *(2 Corinthians 8 and 9)* 2 Corinthians 9 is the body of a separate advisory letter with *exordium* (vv. 1-2), *narratio* (vv. 3-5a), *propositio* (v. 5b-c), *probatio* (vv. 6-14: thesis and five proofs), and *peroratio* (v. 15). Epistolary prescript and postscript are, of course, omitted by the editor who combined the fragments, i.e., chs. 8 and 9. However, besides justified doubts regarding the general view of ch. 9 as a separate letter arranged as a classical discourse, one should not take v. 5bc as a *propositio* or accept the division of vv. 6-14 into a thesis and five distinct proofs. Moreover, few scholars are willing to see v. 15 as Paul's intonation of a thanksgiving, the first line of a hymn that the Corinthians will spontaneously continue when the letter is read.

True, at first sight 9:1, with its stereotypical formula, presents itself as the beginning of a letter. Yet many facts indicate that ch. 9 is not a second letter but the continuation of the previous chapter. (1) In v. 1 Paul writes "it is superfluous for me to" followed by the present infinitive *graphein*, which itself is preceded by the anaphoric article *to* ("the, 'this' writing"). This appears to mean: there is no need for me "to go on writing." Moreover, the article *tēs* before "service for the saints" may also be anaphoric: "this" collection. All this connects 9:1 with what precedes. (2) The absence of any qualification of "the brothers" in vv. 3 and 5 makes one suppose that there is a reference to 8:16-24. (3) The explaining or grounding *gar* ("for") in v. 1 connects chapter nine with what precedes.

(4) It seems likely that in v. 1 *men* ("on the one hand") at the beginning is to be connected with the particle *de* ("on the other hand") of v. 3. In such a construction the *men* clause can be concessive. In a paraphrase the line of thought in vv. 1-3 would then be as follows: "although it is superfluous to go on writing to you about this collection—since I know your desire, of which I am boasting to the people of Macedonia—yet I still want to explain the implication of the sending of the brothers beforehand." In ch. 8 Paul has not given all the reasons for that mission (cf. 8:20-21). Now he adds: I am sending the brothers ahead of me (and possibly of some Macedonians), lest my boast about you may prove empty, lest we—I myself and you—may be put to shame.

(5) "Boasting" in vv. 2-3 almost certainly refers back to "boasting" in 8:24. Paul has to indicate the implications of that boasting. If at the arrival

of Paul (and perhaps some Macedonians with him) the collection is not ready, the boasting will prove empty; both Paul and the Corinthians will be disgraced. Obviously 8:24 and 9:1-5 belong together. (6) Moreover, in 8:1-5 the recent completion of the collection among the Macedonians is an example for the Corinthians. In addition, 9:2 can be seen as a compliment that will please the addressees: it was the readiness of the Corinthians (cf. 8:10) that initially stimulated the Macedonians.

(7) The vocabulary in 9:2, "eagerness" and "ready since last year," is also present in 8:10-12. (8) The exhortation of 9:6-13, with its emphasis on generosity, is not a real repetition of that in 8:7-15, which focuses on equality and completing the collection willingly. (9) Just as in 8:1, Paul employs the phrase "the grace of God" in 9:14. Although the meaning of the phrase in 8:1, concretely referring to the collection, is more restricted than that in 9:14 where it points to the whole of God's salvation, one may consider the two uses as an inclusion that frames the two chapters. In summary, the convergence of these nine points very much suggests that chs. 8 and 9 originally belong together.

Furthermore, in the Notes a reason has been offered for the presence of the name of the province "Achaia" in v. 2: Achaia corresponds with the other Roman province mentioned, Macedonia; its inhabitants, "the Macedonians," are mentioned in the same verse. "Corinth" may be meant, or at least included in "Achaia." On the other hand, some Christians must have lived outside that city, in the province (cf. 1:1). Nor should we see a contradiction between the rhetorically exaggerated praises of the Macedonians and the equally forced praise of Achaia. Finally, the somewhat repetitious character of ch. 9 and the length of both chapters witness to the importance Paul attached to the collection for Jerusalem and equally to its delicacy.

In ch. 9 Paul's further appeal, three sections can be distinguished: vv. 1-5 (do not put me to shame); vv. 6-9 (give liberally); and vv. 10-15 (thanksgivings will accompany your gifts). The end of v. 5 announces the theme of the second section, and this second section is finished off beautifully by the quotation in v. 9. In vv. 1-5 Paul informs his addressees of what he had told the Macedonians about the Corinthians: Achaia has been ready since last year. Yet, since some Macedonians might come with him to Corinth, Paul fears that he might be put to shame if it becomes evident that, as a matter of fact, the "promised" collection is not ready. Therefore, by way of precaution, he has sent "the brothers" ahead of him. One can hardly miss the point: this first section already contains an implicit exhortation. This exhortation, then, becomes explicit and more specific in the second section (vv. 6-9). Paul urges the Corinthians to give in a generous way. He uses the image of sowing and reaping; he emphasizes that God will lavishly provide the Corinthians with all kinds of gifts and will take care of them, so that there will be enough of everything for an independent, self-sufficient life, enough also for doing even more good works. Their generosity, Paul adds, will be remembered forever. In the third section (vv. 10-15) God is the central figure. God "creates," as it were, the generosity of the Corinthians. The result is that their liberality will bring with it much thanksgiving on the part of those who receive the collection.

b. *Characteristics.* It is rather striking that within chs. 8 and 9 no "neutral" word is used for the collection (cf. 1 Cor 16:1: *logeia*). In ch. 8 Paul calls it mostly *charis* ("grace, gracious work"; see vv. 1, 6-7, 19). In ch. 9 one finds the terms *diakonia* ("service"; see vv. 1, 12-13; cf. 8:4) and *eulogia* ("blessing"; see vv. 5-6). He refers to it also as *dikaiosynē* ("righteousness"; see vv. 9-10) and *haplotēs* ("simplicity"; see vv. 11 and 13, but also earlier, in 8:2). Furthermore, the style in 9:3-4, 5, 10-11, 13-14 is undeniably heavy. One cannot avoid the impression that to a certain extent such a constrained way of writing was intentional.

c. *Theological Reflection.* If "the saints" of v. 12 are the subject of the verb in v. 13, Paul further deals with their actions: they will glorify God for the Corinthians' obedient Christian life and for the Corinthians' generosity, and they will pray for them and even long for them because of God's surpassing grace given them. Yet according to the translation that is grammatically more defensible the Corinthians themselves will glorify God by their obedience to the gospel and also, of course, by their generous giving. Paul then announces that the Jerusalem Christians, in their prayer, will long for the Gentile Christians because of the grace of God, i.e., the salvation that is also given to the Gentiles. Paul thanks God for this inexpressible gift. One sees how in both interpretations this third section becomes more general, almost all-embracing.

When the two collection chapters are taken together Paul's inventiveness in exhorting his Christians to generous giving catches our attention. He refers to the example of the churches of Macedonia and, quite unexpectedly, even to the example of Christ emptying himself in becoming human. He appeals to the Corinthians' well-known eagerness and fervor. He announces that he is going to "test" the genuineness of their love. He tells his readers that he is boasting of their work before the Macedonians: "since last year it has been ready." This, however, is an exaggeration, and Paul immediately adds that out of fear of being shamed he has sent Titus and the other two brothers ahead of him to complete the collection before he arrives (and perhaps some Macedonians are coming with him). Above all he speaks of God, who is the creative source of their generosity and who also is continually giving in abundance, God who will be glorified by the Corinthians' obedience to the gospel and by the collection itself, and finally God who also will be exceedingly thanked by "the saints" for what the Corinthians are doing, for the grace given to them.

d. *Paul's Vision.* From the last verses of these chapters emerges a great expectation, the grandiose dream of Paul. The collection is more than a gathering of money; it means more than material help to the poor. Not only is Paul certain that "the saints" of Jerusalem will thank God for what they receive; he also inwardly hopes that through their reception of this collection his apostolic work among the Gentiles will be recognized. It is a dream of final reconciliation and mutual appreciation; it is a vision of the sealed union between Jewish Christians and Gentile Christians, of Christian love and prayer and longing for one another.

As far we can judge, this expectation did not materialize, certainly not the way Paul depicted it in 9:10-15 (cf. Rom 15:25-28). The transfer of the collection ended for him in his being put in prison through the maneuvers of the Jews (and also Jewish Christians?). Nowhere in the New Testament is it revealed what happened to the money that was collected.

For Reference and Further Study

See also the bibliography following 8:1-24.
Olson, Stanley N. "Pauline Expressions of Confidence in His Addressees," *CBQ* 47 (1985) 282–295.

V. PAUL'S SELF-DEFENSE (10:1–13:10)

14. *Paul's Defense of His Authority* (10:1-11)

1. I myself, Paul, appeal to you by the meekness and gentleness of Christ—I who admittedly (am) humble when face to face among you, but when absent bold toward you. 2. Yet I ask (you) that when present I do not need to be bold (toward you) with the confidence with which I intend to show daring against certain people who think that we are walking according to the flesh. 3. For although we are walking in the flesh we are not waging war according to the flesh, 4. for the weapons of our warfare are not fleshly, but powerful to God for the destruction of strongholds. We destroy sophistries 5. and every obstacle that sets itself

up against the knowledge of God, and we take captive every thought (to bring it) to the obedience of Christ, 6. and we are ready to punish every disobedience, once your obedience has been made perfect.

7. Look at what is before your eyes. If anyone is convinced in himself that he belongs to Christ, let him consider, again by himself, that just as he belongs to Christ, so we too. 8. For if I am going to boast rather much about our authority, which the Lord gave for building you up and not for destroying you, I shall not be put to shame.

9. I do not want to seem as if I were frightening you with letters. 10. For someone says, "His letters are weighty and strong, indeed, but his bodily presence is weak and his speech amounts to nothing." 11. Let this individual realize that just as we are in word by letters when absent, so (we will be) in action when present.

NOTES

1. *I myself, Paul, appeal to you by the meekness and gentleness of Christ:* The double pronoun (cf. 12:13) at the beginning heightens the emphasis already present in the mention of the proper name. For an expressive *egō* and the mention of "Paul," cf. 1 Thess 2:18 and Gal 5:2. Does Paul wish to make a distinction here between his fellow workers and himself? This may be the case. The context of accusation against Paul alone, to the exclusion of his coworkers, and his vehement reply in chs. 10–13 make the emphatic quality of the phrase "I myself, Paul" easily understandable.

The verb *parakalō* ("I appeal") often stands at the beginning of a paraenetic section in the Pauline letters (see especially 1 Thess 4:1 and Rom 12:1). By the expression "by the meekness and gentleness of Christ" Paul seems to suggest that these exemplary virtues that belong to Christ are to a certain degree his own and should also become virtues of the Corinthians, yet the relative clause that follows interrupts the train of thought.

I who admittedly (am) humble when face to face among you, but when absent bold toward you: The whole of v. 1b alludes to a reproach, the content of which subsequently becomes clearer in v. 2 and especially in v. 10. According to Hans Dieter Betz *(Der Apostel Paulus)* v. 1b is not simply an anticipation of the accusation quoted in v. 10. In v. 1b Paul is already answering the reproach and defending himself. He acknowledges the data that gave rise to that accusation, but he cannot accept the interpretation of the data.

"Face to face" means "in person." Attention should be given to the negative connotation here of the term *tapeinos* ("humble"), which connotation is rather exceptional in the biblical use of the term (cf. also the verb *tapeinoō* in 11:7). The verb "am" must be supplied in the first part of v. 1b. In the light of vv. 9-11 one should already see here in "but when absent am bold toward you" a reference to his letters, and probably more particularly to the so-called severe letter (cf. 2:4 and 7:8).

2. *Yet I ask (you) that when present I do not need to be bold (toward you) with the confidence:* The literal translation of this clause is as follows: "But I ask not when

present to be bold with the confidence." It is not at all clear that "I ask" simply resumes, softens, or complements the "I appeal" of v. 1a. What Paul wanted to say in v. 1a is, as it were, forgotten; v. 2, by way of a personal reaction, continues the digression present in v. 1b.

The text itself seems to require the addition of another verb: "I ask you not 'to compel me' (or: I ask you 'that I do not need') to be bold. . . ." The infinitive phrase "not (need) to be bold when present" is substantivized by means of the article *to*; the whole becomes the equivalent of a purpose clause. "To be bold" and "to show daring" (v. 2b) are both aorist infinitives; they point to the future (Paul's third visit). "Confidence" is Paul's apostolic self-assurance.

with which I intend to show daring against certain people who think that we are walking according to the flesh: The nuances in the two uses—a play on words?— of *logizomai* ("to count, to reckon") in v. 2 are slightly different. In the first use it means "to intend," while in the second we should take it rather as "to think." It is probable that the phrase "against certain people" indicates not only the rival apostles but also the anti-Pauline members of the Corinthian community. The translation has to omit the particle *hōs* ("as if"), which refers here to the subjective and false opinion of those other people.

In our translation of vv. 2-4 we retain the terminology of "flesh" (and "walking") because of Paul's word-play. Although for Paul "to live according to the flesh" normally means to live a sinful life, the expression in vv. 2-3 is most probably without such a nuance. It possesses the somewhat more neutral though nonetheless negative sense of "according to worldly standards." The fact that Paul "has been weak and cowardly in his personal dealings with the Corinthian church" has been taken "as evidence of his bondage to the flesh and of his lack of charismatic power and authority" (Furnish, *II Corinthians* 461). One should note the shift to the first person plural at the end of the sentence.

3. *For although we are walking in the flesh, we are not waging war according to the flesh:* The "although" clause admits Paul's "fleshly" condition, but "for" grounds his future boldness, his confidence. The whole of the verse introduces the reply to the reproach contained in v. 2. That reply partly contains the same wording as the accusation. By the phrase *"in* the flesh" as distinguished from *"according to* the flesh" he refers to the limitations of a human creature (cf. "clay vessels" in 4:7). The first use of "flesh" in v. 3 is thus neutral (cf. "in the world," 1:12). The second use (with *kata*) is not without a negative nuance; yet, as is the case with the similar usage in v. 2, it probably does not contain the specific Pauline sense of sinful behavior. In v. 3b the verb "walking" is replaced by "waging war"; thus metaphorical war language comes to the fore.

4. *for the weapons of our warfare are not fleshly but powerful to God for the destruction of strongholds:* This second "for" clause further explains v. 3b. Cognate forms of the same words are used. "To God" can be understood as a dative of interest (= in God's service; God can use them). However, the phrase can also

be seen as the equivalent of "spiritual," which we might expect here as the opposite term to "fleshly" in v. 4a; in this case the dative rather reinforces "powerful": mightily powerful, effective. Many exegetes—and it would seem rightly so—find in this verse an allusion to Prov 21:22: "A wise man attacks strong cities and brings down the stronghold in which the ungodly trusted." *We destroy sophistries:* It is preferable to take the three participles of v. 4 (at the end: "destroying"), v. 5 ("taking captive") and v. 6 ("being ready") as grammatically independent from v. 3 and as equivalent to indicatives. Verses 4b-6 illustrate and concretize the final expression of v. 4a, "for the destruction of strongholds." The context suggests that the term *logismoi* ("arguments, reasonings") has a negative meaning: false arguments. The strongholds are thus sophistries.

5. *and every obstacle that sets itself up against the knowledge of God:* "Obstacle" is (after "sophistries") the second direct object of "we destroy" (v. 4b); "obstacle" is but a weak translation of *hypsōma* (literally "height"). The two direct objects are descriptive and complementary terms and, as such, point to the same arrogant mentality. Note the concentration of "every" in vv. 5-6: Paul does not lack determination in his writing. For "the knowledge of God" cf. 2:14 and 4:6. We might paraphrase: "against the 'real' knowledge of God"; the opponents do not understand God as he is revealed in Christ.

and we take captive every thought (to bring it) to the obedience of Christ: With "taking captive" the war imagery continues but then, just as at the end of v. 4, the metaphorical language gives way to plain speech. Like "sophistries" in v. 4 "thought" has here a negative connotation. "Of Christ" is an objective genitive: so that they obey Christ.

6. *and we are ready to punish every disobedience, once your obedience has been made perfect:* The expression *en hetoimǭ echo* seems to be a Latinism: *in promptu habeo* ("to stand at the ready"). Because of v. 6b, which alludes to a completed obedience on the part of the addressees, the disobedience in v. 6a probably refers mainly to the activity of the opponents. Paul will proceed to punish that disobedience (only) after the Corinthians' obedience "shall have been completed" (or: "made perfect"). The time difference between v. 6b and v. 6a is strange and not without tension.

7. *Look at what is before your eyes:* The apparently similar phrases *ta kata prosōpon* (v. 7: "the things before the eyes," direct object) and *kata prosōpon* (v. 1: "face to face," an adverbial expression) are different in meaning. We must, moreover, ask whether the mood of *blepete* is imperative or indicative. The imperative contains a call: "face plain facts"; these things can provide positive evidence! The indicative would mean: "You are looking at things as they are on the outside," which implies: you ought not to see the outward appearance, but the reality below the surface. Both possibilities could make sense in the context. Elsewhere (e.g., 1 Cor 8:9; 10:18; Gal 5:15; Phil 3:2) *blepete* as an imperative normally occupies the first position in the sentence, but this is hardly a sufficient reason for taking the verb here as an indicative. Because of the context a slight preference is given to the imperative.

If anyone is convinced in himself that he belongs to Christ: "Anyone" can be taken as a generalization (cf. "some people," v. 2), or in employing this term Paul might be referring in a vague way to a particular person. The translation adopts the second possibility and supposes, probably rightly, that this person is a man. It is to be assumed, however, that among Paul's opponents there were powerful women as well. The dative *heautǭ* is not clear: "with regard to himself" (dative of respect), "for himself" (dative of interest), or "in himself"? Both dative and verb seem to point to an excessive self-assurance. The expression "to belong to Christ" cannot but remind us of the parties in 1 Cor 1:12: I belong to Paul, I belong to Apollos, I belong to Cephas, I belong to Christ. But does 2 Cor 10:7 contain a reference to parties? It seems difficult to assume that Paul himself is stating in v. 7b that he belongs to the Christ party. Nor can the expression simply mean "being a Christian," for it cannot easily be supposed that opponents said that Paul was not a Christian. For these reasons "being Christ's person (apostle, servant, or minister)" probably renders the right sense. It is a matter of title (cf., for example, 11:23), of apostolic qualification and authority. In fact, v. 8 will resume the motif of authority.

let him consider, again by himself, that just as he belongs to Christ, so we too: Touto ("this," not translated) stands before the main verb; it announces the following *hoti* ("that") clause in an emphatic way. The verb "to consider" is the same as that translated by "to intend" and "to think" in v. 2 (cf. also v. 11), *logizomai.* Taking into account the present tense of the imperative, one might propose as a version: "let him go on to consider." "Again" should probably be read not with the verb but with "by himself" (cf. v. 7b: "in himself"). The comparison "just as he . . . so we . . ." is somewhat repetitious after v. 7b, but it does heighten the emphasis and in its own way helps to manifest Paul's emotion and anger.

8. *For if I am going to boast rather much about our authority:* This is the first of many occurrences of the verb "to boast" (and its derivatives) within chs. 10–13. The whole of v. 8 looks to the future. Verse 8a refers to what Paul is going to do in this letter. He begins with an *eventualis* (*ean* + subjunctive, "if"), but in v. 8c he ends with a confident assertion ("I shall not be put to shame"). *Perissoteron ti* can mean either "somewhat abundantly, rather much, too much" or "more abundantly." If there is a real comparison ("more than," second meaning), we should ask whether the phrase refers to vv. 3-6, where Paul is already somewhat boasting, or to v. 7 (a further boast, i.e., beyond that of stating that he belongs to Christ). Yet the first meaning ("rather much") seems preferable. "Authority" is a key concept in ch. 10; it is Paul's apostolic commission to preach the gospel and to take care of the communities he founded.

which the Lord gave for building you up and not for destroying you: Almost the same clause occurs in 13:10. Paul apparently refers to his vocation and mission (see Galatians 1–2). The term *oikodomē* is metaphorically used and in this instance points to the process of building (not to the result, the building as product). For "destroying," compare v. 4. There appears to be an allusion to the prophet Jeremiah, more precisely to Jer 1:10: "See, today I appoint you over nations and over kingdoms, to pluck up and to pull down, to destroy and to overthrow, to build and to plant." However, for himself Paul retains only the positive side of the enterprise (yet see vv. 3-6 in this pericope). Moreover, with "and not for destroying you" Paul possibly points to the destructive work of his opponents.

I shall not be put to shame: The passive form of the verb may be a *passivum divinum*: "put to shame 'by God'" (cf. v. 10: the Lord commends). The change within v. 8 from first person plural to singular should be noted; one remembers that the opposite occurred in v. 2.

9. *I do not want to seem as if I were frightening you with letters:* The charge is that in his letters Paul claims more authority than he is able to demonstrate when he is present. *Hōs an* (or *hōsan* in one word) between the verbs "to seem" and "to frighten" makes the grammatical construction somewhat irregular. Moreover, the syntactical position of this purpose clause with *hina mē* ("in order that not," "lest") at the beginning is much discussed. One possibility is to connect the clause with the preceding v. 8 (e.g., with "not for destroying you": my authority was given not for destroying you lest I should seem as if I were frightening you). Because such a connection seems rather artificial, some connect v. 9 with v. 11 and regard v. 10 as a parenthesis: "That I may not seem to frighten you . . . let such a person consider. . . ." But again this is forced. Other commentators suggest that Paul, being under emotional stress, has left out a connecting statement: "(but I am not going to boast) lest I. . . ." The problem with this solution in terms of a negative ellipsis is that Paul as a matter of fact is going to do precisely that.

The best solution remains to take *hina* as an imperative particle. Such a construction, not unknown in the New Testament, is a substitute for the imperative. The punctuation after "I shall not be put to shame," then, should be a full stop. There is a new start and, at the same time, some degree of interruption in the train of thought: "Let me not look as if. . . ."

10. *For someone says, "His letters are weighty and strong, indeed":* This verse explains ("for") what is stated in v. 9: "as if I were frightening you with letters." The singular *phēsin* is to be preferred to the plural *phasin* (variant reading). For "someone says" (better, it would seem, than the impersonal "one says = they say"), see v. 11 (*ho toioutos*, "such a person, this individual"; cf. also v. 7). It has been suggested that this person was perhaps a kind of leader, a "ringleader" of Paul's opponents. *Barys* ("heavy") metaphorically means "weighty, impressive" (or possibly "exacting"). The plural "letters" may above all refer to Paul's supposedly strongly worded and stern letter of tears (cf. v. 1).

"but his bodily presence is weak and his speech amounts to nothing": "Of the body" is a Hebrew genitive, hence "bodily" presence. For "speech" see also 11:6. There appears to be some connection here between the accusation of weakness and a certain deficiency in oratorical powers, a deficiency that Paul seems ready to admit. Note the chiasm in the use of the contrasting pairs: "weighty" over against "contemptible" ("amounts to nothing, light") at the extremes and in the middle "strong" over against "weak."

11. *Let this individual realize that just as we are in word by letters when absent, so (we will be) in action when present:* In "let the person in question realize" the same

verb *logizomai* is employed as in vv. 7 and 2. As in v. 7, the emphatic *touto* ("this"), which anticipates the *hoti* ("that") clause, could not be translated. In v. 10 the *logos* is the spoken word of the physically present Paul; here the term points to the written word in his letters. In v. 11 the chiastic antithesis is between word and deed, i.e., between letters when absent and bodily presence. For "absent" and "present" see vv. 1-2; this vocabulary thus "frames" the passage. It is preferable to supply "we will be" in v. 11b and see here again (cf. v. 2) a reference to Paul's future visit. Others supplement "we are" and would not confine that attitude to the intended visit.

INTERPRETATION

a. *Structure and Line of Thought.* Chapters 10–13 of 2 Corinthians can be taken as a unit, with a style and a tone all their own that distinguish them from the rest of the letter (see also Introduction, pp. 7–11). The style is vivid and emotional: pleading and paraenesis, biting irony and bitter sarcasm, threat and condemnation go hand in hand. The tone is both apologetic (self-defense *vis-à-vis* the faithful of Corinth) and indirectly polemical (attack against the opponents, the intruders). Moreover, Paul's way of reasoning in these chapters has paradoxical, if not contradictory, features. In 10:12 he states that he does not wish to compare himself with some of those who rate themselves so highly, but as a matter of fact already in 10:13-16 and further in chs. 11 and 12 he does compare himself with his opponents. Again Paul stresses that boasting is foolish, and yet he must boast; he is compelled to do it. Nonetheless then, paradoxically as it is often said, what he ultimately boasts of is his weaknesses. Is this still "foolish" boasting? Furthermore, the majority of the sections in chs. 10–13 can be regarded as apologies, and indeed apologies they are, but Paul himself protests in 12:19: "Are you thinking again that we defend ourselves before you? In God's sight we speak in Christ; beloved, all (is done) for your upbuilding." In chs. 10–13 Paul contends for the true notion of apostleship: its authority and vulnerability, its power and weakness. Notwithstanding the fact that, in contrast to 2:14–7:4, almost no teaching is given in chs. 10–13 and the tone is so different, numerous relationships in ideas do exist between these two apologetic and pleading sections. This would seem to argue for 2 Corinthians as one letter.

Chapter 13 refers back to ch. 10 in many respects. The two chapters can be considered, to some degree, as framing and including the middle chs. 11 and 12. A number of motifs are present in both ch. 10 and ch. 13:

(1) Paul speaks of his absence and presence at Corinth (10:1, 2, 11; 13:2, 10) and of his future (third) coming (10:2, 4-6, 11; 13:1, 2, 10).

(2) In both chapters he threatens to show boldness, to be severe and not to spare anyone at his coming (10:2, 11; 13:2, 10). It should, however,

be noted that in ch. 13 Paul has in mind not only those Corinthians who favor his opponents, but also those who have gravely sinned previously and do not repent (13:2; cf. 12:20-21).

(3) The motif of obedience/disobedience on the part of the Corinthians, which is explicitly spoken of in 10:6, also seems present in 13:1-2, 5, 9-10.

(4) Paul mentions in 10:9-11 and also in 13:10 his earlier letters and/or his actual writing.

(5) In both chapters Paul contrasts the themes of weakness and power.

(6) Moreover, by means of an almost identical wording borrowed from Jeremiah, in 10:18 and 13:10 he points to the authority the Lord has given him for building up and not for tearing down.

(7) In 10:18 we meet the motif of test and approval, which is dominant in ch. 13 (see 13:3, 5-7).

(8) "To belong to Christ" in 10:7 recurs in the slightly different expressions of 13:5: to be living in the faith; Jesus Christ is in you (cf. 13:3: "Christ is speaking through me").

In view of the presence in both chapters of all these motifs it should not surprise us that there is a similarity in their respective vocabularies as well: e.g., present and absent, power and powerful, authority and building up, "not for destruction," letters or writing, faith and test. Finally, in contrast to chs. 11–12, which contain Paul's "foolish" boasting about what he was and is and all that he has done and suffered in the past, ch. 10 as well as ch. 13 look to the future. Paul announces a future visit to Corinth. He states what he is going to do there and what his attitude will be. In an entreating, warning style he writes to the Corinthians about what he expects from them, too: self-examination and improvement. All this primarily concerns the future.

Although no strict, obvious division can be discovered within ch. 10, two subunits present themselves: vv. 1-11 and vv. 12-18. The first is held together by the motif of Paul's future coming (see v. 2 and v. 11) and by the reproaches referred to or quoted in v. 1 and v. 10. The second subunit, although connected to the preceding by *gar* ("for") in v. 12 (which probably refers back to v. 8), forms a kind of excursus, a seemingly independent consideration in which the themes of commendation (vv. 12, 18) and boasting (vv. 13, 15, 16, 17) are developed by Paul; he explains how he envisages his apostolic authority in relation to the field of his work. Moreover, by its motif of boasting this second pericope is clearly related to chs. 11 and 12.

b. *An Interruption in v. 1?* Paul begins ch. 10 with a very emphatic expression: "I myself, Paul, appeal to you by the meekness and gentleness of Christ" (v. 1a). This sentence, however, remains incomplete. Paul appears to announce a moral exhortation. He mentions Christ who is the basis of his authority and whose qualities of meekness and gentleness are exemplary for Christians (and Paul himself)—at least that is our impression. But from v. 1b onwards he speaks of an accusation brought forward against him and he defends himself; he denies what the opponents say. Inimical intruders and critics of his person have entered the scene; this is manifest in v. 2b. At the beginning of the pericope one expects that the Corinthians would be exhorted to a better Christian life, but from v. 1b onward Paul seems to be very much occupied with himself and his enemies; he indicates how he himself acts and will act as an apostle. Paul is able to show that he does not lack boldness; he will oppose his enemies and demolish their arguments and pretensions; his weapons will prove powerful for God.

New topics are introduced after vv. 1-6, yet three factors make it rather difficult to determine the exact function of vv. 7-9 within Paul's line of thought. (1) Can we assume that the expression "belonging to Christ" in v. 7 is more or less the equivalent of the term "authority" in v. 8, so that both verses would deal with apostolic self-assurance? (2) What is the meaning of *perissoteron ti* in v. 8? In the Notes we asked whether the phrase means "somewhat excessively" or indicates that Paul is making a "further boast," i.e., a boast beyond that of "being of Christ." In the second understanding v. 8 would introduce a theme different from that in v. 7, while this is not necessarily so in the first interpretation. (3) What is the logical connection of the *hina* clause in v. 9 with v. 8? Is v. 9 dependent on a verb or an idea in v. 8, or does v. 9 constitute, as far as grammar and content are concerned, an independent sentence? The option of this commentary is for the second alternative. Paul comes back to the topic of his so-called threatening letters.

Notwithstanding these uncertainties what cannot be doubted is the introductory function of v. 8 in relation to vv. 12-18. In v. 8 (and perhaps already in v. 7) Paul speaks of the apostolic authority given to him by the Lord. He prepares the reader for his "boasting" of this authority that will follow in vv. 12-18. He will use his own building up of the Corinthians as the basis of his self-commendation. It would seem, then, that the annunciatory character of v. 8 has become evident, but this, in turn, entails that vv. 9-11 now appear as a kind of interruption.

c. *Theological Reflection.* We thus find in 2 Corinthians 10 two main points in the argument. In this chapter Paul first defends himself against the claim that he is bold and strong only when absent, that is, in his letters. His timidity, however, must not be misinterpreted. If necessary he will show boldness and a forceful, daring attitude when present: see vv. 1-6 and 9-11. In vv. 7-8 (and vv. 12-18) there appears a second point. Here

Paul deals with what he really is (he belongs to Christ and is his minister, v. 7), and with the authority that the Lord has given him (he will boast of it and will not be put to shame, v. 8).

Most probably Paul's original intention while writing 10:1a was to begin an exhortative section that might have contained diverse items of moral behavior, but all of which could have constituted an imitation of Christ's meekness and gentleness. In any case that appeal or exhortation would have meant more than just Paul's begging for "obedience" to himself (10:6). It must be stressed, on the other hand, that reconciliation with God (cf. 5:20 and 6:1-2) and peace with one another (cf. 13:11) certainly also imply reconciliation of the Corinthians with Paul and their obedience to him (10:6; cf., for example, 7:3-4). In view of Paul's return to that exhortation in 12:19–13:11 (especially 13:11), the whole of 10:1b–12:18 (or 10:1b–12:10, or even 10:1b–13:10) should perhaps be considered as a kind of lengthy excursus. Pleading, attacks, and foolish boasting are not the usual paraenesis. Is 10:1b–12:18, therefore, not somewhat analogous to the equally major (but, of course, quite different) excursus of 2:14–7:4? One is also tempted to compare 10:1a with Rom 12:1 and 1 Thess 4:1. Was 2 Cor 10:1a not originally intended as the beginning of the final paraenetical section of the letter, just as those two other verses are? This constitutes but one more, admittedly quite hypothetical element in the argumentation for the unity of the letter.

d. *The Meekness and Gentleness of Christ.* A last observation should be made. In 2 Cor 10:1a Paul appeals to the Corinthians "by the meekness and gentleness of Christ." Although in some New Testament texts (Phil 4:5; Titus 3:2) the general signification of "gentleness" *(epieikeia)* is almost interchangeable with other terms that express goodness, it has been claimed that the term here retains a connotation of condescension. The meaning is not exactly the same as that of the first term in the expression ("meekness"), but the nuance of the condescendent gentleness of a lord is present (cf. Adolf von Harnack: "die 'Milde Christi als des Herrschers,'" quoted by Leivestad, "Meekness," 116). In 10:1a, therefore, there would be no reference to Jesus' behavior during his earthly life. As a matter of fact Paul uses the title "Christ," not Jesus. As is well known, in his letters Paul does not provide us with many data about the earthly career of Jesus. In 2 Cor 8:9 as well as Phil 2:6-8, moreover, Paul refers to the incarnation or *kenōsis*, not to the example of Jesus on earth (but it could be asked: not at all?). This data, however, should probably not lead the reader to suppose that by the mention of "the meekness and gentleness of Christ" Paul is in no sense pointing to Jesus' earthly behavior and example.

FOR REFERENCE AND FURTHER STUDY

2 Corinthians 10–13 as a whole:
Betz, Hans Dieter. *Der Apostel Paulus und die sokratische Tradition. Eine exegetische Untersuchung zu einer "Apologie."* 2 Korinther 10–13. BHT 45. Tübingen: Mohr-Siebeck, 1972.

Carson, Donald A. *From Triumphalism to Maturity. An Exposition of 2 Corinthians 10–13.* Grand Rapids: Eerdmans, 1984.

Chevallier, Max-Alain. "L'argumentation de Paul dans II Corinthiens 10 à 13," *RHPhR* 70 (1990) 3–15.

DiCicco, Mario M. *Paul's Use of Ethos, Pathos, and Logos in 2 Corinthians 10–13.* Biblical Press Series 31. Lewiston: Edwin Mellen, 1995.

Fitzgerald, John T. "Paul, the Ancient Epistolary Theorists, and 2 Corinthians 10–13" in David L. Balch, Everett Ferguson, and Wayne A. Meeks, eds., *Greeks, Romans, and Christians. FS A. J. Malherbe.* Minneapolis: Fortress, 1990, 190–200.

Forbes, Christopher. "Comparison, Self-Praise and Irony. Paul's Boasting and the Conventions of Hellenistic Rhetoric," *NTS* 32 (1986) 1–30.

Heckel, Ulrich. *Kraft in Schwachheit. Untersuchungen zu 2. Kor 10–13.* WUNT 56. Tübingen: Mohr-Siebeck, 1993.

Holland, Glenn. "Speaking Like a Fool: Irony in 2 Corinthians 10–13" in Stanley E. Porter and Thomas H. Olbricht, eds., *Rhetoric and the New Testament. Essays from the 1992 Heidelberg Conference.* JSNT.S 90. Sheffield: Sheffield Academic Press, 1993, 250–264.

Judge, Edwin A. "Paul's Boasting in Relation to Contemporary Professional Practice," *ABR* 16 (1968) 37–50.

Käsemann, Ernst. "Die Legitimität des Apostels. Eine Untersuchung zu II Korinther 10–13" in K. H. Rengstorf, ed., *Das Paulusbild in der neueren deutschen Forschung.* WdF 24. 2nd ed. Darmstadt: Wissenschaftliche Buchgesellschaft, 1969, 475–521.

Lambrecht, Jan. "Dangerous Boasting. Paul's Self-Commendation in 2 Corinthians 10-13" in Reimund Bieringer, ed., *The Corinthian Correspondence.* BEThL 125. Leuven: Leuven University Press/Peeters, 1996, 325–346.

Lohse, Eduard. *Verteidigung und Begründung des apostolischen Amtes (2 Kor 10–13).* Benedictina 11. Rome: Abbazia San Paolo fuori le mura, 1992.

Loubser, J. A. "A New Look at Paradox and Irony in 2 Corinthians 10–13," *Neotest.* 26/2 (1992) 507–521.

Marshall, Peter. *Enmity in Corinth: Social Conventions in Paul's Relation with the Corinthians.* WUNT II/23. Tübingen: Mohr-Siebeck, 1987.

Murphy-O'Connor, Jerome. "The Date of 2 Corinthians 10–13," *ABR* 39 (1991) 31–43.

Schütz, John Howard. *Paul and the Anatomy of Apostolic Authority.* MSSNTS 26. Cambridge: Cambridge University Press, 1975.

Spencer, Aida Besançon. "The Wise Fool (and the Foolish Wise): A Study of Irony in Paul," *NT* 23 (1981) 349–360.

Travis, Stephen H. "Paul's Boasting in 2 Corinthians 10–12," *StEv* 6 (TU 112). Berlin: Akademie-Verlag, 1973, 527–532.

Watson, Francis. "2 Cor. x–xiii and Paul's Painful Letter to the Corinthians," *JThS* 35 (1984) 324–346.

Welborn, L. L. "The Identification of 2 Corinthians 10–13 with the 'Letter of Tears,'" *NT* 37 (1995) 138–153.

Zmijewski, Josef. *Der Stil der paulinischen 'Narrenrede'. Analyse der Sprachgestaltung in 2 Kor 11,1–12,10 als Beitrag zur Methodik von Stilundersuchungen neutestamentlicher Texte.* BBB 52. Cologne and Bonn: Peter Hanstein, 1978.

2 Cor 10:1-11

Dewey, Arthur J. "A Matter of Honor: A Social-Historical Analysis of 2 Corinthians 10," *HThR* 78 (1985) 209–217.

Lambrecht, Jan. "Paul's Appeal and the Obedience to Christ: The Line of Thought in 2 Corinthians 10:1-6," *Bib.* 77 (1996) 398–416.

Leivestad, Ragnar. "'The Meekness and Gentleness of Christ' II Cor. X.1," *NTS* 12 (1965–1966) 156–164.

Malherbe, Abraham J. "Antisthenes and Odysseus, and Paul at War," *HThR* 76 (1983) 143–173.

15. *Wrong and Right Commendation* (10:12-18)

12. For we do not dare to class or compare ourselves with some of those who recommend themselves; yet when they themselves measure themselves with one another and compare themselves with one another, they are not wise.

13. We, however, will not boast beyond measure, but (only) according to the measure, i.e., the competence that God has apportioned to us, namely to come even as far as to you. 14. For we are not overstretching ourselves as not being able to reach you, for even to you were we the first to come with the gospel of Christ. 15. We are not boasting beyond measure in the labors of others, but we have hope that, as your faith goes on increasing, we may be enlarged among you, according to our competence, abundantly, 16. (and) preach the gospel farther than among you, (yet) not boast of things ready at hand within someone else's competence.

17. "Let the one who boasts, boast of the Lord" (Jer 9:22-23). 18. For (it is) not the one who recommends himself who is approved, but the one whom the Lord recommends.

NOTES

12. *For we do not dare to class or compare ourselves with some of those who recommend themselves:* Verse 12a is decidedly ironic. The verb "to dare" is taken up from v. 2, as well as the indefinite pronoun *tines* ("some"), which refers here to the

opponents. For "to recommend" plus the reflexive pronoun see 3:1; 5:12 (cf. 12:11, passive). Note also the play on words: *enkrinai/synkrinai*. Alfred Plummer renders as follows: "Well, I really cannot muster courage to pair myself or compare myself with certain persons who are distinguished by much self-commendation." He comments that the translation "'pair' and 'compare' fairly well preserves the similarity of sound and change of meaning" (*Commentary*, 285–286). The *"synkrisis"* is a well-known figure of speech in ancient Greco-Roman literature.

In 2 Corinthians the typical verb *synistanō* ("recommend") mostly occurs in passages that relate to the opponents: see 3:1; 4:2; 5:12; 10:12, 18; 12:11.

yet when they themselves measure themselves with one another and compare themselves with one another, they are not wise: At the end of v. 12 and the beginning of v. 13 a number of variant readings are present in the manuscript tradition. Of the six readings indicated in the apparatus of the *Greek New Testament*[4] two readings should be discussed, the longer and the shorter.

In the short reading four words are missing at the end of v. 12 and the beginning of v. 13: *ou syniasin. hēmeis de* ("they are not wise. We, however"; literally: "they are not understanding. But we"). The text of vv. 12b-13a runs then as follows: "but by measuring ourselves by ourselves and comparing ourselves with ourselves we will not boast beyond measure, but (only) according to the measure" (note that v. 12b, too, has the first person plural). This variant is present in D*, some Old Latin manuscripts and also in some early Christian authors. It is preferred by a number of exegetes (e.g., Hans Windisch [*Zweite Korintherbrief*], Rudolf Bultmann [*Second Letter*], Jean Héring [*Second Epistle*], Ernst Käsemann [*"Legitimität"*]). Four reasons are advanced, not all, however, by the same commentators. (1) According to some of them the short reading is the more difficult. (2) It provides a more balanced "not . . . but" construction in v. 12. (3) Its sense fits in with what Paul says elsewhere. (4) "They are not understanding," without a direct object in the longer reading, is too weak and, moreover, unclear as a criticism of the opponents. These reasons, however, are hardly convincing.

The longer reading is supported by manuscripts of the highest textual authority (e.g., B 33; also the old but not always reliable 𝔓[46]). (1) This reading is not less difficult than the shorter. (2) The "but" (or "yet") at the beginning of v. 12b introduces an interruption of the train of thought. (3) The long reading is even more Pauline and fits very well in its immediate context. (4) The clause "they are not understanding" (no direct object) is rather impressive (cf. the same absolute use of the verb in Mark 8:17).

Moreover, two hypotheses could account for the origin of the shorter reading. It could be haplography (from *ou* to *ouk*), or a misinterpretation of the reflexive pronoun: in Hellenistic Greek *heaut-* was common to all persons; one could have understood it in v. 12 as "ourselves" and then dropped the third person "they are not understanding" (at the end of v. 12) as unintelligible, and "but we" (at the beginning of v. 13) as superfluous.

Verse 12b explains the last expression of v. 12a: those who are commending themselves. Although the opponents are not dignified by direct reference, the pronoun *autoi* ("they themselves") is very emphatic. Note may be taken of the chiastic structure in Greek: (1) *en heautois* ("by one another"), (2) *heautous* ("themselves"), (3) *metrountes* ("measuring") and (3) *synkrinontes* ("comparing"), (2) *heautous* ("themselves"), (1) *heautois* ("with one another"). It is probably better to take the two datives *(en) heautois* here not as purely reflexive but as reciprocal (which is possible already in classical Greek). There is then a mutual measuring and comparing. What is the exact nuance of the participles: only time ("when" they measure and compare) or also cause ("because" they measure and compare)? It would seem that the causal nuance cannot be absent.

Peter Marshall points to the fact that in v. 12 three "technical" terms (compare, recommend, and measure) are employed together. He stresses that among Greeks the "comparison" is a rhetorical device and that its content above all reflects familiar encomiastic topics: "*synkrisis* was a method by which a person amplified his own virtues and achievements and depreciated those of his enemies" (*Enmity* 325). In his opinion the rival apostles are "self-commenders"; they compare themselves not only with one another but also with Paul: "they consider themselves superior to Paul" (*Enmity* 200; cf. also Forbes, "Comparison, Self-Praise, and Irony"). However, the last idea is not explicitly given in the Pauline text.

13. *We, however, will not boast beyond measure:* In the preceding v. 12 Paul attacks the self-commendation of the opponents and their senseless reciprocal comparison; from v. 13 to v. 16 he rather counters their false claims with regard to the church of Corinth. However, v. 13a can be taken as a resumption of v. 12a (cf. negation, first person plural, similar content). The future tense "we will not boast" now announces what Paul intends not to do. The adjective *ametron* (literally: "without measure") takes up the idea of measure present in the verb *metrountes* ("measuring") of v. 12b; it will itself be followed by the noun *metron* ("measure") in v. 13b. *Ta ametra* can be translated "things without measure." In view of the cognates in v. 12b and v. 13b it would seem that a literal sense of the phrase *eis ta ametra* should be retained as much as possible: "beyond measure." According to Marshall, *Enmity*, Paul in vv. 12-13 is drawing upon the conventional language of moderation and immoderation; he accuses his rivals of excess in their behavior. Marshall is of the opinion that Paul sees and characterizes his enemies as "hybrists" in the Greek sense of the term. However, this may be an overinterpretation.

but (only) according to the measure, i.e., the competence which God has apportioned to us, namely to come even as far as to you: Alla corresponds with the *ouk* ("not") of v. 13a and has the sense here of "but (only)." Within this context *metron* is not the means used to measure but the measured quantity, i.e., the amount of authority. *Kanōn* can be the measuring rod or, metaphorically, the rule, norm, statute, canon, or standard. In Gal 6:16 the sense is clearly metaphorical: "the rule." The same word occurs three times in the pericope of 2 Corinthians 10: in vv. 13, 15, and 16. In our translation we prefer its metaphorical meaning and choose, not without hesitation, the term "competence" (which is close in meaning to "norm" and "jurisdiction"). Many commentators, however, want to find in *kanōn* a nuance of place: what is enclosed in boundaries, the field or province. By this word Paul would refer to his province of apostolate, his missionary field. It is questionable, however, whether *kanōn* in itself possesses such a local connotation. Some authors, following Edwin A. Judge ("Paul's Boasting"), are of the opinion that in the early first century C.E. edict of Sotidius, governor of Galatia, *kanōn* refers to both the schedule of services and the territorial limits of the services. Paul's language in 2 Cor 10:13-16 could then reflect these two meanings of the term apparently borrowed from the language of public service. Scott Hafemann, "'Self-Commendation,'" criticizes this opinion, and it would seem rightly so. He very much doubts that a "geographical" meaning of *kanōn* has been found. Still, the local nuance, it must be stressed, is present through the immediate context.

The grammar of this sentence is strained and notoriously difficult. The relative pronoun *hou* (genitive) is attracted to *kanonos* (genitive). *Kanonos* itself may be taken as epexegetical: the measure *(metron)*, i.e., the *kanōn*, the "competence" God assigned to us "as measure." The infinitive "to come to" is equally epexegetical ("namely") and loosely attached to what precedes. The *kai* means "even" here, "even to you."

14. *For we are not overstretching ourselves as not being able to reach you:* Verses 14-16 constitute one long, grammatically overloaded sentence. The picturesque image present in the verb "we are not overstretching ourselves" should be noticed. The present tense is somewhat strange here. Paul may (also) be pointing to what he is actually doing, i.e., writing to the Corinthians. Most translations render *ephiknoumenoi* by a past tense: "as if we did not reach you," but this is hardly correct.

for even to you were we the first to come with the gospel of Christ: The phrase "even to you" is resumed from v. 13b. The preposition *en* before "the gospel" probably has a sociative meaning here: "with." The verb *phthanō* differs from "to come, to arrive" in v. 13b; the nuance is "to come first." Regarding the content we may refer to 1 Cor 3:6 and 10: "I planted, Apollos watered, but God gave the growth. . . . According to the grace of God given to me, like a skilled master builder I laid a foundation, and someone else is building on it" (cf. also 1 Cor 4:15).

15. *We are not boasting beyond measure in the labors of others:* The participles *kauchōmenoi* ("boasting") and, in v. 15b, *echontes* ("having") are perhaps absolute; if so, they introduce independent clauses. In Paul *kopos* often means apostolic work, hence our translation "labors." In the phrase "beyond measure," taken up from v. 13b, we should assume a slight shift in meaning; after vv. 13b-14 "measure" now concretely points to the mission territory assigned to the apostle. For *allotrios* ("belonging to another") see Rom 15:20 (different image but parallel idea): "lest I build on the foundation of another."

but we have hope that, as your faith goes on increasing, we may be enlarged among you, according to our competence, abundantly: Three infinitives depend on "we have hope" (literally "having hope"): "to be enlarged" (v. 15b), "to preach (the gospel)" (v. 16a) and "to boast" (v. 16b). The grammatical subject is that of the main verb in v. 14b ("we were the first to come") and of the (absolute?) participles in v. 15: Paul. The growth in faith is to be understood as a qualitative growth, a deepening of faith (cf. 10:6: "once your obedience has been made perfect"). It would seem that in vv. 15b-16 there is a degree of evolution in Paul's reasoning. "When your faith grows, I hope to be magnified in you (= in your estimation)," i.e., praised and commended by you. But under the influence of *kata ton kanona* ("according to our competence") and even more of *eis perisseian* ("abundantly," a phrase further explained by v. 16) the verb "to be enlarged" already has a connotation of being able to go "farther than you." "Abundantly" must thus be understood in a geographical sense; it refers to evangelization in other regions. In this interpretation "among you" characterizes the verb "to be enlarged," which in the Greek text comes after this expression.

16. *(and) preach the gospel farther than among you:* Verse 16a determines the understanding of v. 15b, which without it could have been differently (or not) understood. In the translation the geographical connotation is made explicit: "farther than among you."

   (yet) not boast of things ready at hand within someone else's competence: There is no conjunction between v. 16a and v. 16b; from a stylistic point of view the asyndeton is harsh, hence our addition of "yet." Because of its immediate context, and especially because of the expression "within someone else's *kanōn*," which in the Greek text comes before *eis ta hetoima,* the term *hetoimos* ("ready at hand") means here "prepared by others." Again, because of that context one should not lose sight of the geographical nuance present here in "competence."

17. *"Let the one who boasts, boast of the Lord":* For Paul "the Lord" here probably points to God, not Christ. The same saying is present in 1 Cor 1:31 where it is introduced as an Old Testament quotation by "therefore, as it is written." Most interpreters refer to Jer 9:22-23 (LXX): "Thus says the Lord: Let the wise man not boast of his wisdom, and let the strong man not boast of his strength, and let the wealthy man not boast of his wealth, but let the one who boasts, boast of this, (namely) that he understands and knows that I am the Lord, who do mercy and judgment and righteousness on the earth." Paul has drastically shortened the Old Testament text; the negative half is omitted and "in the Lord" replaces the knowledge of the Lord. While in 1 Cor 1:31 Paul applies the saying to the attitude that the Corinthians should adopt, here in 2 Cor 10:17 Paul uses it as a criterion for the true apostle.

18. *For (it is) not the one who recommends himself that is approved, but the one whom the Lord recommends:* For "to recommend" see v. 12a. *Dokimos* means "tested and approved, accepted." In ch. 13 the term and its cognates will be frequently employed. Just as in the quotation in v. 17, so also in v. 18b *kyrios* ("Lord") most probably designates God (compare *kyrios* of v. 18 with *ho theos,* "God," in v. 13).

a. *Structure and Line of Thought.* In the previous passage the introductory function of 10:8 in relation to 10:12-18 was mentioned. In v. 8 (and perhaps already in v. 7) Paul speaks of the apostolic authority given to him by the Lord. Although in vv. 12-15 the verbs are often preceded by a negation, with the positive v. 8 Paul prepares the reader for his actual boasting that, after all, is present in vv. 12-18. He will use his building up of the Corinthians as the basis of his self-commendation. One should also consider the parallelism of both vocabulary and motif:

Verse 8	Verses 12-18
rather much	not beyond measure (vv. 13, 15)
I am going to boast	we will not boast (v. 13)
our authority	the measure, i.e., the competence (v. 13; cf. vv. 15-16)
that the Lord gave	that God has apportioned (v. 13)
for building up	evangelization (vv. 14-16)
I shall not be put to shame	the one (= Paul) whom the Lord recommends (v. 18).

What is the structure and the line of thought of vv. 12-18? The framing function of v. 12 and vv. 17-18 can scarcely be denied. There are the terminological elements that form an inclusion: compare "some of those who recommend themselves" in v. 12 with "not the one who recommends himself" in v. 18a. There is also the correspondence in content between two negative assertions: "they are not wise" (v. 12) and "not . . . approved" (v. 18a). In the beginning and at the end of the passage Paul accuses his opponents of self-commendation and comparison with one another; he stresses the non-sense, the worthlessness of such an attitude (v. 12). The wrong sort of boasting and commendation (vv. 17-18) consists precisely in the fact that the opponents measure themselves by themselves and compare themselves with one another. Verses 13-16 comprise the core of the pericope (surrounded by v. 12 and vv. 17-18). In this middle part Paul speaks of himself, of what he has done and what he hopes to do. He does not boast of work that is not his own. In stating what he is doing and not doing he is defending himself and, in a veiled and polemic way, comparing himself with others, the intruders. They are explicitly referred to in v. 12 and the allusion to them in vv. 17-18 can hardly be missed. Therefore the structure of the passage appears to be concentric: v. 12 *(a)*, vv. 13-16 *(b)*, and vv. 17-18 *(a')*. How then does the argumentation in this pericope proceed?

If it is correct to see v. 12 as linked by its *gar* ("for") to v. 8, then Paul intends to begin the boasting about his authority that he announced in that verse. His boasting will not, however, take the form of an explicit comparison with his opponents who commend themselves, for their commendaton consists in reciprocal measuring and comparing and this senseless action leads to a lack of understanding and wisdom.

Paul's standard of boasting is the authority given to him by God. In the unfolding of vv. 13-16 it becomes clearer how Paul concretely sees that authority. It is a *kanōn*, a competence assigned to him by God. This competence is connected with the regions where Paul has to proclaim the gospel and is thus entitled to do so. Corinth belongs to his competence. Paul has not exceeded his legitimate measure and he has not taken credit for what others have done. Verses 14-16 are partly a repetition of v. 13; at the same time, each verse goes a step farther in the concretization:

> 13a We will not boast beyond measure, but (only) according to the measure, i.e., the competence
>> 13b that God has apportioned to us, (namely) to come even as far as to you.
> 14a For we are not overstretching ourselves as not being able to reach you,
>> 14b for even to you we were the first to come with the gospel of Christ.
> 15a We are not boasting beyond measure in the labors of others,
>> 15b but we have hope that, as your faith goes on increasing, we may be enlarged among you, according to our competence, abundantly,
> 16a (and) preach the gospel farther than among you,
> 16b (yet) not boast of things ready at hand within someone else's competence.

The parallelism between vv. 13a, 14a, and 15a (cf. also v. 16b) is striking. All these clauses are negatively formulated and have verbs in the first person plural. All contain either the theme "without measure" (vv. 13 and 15a) or a *hyper* ("over, beyond") construction (v. 14a; cf. v. 16a). The negations in vv. 13a, 14a, and 15a are followed by a positive corrective or explanatory assertion. The rather static and apologetic reference to Paul's past missionary activity in Corinth of vv. 13-15a gives way, in vv. 15b-16, to a glance into the future. Paul cherishes the hope of preaching the gospel in regions beyond that of the Corinthians, once their faith is increased.

In vv. 17-18 Paul concludes. The thesis sentences are put in the third person, but Paul certainly has himself in mind as well as his opponents. By measuring themselves against one another and by boasting of others' work and commending themselves, the opponents show their lack of good sense (cf. the end of v. 12); they will not be approved. The addressees of the letter are implicitly invited to compare Paul with the intruders and draw the appropriate conclusion. "For (it is) not the one who recommends himself that is approved, but the one whom the Lord recommends" (v. 18).

b. *Geographical Overtones.* It can hardly be assumed that the term *kanōn* in vv. 13, 14, and 16 by itself means field or province. However, the geographical overtones present in the context must be taken into account. In this pericope Paul stresses that he has reached Corinth and that he was the first to proclaim the gospel there. He further hopes that the growth of the Corinthians' faith will allow him to go to other regions that have not yet received the gospel.

c. *Theological Reflection.* We cannot but see in this pericope a reference to Paul's famous principle of non-intervention—a principle that is more explicitly formulated in Rom 15:14-33. Moreover, it would seem that the Romans passage itself has to be explained in terms of Gal 2:6-10 (the Jerusalem agreement). Ultimately, authority and competence are based on divine commission (cf., for example, Gal 1:15-16). Paul's understanding of his mission and founding function, as well as his missionary planning, depend upon his vocation as apostle of the Gentiles (cf. Rom 11:13; see also, e.g., 1 Cor 1:17: "Christ did not send me to baptize, but to proclaim the gospel").

But what about Paul's barely concealed self-commendation? We should realize that the situation in Corinth was most critical for him. He is said to be weak when present. His speech is poor and weak; only his letters are weighty and strong, but when writing, of course, he is absent. Apparently other missionaries display more strength, more rhetorical skill. Paul's authority in Corinth is no longer beyond dispute. For his own part Paul does not want to show boldness, but nonetheless he will be ready to punish every disobedience at his future coming (see 10:6 and cf. 13:2).

Because of these concrete circumstances Paul refers in 10:8, 13-16 to the authority the Lord has given to him. He mentions his personal commission, the evangelization of the Gentiles. This commission includes his work among the Corinthians. He was the founder of their Christian community; he was the first to reach Corinth with the gospel of Christ. Hence he is not overstretching himself, not overstepping his measure and competence. On the contrary, the very existence of the Corinthian church, i.e., the fruit of his missionary work, is his true recommendation and his rightful, legitimate boast (cf. also 3:2-3).

d. *Actualization.* Paul's emphatic argumentation in 2 Cor 10:12-18 brings the reader to the obvious conclusion that not all self-commendation, not all boasting of personal achievement is wrong. One cannot but apply what is said in vv. 17-18 also to Paul himself. Because in Corinth he has built under God's commission, the work he did was God's work. His boasting of the Corinthians' faith as the result of his efforts is at the same time a boasting in the Lord. Through this accomplishment he is recommended by the Lord. Self-commendation and recommendation by God here coincide. Scott Hafemann comments: Paul's "boast concerning his authority is, in reality, merely the appropriate human counterpart to the 'Lord's commendation' upon which one's approval ultimately rests" ("'Self-Commendation,'" 75).

God's commission provided Paul with authority; that commission was carried out by Paul and resulted in a visible church. The Corinthian church, therefore, legitimates the apostle. True, Paul does not like to boast of that authority (see 10:8); true, his boasting is forced upon him through the critical and sad situation in Corinth (see 10:13-16); true, vv. 17-18 are meant in the first place as a charge against the unjustified boasting of his opponents. Yet according to 2 Cor 10:8, 12-18, because the Lord commends him Paul is approved. He can boast of his authority and achievements in a legitimate way.

For Reference and Further Study

See also the bibliography following 10:1-11.

Hafemann, Scott J. "'Self-Commendation' and Apostolic Legitimacy in 2 Corinthians: A Pauline Dialectic?" *NTS* 36 (1990) 66–88.

Henning, John. "The Measure of Man: A Study of 2 Cor. 10:12," *CBQ* 8 (1946) 332–343.

Lambrecht, Jan. "Dangerous Boasting. Paul's Self-Commendation in 2 Corinthians 10–13" in Reimund Bieringer, ed., *The Corinthian Correspondence.* BEThL 125. Leuven: Leuven University Press/Peeters, 1996, 327–335.

Marshall, Peter. *Enmity in Corinth: Social Conventions in Paul's Relation with the Corinthians.* WUNT II/23. Tübingen: Mohr-Siebeck, 1987.

Schreiner, Josef. "Jeremia 9,22.23 als Hintergrund des paulinischen 'Sich-Rühmens'" in Joachim Gnilka, ed., *Neues Testament und Kirche. FS R. Schnackenburg.* Freiburg, Basel, and Vienna: Herder, 1974, 530–542.

Strange, James F. "2 Corinthians 10:13-16 Illuminated by a Recently Published Inscription," *BA* 46 (1983) 167–168.

Wong, Kasper. "'Lord' in 2 Corinthians 10:17," *LouvSt* 17 (1992) 243–253.

16. *Paul, the Corinthians, and the Super-Apostles* (11:1-15)

1. If only you would tolerate me in a little foolishness; yes, do tolerate me. 2. For I am jealous for you with God's jealousy, because I betrothed you to one husband in order to present you as a chaste virgin to Christ.

3. But I am afraid that somehow, just as the serpent deceived Eve by his cunning, your minds may be led astray from the sincerity and the purity (you have) toward Christ. 4. For if a newcomer preaches another Jesus whom we did not preach, or if you receive a different spirit whom you did not receive, or a different gospel that you did not accept, you tolerate (that person) well enough.

5. But I think that I am in no way inferior to these super-apostles. 6. Even if I am unskilled in speech, (I am) certainly not in knowledge; but we have made (that) clear to you in every way and in all things. 7. Or did I commit a sin in humbling myself so that you may be exalted, in that I preached the gospel of God free of charge? 8. I robbed other churches by taking support in order to serve you, 9. and while I was with you and had become needy, I did not burden anyone, for the brothers who had come from Macedonia supplied what I still needed. I kept and will keep myself from being a burden to you in every respect. 10. The truth of Christ is in me: this boasting will never be stifled in me in the regions of Achaia. 11. Why? Because I do not love you? God knows (that I do). 12. What I am doing I will also continue to do in order that I may take away the opportunity from those who desire (such) an opportunity to be regarded as our equals in what they are boasting about.

13. For such people (are) false apostles, deceitful workers who are disguising themselves as apostles of Christ. 14. And no wonder, for Satan himself disguises himself as an angel of light. 15. It is no great (thing), then, if his servants too disguise themselves as servants of righteousness; their end will be according to their works.

NOTES

1. *If only you would tolerate me in a little foolishness:* Paul begins this new pericope by expressing an unfulfillable wish (*ophelon:* "if only"). In this construction the imperfect *aneichesthe* (literally "you tolerated") refers to the present. V. 1b, however, will modify this unattainability and show that in fact Paul regards his wish as realizable. One could take the *mou* as qualifying the expression "a little foolishness." In this case the whole phrase *mou mikron ti aphrosynēs* is the direct object of the verb. The translation of v. 1a then would be "if only you would tolerate a little foolishness of mine." Yet in v. 1b *mou* ("me") goes with the verb "to tolerate" and therefore most probably this is the case also in v. 1a. The vocabulary of "foolishness" occurs here for the first time in chs. 10–13.

   yes, do tolerate me: Depending on whether *anechesthe* is considered to be an imperative or an indicative, the meaning of *alla* differs: "yes (copulative force), do tolerate me," or "but in truth (adversative force), you already tolerate me." An imperative is more likely here. The *kai* ("and") emphasizes the following verb; hence our translation: "do" tolerate me.

2. *For I am jealous for you with God's jealousy:* "Jealousy" is meant here rather than "zeal." The term pertains to the marriage imagery that is clearly dominant in

the remainder of v. 2. Paul's jealousy for the Corinthians is not on his own behalf; his jealousy is God's jealousy ("of God" is more than just a Hebrew genitive: "divine" jealousy). God is involved in this matter. We are reminded of the OT language that depicts Israel as the bride of YHWH (cf., for example, Isaiah 50, 54; Jeremiah 3; Ezekiel 16; Hosea 1–3).

because I betrothed you to one husband in order to present you as a chaste virgin to Christ: The emphatic dative "to one husband" goes with the verb "I betrothed" (a middle with active meaning, used here not of betrothing oneself, but of betrothing another person); "to Christ" depends on "to present," which is an infinitive of purpose.

Paul's jealousy is qualified by two facts. One lies in the past (the betrothal), one in the future: the presentation (for marriage). We should think of two specific moments in the Christian life: conversion (baptism) and Parousia (encounter with Christ). Paul's jealousy consists in his watching over the bride's conduct in the interval between betrothal and marriage. According to Jewish custom betrothal (with solemn promise) is already part of the "marriage," although the bride's introduction into the home of the bridegroom has not yet taken place. The church at Corinth lives in a nuptial state between its inchoative and completed phases (see Infante, "Immagine"). It is true that the Lord is present in both historical memory and the immediate encounter with the Spirit; yet in addition the present Spirit is the betrothal gift, a pledge that the wedding will be performed at the Parousia.

3. *But I am afraid that somehow, just as the serpent deceived Eve by his cunning:* Note Paul's pastoral concern. In view of 11:14 one may probably assume that Paul identifies the serpent with Satan (cf. Wis 2:24). Alternatively the serpent could also be Satan's representative. In Gen 3:1 the text says that the serpent *ēpatēsen* ("betrays"). Paul employs the compound *exapateō* ("to deceive," which in this context means "to cause disobedience to God's command"). There is no agreement among scholars as to whether Paul is alluding to the Jewish Haggadah on the paradise narrative according to which the serpent seduced Eve to unchastity and infidelity. The term *panourgia* ("craftiness, cunning") is an abusive word. Paul uses it to refer to Genesis 3, but perhaps also to contemporaneous practices among sophists and religious propagandists.

your minds may be led astray from the sincerity and the purity (you have) toward Christ: In the manuscripts there are two long readings ("sincerity and purity" or "purity and sincerity") and two short ones ("sincerity" or "purity"). In Greek the two words are almost the same; only the second and third letters are different, and as capital letters very slightly different: *haplotēs, hagnotēs.* The origin of the longer reading could be a sort of dittography (*APL* and *AGN*). However, in view of such witnesses as 𝔓⁴⁶, ℵ*, B, and 33 the first longer reading is often retained, although with some hesitation.

The term "minds" is not to be taken as a purely intellectual notion. "Sincerity" points to an attachment and devotion of the whole person. "May be led astray from" may have a moral connotation. This translation renders rather freely a contracted construction. A literal translation would read "may be corrupted away from." The passive form without indication of the expected agent (the serpent) has perhaps been chosen on purpose, since in vv. 13-15 there will be visible, human agents. The paraphrastic translation with "(you have) toward" respects the attributive construction *tēs eis ton Christon*.

4. *For if a newcomer preaches another Jesus whom we did not preach, or if you receive a different spirit whom you did not receive, or a different gospel that you did not accept:* The lengthy conditional period of v. 4 is a *realis*. The *men* ("on the one hand") has no corresponding *de* ("on the other hand"). Note the variations within the repetition:

> if a newcomer preaches another Jesus
>   whom we did not preach,
> or if you receive a different spirit
>   whom you did not receive,
> or a different gospel
>   that you did not accept.

There is a change of persons (from third singular and first plural to second plural), a shift from *allos* ("another") to *heteros* ("different"), probably without a change of meaning (otherwise in Gal 1:6-7), and also a shift from *lambanō* ("to receive") to *dechomai* ("to accept"), again probably without a change of meaning. The singular *ho erchomenos* ("the coming one") may point back to the singular in 10:7, 10, 11 (a ringleader among the opponents? So Barrett, "Paul's Opponents") or may rather be generic. The past tenses refer to the time of the Corinthians' conversion. The triad "Jesus, spirit, gospel" does not occur elsewhere in Paul's letters. It remains difficult to guess exactly what Paul means by "another Jesus." We quote from the summary of an article by Jerome Murphy-O'Connor who, however, could be overinterpreting the expression: "In addition to connoting the earthly existence of Christ, 'Jesus' in 2 Cor 11:4 carries the specific nuance of humiliation and suffering culminating in death. Paul uses it to counteract the propaganda of those whose distaste for a crucified Christ led them to invent 'another Jesus'" ("'Another Jesus,'" 238). "Another Jesus" implies, of course, a "different spirit" and a "different gospel." Is the Jesus of the opponents (only) the risen Lord of glory, their "spirit" (only) one of power and ecstasy, their "gospel" a message that neglects the cross? Many commentators explain v. 4 along these lines, but one must not lose sight of the hypothetical elements in such a reconstruction.

you tolerate (that person) well enough: The manuscripts are divided as to the tense of the verb. If the imperfect (א, vg, and other manuscripts) is to be accepted it should be taken as an *irrealis:* "you would tolerate him well enough." Yet since the protasis is a *realis*, a *realis* in the apodosis as well is more probable and so the present (𝔓⁴⁶ B D* 33) should be preferred here (cf. the same construction in 11:20). The unexpressed direct object could be "the newcomer," *ho erchomenos*, of the first clause.

5. *But I think that I am in no way inferior to these super-apostles:* It is tempting to suggest that an ellipsis regarding the *gar* ("for") at the beginning should be postulated: "(bear also with me), for. . . ." Sometimes, however, the particle *gar* possesses an adversative nuance; cf. our translation "but." The position of

"in no way" is emphatic in the Greek text. The phrase *hoi hyperlian apostoloi* ("the super-apostles") recurs in 12:11. It is possible that *hyperlian* (literally "abundantly") was current in colloquial language; however, according to Alfred Plummer *(Commentary)* Paul himself may have coined this term. These super-apostles are most probably not the apostles of Jerusalem or the leaders among the Twelve, but the intruders in Corinth of whom Paul speaks in v. 4. The perfect *hysterēkenai* ("to have fallen short") points to past and continuous inferiority.

6. *Even if I am unskilled in speech, (I am) certainly not in knowledge:* The grammatical construction is somewhat irregular. The two clauses, protasis and apodosis, both lack a verb. The first *alla* ("but") in v. 6b introduces the *apodosis* and reinforces what follows; hence our translation: "certainly." Originally *idiōtēs* referred to those who confined themselves to their own affairs *(ta idia)* and did not take part in public life. Later it came to mean a person without training or skill. The expression "unskilled in speech" is possibly a slogan used by the opponents that Paul takes up and admits. Hans Dieter Betz *(Der Apostel Paulus)*, however, is of the opinion that the expression belongs to Paul's own language (cf. the same opinion with regard to 10:1b).

Paul Barnett claims that Paul's "verbal skills must have been, at the very least, adequate, and, quite possibly, considerable, even though he lacked the high professionalism of the trained rhetorician" *(Second Epistle* 510). There are, however, commentators who think that Paul is referring here to a physical or psychological impediment in speech; some of them even suggest that this is the very "thorn in the flesh" mentioned in 12:7.

The distinction between "word, speech" (form) and "knowledge" (content) is possibly anti-sophistic, as in its use by Cynic philosophers (so Betz, *Der Apostel Paulus*). Or was Paul responding to the pretension of "gnosticizing" opponents who thought that they alone possessed true wisdom? One should not, of course, too hastily characterize Paul's rivals as "gnostic."

but we have made (that) clear to you in every way and in all things: Plural ("we") and singular ("I") clash in this v. 6. The plural participle of v. 6c ("having made clear," literally: "having manifested") could be regarded as in apposition to the subject of the verb that is to be supplied in v. 6b ("I am"). Yet it would seem, also in view of the plural, that with the second *alla* ("but") an independent sentence begins. One should take the participle as absolute, i.e., as the equivalent of a finite verb in the indicative: "we have made clear." Some assume that the text of this clause is corrupt. A direct object must be supplied. So a clause could be added: we have made clear "that we are not without knowledge," or perhaps a personal object: we manifested "ourselves." Note that the phrase *en panti* ("in every way") is frequently employed in 2 Corinthians (4:8; 6:4; 7:5, 16; 8:7; 9:8, 11; 11:9). As far as the content of the clause is concerned, see 4:2.

7. *Or did I commit a sin in humbling myself so that you may be exalted:* The change of topic is abrupt. Paul uses strong, sarcastic language. It seems probable that by this rhetorical question he is answering a charge brought forward in Corinth against him. Paul's opponents and the Corinthians may have despised

the apostle because he refused maintenance and was doing manual labor. This verse and Rom 4:8 are the only instances where Paul uses *hamartia* in the singular to refer to an *Einzelsünde,* a particular sin, not sin as such or personified sin. "Sin" here may point to his alleged lack of love (cf. v. 11) or to disobedience to a saying of the Lord (cf. 1 Cor 9:14), though the language may simply be ironical.

Tapeinōn ("humbling"; cf. 10:1b: *tapeinos*) is to be taken in a negative sense. It is perhaps a reference to Paul's physical work, which in Corinth might have been regarded as a humiliating occupation. The nature of the corresponding exaltation on the part of the Corinthians is not clear. The contrasting terms "to humble/to exalt" occur in a saying of Jesus (Luke 14:11; 18:14; Matt 23:12); see also Phil 2:8-9 in the christological hymn (with the compound *hyperypsoō,* however). Paul may be alluding to these passages, or one of them, yet in those references, in contrast to what we have in 2 Cor 11:7, it is the same person who humbled himself or herself and is later exalted. The emphatic "you" manifests the missionary aim of Paul's conduct.

in that I preached the gospel of God free of charge? The particle *hoti* can be taken as dependent on "did I commit a sin." Then it explains wherein the sin consists ("in that I . . ."). Otherwise, it might give the reason why there could be a sin ("because I . . ."). The clause may possibly be considered an illustration of "lowering oneself": Paul's act of humbling himself is his preaching for nothing (together with his manual work?). The position in the original Greek of both "of God" and "free of charge" is emphatic, and the repetitive sequence *euangelion euēngelisamēn* ("I preached the gospel") is by no means accidental.

8. *I robbed other churches by taking support in order to serve you:* The verb *sylaō* ("to rob") is very strong and used here ironically; it is a *hapax legomenon* in the NT. (Cf. *hierosyleō* in Rom 2:22, "to rob temples"). Together with *opsōnion* ("wages") it suggests military language: we are reminded of 10:3-6 and of 1 Cor 9:7a ("Who serves as a soldier at his own expense?"). The plural "churches" (in Macedonia; cf. v. 9) is somewhat strange in the light of Phil 4:15-16 where it is said that Philippi is the only exception in the matter of support ("no church . . . except you only").

9. *and while I was with you and had become needy, I did not burden anyone:* The verb *katanarkaō* (with genitive) may originally have been a medical term ("to stupefy, to make slow and insensible"), but here it seems to mean "to burden, to weigh down." See the apparently parallel expression in v. 9c: *abarē emauton . . . etērēsa* (literally: "I kept myself 'not heavy'"). The only other occurrences of this verb in the New Testament are in 12:13, 14. The aorist tense is global; it refers to the whole of Paul's stay in Corinth.

for the brothers who had come from Macedonia supplied what I still needed: We may here refer to Phil 2:25 and 4:10-20. The first preposition in the compound *pros-ana-plēroō* ("to supply 'in addition'") probably alludes to Paul's own earning activity, which seems to have been insufficient for his needs. Hence the "still" in the translation.

I kept and will keep myself from being a burden to you in every respect: "From being a burden" renders *abarēs* ("not burdensome"), a *hapax legomenon* in the whole Greek Bible. Compare, however, 1 Thess 2:9 (*pros to mē epibarēsai tina hymōn:* "in order not to burden any of you," also in 2 Thess 3:8).

10. *The truth of Christ is in me: this boasting will never be stifled in me in the regions of Achaia:* Verse 10a probably contains an oath formula. Cf. Rom 9:1: "I am speaking the truth in Christ" and 2 Cor 1:18: "God is faithful." We note the noun "boasting" and the verb "to boast" in v. 12 (cf. 10:8 and 10:12-18); the boasting terminology will become very important in what follows, from 11:16 onwards.

The verb *phrassō* means "to dam (a river), to barricade (a road)"; hence "to stop (a mouth), to silence." Cf. Rom 3:19: "so that every mouth may be stopped." The explicit mention of "Achaia" could suggest that Achaia is the only region where Paul has radically refused support. (But cf. Phil 4:15, which, however, is not too clear: "and you Philippians yourselves know that in the beginning of the gospel, when I left Macedonia, no church entered into partnership with me in giving and receiving except you only"; is the emphasis on "in the beginning"?)

11. *Why? Because I do not love you? God knows (that I do):* The style is elliptic. The first, false reason may reflect a Corinthian misunderstanding of Paul and/or a suggestion of the opponents. God knows that he cares about the Corinthians! The language is very emotional. The asseveration formula "God knows" adds emphasis (cf. 11:31; 12:2, 3).

12. *What I am doing I will also continue to do:* Verse 12 concludes the section on Paul's refusal of recompense. It answers the question with which v. 11 began: "why"? After the negation in v. 11 Paul presents the real reason in v. 12. The motivation mentions the opponents and thus v. 12 can also be considered a transition to the invectives against the false apostles in vv. 13-15. One could translate v. 12a in two different ways: "What I am doing I will also continue to do in order that I take away . . ." or (less correctly, it would seem): "What I am doing and will also continue to do (is intended) that I may take away. . . ." Furthermore, what does *ho* ("what") in the first rendering refer to?—to v. 11 (Paul's love) or, almost certainly, to vv. 7-10 (i.e., his refusal of support)?

in order that I may take away the opportunity from those who desire (such) an opportunity to be regarded as our equals in what they are boasting about: "in order that I may take away" and "to be regarded" each translate a *hina* ("in order that"); both v. 12b and v. 12c are thus purpose clauses. According to the understanding of this translation the second *hina* clause is not parallel to the first. Verse 12c depends on "who want (such) an opportunity" in v. 12b. It must be conceded that the grammar of this lengthy sentence is strained to the utmost, yet the text as it stands does make sense. There is no reason for supposing it corrupt, as some interpreters do.

The commentators who defend the parallelism between v. 12c and v. 12b see in both clauses the expression of Paul's intention. The second purpose clause, then, clarifies the first: Paul's intention with his refusal of support (v. 12a) is to take away from his opponents the opportunity they want to have (v. 12b), i.e., to force them in the matter of boasting to become ("to be found") as he is (v. 12c). Yet within the whole context there is nothing that leads one to assume a Paul who tries to reform his enemies so that they too will refuse support.

Grammatically speaking the clause "those who want an opportunity" in v. 12b requires a complement. This is given in 12c, which therefore depends on v. 12b. Verse 12c expresses the intention not of Paul but of the opponents. According to this preferable (and first) interpretation one has to suppose that the boasting of the opponents concerns their social position in Corinth. By accepting gifts and money from the Corinthians they cultivate friendship with them; in this way they honor the appreciation of the hosts. The opponents would like Paul to act in the same way and thus become their equal. By preaching free of charge, however, he takes away that opportunity.

Nonetheless, it is true that v. 12c remains strange. Both the aorist tense and the third person plural (*heuretōsin*, "be found") would seem to point to the opponents' entrance into a new state. But this idea is not at all suggested by the context. Paul has perhaps been somewhat imprecise in his writing here.

13. *For such people (are) false apostles, deceitful workers who are disguising themselves as apostles of Christ:* Hans Windisch (*Zweite Korintherbrief*) calls vv. 13-15 a *Scheltrede* (invective). Persons of this kind (grammatical subject) are false apostles (= predicate). The term *pseudapostoloi*, perhaps coined by Paul himself, can mean either an apostle who is not really an apostle, or a (so-called) apostle who speaks what is false and proclaims a "different" gospel, or both. The qualification that follows in this verse explains what is meant by the term "false apostles."

In 1 Cor 4:6 the same verb *metaschēmatizomai* occurs; its exact meaning there is debated. In Phil 3:21 Paul uses it to speak of the transformation of the body. In 2 Cor 11:13 the meaning is clearly pejorative; the voice is middle: "fashioning themselves, disguising themselves." While in 10:7 Paul seems to accept that the opponents belong to Christ, here and in vv. 14-15, their real identity is manifest.

14. *And no wonder, for Satan himself disguises himself as an angel of light:* The Jewish Haggadah is mentioned in the Notes on v. 3, although with hesitation. Here its influence is more probable. The references to Satan changing himself into the form of an angel, or wearing the brightness of an angel, are found in the *Apocalypse of Moses* 17.1-2 and the *Life of Adam and Eve* 9.1.

15. *It is no great (thing), then, if his servants too disguise themselves as servants of righteousness:* Compare the introductory clause *ou mega* ("no great [thing]") with the phrase at the beginning of v. 14 (*ou thauma*, "no wonder"). The reasoning pattern is *a fortiori*. Such a *qal waḥomer* ("light and heavy") is a well-known rabbinic argumentation. Note the construction *hōs diakonoi* ("as servants"), different from that with *eis* (literally "into") with the accusative in vv. 13 and 14. After "his servants" ("his" referring to Satan) one expects servants "of

Christ" rather than "of righteousness." It is difficult to decide whether this last genitive is descriptive (like "of light" in v. 14?), thus "righteous servants," or objective, "servants who serve righteousness." The typically Pauline sense of righteousness, i.e., justification, is not present here. Many commentators hold that in Corinth the opponents called themselves "apostles" and "workers" (v. 13), and "servants" (v. 15). Peter Marshall *(Enmity)* maintains that not properly naming the enemies is a rhetorical device.

their end will be according to their works: This eschatological statement at the end contains a hidden threat. Compare 5:10 where Paul also concludes a paragraph with a reference to the judgment. For similar expressions see Rom 2:6 and Phil 3:19. One cannot but be surprised by Paul's outburst in vv. 13-15, and by the bitter, severe language of this invective.

INTERPRETATION

a. *Structure and Line of Thought.* The internal division of 11:1-15 is often made at vv. 7 and 12, so that the three small text units would be vv. 1-6, vv. 7-11, and vv. 12-15. This presentation, however, may be questioned, and in any case one could ask whether a too strict structuring is appropriate for Paul's lively and heated style here.

The line of thought in 11:1-6 is rather unclear. Verses 2, 4, and 5 are each introduced by the particle *gar* ("for"). According to Rudolf Bultmann *(Second Letter* 200–201) and C. K. Barrett, for example, these verses give the three grounds for Paul's appeal in v. 1. Barrett paraphrases the text as follows: "I ask you to put up with me: for I am, and have reason to be, really concerned about you (v. 3); for you put up with a false apostle who preaches a false Gospel (v. 4); for I am equal to the highest apostles of all (v. 5)" *(Commentary,* 278). Against this interpretation the following data should be noted. (1) In vv. 2-4 Paul is actually not boasting of himself. His boasting starts in vv. 5-6 (I am not inferior to the super-apostles and I do possess knowledge); it continues in vv. 7-10. (2) To be sure, in v. 7 the theme of boasting changes, but the *ē* ("or") connection between v. 6 and v. 7 does not represent a major break. Preaching the gospel without cost to the Corinthians (v. 7) could be regarded as a proof and example of his openness (v. 6b). (3) Moreover, with *anechesthe* ("you tolerate"), the concluding word of v. 4, Paul rounds off the unit he opened in v. 1 with the same verb and motif. For these reasons it might seem preferable to assume a (small) caesura after v. 4, and to read vv. 5-6 together with vv. 7-10 (although the mention of the "super-apostles" and possibly the *gar*—see Notes—in v. 5 might seem to link this verse with v. 4).

In v. 10 Paul solemnly states that he will not change his behavior (cf. already v. 9bc). Thereafter, in vv. 11-12, he provides the motivation: v. 11 rejects a false explanation and v. 12 presents the real reason. Both verses belong together, and likewise both, structurally speaking, depend on v. 10. Moreover, the future "I will . . . continue to do" in v. 12 corresponds to the future "I will keep" in v. 9c; "boasting" in v. 12 reminds the reader of "this boasting" in v. 10. Notwithstanding the fact that v. 12 is also transitional—the opponents spoken of in vv. 3-4 reappear here already, see vv. 13-15—it seems better not to separate v. 12 from v. 11 and, furthermore, to connect both verses with the "boasting unit" of vv. 7-10.

The pericope 11:1-15 thus consists of three minor sections: vv. 1-4; vv. 5-12; and vv. 13-15. The structure can be seen as concentric: *a–b–a'*. The *a–a'* elements have a number of striking similarities which characterize them as corresponding and including parts:

a	*a'*
v. 3: "the serpent,"	cf. v. 14: "Satan"
v. 3: idea of deceiving,	cf. vv. 13-15: idea of falseness
v. 4: opponent,	cf. vv. 13-15: opponents.

However, the differences between *a* and *a'* should not be overlooked. On the one hand, in *a* Paul addresses the Corinthians with an appeal; using the betrothal imagery he points to his apostolic relationship to them and expresses his fears concerning them. The opponent (singular) is spoken of only in function of this appeal and of the danger he poses for the Corinthians. The whole of *a'*, on the other hand, is devoted to a depiction of the opponents (plural) and their methods. The second person plural has given way to the third person plural. The middle unit *b* is rather long: vv. 5-12. The subject matter is twofold: Paul's knowledge (vv. 5-6) and Paul's refusal of support (vv. 7-12). These last verses should be divided into three subsections: Paul explains his past behavior (vv. 7-9); Paul formulates his intention concerning his future behavior (v. 10); and Paul motivates this way of acting (vv. 11-12).

In the treatment above of the structure of 11:1-15 much has already been said regarding the line of thought. One could characterize the paragraph 11:1-15 by stressing that it has still something of an introductory function *vis-à-vis* the remainder of chs. 11 and 12. Although there is already boasting on the part of Paul (and therefore foolishness), the really foolish boasting will take place in subsequent passages like 11:22-23 and 12:2-4, and the corresponding theme of weakness will only appear in 11:30-33 and 12:5-10. In 11:1-15 Paul is still defending himself in an indirect, polemical way, comparing himself with his opponents, and also reproaching the Corinthians.

In vv. 1-4 the appeal to the Corinthians to bear with him looks forward to Paul's later boasting. Paul motivates this appeal by referring to what he has done for them: he betrothed the Corinthians to one husband in order to present them (at the parousia) as a pure virgin to their husband, to Christ. However, he is afraid that they will abandon their sincere devotion to Christ, for they readily bear with the person who preaches another Jesus and they readily receive and accept a different spirit and gospel. Paul's pastoral care comes to the fore here. His reproach is meant as an exhortation to the Corinthians to abandon their wrong attitude. Note that the *gar* ("for, since") of v. 4 could have a double function: it could motivate the appeal of v. 1 (you should submit to me *since* you submit to that other person), and it could (at the same time?) expound and motivate Paul's fear (v. 3) that the Corinthians will be led astray. For our understanding of the betrothal image and the characterization of the different Christ, gospel and spirit, see the Notes.

In vv. 5-12 Paul says of himself that he is not unskilled in knowledge; he also emphasizes that in the regions of Achaia he was and is and will be unwilling to charge the faithful for his preaching. Many commentators assume that Paul is responding here to accusations brought against him. The opponents (and some Corinthians under their influence) must have regarded Paul as inferior because his speaking was poor and, so they thought, his knowledge as well. Were the same opponents, or above all the Corinthians, also thinking less of Paul because he refused to accept (financial and material) support? It would seem that to a certain extent these verses can be used to reconstruct a historical picture of the opponents (see b). The tone is decidedly apologetical and self-confident.

In vv. 13-15 the catchword is the verb *metaschēmatizomai* ("to disguise oneself"), which links the opposing characterizations:

v. 13: false apostles	apostles of Christ
v. 14: Satan	angel of light
v. 15: servants (of Satan)	servants of righteousness.

Verses 13-15 are very much like an angry outburst. They contain an attack against the opponents that interrupts the flow of the discourse. In vv. 16-20 Paul will return to his main theme: cf. the vocabulary that links up with that of 11:1-12: foolish, a little, to boast (v. 16); foolishness, boast (v. 17); to boast (v. 18); foolish, to bear with (v. 19 and v. 20). Regarding vv. 13-15 one might, therefore, ask to what degree Paul has been carried away by his anger. This is hardly an objective descriptive language, completely true to what the opponents really were. In vv. 22-23 of the same chapter Paul will call them not only Hebrews, Israelites, and descendants of Abraham but also "servants of Christ." Strangely enough, he does not seem to refuse them this last title.

The pericope 2 Cor 11:1-15 is the first within chs. 10–13 in which the term "foolishness" (*aphrosynē*) occurs: see v. 1. The term, or one of its cognates, is thereafter repeated quite frequently in chs. 11 and 12: see 11:16, 17, 19, 21 and 12:6, 11. Paul is foolish because he is going to boast. The glorying of 10:8, 12-18, based on Paul's vocation and his apostolic authority, is somewhat different from what he will boast of in chs. 11 and 12.

b. *The Opponents.* In 11:1-15 Paul mentions the opponents at two points: see vv. 4-5 and vv. 13-15. This is the first time in chs. 10–13 (yet see 10:12) that some particular characteristics of the opponents are so clearly pointed out. The portrait of the opponents thus takes on a more concrete form. To be sure, the identification of Paul's opponents remains a difficult and hazardous task (also because of the lack of information concerning the situation in Corinth). Yet in this passage Paul depicts the opponents as people who by their preaching of another Jesus, a different spirit, and a different gospel corrupt the minds (and moral life?) of the Corinthians. (For a hypothetical reconstruction, see the Notes.) They are false apostles, deceitful workers, servants of Satan who change themselves to look like apostles of Christ. In light of Paul's attack in 11:13-15 and, more particularly, of 11:12 one may assume that these apostles were also opposed to Paul on the question of remuneration. They could not have criticized Paul for refusing maintenance unless they accepted it themselves. Furthermore, because of Paul's insistence on his not burdening the Corinthians and in light of expressions such as are present in 11:20, we are led to see the opponents as people who, in defending their right of maintenance by the church, behaved in a covetous and greedy way. It is not unlikely that these opponents disguised their objectionable attitude by means of accusations against Paul and by their defense of a different understanding of apostleship.

c. *Theological Reflection.* In speaking of his refraining from burdening the Corinthians, Paul strikingly contrasts the concepts "sinning" and "boasting" (11:7 and 10). What the Corinthians could neither accept nor approve was for Paul precisely a reason for glorying. The two positions are opposite. What is the specific background of this difference of approach? What are Paul's motivations for his personal behavior? Paul treats the matter of financial support in other passages besides 2 Cor 11:7-12. An exhaustive survey of the relevant texts should involve 1 Thess 2:5-12; 1 Cor 9:1-23 (perhaps also 1:12); 2 Cor 11:7-12 and 12:13-18; Phil 4:10-20 (cf. also 2 Thess 3:7-9). Besides these Pauline data, mention must also be made of Acts 20:33-35, the conclusion of Paul's farewell discourse at Miletus, where he stopped on his way back to Jerusalem at the end of his third missionary journey and addressed the elders of the church of Ephesus. Finally, there is the saying of Jesus that is to be found in both Matt 10:10b and Luke 10:7b (and "quoted" by Paul in 1 Cor 9:14: "the Lord commanded that those who proclaim the gospel should get their living by the gospel"). We shall mainly focus here on the Corinthian correspondence.

First Corinthians 9 is part of a larger unit that runs from 8:1 to 11:1 and deals with the topic "food sacrificed to idols." Are Christians permitted to eat such food? This matter was heatedly discussed. There were two positions, that of those who had "knowledge" and felt free to eat, and that of those whose "weak" conscience led them to think that such eating was prohibited. Paul himself has "knowledge," but for him this is not the whole matter. Love is more important than knowledge. Out of consideration for the weak brothers and sisters Christians must be prepared not to use their rights, their freedom and privileges. In ch. 9 Paul goes on speaking of himself. He mentions the rights of the apostles and shows how he himself refrains from using them. Paul thus limits his apostolic liberty for the sake of the gospel. Similarly the Corinthians who have knowledge are to imitate Paul by limiting, for the sake of love, their own freedom regarding eating food sacrificed to idols, i.e., by laying no stumbling-block before the weak brothers and sisters. In 1 Corinthians 9 Paul first defends the apostles' right to support (vv. 4-12a and 13-14). Four different arguments are adduced: human analogies (v. 7), Scripture (vv. 8-12a), religious practice (v. 13) and a saying of the Lord (v. 14). In vv. 12b and 15-23, Paul then provides four other reasons for his renunciation of that right: no obstacle is to be put in the way of the gospel (v. 12b), renunciation is a ground for boasting (vv. 15-18), it gives Paul freedom for adaptation (vv. 19-22); finally, he briefly mentions his personal salvation (v. 23).

Second Corinthians 11:7-12 is both similar to 1 Corinthians 9 and different from it. The following data are parallel. In both passages it is explicitly stated that Paul preaches the gospel for nothing. (Compare v. 7b with 1 Cor 9:18b). In both passages Paul says that this way of evangelizing is his ground for boasting (compare the boasting terminology in v. 10 and v. 12 with that of 1 Cor 9:15-16). In both texts, too, Paul indicates his firm decision not to change his behavior in the future (compare vv. 10 and 12 with 1 Cor 9:15). Yet divergent data must also be listed. First, differently from 1 Corinthians 9, Paul in 2 Corinthians 11 does not explicitly mention his manual labor (but are there allusions in vv. 7 and 9?). Second, in 2 Cor 11:8-10, Paul admits that he received support from "other churches," from "Macedonia." In v. 9 he mentions his needs during his (long!) stay in Corinth. This seems to imply that the earnings from his manual work were not sufficient. Nothing is said about this in 1 Corinthians 9 (but see Phil 4:14-19). Third, only in 2 Cor 11:10 is mention made of the restriction "in the regions of Achaia." Paul's decision not to burden the Christians is thus not so radical or general as the reader of 1 Corinthians 9 might have supposed. "The regions of Achaia" are not to be taken in too strict a sense (cf. 1 Thess 2:9). Fourth, from 2 Cor 11:7, 11 it is obvious that there was opposition to Paul's rejection of his right to support in Corinth. This opposition is not so evident in 1 Corinthians 9, and were it not for 2 Corinthians one would hardly think of it. Fifth, although already in 1 Cor 9:3 ("this is my defense to those who would examine me") criticism with regard to Paul's apostleship comes to the surface, the role of the opponents in this matter is much more obvious in 2 Cor 11:12 (and throughout the whole letter). In 11:12, moreover, Paul gives an additional reason for his refusal to use the right to support: he wants to distance himself from his opponents. Sixth, in 2 Corinthians 11 there is no reflection on the foundation of the apostle's right to maintenance such as is amply given in 1 Cor 9:3-14.

Second Corinthians 12:13-18, finally, is very much like 11:7-12. In 12:13 Paul refers to other churches and at the same time points to Corinth's special situation. In the same verse the clause "forgive me this injustice" recalls the beginning of 11:7 "did I commit a sin?" In 12:14 Paul restates his intention concerning his future attitude. The theme of "love of the Corinthians," which was mentioned in 11:11, reappears in 12:15. Yet there are also new elements: the image of the parents in 12:14 (cf. 1 Thess 2:7 and 11, "mother" and father), the collection (from 12:16-18 it would seem that its organization has been misunderstood by some Christians), and, in 12:19a, the apology terminology (cf. 1 Cor 9:3).

The situation of the church in Corinth must have changed after 1 Corinthians, and this forced Paul in 2 Corinthians to speak of his preaching for nothing two times. The Corinthian Christians now appear to be influenced by the activity of intruders. Paul has to defend his apostleship, more specifically his own conception of true apostleship. What were the charges against Paul and why did he refuse support from the Corinthians?

Because Paul stresses disinterestedness and the absence of greed as well as his strong determination not to burden the churches we might think that the reproach concerned the support itself, i.e., the heavy "burden" it brought with it for the Corinthians. However, at least in 1 and 2 Corinthians the whole drift of the texts betrays no such opposition. In the light of 2 Cor 12:16-18 it would seem that some people in Corinth did not trust Paul in connection with the collection. While they had to admit that Paul himself was not a burden, they still regarded him as insincere, as one who used indirect methods to defraud his Christians. Although it is possible that such an accusation was in fact leveled against Paul, we have most probably not yet reached the real point of the animosity against him. Moreover, Hans Dieter Betz, who is not willing to accept the existence of these first two charges *(Der Apostel Paulus),* cautions us that according to the rules of rhetoric Paul's defense against accusations that were not made against him may be meant as an insinuation aimed at his opponents.

The Corinthians seem to have been humiliated because Paul refused to accept their support. They took it as a proof of his lack of love for them. They may also have despised him precisely because he preached for nothing; as a missionary he should have requested financial remuneration in order to show the importance of his preaching. Other legitimate missionaries acted in this way. And there is, of course, the word of Jesus (cf. 1 Cor 9:14). Gerd Theissen notes: "Whether Paul is coming to terms with the followers of Peter and Apollos in 1 Corinthians or with newly arrived missionaries in 2 Corinthians, in either case he must defend himself against the charge that he did not act like a real apostle and allow himself to be supported by the community . . ." ("Legitimation," 40–41). Theissen also stresses—perhaps in an exaggerated way—the "apostolic duty," i.e., "the obligation of missionaries to practice charismatic poverty." Paul's "work as a craftsman displays a lack of trust." Of course, charismatic poverty could not be practiced without financial and material support. Paul has "offended against the norm of the primitive Christian ideal of itinerant charismatics set down by Jesus himself" ("Legitimation," 43). Yet times and circumstances have changed. Besides this original type of missionary rooted in rural, Palestinian soil there are now also the "community organizers" such as Paul and Barnabas, "a type which is firmly established in the urban, Hellenistic world." They do not claim support but are dependent on their manual labor (cf. "Legitimation," 57–58). Corinth does not agree with this evolution.

Peter Marshall analyzes the Pauline text with the assumption that Paul's strained relationship with the Corinthians can partly be explained in terms of Graeco-Roman conventions. He sees Paul's refusal of the Corinthians' gifts—their support—as a rejection of their friendship. "Paul, by his refusal, had shamed and dishonoured them and was held to be responsible for the hostilities which followed" (*Enmity*, 177). Paul's enemies in Corinth must have associated themselves with the rival apostles, the intruders; it was a hostile alliance. Furthermore, it is not unlikely that the fact that Paul accepted assistance from other churches was a sort of slap in the face to the Corinthians, which they might have called a "sin" and an "injury." Marshall's conclusions should be duly considered, notwithstanding their inevitably hypothetical character.

d. *Actualization.* Modern readers ask themselves about Paul's example and its possible inspiration for ministers today. The data of Paul's letters show that "no support" was not a rule to be observed always and everywhere, yet the Corinthian correspondence sets before all of us a Paul who is radical to the extreme. In 1 Cor 9:12 he writes: "we have not made use of this right (= of support), but we endure anything rather than put an obstacle in the way of the gospel of Christ." Paul's motivation must have had a thoroughly apostolic dimension (cf. also 9:19-23).

The deepest motive, however, is still to be uncovered. Apparently the gospel itself demanded this concrete lifestyle from Paul. For him such behavior was much more than an apostolic strategy. The ultimate justification of his attitude was christological. A concrete pattern of ministerial life, even, if necessary, to the point of refusing support, was experienced by Paul as a condition for his "belonging to Christ" (2 Cor 10:7).

FOR REFERENCE AND FURTHER STUDY

Barrett, C. K. "Paul's Opponents in II Corinthians" in idem, *Essays on Paul*. London: S.P.C.K., 1982, 60–86.

_____. "*PSEUDAPOSTOLOI* (2 Cor. 11.13)" in idem, *Essays on Paul*. London: S.P.C.K., 1982, 87–107.

Caragounis, Chrys C. "*OPSŌNION:* A Reconsideration of Its Meaning," *NT* 16 (1974) 35–57.

Fee, Gordon D. "'Another gospel which you did not embrace': 2 Corinthians 11.4 and the Theology of 1 and 2 Corinthians" in L. Ann Jervis and Peter Richardson, eds., *Gospel in Paul. Studies on Corinthians, Galatians and Romans. FS for Richard N. Longenecker*. JSNT.S 108. Sheffield: Sheffield Academic Press, 1994, 111–133.

Infante, Renzo. "Immagine nuziale e tensione escatologica nel Nuovo Testamento. Note a 2 Cor. 11,2 e Eph. 5,25-27," *RivBib* 33 (1985) 45–61.

McClelland, Scott E. "'Super-Apostles, Servants of Christ, Servants of Satan,'" *JSNT* 14 (1982) 82–87.

Marshall, Peter. *Enmity in Corinth: Social Conventions in Paul's Relation with the Corinthians*. WUNT II/23. Tübingen: Mohr-Siebeck, 1987.

Murphy-O'Connor, Jerome. "'Another Jesus' (2 Cor 11:4)," *RB* 97 (1990) 238–251.

Pratcher, Wilhelm. "Der Verzicht des Paulus auf finanziellen Unterhalt durch seine Gemeinden: ein Aspekt seiner Missionsweise," *NTS* 25 (1978–1979) 284–298.

Theissen, Gerd. "Legitimation and Subsistence: An Essay on the Sociology of Early Christian Missionaries" in idem, *The Social Setting of Pauline Christianity: Essays on Corinth*. Translated by J. H. Schütz. Edinburgh: T & T Clark, 1982, 27–67.

Thrall, Margaret E. "Super-Apostles, Servants of Christ, and Servants of Satan," *JSNT* 6 (1980) 42–57.

17. *Paul's Foolish Boasting* (11:16-33)

16. I repeat, let no one think that I am a fool; but if (you think) otherwise, then accept me, even if (you can accept me only) as a fool, in order that I too may boast a little. 17. What I am saying I do not say according to the Lord, but as in folly, with regard to this matter of boasting. 18. Since many boast according to the flesh, I too will boast (in the same way).

19. After all, you gladly tolerate fools since you are (so) wise! 20. For you tolerate (it) when someone enslaves you, when someone devours (you), when someone takes advantage (of you), when someone puts on airs, when someone slaps you in the face. 21. To (my) shame I admit that we have been too weak (for that).

Yet whatever anyone may dare (to boast of)—I am speaking in folly—I too dare (to boast of).

22. Are they Hebrews? So am I. Are they Israelites? So am I. Are they descendants of Abraham? So am I. 23. Are they servants of Christ?—I am talking as if out of my mind—I am more: more often in hard labor, more often in prison, with countless floggings, many times in danger of death. 24. Five times I received from the Jews the forty lashes minus one; 25. three times I was beaten with rods; once I was stoned; three times I was shipwrecked; I spent a night and a day in the open sea. 26. Often traveling, in danger from rivers, danger from robbers, danger from my fellow-countrymen, danger from Gentiles, danger in the city, danger in the wilderness, danger at sea, danger from false brethren. 27. In hard labor and toil, often without sleep, in hunger and thirst, often without food, in cold and nakedness. 28. Apart from the other things (there is) the daily pressure on me, the concern for all the churches. 29. Who is weak, and I am not weak? Who is made to fall, and I do not blaze (with indignation)?

30. If boasting there must be, I will boast of the things (that manifest) my weakness. 31. The God and Father of the Lord Jesus—he who is blessed for ever!—knows that I am not lying.

32. In Damascus the ethnarch of King Aretas was guarding the city of the Damascenes in order to arrest me, 33. and through a window in the wall I was lowered in a basket and escaped his hands.

NOTES

16. *I repeat, let no one think that I am a fool:* With "I repeat" Paul refers back to 11:1. As a matter of fact, the negative injunction that immediately follows in v. 16 ("let no one think that I am a fool") is not found in the preceding vv. 1-15. So there is no strict repetition here. The verb *doxę* ("think, suppose") is an aorist subjunctive and looks to the future. This could imply that up till now Paul has not yet acted as a fool. The Fool's Speech is yet to begin. "No one" indicates the members of the Corinthian community. Paul is indebted here to Greek categories. The true philosopher was often seen as a fool, especially by the sophists.

One might refer to the appeal in 11:1 (wish and command: "do tolerate me") and consider "I say again" as announcing a kind of repetition of that appeal, yet the content of what follows in v. 16 is different: "Let no one think that I am a fool." Grammatically speaking it is a negative purpose clause introduced by *mē* ("lest"), but it probably functions as an independent and direct prohibition. Later in v. 16 we have the command "accept me," which can be seen as the equivalent of "do tolerate me" in v. 1. Besides the themes of tolerating or accepting and that of foolishness, both v. 1 and v. 16 also contain the expression "a little." It would seem, therefore, that a connection between v. 16 and v. 1 is to be assumed.

but if (you think) otherwise, then accept me, even if (you can accept me only) as a fool: Paul's style is compact. The expression *ei de mē ge* means "but if (you think) otherwise"; it is common in classical Greek and occurs quite frequently in the New Testament, yet it is a *hapax legomenon* in Paul. The expression as a whole may possibly be taken more or less as a particle with the sense of "otherwise" (already thus in classical Greek). However, its presence in this verse, just as in Matt 6:1, surprises the reader somewhat, since one expects a positive clause before that phrase (cf., for example, Matt 9:17), not a negative one. The *kan* (= *kai ean*, "even if") in the main clause is also elliptic. The words in parentheses—"you can accept me only"—are one possible supplement; others have been proposed. *Kan,* too, has become the equivalent of a particle with the meaning of "at least": at least accept me as a fool. To accept Paul is to accept his speaking, his words. For the verb *dechomai* ("accept") cf. 11:4.

in order that I too may boast a little: For the verb "boasting" cf. 11:12. In v. 15 Paul brings together "fool" (cf. "folly" in 11:1) and "boasting." So we can expect that he is finally going to "boast foolishly." For *mikron ti* ("a little," here most probably direct object) see 11:1.

17. *What I am saying I do not say according to the Lord, but as in folly, with regard to this matter of boasting:* The start is asyndetic; there is no connecting particle between v. 16 and v. 17. Verses 17 and 18 belong together. The double *lalō* ("I speak") in v. 17 seems to point to the announced act of boasting and has a somewhat negative ring (as in v. 23). The expression *kata kyrion* ("according to the Lord") should be taken as the opposite of *kata sarka* ("according to the flesh," v. 18), and is thus more or less the equivalent of *kata pneuma* ("according to the Spirit"), not present here. The provisional opposition in v. 17 is between "according to the Lord" and "as in folly." Translations such as "at the Lord's command" or "with the Lord's authority" seem to somewhat overemphasize the Lord's activity in this matter. Some commentators suggest, wrongly it would seem, that Paul is thinking here of Christ's example of "gentleness and meekness" (10:1). As in v. 16, with the use of *hōs* ("as") Paul informs the readers that his "foolishness" will be fictitious.

The word *hypostasis* means "standing ground, foundation, essence, reality, real being" (cf. Heb 1:3: "The Son is the very stamp of God's being") but also "confidence, assurance, conviction" (cf. Heb 11:1: Faith is the assurance, i.e., the firm confidence of things hoped for). If in our verse this second meaning is to be supposed, then the genitive is descriptive: "in this 'boastful' confidence." It is, however, possible, and indeed probable that in v. 17 *hypostasis* has the weakened sense of "thing, matter." This justifies the rendering: "with regard to (= in) this matter of boasting."

18. *Since many boast according to the flesh, I too will boast (in the same way):* By "many" Paul refers to his opponents. Are they quite numerous (cf. 2:17)? The meaning of "according to the flesh" is decidedly negative, but in this context without the connotation of sin (Paul himself will boast in that way). We should probably not think at once of what Paul will boast of, but rather see before us the type of boasting, i.e., foolish boasting. In v. 18b one has, of course, to supply mentally "according to the flesh," i.e., "in the same way."

19. *After all you gladly tolerate fools since you are (so) wise!* The *gar* ("for") at the beginning of this verse does not, strictly speaking, give the reason for what is stated in v. 18. It rather motivates the appeal of v. 16. We translate the particle "after all," and regard it as introducing an interruption. The adverb *hēdeōs* ("gladly") is emphatic. In the Greek text Paul juxtaposes and contrasts "fools" and "wise (persons)." "The verbal contrast might be preserved with 'senseless' and 'sensible', but *phronimos* means a good deal more than 'sensible'" (Alfred Plummer, *Commentary*, 315). For "tolerate" see 11:1 and 4. One could hesitate as to the connotation present in the participial phrase *phronimoi ontes* ("being wise"). It is presumably *"because* you are wise" (ironically stated). Verse 20 will identify the "fools" as Paul's opponents, as the rival apostles. Regarding the content one might refer to 1 Cor 4:10 ("we are fools for the sake of Christ, but you are wise in Christ"). In both verses Paul's sarcasm is bitter and biting.

20. *For you tolerate (it) when someone enslaves you, when someone devours (you), when someone takes advantage (of you), when someone puts on airs, when someone slaps you in the face:* The *gar* ("for") explains v. 19. With five short *ei tis* ("if someone") clauses Paul now says what the Corinthians are tolerating. "Each clause of this splendid series of anaphorae . . . operates as a whiplash" (Windisch, *Zweite Korintherbrief*, 347). The tone is very ironic and sarcastic. Note the presence of "you" in both the first and the last clauses; they frame the fivefold attack. "You" has to be mentally supplied after "devours" and "takes advantage" (what about "puts on airs"?). The use of "someone" is generic here. For the *realis* construction of the sentence cf. 11:4.

Galatians 2:4 is the only other passage in the New Testament where the compound *katadouloō* ("to enslave") occurs. (The prefix *kata* increases the pejorative sense.) There the slavery consists in the mistaken forced observance of the Law (the false brethren "might bring us into bondage"). In 2 Cor 11:20 the meaning is not so obvious (but compare 1:24). The vague idea of slavery is probably specified by the following verbs. Yet what about the exact meaning of "devours"? Presumably we have to add the idea of "your substance, your riches" (cf., of the scribes, Mark 12:40 and Luke 20:47). How is "takes advantage" to be understood? We mention three possibilities: "takes you, so that you become that person's disciples" or "takes your possessions from you" or "lays hands on you" (which may imply violence). The verb rendered by "puts on airs" could also signify "uplifts oneself over you, lords it over you" (cf. the same verb in 10:5 with *kata*). A metaphorical interpretation of "slaps you in the face" may be assumed: "if someone despises, disgraces you."

21. *To (my) shame I admit that we have been too weak (for that):* "My" is not present in the Greek text. Some prefer, against the context, it would seem, "to 'your' shame." The *hōs hoti* (literally: "as that") is probably the equivalent of *hoti* ("that"). Or should we paraphrase: "to my shame, I must say—'as' it is said by others—'that' we were too weak"? In each case the pronoun "we" is emphatic. Over against "you" in v. 20 Paul now writes "we", yet he stresses the opposition with the "someone" of v. 20, i.e., the "many" of v. 18, the so-called strong opponents who boast according to the flesh. Again the language is sarcastic. It is the first time in chs. 10–13 that Paul speaks of his own weakness. Obviously for him "weak" has another meaning than for the Corinthians, yet notwithstanding his weakness, Paul is going to boast.

Yet whatever anyone may dare (to boast of)—I am speaking in folly—I too dare (to boast of): With this sentence Paul finally introduces his actual boasting. For *tis* ("anyone") see the indefinite pronoun five times in v. 20; for "to dare" see 10:1, 12; for "in folly" see v. 17 (with *hōs*, "as"). Paul will employ *kagō* (= *kai egō*, literally "I as well") three more times in v. 22. "To boast of" must be supplied twice. "I am speaking in folly" interrupts the sentence and again (cf. vv. 16 and 17) manifests Paul's embarrassment, just before the actual boasting begins.

22. *Are they Hebrews? So am I. Are they Israelites? So am I. Are they descendants of Abraham? So am I:* One feels the staccato style in this verse as well as in v. 23a (and cf. already in v. 20). There is no answer to the questions—they function as if-clauses—but the implicit answer is evidently "yes." By his *kagō* ("so am I") Paul reacts to that "yes" answer. It is rather unlikely that by means of the term *hebraios* ("Hebrew") Paul (also) wishes to point to his knowledge of the Hebrew language (or a similar knowledge on the part of the opponents). Neither is it certain that an affirmation concerning his birth (or, better, former residence) in Palestine must be seen in his use of this term. By the rather archaic title Paul simply means "a Jew" (cf. Phil 3:5: "a Hebrew born of Hebrews"). After the "racial" term Paul uses a "religious" category. Both the opponents and Paul are "Israelites"; they belong to the chosen people of God (cf. Rom 11:1; Phil 3:5, "a member of the people of Israel"). One might perhaps call the third title, "descendants of Abraham," a "theological" category. The mention of Abraham makes us think of Abraham's call and election, as well as the promises made to him: all theological data. The term *sperma* ("seed") has a collective meaning here (cf. Rom 11:1, *ek spermatos Abraam*: "a descendant of Abraham"; in Gal 3:16, 19 it points to one person, Christ). See the Interpretation below.

23. *Are they servants of Christ?—I am talking as if out of my mind—I am more:* For "servants of Christ" see the Note on 11:15 ("servants of righteousness"). Paul may avoid the title "apostle" in v. 23. In any case it would have been difficult to write that title after 11:13 ("false apostles"). The interrupting clause "I am talking as if out of my mind" is probably still stronger than that in v. 21 ("I am speaking in folly"). The clause points to what follows, i.e., Paul's rejoinder "I

am more," not to the preceding questions (and answers). The verb *para-phroneō* ("to be beside oneself") is a *hapax legomenon* in the New Testament.

After the threefold *kagō* in v. 22 (six occurrences in all in this pericope: see also vv. 16, 18, and 21) Paul changes his formulation. He is not only the equal of his opponents; he has accomplished and suffered more than they have. The adverbial use of the preposition *hyper* ("above") is also a *hapax legomenon* in the NT (literally it means "I above"). The meaning is not "I am more than a servant of Christ," but "I am more a servant of Christ than they are." However, it is not so clear that Paul really recognizes that his opponents are "servants of Christ" (cf. 11:15, where he implies that they are servants of Satan).

By this self-assured statement Paul introduces a whole "list of circumstances," a *Peristasenkatalog*, which has to do only with hardships, sufferings, and care. This catalogue of trials should provide proof of Paul's daring conviction "I am more!" but that comparison with the opponents will recede into the background. At this point, however, we are reminded of 1 Cor 15:10 where Paul compares himself with the other apostles. Therefore it is understandable that scholars who (wrongly, it would appear) think that in 2 Cor 11:22-23 Paul is speaking of the Jerusalem leaders refer to this passage.

more often in hard labor, more often in prison, with countless floggings, many times in danger of death: Four verbless clauses constitute the beginning and the heading of the list. It is possible that the Greek term *kopos*, here translated by "hard labor," means apostolic preaching and not manual work (cf. v. 27). Otherwise than in 10:8 *perissoterōs*, here an adverb, probably retains its comparative sense (literally "more abundantly"). The adverb *hyperballontōs* ("excessively, without number") is a *hapax legomenon* in the New Testament. It should, however, be noted that, as elsewhere, Paul also frequently employs compounds with *hyper* in 2 Cor 10-13 (see 10:14; 11:5; 12:7). The fourth clause, which mentions the danger of death, may function as a climax: "even . . . in danger of death."

24. *Five times I received from the Jews the forty lashes minus one:* In vv. 24-25 Paul's sentence structure is grammatically more regular. The position of "from the Jews" at the beginning of v. 24 is emphatic. The Jewish character of the flogging punishment is indicated by the idiom "forty minus one" (cf. Deut 25:1-3: the maximum of forty stripes).

25. *three times I was beaten with rods; once I was stoned; three times I was shipwrecked; I spent a night and a day in the open sea:* "Beaten with rods" is a Roman and thus Gentile punishment for people who were not Roman citizens *(Lex Julia;* cf. Acts 16:22-24, 37; 22:23-29). So the reference to Gentiles follows that to Jews; both are equally opposed to Paul. To receive a stoning is, of course, still more serious than to be beaten (cf. Acts 14:19).

26. *Often traveling, in danger from rivers, danger from robbers, danger from my fellow-countrymen, danger from Gentiles, danger in the city, danger in the wilderness, danger at sea, danger from false brethren:* After sea hardships Paul mentions his traveling by land (or in general?). What follows in the rest of v. 26 illustrates the sort of journeys Paul means: their dangers and "circumstances." In the first pair of deadly perils "rivers" and "robbers" may be taken as genitives of

origin. Then, as in vv. 24-25a, Paul's own people and the Gentiles are paralleled. Regarding "city" and "wilderness" Barrett emphasizes the contrast: "dangers in crowded cities, dangers in the lonely country" (*Commentary*, 299). By the seventh danger Paul refers back to the shipwrecks of v. 25. The eighth and last danger is striking. Its position at the end is deliberate and climactic and indicates how much Paul must have suffered on the part of the *pseudadelphoi* ("false brethren"; the term also occurs in Gal 2:4), since they are Christians. Paul's care for the churches is thus announced (see vv. 28-29).

27. *In hard labor and toil, often without sleep, in hunger and thirst, often without food, in cold and nakedness:* For the combination of the first two terms see 1 Thess 2:9 (cf. 2 Thess 3:8); for the first term *(kopos)* see also v. 23d. Verse 27 strongly suggests that "working" refers to manual work in v. 23 also. The "sleepless nights" referred to here are probably to be seen as the consequence of Paul's "hard labor and toil." In an analogous way "fasting" could be connected with "hunger and thirst," or Paul may be referring to voluntary fasts. Like the other hardships in v. 27, "cold and nakedness" must be regarded, at least partly, as a consequence of Paul's refusal of support.

28. *Apart from the other things (there is) the daily pressure on me, the concern for all the churches:* Two translations have been proposed for *chōris tōn parektos:* "apart from such external matters" and, probably to be preferred, "apart from the things I omit." The second phrase, "the concern for all the churches," explains the first ("the daily pressure on me"). *Ekklēsiōn* ("for the churches") is an objective genitive. Verse 28 provides the apostolic context for the whole list that precedes. In view of the present tenses in v. 29, a present may be supplied in v. 28: "is."

29. *Who is weak, and I am not weak?* Verse 29 is closely connected with v. 28. What Paul speaks of here is part of the pressure and care. One is reminded of Paul's will to adapt himself. See 1 Cor 9:19-23, more specifically, 9:22a: "To the weak I became weak, that I might win the weak," where "weak" in the first clause means weak in knowledge, conscience-ridden, scrupulous regarding the eating of food and the like. In 2 Cor 11:29 the meaning of "being weak" in its first clause may be wider: various kinds of weaknesses, spiritual and physical infirmities, seem to be included. Paul's "weakness" in the second clause is only partially the same as that alluded to in the first clause.

Who is made to fall, and I do not blaze (with indignation)? Note the emphatic *egō* in v. 29b. Do we have here a new idea, or is Paul making clear what he means by "weak people," i.e., those who are "scandalized," "are made to stumble" by the (too free) behavior of fellow Christians (cf. 1 Cor 8:13)? The first alternative may be preferred. Paul's reaction to scandal is "to burn, to become indignant."

30. *If boasting there must be, I will boast of the things (that manifest) my weakness:* Compare this verse with 12:1a (where the conditional formulation is dropped: "there must be boasting") and 12:5b ("I will not boast about myself, except about my weaknesses"). The future tense in 11:30b is not to be taken in an exclusive sense as pointing only to what follows. The expression "the things

(that manifest) my weakness" takes up and characterizes as "weak" what is expounded in 11:23d-29, as well as announcing as "weak" what will be said in 11:32-33.

31. *The God and Father of the Lord Jesus—he who is blessed for ever!—knows that I am not lying:* Again, as with "weakness" in v. 30, there is no reason "to confine this to what follows. Like *kauchēsomai*, it looks both ways" (Plummer, *Commentary*, 332). Paul's assertion of truthfulness is very solemn and emotional; cf. 11:10. Paul has already used the expression "the God and Father of the Lord Jesus (Christ)" at the beginning of the letter: see 1:3. For "I am not lying" and the mention of Christ or God, cf. Rom 9:1 and Gal 1:20.

Blessings such as "blessed is (or: be) he forever!" appear to have been common among the Jews. The nominative *ho ōn* ("he who is") is in apposition to "the God," not to "the Lord Jesus." Compare with Rom 1:25 and, more especially, with 9:5. Even in Rom 9:5 it is not certain that the doxology refers to Christ; *ho ōn* in this verse of Romans may be a loosely attached blessing of God.

32. *In Damascus the ethnarch of King Aretas was guarding the city of the Damascenes in order to arrest me:* The narrative and prosaic vv. 32-33, "cette petite anecdote" (Allo, *Seconde épître*), have in the past been thought by some scholars to be an interpolation. It is probably not true that they are an illustration only of the weakness and humiliation of which Paul boasts, and not of his endurance. It is, moreover, quite uncertain that both hostile Corinthians and opponents made use of the incident so as to make a fool of Paul. E. A. Judge writes: "If it is realized that everyone in antiquity would have known that the finest military award for valour was the *corona muralis,* for the man who was first up the wall in the face of the enemy, Paul's point is devastatingly plain: he was the first down" ("Conflict," quoted in Travis, "Boasting," 530).

Because of the mention of "Damascus" and, again, of "the city of the Damascenes" the sentence catches the readers' attention. The aorist infinitive *piasai* ("to seize, to apprehend") is an infinitive of purpose. Aretas IV was king of the Nabataean Arabs from about 9 B.C.E. to 39 C.E. Was his ethnarch attacking and guarding (from outside) Damascus which was under Roman rule? Or, more probably, was Aretas governing the city through his ethnarch (cf. "in Damascus") at that time (so recently Justin Taylor, "Ethnarch")? If this incident could be dated, it would be of great use to Pauline chronology.

33. *and through a window in the wall I was lowered in a basket and I escaped his hands:* See Acts 9:23-25 on the same incident. The (partial) identity attracts our attention: *dia tou teichous* ("through the wall") and *chalazō* ("to lower") in both texts. Note, however, the differences as well. The Jews are Paul's enemies in Acts; they "were watching the gates" (Acts 9:24b; thus inside the city); no window is mentioned in Acts (but this should, of course, be understood); in Acts 9:25 Luke writes *en spyridi* ("in a basket") while Paul writes *en sarganē* in v. 33; and the whole atmosphere in Acts differs from that in 2 Corinthians. A literary dependence on the part of Luke should not be postulated.

It seems that Paul boasts of his miraculous liberation (in utter helplessness as well as God-given endurance) more than of a so-called humiliation.

INTERPRETATION

a. *Structure and Line of Thought.* In 11:16-33 the division between vv. 16-21 and 22-33 is obvious. In the second half we find Paul's actual boasting; in the first he announces this boasting and excuses himself for doing it. The expression *palin legō* ("I say again, I repeat") in v. 16 undoubtedly indicates a new start. With "there must be further boasting" in 12:1 another new beginning is clearly marked.

The structure and line of thought in vv. 16-21 must be analyzed in greater detail. In vv. 16-18 and 21b one can distinguish five elements:

(1) Paul makes an explicit appeal in v. 16: "accept me."

(2) Paul manifests his decision to boast, already indirectly at the end of v. 16: "so that I too may boast a little," then directly in v. 18b: "I too will boast (in the same way)," and again in v. 21b: "I too dare (to boast of)"; see also v. 30b: "I will boast of the things (that manifest) my weakness."

(3) Paul considers boasting a foolish action and excuses himself by admitting it, so in v. 17: "what I am saying in this matter of boasting, I do not say according to the Lord, but as in folly," and in v. 21b: "I am speaking in folly"; see also v. 23b: "I am talking as out of my mind."

(4) Paul is convinced that properly speaking he is not a fool: "let no one think that I am a fool" (v. 16). Compare the particle *hōs* in v. 17: "but *as* in folly"; see also v. 31 where Paul emphasizes his veracity. In 12:6 ideas of not being a fool and of speaking the truth are brought together.

(5) Paul refers to other people. He is going to use their own weapons against them. See v. 18: "since many boast according to the flesh, I too will boast," and v. 21: "yet whatever anyone may dare (to boast of) . . . I too dare (to boast of)."

The connection between the five elements can be paraphrased in the following way: Although I am not really a fool, if you think I am, accept me then as a fool, for I want to boast; I admit that boasting is not appropriate, but since others glory I am going to do it as well.

The ironic, biting vv. 19-21a provide a motivation for the Corinthians' unwillingness to "accept" Paul (v. 16): they bear with others (= the opponents). One is reminded of the way Paul motivates his appeal of 11:1 in 11:4 (the second motivation after the initial one in v. 2). Paul refers to the opponent(s) with the same verb *anechomai* ("to tolerate"). Verses 19-21a do not immediately follow the appeal of v. 16; consequently their motivating force remains somewhat implicit. Moreover, these verses could also be regarded as a brief excursus (v. 21b takes up v. 18). In v. 21a, by the clause "we have been too weak (for that)" Paul seems to allude to an accusation of a lack of strength made against him by hostile Corinthians and rival apostles.

The following concentric structure can be detected in vv. 16-21 (the announcement of boasting): *a:* Paul's intention to boast (vv. 16-18); *b:* Paul's reproach (vv. 19-21a); *a':* Paul's intention to boast (v. 21b).

No such cyclic arrangement is to be found in vv. 22-33. Three items should be briefly developed.

(1) In v. 23b one comes across Paul's last excuse: "I am talking as if out of my mind." It should be noted that at this point there is a double shift in his boast. In vv. 22-23a titles that refer to a status are mentioned; from v. 23b onward Paul enumerates his apostolic hardships. In vv. 22-23a Paul compares himself with the opponents; from v. 23b onward the opponents do not seem to occupy his attention any longer.

(2) In v. 30a we meet for the first time the idea of necessity: "If boasting there must be." See also 12:1: "There must be further boasting" (the conditional construction, however, is lacking here); and 12:11b: "You forced me (to it)."

(3) The term "weakness" in v. 30b sums up what is developed in vv. 23d-29, but, connected with the verb "I will boast," it also anticipates what follows. In vv. 32-33 Paul proceeds to illustrate by means of one particular event what it means for him to be "weak" and yet to experience God's effective help. The verb "to be weak" occurs in v. 21 and v. 29 (twice), the noun "weakness" in v. 30. The meaning, however, is somewhat different in each case. In v. 21 Paul admits a kind of weakness in his behavior *vis-à-vis* the Corinthians (i.e., his refraining from a harsh, tyrannical attitude). In v. 29 he points to his adaptation to those who are actually weak. In v. 30 the noun "weakness" summarizes all sorts of situations wherein Paul feels himself helpless but assisted by God.

Verses 22-33 contain Paul's actual boasting. In this passage we might distinguish vv. 22-23a (titles), vv. 23b-29 (hardships and apostolic care), v. 30 (mention of weakness), v. 31 (Paul is not lying), and vv. 32-33 (Paul's escape from Damascus).

b. *Stylistic Characteristics.* The Fool's Speech in its entirety extends from 11:22 to 12:10. However, the manner in which Paul composed vv. 22-29 merits special attention. Verses 22-23a and 23b-29 should be treated separately.

Verses 22-23a certainly belong to the discourse. There are four questions; no direct answer is given, but Paul implicitly admits a positive answer and immediately continues with "so am I." The fourth clause breaks the monotonous repetition and, by its variation ("I am more") and the interruption ("I am talking as if out of my mind"), forms the climax:

> 22   Are they Hebrews?
>   So am I.
>   Are they Israelites?
>   So am I.

> Are they descendants of Abraham?
> So am I.
> 23a   Are they servants of Christ?
> —I am talking as if out of my mind—
> I am more.

Until v. 23a Paul's boasting has not referred to hardships, only to "titles." The list of trials itself begins in v. 23b. Differently from 6:4-10, no virtues or antitheses are mentioned, only hardships. One can distinguish five strophes, more on the basis of the construction than on that of a neatly differentiated content:

(1)   23b   more often in hard labor,
              more often in prison,
              with countless floggings,
              many times in danger of death.

(2)   24   Five times I received from the Jews the forty lashes minus one;
       25   three times I was beaten with rods;
              once I was stoned;
              three times I was shipwrecked;
              I spent a night and a day in the open sea.

(3)   26   Often traveling,
              in danger from rivers,
              danger from robbers,
              danger from my fellow-countrymen,
              danger from Gentiles,
              danger in the city,
              danger in the wilderness,
              danger at sea,
              danger from false brethren.

(4)   27   In hard labor and toil,
                   often without sleep,
              in hunger and thirst,
                   often without food,
              in cold and nakedness.

(5)   28   Apart from the other things, (there is)
                   the daily pressure on me,
                   the concern for all the churches.

       29   Who is weak,
                   and I am not weak?
              Who is made to fall,
                   and I do not blaze (with indignation)?

In (1), the first strophe (v. 23b), there are four substantives. After two parallel occurrences of "more often," Paul changes to "countless" and "many times." This first strophe is, as it were, the heading of the whole list. What follows in vv. 24-28 is illustration and concretization of v. 23b. "Hard labor" is mentioned again in v. 27; being "in prison" can be presumed in vv. 24-25ab, which verses also vividly depict the "floggings"; "danger of death" is broadly elaborated in vv. 25cd-26.

In (2), the second strophe (vv. 24-25), the first four clauses are related through numeral adverbs (five times, three times, once, three times); they indicate different punishments. The fourth, which is continued by the fifth, deals with shipwrecks. All five clauses have verbs in the first person singular. The longer clauses, one and five, frame the shorter middle clauses.

(3) The third strophe (v. 26) might be entitled "travel dangers": eight "dangers." The introductory term *hodoporiai* probably points to journeys on land. The rhythmic repetition of eight "dangers" follows. First we have three pairs: rivers and robbers, Jews and Gentiles, city and wilderness. Although the same construction continues, it is not certain that "at sea" is to be linked with the third pair (city, country, and sea). With "false brethren" Paul concludes the series. The second pair mentioned Jews and Gentiles; the position of the false brethren (= Christians) at the end of the series is very emphatic and, moreover, returns to the idea of trouble.

(4) The fourth strophe (v. 27) contains five expressions. One, three, and five on the one hand (each involving a pair of nouns in the singular) and two and four on the other (with only one term—a plural noun in Greek—followed by "often") are symmetric. The hardships here are not so "external" as in the three first strophes.

(5) The last strophe (vv. 28-29), devoted to apostolic care, is more prosaic in v. 28; in v. 29 it contains two parallel questions that manifest Paul's compassion.

The stylistic composition of the first part of the Fool's Speech is remarkable, yet it is, in a sense, an emotional outburst. One might wonder to what degree Paul consciously intended such a structured text.

c. *Theological Reflection.* In his study "Abraham und Mose im Streit der Meinungen," D.-A. Koch also discusses vv. 22-23a. In his opinion the four names are titles used by Paul's opponents to qualify themselves. The self-designation *Ioudaios* ("Jew"), which Jews employed in communication with non-Jews, is characteristically absent. In the enumeration—that as such, according to Koch, goes back to these opponents—there is a crescendo: from Hebrew (racial) to Israelite (salvation historical) to "seed" of Abraham (theological) to servant of Christ (specifically Christian). Yes, precisely as Hebrews, Israelites, and descendants of Abraham they present themselves to the Gentile Christians of Corinth as "servants of Christ" in order to stress the continuity with Israel. Moreover, because in Jewish tradition Abraham is seen as a blessing for the nations and as the father of many peoples they can, with this third title, address the Gentile Christians: Abraham is *their* father as well.

In Phil 3:5-8 the Jewish past is rejected in a most critical way; in 2 Cor 11:22 Paul only "equalizes" and "minimalizes" the first three titles by means of his threefold "so am I." Otherwise than in Galatians 3 and Romans 4 he does not explain in 2 Corinthians that Abraham was justified by faith without works of the Law. In 11:22-23a Paul's attention goes almost exclusively to the fourth title "servants of Christ." In v. 23a he begins to argue; he states—although not without hesitation—"I am more." The entire list of trials (vv. 23b-29) and what follows (11:30–12:10) is meant to prove this affirmation.

For the list of hardships (vv. 23b-29) see also the Interpretation of 6:1-10, pp. 113–115.

d. *Actualization.* With regard to Paul's boasting one should pay due attention to the three shifts within 11:22-33: at vv. 23b, 27, and 30. These shifts provide us, it would seem, with four types of boasting defined by the object Paul boasts about. (1) In vv. 22-23a, while comparing himself with his opponents and enumerating his Jewish and Christian titles, he visibly boasts "according to the flesh" (11:18). (2) Within the catalogue of hardships itself, in vv. 23b-26, Paul proves his superiority by listing external hardships, adverse circumstances. (3) Within the same list, however, from v. 27 to v. 29, he points to his own toils and labors, his personal "active" apostolic attitude. (4) Finally, in vv. 32-33 a situation is depicted where Paul's utter weakness, i.e., the absence of his own power, is emphasized. Yet attention is also given to his almost miraculous liberation.

For Christians today, one could ask, what type of boasting is legitimate? For a reflection on "foolish boasting" see the Interpretation of 12:1-10, pp. 206–207.

For Reference and Further Study

Andrews, Scott B. "Too Weak Not to Lead: The Form and Function of 2 Cor 11.23b-33," *NTS* 41 (1995) 263–276.

Barré, Michael L. "Paul as 'Eschatologic Person': A New Look at 2 Cor 11:29," *CBQ* 37 (1975) 500–526.

Barrett, C. K. "The Acts—of Paul" in idem, *New Testament Essays.* London: S.P.C.K., 1972, 86–100.

Collins, John N. "Georgi's 'Envoys' in 2 Cor 11:23," *JBL* 93 (1974) 88–96.

Ebner, Martin. *Leidenslisten und Apostelbrief: Untersuchungen zu Form, Motivik und Funktion der Peristasenkataloge bei Paulus.* Würzburg: Echter, 1991, 93–172.

Fitzgerald, John T. *Cracks in an Earthen Vessel: An Examination of the Catalogues of Hardships in the Corinthian Correspondence.* SBL.DS 99. Atlanta: Scholars, 1988.

Harding, Mark. "On the Historicity of Acts: Comparing Acts 9.23-5 with 2 Corinthians 11.32-3," *NTS* 39 (1993) 518–538.

Hodgson, Robert. "Paul the Apostle and First Century Tribulation Lists," *ZNW* 74 (1987) 59–80.

Judge, Edwin A. "The Conflict of Educational Aims in NT Thought," *Journal of Christian Education* 9 (1966) 32–45.

Koch, Dietrich-Alex. "Abraham und Mose im Streit der Meinungen. Beobachtungen und Hypothesen zur Debatte zwischen Paulus und seinen Gegnern in 2 Kor 11,22-23 und 3,7-18," in Reimund Bieringer, ed., *The Corinthian Correspondence.* BEThL 125. Leuven: Leuven University Press/Peeters, 1996, 305-314.

Lambrecht, Jan. "'Strength in Weakness': A Reply to Scott B. Andrews' Exegesis of 2 Cor 11.23b-33," *NTS* 43 (1997) 285–290.

Marshall, Peter. *Enmity in Corinth: Social Conventions in Paul's Relation with the Corinthians.* WUNT II/23. Tübingen: Mohr-Siebeck, 1987.

Schrage, Wolfgang. "Leid, Kreuz und Eschaton: Die Peristasenkataloge als Merkmale paulinischer *theologia crucis* und Eschatologie," *EvTh* 34 (1974) 141–175.

Taylor, Justin. "The Ethnarch of King Aretas at Damascus. A Note on 2 Cor 11,32-33," *RB* 99 (1992) 719–728.

Travis, Stephen H. "Paul's Boasting in 2 Corinthians 10–12," *StEv* 6 (TU 112). Berlin: Akademie-Verlag, 1973, 527–532.

18. *More Boasting: Strength in Weakness* (12:1-10)

1. There must be further boasting. Although it is no use, yet I will come to the visions and revelations of the Lord. 2. I know a person in Christ who, fourteen years ago—whether in the body, I do not know, or out of the body, I do not know, God knows—was caught up to the third heaven, 3. and I know that such a person—whether in the body or without the body, I do not know, God knows—4. was caught up into Paradise and heard ineffable words which a human being is not permitted to tell. 5. About this (person) I will boast, but about myself I will not boast, except about my weaknesses. 6. But if I want to boast I will not be foolish, since I will be speaking the truth; but I refrain in order that no one esteems me above what he or she sees of me or hears from me.

7. Therefore, because of the abundance of revelations—in order that I might not be unduly elated—a thorn was given me in the flesh, a messenger of Satan to beat me, in order that I might not be unduly elated. 8. About this one I begged the Lord three times that he would go away from me. 9. But he said to me: "My grace is sufficient for you, for power is made perfect in weakness." Most gladly, therefore, I rather will boast

of my weaknesses in order that the power of Christ may come to rest upon me. 10 That is why I am well pleased with weaknesses, insults, hardships, persecutions, and constraints (endured) for Christ. For whenever I am weak, then I am strong.

NOTES

1. *There must be further boasting. Although it is no use, yet I will come to the visions and revelations of the Lord:* The translation is that of the *lectio difficilior,* attested in fact by good manuscripts. Among the variant readings one may note *de* or *dē* (instead of *dei*); *sympherei* (instead of *sympheron*); *moi* (instead of *men*) and *gar* (instead of *de*). Different combinations result, of course, in different understandings of this verse. If the *men . . . de* construction in v. 1bc possesses a concessive nuance in its first clause—which is probable—("although it is no use . . ." or: "although it serves no good purpose . . ."), the second clause carries the full weight: "yet I will come to. . . ." For "there must be further boasting" or "it is necessary to go on boasting" (in Greek a present tense) see 11:30 (aorist) and also 11:18. Paul is forced to boast by the behavior of the opponents.

The expression *eis optasias kai apokalypseis* ("to the visions and revelations") is probably a kind of hendiadys. To distinguish here technically between the visible (visionary) and audible (revelatory) sides of the ecstatic experiences would most likely go too far. The plural "visions and revelations" must be taken seriously. It may have been Paul's original intention to mention several such experiences. One is somewhat hesitant with regard to the genitive *kyriou,* which applies to both nouns. Is it a subjective genitive (a genitive of the author: the Lord causes visions and revelations) or an objective genitive (Paul sees and hears the Lord)? Perhaps the objective genitive is to be preferred. According to 1 Cor 9:1; 15:8; Gal 1:16 (cf. 2 Cor 4:6) Paul "saw" the risen Lord at the moment of his conversion/vocation. One may rightly ask whether the later visions and revelations possessed the same significance as that first overwhelming experience for Paul.

2. *I know a person in Christ who, fourteen years ago—whether in the body, I do not know, or out of the body, I do not know, God knows—was caught up to the third heaven:* The expression "a person in Christ" seems here to mean more than just "a Christian," most likely "a person in Christ's power." The use of the third person ("a person") is striking for readers of this pericope. Paul "could doubt his own identity with the recipient rather than doubt the reality of the revelations" (Alfred Plummer, *Commentary,* 339). But is that the point? One must keep in mind Paul's uneasiness in speaking of special graces (cf. 5:13). Moreover, in an ecstatic experience a kind of retreat of the ego, with the consequent possibility of objectification, is supposed to occur.

The exact date, "fourteen years ago," indicates that Paul is referring to one of his revelations. In view of the date "fourteen years ago" (i.e., about the year 40, or somewhat later) this cannot be Paul's seeing the Lord at his conversion or his Temple vision related in Acts 22:17-22.

Narratives of an ascension into heaven (e.g., those of Enoch, Ezra, Baruch, Moses and Levi) were not uncommon in apocalyptic literature. It is not clear how old the traditions are on which the later *maʿaseh merkabah* in rabbinic literature and the equally late visionary mystical *hekhalot* literature depend. One should not follow Hans Dieter Betz ("Christus-Aretalogie") in taking vv. 2-4 as a parody of an ascension narrative (and/or vv. 7b-10 as a "Parodie einer Christus-Aretalogie"); for criticism see, e.g., C. K. Barrett, *Commentary* 307–308; Christian Wolff, *Der zweite Brief* 241; J. D. Tabor, *Things Unattainable* 53 n. 79; Margaret E. Thrall, "Journey," 349–351. Paul appears to refer to an actual event in his own life; the narrative in vv. 2-4 is not a purely literary construct.

The two types of ascensions existed in contemporary literature: "in the body" (more Jewish) and "out of the body" (more Greek?). It is hard to know to what degree Paul has been influenced by such narratives. Peter Schäfer ("New Testament and Hekhalot Literature") refers to the tendency to see parallels between Paul's journey and the journeys present in Merkabah mysticism as risking "parallelomania." The expressions "in the body" and "out of the body" can scarcely be used to claim for Paul's anthropology the possibility of an incorporeal existence. After all, Paul "may be emphasising his total lack of comprehension as to how the event occurred" (Thrall, "Journey," 359).

The participle *harpagenta* ("caught up") stands in apposition to the following *ton toiouton* (literally "that type of [person]"). The agent behind this passive verb is God (or Christ?). Paul has employed the same verb in 1 Thess 4:17. For Paul "the third heaven" is, because of *heōs* ("to") and the parallel "Paradise" in v. 4, almost certainly the "highest" heaven. It is most likely wrong to see in this heaven the place where the (already) risen dead, the righteous departed, await their final destiny.

3. *and I know that such a person—whether in the body or without the body, I do not know, God knows—:* This is the beginning of a major repetition that betrays Paul's awe and hesitation. Notwithstanding some variance of vocabulary, the same incident is intended. Only in v. 4 will something of the content be told; what is said in v. 2 was not yet complete. Some additional information, too, will be given in v. 4: the third heaven is Paradise. There is no real difference of sense between *chōris* ("without," v. 3) and *ektos* ("out of," v. 2).

4. *was caught up into Paradise and heard ineffable words which a human being is not permitted to tell:* The *hoti* ("that") clause in v. 3 replaces the participial construction present in v. 2. Eschatological "Paradise" is meant here as the equivalent of "third heaven." The adjective *arrētos* can mean "inexpressible, unutterable" or (as here?) "not to be expressed and communicated"; cf. what follows: "that a human being is not permitted to tell." "The verbal contradiction *(arrēta rēmata)* may be accidental, but it is probably another instance of playing upon words of which St. Paul is fond" (Plummer, *Commentary* 345). The phrase appears to be unique to him.

5. *About this (person) I will boast, but about myself I will not boast, except about my weaknesses:* Ton toiouton (the same term as in v. 3) refers to the person of v. 2 and v. 3. For Paul the distinction between "this (person)" and "myself" points

to reluctance and uneasiness in the same manner as his repeated statements that this kind of boasting is foolish and that, therefore, he will be regarded as foolish (see 11:1 and 16-21; 13:1). With "I will not boast, except about my weaknesses," the theme of the second unit (vv. 7-10) is announced.

6. *But if I want to boast I will not be foolish, since I will be speaking the truth:* The particle *gar* ("for") sometimes possesses an adversative nuance; hence the translation "but." This verse begins with an *eventualis* condition as protasis (= "in case") and continues with a *realis* apodosis. Paul's use of the terminology *aphrōn* and *alētheia* in v. 6 is different from that in 2 Corinthians 10–13 generally. Normally "foolish" is what must not be done, even if it is true; here "foolish" equals "untrue."

but I refrain in order that no one esteems me above what he sees of me or hears from me: The verb *pheidomai* may mean "I am refraining" or, less probably here, "I am sparing you." The reader of v. 6b remembers, of course, 5:13: "if we have been beside ourselves, it was for God; if we are sober-minded, (it is) for you."

7. *Therefore, because of the abundance of revelations—in order that I might not be unduly elated—:* In v. 6 Paul was dealing with the danger that others might misunderstand him; in vv. 7-9a he has in mind himself and God's care for him. Two variant readings, namely omissions, must be mentioned: *dio* ("that is why") and *hina mē hyperairōmai* ("in order that I might not be unduly elated" at the end of the verse). Both variants, however, seem secondary. That the final words of v. 7 are left out by copyists can easily be understood since they are the repetition of a clause within the same sentence. Of the omission of *dio* it is often said that it happened when copyists no longer saw it as the beginning of a new sentence. This may be correct, yet in the original text *dio* was probably not the beginning, but an interruption. The style in v. 7 is irregular to the extreme, but such a style is in no way uncharacteristic of Paul.

   Therefore, against many interpreters, one may assume that the clause *kai tē hyperbolē tōn apokolypseōn* ("and because of the abundance of revelations") belongs to the sentence that follows. It is better not to consider this dative as a strict dative *pendens*. The construction within v. 7 appears to be interrupted by the anticipative words *dio, hina mē hyperairōmai*. The main sentence structure reads: "and because of the abundance of revelations a thorn was given me in the flesh, a messenger of Satan to beat me, in order that I might not be unduly elated." In the actual text *dio* is explained by the purpose clause that immediately follows. Alternatively, one could regard the initial dative not as cause but as means, a dative that stands in an anticipative way at the beginning and is to be linked with the first "elated": "that I might not be unduly elated by the abundance of revelations." However, in this alternative view *dio* is rather awkward.

a thorn was given me in the flesh, a messenger of Satan to beat me, in order that I might not be unduly elated: Skolops is "thorn" or "stake" (for torture?). The first meaning is to be preferred here. The verb "was given" is probably a divine passive: given by God (or Christ). The aorist tense refers back to a specific date (that of the revelation mentioned in vv. 2-4?). The dative *tē sarki* presumably is local: "in the flesh," yet Alfred Plummer writes: "'*For* the flesh' is on the whole more probable than 'in the flesh'" (*Commentary*, 348).

The clause "a messenger of Satan to beat me" concretizes the thorn. There is an appositional relation between "messenger" and "thorn," i.e., an identification. The infinitive "to beat" renders a *hina* ("in order that") clause. The subject of "to beat" is Satan's messenger. The mention of Satan after a (possible) "divine" dative surprises the reader. It is possible, then, that there is a double agent. God uses Satan's messenger. The second "in order that I might not be unduly elated" is probably grammatically co-ordinated; it is not just an awkward repetition but a clause consciously and emotionally added for the sake of emphasis. Some may defend the position that this purpose clause is gramatically subordinated to the preceding one ("to beat me") and indicates the purpose of the messenger's beating. Although this is less likely, it does not constitute a major alteration of the overall sense.

There is no consensus concerning the kind of suffering Paul is alluding to by "thorn" and/or "a messenger of Satan" in v. 7 (See Interpretation b).

8. *About this one I begged the Lord three times that he would go away from me:* The demonstrative pronoun *toutou* ("this") is most probably masculine (not neuter) and in that case refers back to the messenger in v. 7, who is then also the grammatical subject of "would go away." "The Lord" is Jesus Christ (see v. 9b). This is the only place in his letters where Paul mentions his praying to Jesus (see, however, 1 Cor 16:22 and cf. Rev 22:20); only here in the NT is *parakaleō* ("to beg") used for a petitionary prayer. Some commentators see in "three times" a parallel to Jesus' prayer in Gethsemane (cf. Mark 14:32-42 = Matt 26:36-46). But it is rather unlikely that the word *tris* is intended by Paul as an allusion to this event.

9. *But he said to me: "My grace is sufficient for you, for power is made perfect in weakness."* The verb *eirēken* (perfect tense) connotes that the Lord has said something and that it stands; the reply is final. The grammatical subject is Christ (cf. vv. 8 and 9b). What follows is the only saying of the *risen* Lord in Paul's letters. "Grace" is here presumably more comprehensive than the special conversion grace that made Paul an apostle. The first part of Christ's answer is a refusal; then, in the second part, which brings the motivation, it becomes evident that this refusal contains much more than a possible granting of Paul's request would have brought.

The clause "for power . . ." is better considered as still belonging to Jesus' answer, not as the beginning of Paul's reflection upon it. "Power" and "grace" are synonyms here. Although the reading *mou* ("of me," i.e., "my") after "power" is certainly secondary, it renders the exact sense since it is the power of Christ (cf., again, v. 9b) that comes to perfection in (Paul's) weakness. The verb *teleō* means not only "to complete, to finish" but also "to bring to fullness, to make perfect."

Most gladly, therefore, I rather will boast of my weaknesses in order that the power of Christ may come to rest upon me: For the use of *hēdista* see 12:15: "I will 'most gladly' spend. . . ." The comparative *mallon* ("more, rather") determines "I will boast"; the second member of the comparison must be mentally supplemented: "Most gladly therefore (because of the Lord's reply) will I rather glory in my weaknesses (than pray that they may be removed)" (Plummer, *Commentary*, 355). After the singular "in weakness" (without the article: "weakness" as such), the plural (with the article: "my particular weaknesses") is used here. Many commentators, however, understand: "I will boast in my weaknesses rather than in something else."

The ingressive nuance of the aorist *episkēnōsē* should not go unnoticed: "come to rest." One rightly hesitates in seeing here an allusion to Israel being overshadowed by the divine presence (cf. the probably later *shekinah* speculations). The verb is a *hapax legomenon* in the New Testament (cf. however *skēnoō*, "to dwell," in John 1:14).

10. *That is why I am well pleased with weaknesses, insults, hardships, persecutions, and constraints (endured) for Christ:* Paul concludes the passage. The Lord's answer (v. 9) provides the reason (*dio*, "that is why") for his spirituality of the cross. After the long list of trials in 11:23b-29 Paul here presents a short list. It hardly functions as a concretization of the thorn. In vv. 7-8 Paul seems to think of a specific adversity or, perhaps, of opponents. The hardships mentioned in v. 10 are connected with Paul's apostolate; no illness is present in the list. Some commentators link "for Christ" with *eudokō:* "for the sake of Christ I am well pleased with. . . ." It seems better to read the expression in connection with the tribulations that are then "endured" for Christ.

For whenever I am weak, then I am strong: This clause motivates v. 10a but is at the same time a conclusion drawn from Christ's saying in v. 9. "Whenever" translates *hotan.* Paul speaks here of both his weakness and his own strength. "With this paradoxical outburst of triumph this paragraph closes" (Plummer, *Commentary*, 356). It is also the conclusion of the whole "foolish" discourse (11:22–12:10).

INTERPRETATION

a. *Structure and Line of Thought.* 2 Corinthians 12:1-10 can be structurally divided into two units: vv. 1-6 (rapture into heaven) and vv. 7-10 (the thorn in the flesh). Both units deal with boasting; the whole passage is framed by this theme: see v. 1 and vv. 9-10. In the first unit there is foolish boasting of visions and revelations; in the second Paul most gladly boasts of his weaknesses and is well pleased with them.

Boasting of revelations (vv. 1-6). In v. 1 a new theme for "foolish" boasting (cf. 11:16-33) is announced. Verses 2-4 deal with an example of Paul's visions and revelations. Fourteen years ago God took him up into Paradise. In vv. 5-6 the uneasiness, already manifested by the use of the third person in vv. 2-3 ("I know a person in Christ") and the repetitious style in vv. 3-4, make Paul stop this specific boasting. He turns at the end of v. 5 to another type of boasting (weaknesses). Yet if he wished he could go on in the previous way; he would not be a fool; he would be speaking the truth. But he prefers that the Corinthians consider him a "normal" person (cf. 5:13).

Boasting of weakness (vv. 7-10). God and Christ enter the scene here in a rather unexpected way. God gives Paul a thorn in the flesh against elation; he sends a messenger of Satan to beat him. In v. 7 God acts; in v. 8 Paul reacts and prays to the Lord (Christ) for deliverance; in v. 9abc Christ speaks to him; in vv. 9de-10 Paul, while addressing himself to his readers, draws the conclusion and states that he decidedly prefers his weaknesses.

b. *The "Thorn" and the "Messenger of Satan" (v. 7).* As is well known, many attempts have been made to identify the "thorn" and the "messenger." A brief survey of the main hypotheses may be given.

There is the old hypothesis that thinks of carnal thoughts. This so-called "Latin" interpretation is probably due, to a great extent, to the faulty rendering of the Vulgate: *stimulus carnis* ("the thorn *of* the flesh").

Many suggestions of a physical illness have been made: an eye disease (cf. Gal 4:13-15), epilepsy (cf. Satan's messenger beating Paul), intermittent fevers (malaria, for example), a speech impediment (cf. 2 Cor 10:10: "his speech is contemptible"; and see also 11:6), or chronic migraine headaches.

Mental, psychological suffering has been proposed as well. It could be caused by a nervous depression after visions and revelations, the Jews' refusal of the gospel, persecutions, personal opponent(s) or demon(s).

In his commentary Philip E. Hughes writes appropriately: ". . . the plain fact is that it is impossible to escape the realm of conjecture, which is by its nature the realm of inconclusiveness" (*Paul's Second Epistle* 442). The thorn and the beating of Satan's messenger may be experienced by Paul above all as a hindrance, an obstacle to his apostolic life (cf. v. 10a). All in all, those who read 2 Cor 12:7 more realistically are inclined to see in the "thorn" a physical disability such as an speech impediment or an eye ailment, while those who regard both "thorn" and "angel of Satan" more spiritually think rather of persecutions and opposition.

c. *Theological Reflection.* At the end of the lengthy discourse (11:16-12:10) two questions remain to be raised. How should Paul's foolish boasting be evaluated, and how must we interpret Paul's boasting of weakness?

(1) In Rom 3:28 Paul states that (Jewish) boasting is excluded because all are justified by faith apart from works prescribed by the Law. In Romans 4 he illustrates this basic thesis by means of the example of Abraham. Our ancestor Abraham believed God, and this was reckoned to him as righteousness. In 4:4-5 a "general" principle is clearly pointed out: "To one who works, wages are not reckoned as a gift but as something due.

But to one who without works trusts the one who justifies the ungodly, such faith is reckoned as righteousness." So in Paul's view the beginning of Christian life, i.e., initial justification, comes about "by God's grace as a gift, through the redemption that is in Christ Jesus" (3:24) and, as far as the human subject is concerned, God's righteousness is given "apart from law . . . through faith in Jesus Christ for all who believe" (3:21). There-fore, in regard to justification, boasting of personal merit is radically ex-cluded. Therefore, also, let us boast in God alone (cf. 2 Cor 10:17) and "never boast of anything except of the cross of our Lord Jesus Christ" (Gal 6:14).

The question imposes itself: does this position apply equally to the life after justification, the Christian life of justified people who want to reach final salvation? Many answer this question positively, without any hesi-tation. Yet this may lead, it would seem, to an incorrect understanding of Paul. The apostle does not absolutely reject legitimate boasting and self-commendation, for he himself boasts of his fruitful missionary achieve-ments in Corinth. In his opinion this boasting is equivalent to boasting in the Lord. To be sure, not all boasting is legitimate, certainly not that of his opponents. There is therefore an opposition between sinful, ungodly boasting and rightful, legitimate boasting. But what about Paul's famous "foolish" boasting in 2 Corinthians 11–12? Does it belong to the category of wrongful, sinful boasting? Probably not.

A distinction is frequently made between boasting foolishly, i.e., ac-cording to the flesh (cf. 2 Cor 11:17-18), and boasting that is wise and per-mitted, i.e., boasting in the Lord (cf. 10:17). In 2 Cor 11:1 Paul pleads that his readers tolerate him even when he is a little foolish. In 11:16 he re-peats: no one should think that Paul is a fool, but if they do, then they must accept him as a fool, so that he too may boast a little. Since there are so many who boast "according to the flesh," he will do the same (11:18). What exactly will he do? The Corinthians gladly tolerate fools; he too will act as a fool, he will boast of his Jewish pedigree (11:19-22). He then goes on: he is a much better "servant of Christ" than the opponents (11:23a); then, quite unexpectedly, he provides a list of hardships (11:23b-29). In this list Paul does not mention his glorious accomplishments but insists on lack of power and on misery, trouble, weakness, and care. Therefore in 11:30 he is able to state: "If boasting there must be, I will boast of the things (that manifest) my weakness." This verse may point to the shame-ful escape from Damascus he is about to narrate in 11:32-33 but, as is evident from 12:10a, it also refers back to the hardships mentioned in 11:23b-29. All this would seem another type of boasting than the "foolish" boasting of origin, status, and work in 11:22-23a. Then, in 12:1-4, Paul starts again; he refers to the visions and revelations of the Lord. Appar-ently this is again a boasting in foolishness. However, in 12:5 he repeats:

About myself I will not boast, except about my weaknesses. Then he deals with the thorn in the flesh and the messenger of Satan who torments him (12:7). Three times he begs the Lord that this messenger would go away (12:8). Because the Lord reveals that grace is sufficient for him and that power is strongest when the apostle is weak, Paul even proclaims: "Most gladly . . . I will rather boast of my weaknesses" (12:9b). Thus twice, in ch. 11 as well as in ch. 12, "foolish" boasting gives way to "wise" boasting of weakness.

Still, does Paul really distinguish between two types of boasting, one unwise and the other wise? Is there, for Paul, besides the foolish boasting also a natural, legitimate boasting that is wise and not foolish at all? Is such legitimate boasting above all the so-called paradoxical boasting of weakness? Most probably not. It would seem that Paul considers *all* boasting in a certain sense foolish and also dangerous. In 10:8 one sees some uneasiness or hesitation in the formulation: "If I am going to boast rather much about our authority . . . I shall not be put to shame." In 11:30, too, there is a sort of reluctance also with regard to boasting of weakness: "If boasting there must be. . . ." The fact that in 12:9 Paul will boast most gladly of his weaknesses probably does not mean that he sees this boasting as normal and free of danger. After all, in regard to his boasting in 2 Corinthians 10–12, that on origin and privileges, as well as that on weaknesses, he confesses: "I have become foolish; you forced me (to it)" (12:11). So one is brought to the conclusion that all boasting, whether of status and accomplishment or of poor condition, is foolish and not without danger. Only boasting in the Lord or in Christ is excluded (cf., for example, 10:17 and Phil 3:3).

It should also be noted that Paul's boasting is not a primary, immediate reaction but only a secondary and later one, upon reflection and in a state of some conflict. Boasting can hardly be called Paul's permanent attitude toward hardships. If after all Paul must boast and is forced to do it, he clearly expresses his preferences. However, one cannot but assume that some danger of ungodly self-praise and self-exaltation is present in any type of boasting.

(2) A further reflection on the delicate problem of Paul's boasting of weakness can hardly be avoided. Is Paul only boasting of his human lack of power, his radical incapacity, his weakness as such? True, one should keep in mind what Paul says about the "treasure in clay jars" and its function: "in order that the exceeding power be God's and do not come" from the apostle himself (4:7). There can be, moreover, no doubt that in 11:23b-33 and 12:7-8 Paul emphasizes the absence of powerful glory. Yet it would be wrong, as already said, to eliminate every nuance of Paul's faithful, active endurance and in this sense a certain kind of God-given success. Just as Paul stresses in 1 Cor 15:10 that "by the grace of God" he is what he is,

so it is also by God's grace that Paul can endure hardships and suffering. The grace that God gave him has not been without effect. Through it Paul has been admirably, heroically strong. Paul is convinced that in the midst of his weakness God's extraordinary power and the life of the risen Jesus are made visible in him (cf. 4:7-11 and 16; and 6:8-11). Nonetheless, one may assert that Paul does not like to boast of that mysterious reality; boasting makes him uneasy. He realizes that such boasting is foolish and dangerous, although it would not be contrary to truth (cf. 12:6).

In 12:9 the distinction between Paul's weakness and the power of Christ is very evident. The Lord says to Paul: "My grace is sufficient for you, for power is made perfect in weakness." Paul draws the conclusion: "Most gladly, therefore, I rather will boast of my weaknesses in order that the power of Christ may come to rest upon me." The distinction between Christ and Paul himself, however, disappears in the paradoxical language of 12:10b: "For whenever I am weak, then I am strong." One knows that paradoxical language intends to be provocative. A paradox mentions only the antithesis and does not offer a complete presentation of the case. A paradox is never absolute. Weakness is not strength. The paradox ought to lead to reflection; by reflection the discerning listener or reader should find the solution. So one might paraphrase v. 10b: Whenever, as a creature and a sinner, I am weak, then the strength of Christ is strong in me.

Still, even this paraphrase could become an understatement; moreover, it runs the risk of being misunderstood. For it is Paul himself who in Christ and through Christ proves also to be humanly strong notwithstanding his weakness. It is precisely of that "strength in weakness" that Paul in 12:9-10 is legitimately, yet foolishly and dangerously, boasting in the Lord. Such foolishness and danger will entirely disappear only in the eschaton, at the Parousia. In 1:13-14 Paul writes: "I hope you will understand fully—as you have understood us in part—that we are your boast as you, too, (are) ours in the day of the Lord Jesus."

d. *Actualization.* The whole of 2 Cor 12:9-10, more specifically the saying of the risen Lord "My grace is sufficient for you, for power is made perfect in weakness" in v. 9, is one of the most frequently used texts in Christian spirituality. In vv. 9b-10 Paul speaks of his own apostolic weakness and strength. Yet we may ask whether these words are (implicitly) not also meant for the sake of the Corinthians and all Christians. The saying is universally applicable.

Weakness is not described here as a prior condition for the manifestation of God's strength. Paul states that while he is weak the power of Christ is active in him. He stresses the simultaneity of weakness and power. Of course, as for Christ, ultimately resurrection will follow death, and in this sense death is a condition of resurrection (cf., for example, 13:4), but in Paul's apostolic existence Christ's powerful life is already present in the midst of experiences of dying. Paul emphasizes that coincidence in both v. 9a ("power is made perfect in weakness") and v. 10b ("whenever I am weak, then I am strong").

One rightly wonders whether every Christian cannot appropriate what Paul says in 12:9b-10 and whether Paul's weakness (in strength) cannot be expanded to all human suffering that is endured in and for Christ.

FOR REFERENCE AND FURTHER STUDY

Baird, William. "Visions, Revelation, and Ministry. Reflections on 2 Cor 12:1-5 and Gal 1:11-17," *JBL* 104 (1985) 651–662.

Barré, Michael L. "Qumran and the Weakness of Paul," *CBQ* 42 (1980) 500–526.

Betz, Hans Dieter. "Eine Christus-Aretalogie bei Paulus (2 Cor 12,7-10)," *ZThK* 66 (1969) 288–305.

Bowker, John W. "'Merkabah' Visions and the Visions of Paul," *JSSt* 16 (1971) 157–173.

Cambier, Jules. "Le critère paulinien de l'apostolat en 2 Cor. 12.6s," *Bib.* 43 (1962) 481–518.

Goulder, Michael. "Vision and Knowledge," *JSNT* 56 (1994) 53–71.

Heckel, Ulrich. "Der Dorn im Fleisch. Die Krankheit des Paulus in 2 Kor 12,7 und Gal 4,13f," *ZNW* 84 (1993) 65–92.

Herrmann, Léon. "Apollos," *RevScR* 50 (1976) 330–336.

Himmelfarb, Martha. *Ascent to Heaven in Jewish and Christian Apocalypses*. New York: Oxford University Press, 1993.

Jegher-Bucher, Verena. "Der Pfahl im Fleisch. Überlegungen zu II Kor 12,7-10 im Zusammenhang von 12,1-13," *ThZ* 52 (1996) 32–41.

Klauck, Hans-Josef. "Die Himmelfahrt des Paulus (2 Kor 12,2-4) in der koptischen Paulusapokalypse aus Nag Hammadi (NHC V/2)," SNTU.A 10 (1985) 151–190.

Leary, T. J. "'A Thorn in the Flesh'—2 Corinthians 12:7," *JThS* 43 (1992) 520–522.

Lincoln, Andrew T. *Paradise Now and Not Yet. Studies in the Role of the Heavenly Dimension in Paul's Thought with Special Reference to his Eschatology*. Cambridge: Cambridge University Press, 1981, 71–86.

McCant, Jerry W. "Paul's Thorn of Rejected Apostleship," *NTS* 34 (1988) 550–572.

Morray-Jones, C. R. A. "Paradise Revisited (2 Cor 12:1-12): The Jewish Mystical Background of Paul's Apostolate," *HThR* 86 (1993) 177–217, 265–292.

Mullins, Terence Y. "The Thorn in the Flesh," *JBL* 76 (1957) 299–303.

Nielsen, Helge Kjeer. "Paulus' Verwendung des Begriffes *Dynamis*. Eine Replik zur Kreuzestheologie" in Sigfred Pedersen, ed., *Die Paulinische Literatur und Theologie*. Teologiske Studier 7. Aarhus: Forlaget Aros, and Göttingen: Vandenhoeck & Ruprecht, 1980, 137–158.

O'Collins, Gerald G. "Power Made Perfect in Weakness: 2 Cor 12:9-10," *CBQ* 33 (1971) 528–537.

Park, David M. "Paul's *SKOLOPS TĒ SARKI:* Thorn or Stake? (2 Cor. XII.7)," *NT* 22 (1980) 179–183.

Price, Robert M. "Punished in Paradise (An Exegetical Theory on II Corinthians 12:1-10)," *JSNT* 7 (1980) 33–40.

Rowland, Christopher. *The Open Heaven: A Study of Apocalyptic in Judaism and Early Christianity.* London: S.P.C.K., 1982.

Schäfer, Peter. "New Testament and Hekhalot Literature: The Journey into Heaven in Paul and in Merkavah Mysticism," *JJSt* 36 (1984) 19–35.

Smith, Morton. "Ascent to the Heavens and the Beginning of Christianity," *Eranos Jahrbuch* 50 (1981) 147–222, 403–430.

Tabor, James D. *Things Unutterable: Paul's Ascent to Paradise in Its Greco-Roman, Judaic, and Early Christian Contexts.* Lanham, Md.: University Press of America, 1986.

Thrall, Margaret E. "Paul's Journey to Paradise: Some Exegetical Issues in 2 Cor 12, 2-4" in Reimund Bieringer, ed., *The Corinthian Correspondence.* BEThL 125. Leuven: Leuven University Press/Peeters, 1996, 347–363.

Trakatellis, Demetrios. "Power in Weakness—Exegesis of 2 Cor 12,1-13" in Eduard Lohse, ed., *Verteidigung und Begründung des apostolischen Amtes (2 Kor 10–13).* Benedictina 11. Rome: Abbazia San Paolo fuori le mura, 1992, 65–86.

Woods, Laurie. "Opposition to a Man and His Message: Paul's 'Thorn in the Flesh' (2 Cor 12:7)," *ABR* 39 (1991) 44–53.

Zmijewski, Josef. "Kontextbezug und Deutung von 2 Kor 12,7a. Stilistische und strukturale Erwägungen zur Lösung eines alten Problems" in idem, *Das Neue Testament—Quelle christlicher Theologie und Glaubenspraxis. Aufsätze zum Neuen Testament und seiner Auslegung.* Stuttgart: Katholisches Bibelwerk, 1986, 157–167.

19. *Self-Defense and Apostolic Concern* (12:11-21)

11. I have become foolish; you forced me (to it). In fact, I ought to be commended by you, for I was in nothing inferior to the super-apostles, even though I am nothing. 12. The signs of the apostle were done among you with utmost endurance: signs, wonders, and miracles. 13. For in what were you treated less than the other churches, except that I myself did not burden you? Forgive me this wrong.

14. Now I am ready to come to you for the third time, and I will not burden (you), for I do not seek what is yours, but you. For the children ought not to save up for the parents, but the parents for the children. 15. But I will most gladly spend and be spent for your souls. If I love you more, am I loved less? 16. Be this as it may, I did not burden you, but (as you say), unscrupulous as I am, I caught you by deceit. 17. Did I defraud you through one of those I sent to you? 18. I urged Titus and, together (with him), I sent the brother. Surely Titus did not defraud you, did he?

Have we not lived in the same spirit? (Have we not taken) the same steps?

19. Are you thinking again that we defend ourselves before you? In God's sight we speak in Christ; beloved, all (is done) for your upbuilding. 20. For I fear that when I come I may not find you the sort of people I wish, and I may be found by you the sort of person you do not wish; that (there may be) rivalry, jealousy, outbursts of anger, ambitions, words of slander and gossip, manifestations of conceit, arrogance, and disorder. 21. (I fear) that, when I come, my God may again humble me before you and I may grieve over many who sinned before and have not repented of the impurity, fornication, and debauchery they have practiced.

NOTES

11. *I have become foolish; you forced me (to it):* The Fool's Speech is finished. Paul looks back at what he has been doing: being a fool while boasting all along. The "you" at the beginning of the second clause is very emphatic. For the vocabulary of "foolish, foolishness," cf. 11:1, 16-19, 21, 23; 12:6.

In fact, I ought to be commended by you, for I was in nothing inferior to the super-apostles, even though I am nothing: The motivating *gar* ("for") supposes an elliptical construction. A thought such as "I would not have done it by myself, for . . ." seems to be missing. The translation avoids this ellipsis; "for" becomes a simple "in fact."

The Greek aorist "I was in nothing inferior" is global: Paul refers back to the whole of his career in Corinth. It is hardly by accident that there is a double *ouden* ("nothing"), one at the beginning and the other near the end of this motivation. Does the clause "even though I am nothing" point to a reproach on the part of the Corinthians, an attack on his apostleship ("you are really nothing"; cf. the term *exouthenēmenos*, "of no account," in 10:10)? Or does Paul here in the first place employ a well-known Greek "topos" and by means of it express his own deepest conviction before God and his fellow Christians? This second interpretation may be preferred.

The verb *synistasthai* is an infinitive passive; the present tense points to continuity: "to be commended," not "to have been commended" (as is found in some translations). For this verb cf. 10:12, 18, and 3:1-2; 4:2; 5:12; 6:4. For "to be inferior" and "super-apostles" (= opponents, "false apostles") see 11:5.

12. *The signs of the apostle were done among you with utmost endurance: signs, wonders and miracles:* At the beginning of this sentence the Greek has a *men* ("on the one hand") but no corresponding *de* ("on the other hand") follows; the *men* could point to the concessive nature of the sentence, e.g., "It is true that signs of the apostle were performed among you (but that did not take away my weakness)" (cf. the end of v. 11 and "with utmost endurance" in v. 12). In v. 13a Paul will resume the idea of "not being inferior" that is present in v. 11.

"Signs" (first use) means evidence, criteria, marks, proofs, and more concretely, "miracles" as is explained later in this verse. Was the expression "the

signs of the apostle" current in Corinth? This is not so certain, nor is the hypothesis likely that such signs accredited a person as apostle. "Were done" could
be a "divine" passive; the aorist in Greek refers back to Paul's stay in Corinth.
The phrase *en pasē hypomonē* (literally "in all endurance") is inserted; this patience or endurance of sufferings prevented any kind of triumphalism in
Paul. Compare *en hypomonē pollē* ("with great endurance") at the beginning of
the second list of trials in 6:4.

It strikes the reader that "signs" is repeated; yet in the repetition the term
is part of the traditional expression *sēmeia kai terata* ("signs and wonders"),
which in the LXX mainly refers to the Lord's wonderful liberation of the
people of Israel during the Exodus. By adding "miracles" *(dynameis)* Paul further intensifies the importance of that expression. Systematic theologians note
that the three nouns indicate the basic aspects of any true "miracle": a miracle (1) witnesses to God's transcendent power (mighty work: *dynamis*); (2) by
its exceptional nature it calls for attention (portent: *teras*); (3) it equally refers
to a deeper reality (sign: *sēmeion*).

The rather strange dative (literally *"with* signs, wonders, and miracles")
could be sociative: the endurance was accompanied by signs, wonders, and
miracles. Another explanation is not to be excluded, namely a dative of
means. One might assume that Paul, as it were, forgot the mention of "signs"
at the beginning of the sentence. The train of thought, then, is more or less as
follows: "To be sure, the signs of the apostle were done among you with great
endurance; (my authentic apostleship was proved) *by* signs, wonders, and
miracles." A third explanation is most likely erroneous, namely that the first
use of "signs" is more general (all true marks of Paul's apostleship) while the
second use refers to miracles as such and is included in the first.

In order to evaluate correctly Paul's view of his miraculous deeds several
points in v. 12 must be taken together: the passive verb may indicate that it is
God who works the miracles (through Paul); only here and in Rom 15:19 does
Paul mention his miracles (briefly); in 2 Cor 12:12 as well as Rom 15:19 the
text remains general: no specific miracle is named; within the context of 2
Corinthians 11–12 the mention of the "signs of the apostle" comes late, outside the discourse proper, after his actual boasting; finally, by means of "in all
endurance" Paul refers at the same time to his sufferings. Although the signs
certainly legitimate the apostle, for Paul they are obviously not the most important criterion.

13. *For in what were you treated less than the other churches, except that I myself did not
    burden you? Forgive me this wrong:* Paul speaks here (especially with "forgive
    me this wrong") in an ironic and even sarcastic way. Paul refused financial
    support from the church in Corinth (cf. 11:7-12).

    For *hēssomai* ("to be treated less") see the adverb *hēsson* ("less") later in
    12:15. For the verb *katanarkeō* ("to burden," literally "to stupefy") see 11:9 and
    further again in 12:14. For the emphatic "I myself" (here in regard to his op-
    ponents) cf. 10:1. For "this wrong" cf. 11:7 ("sin").

14. *Now I am ready to come to you for the third time, and I will not burden (you), for I
    do not seek what is yours, but you:* As can be seen from 13:1, *triton* ("for the third

time") qualifies "to come," not "I am ready" (which then would have the odd meaning: I am ready for the third time). The grammatical construction, here and in 13:1, seems to result from a conflation of two clauses: "This is the third time" and "I am ready [a possible Latinism, cf. 10:6] to come to you." Earlier Paul refrained from going (a third time) to Corinth so as not to make another painful visit (cf. 1:23–2:1). Now, however, he is ready; he is even on the way (cf. 7:5-6). In 12:14 (differently from 13:1) the announcement of that visit is not the main issue; it is subordinated to the decision of "not burdening" the Corinthians. For the same firm decision cf. 11:9 (end) and 11:12. The phrase *ta hymōn* ("what is yours") and the pronoun *hymas* ("you") contrast with one another.

For the children ought not to save up for the parents, but the parents for the children: The saying about parents and children is a well-known principle. In quoting it Paul indicates that he considers himself the "father" and "mother" of the Christians in the churches he founded. For "father" see, e.g., 1 Cor 4:15 and cf. 1 Thess 2:11; for "mother" see Gal 4:19 and cf. 1 Thess 2:7.

15. *But I will most gladly spend and be spent for your souls. If I love you more, am I loved less?* The different punctuations and the choice between the variants *ei* ("if") and *ei kai* ("even though"), as well as between the other variants *agapō* (indicative present: "I love") and *agapōn* (participle: "loving"), make a number of readings possible in this verse. (1) Verse 15 is one sentence: "I will most gladly spend and be spent for your souls even though, loving you more, I am loved less." The other three possibilities have a full stop after "for your souls": (2) "Loving you more, I am loved less" (statement); (3) "Loving you more, am I loved less?" (question); and (4) "If I love you more, am I loved less?" (question). The well attested third reading is the *lectio difficilior* and may provide the original text; however, the fourth is preferred by many commentators and translators because of its smoother sense and more regular grammar.

For "most gladly" cf. 12:9. Note that after the active *dapanēsō* ("I will spend") the second verb is in the passive and it is a compound in Greek: *ekdapanēthēsomai* ("I will be spent"). Paul's spending and, even more, his being spent entail much more than money. In a loving way Paul gives himself completely for the Corinthians. "Soul" signifies the whole person; the broad expression "for your souls" certainly adds emphasis. One should not assume that *hyper* ("for, on behalf of") possesses a substitutionary sense here. For the adverb *hēsson* ("less," a comparative without a corresponding positive) see the verb *hēssomai* ("to be treated less") in v. 13. Paul stresses that his refusal of financial support should not be interpreted as a lack of love.

16. *Be this as it may, I did not burden you, but (as you say), unscrupulous as I am, I caught you by deceit:* The first verb *estō* means literally "let it be (so)." The Corinthians will easily admit that Paul did not burden them. Paul goes on and makes explicit what they may be thinking: but you (and the opponents) say that, since I was unscrupulous, I took you in by subterfuge. Attention should be paid to the causal nuance of the clause *hyparchōn panourgos* ("being unscrupulous"). Compare the adjective *panourgos* (literally: "capable of anything") with the noun *panourgia* ("cunning") in 11:3 and 4:2 (in this last verse *doloō*, "falsify," must also be compared with *dolos*, "deceit," in 12:16).

17. *Did I defraud you through one of those I sent to you?* The literal translation is: "Any of those whom I sent to you, have I defrauded you through him?" The accusative *tina* ("someone," or "any of those") has no function in the Greek sentence *(casus pendens)* and is resumed by *di' autou* ("through him").

"I sent" in the Greek text is a perfect, which implies that Paul is "a sender" and has sent fellow workers or messengers from time to time. The answer expected by the introductory *mē* is: "of course not!"

It is not obvious that one can conclude from v. 17 (and v. 18) that not only Paul but also his fellow workers have been accused of fraud.

18. *I urged Titus and, together (with him), I sent the brother. Surely Titus did not defraud you, did he? Have we not lived in the same spirit? (have we not taken) the same steps?* The first two verbs are possibly so-called "epistolary" aorists; they are used from the point of view of the addressees (cf. 8:17, 18, 22). For Paul the action lies in the present, so a translation with present tenses is defensible: "I am urging Titus (to go) and I am sending the brother with him." Then the question "surely Titus did not defraud you, did he?" points to an earlier visit. C. K. Barrett, for example, maintains the reference of these aorists to the past; for him chs. 10–13 constitute a later letter (see *Commentary,* 325). Not only the use of the tense is confusing; it is also strange that only one brother is mentioned here, in comparison to two in 8:16-24 (cf. 9:3).

"Titus did not defraud you" must refer to Titus's past visit. Compare the three questions: the first introduced by *mēti* (a strengthened form of *mē*; expected answer: "no"); the other two by *ou* (expected answer: "yes"). The term "spirit" certainly points to the human spirit of (apostolic) responsibility, not to the Holy Spirit.

19. *Are you thinking again that we defend ourselves before you? In God's sight we speak in Christ; beloved, all (is done) for your upbuilding:* Verse 19a could also be a statement, not a question, but either way Paul claims that he is not defending himself. Yet he can hardly deny that his words are also a kind of apology. Self-defense and "for your upbuilding" are not mutually exclusive.

For the adjective *agapētoi* ("beloved," in the vocative), compare the double use of the verb *agapaō* ("to love") in v. 16. Even Paul's foolish boasting is a speaking in Christ and has an apostolic purpose. Compare the identical vocabulary at the end of 2:17: "In God's sight in Christ we speak." In its own way such a repetition in 12:19 suggests the unity of the letter. For the term *oikodomē* ("upbuilding") see 10:8 and, later in the letter, 13:10.

20. *For I fear that when I come I may not find you the sort of people I wish, and I may be found by you the sort of person you do not wish:* Paul's pastoral solicitude comes to the fore. His language here has an apprehensive tone. The translation "the sort of people" and "the sort of person" constitutes an attempt to render the nuance present in *hoious* and *hoion*. The second clause ("and I may be found . . .") has the appearance of a needed afterthought, yet it may be meant as an allusion to his severe threat (cf. 10:11 and further in 13:10).

that (there may be) rivalry, jealousy, outbursts of anger, ambitions, words of slander and gossip, manifestations of conceit, arrogance, and disorder: This second *mē pōs* ("that," a verb is missing) continues Paul's basic concern: the moral life of the Corinthians. Here (and in v. 21) Paul speaks of a present deplorable situation in Corinth. The list of sins contains eight nouns, the first two in the singular, the others in the plural. In the translation "outbursts of," "words of," and "manifestations of" are used to indicate these plurals.

21. *(I fear) that when I come my God may again humble me before you:* After the two *mē pōs* in v. 20, Paul now writes *mē* (after a verb of fearing: "that"); the reader must mentally supply the verb from v. 20. Notwithstanding the position of "again" before "to come" in the Greek text this adverb probably goes with the verb "to humble." Paul seems to be referring to a first humiliation (during the intervening visit?). God as the subject of the verb "to humble" is rather strange. Did Paul too easily detect God's activity in what occurs in this world?

and I may grieve over many who sinned before and have not repented of the impurity, fornication, and debauchery they have practiced: In the original Greek text the genitive after "many" is presumably less correct. Paul is going to mourn over *all* those who sinned before and have not repented (not: over *many* of those who . . .). Paul seems to mean: "Among those who sinned before there are many who have not repented; I may have to grieve over those many."

In the Greek text there is, not accidentally, a shift from the perfect tense (*proēmartēkotōn*, "having sinned") to the aorist (*metanoēsantōn*, "having repented"). The sinning has persisted until now; a past opportunity to repent (during the intervening visit?) was not taken.

The three sins (nouns in the singular, introduced by only one article) all point to sexual misbehavior. They were not mentioned in the list in v. 20 nor are the sins of that list repeated in v. 21. Therefore some commentators think of two different groups of sinners in Corinth: in v. 20 those who, influenced by the opponents, cause divisions and strife; in v. 21 those who still cling to pre-Christian immorality (cf. 1 Cor 5:1-11 and 6:12-20). The sexual sins make one think of the slogans of the "Christian" immoral people in 1 Cor 6:13: "All things are lawful for me" and "food is meant for the stomach and the stomach for food." The unexpected naming of grave immorality in Corinth here at the very end of the letter and in connection with the third visit (cf. also 13:2) cannot but surprise the readers (however, see 2 Cor 6:14–7:1).

INTERPRETATION

a. *Structure and Line of Thought.* 2 Corinthians 12:11-21 can be divided into three subsections: vv. 11-13 (Paul is not inferior to the others), vv. 14-18 (Paul is no burden to the Corinthians; cf. already in v. 13bc), vv. 19-21 (Paul is concerned about the moral behavior of the Corinthians).

In comparison to 11:1–12:10 three characteristics of 12:11-21 may be pointed out:

(1) To some extent this pericope runs parallel to the three text units in 11:1–12:10: there is again a new start in 12:11a ("I have become foolish");

there is an excuse on the part of Paul: boasting is the work of a fool, but you forced me to it. Subsequently in 12:11c (no inferiority to the super-apostles) and in 12:12 (signs) there again is actual boasting. However, this is no longer the Fool's Speech proper.

(2) The pericope has its own repetitions and therefore seems to have a framing function. In 12:13-18 Paul speaks of the fact that he has not been a burden to the church of Corinth: see 11:7-11 (even "this wrong" in 12:13 reminds the reader of the "sin" in 11:7). Furthermore, the motif of self-commendation in 12:11 recalls 10:12-18 where the same motif was dealt with in more detail. In 12:16 we find an accusation brought forward by the Corinthians: Nevertheless, you say that, since I was crafty, I took you in by deceit. This reminds the reader of the reproach in 10:10 (cf. 10:1b and 2b).

(3) Finally, especially toward the end, the pericope is obviously transitional. By means of the motifs of his future visit (v. 14: "Now I am ready to come to you for the third time," cf. v. 20: "when I come") and of "up-building" (v. 19; cf. 10:8 and, further, 13:10) and via the glance to the future in 12:20-21 Paul already makes the transition to the main themes of ch. 13.

In light of these three characteristics (new boasting, repetitions, transition) it is better to take 12:11-21 as a text unit on its own, similar to yet different from the three preceding pericopes in 11:1–12:10, as well as from the following one in ch. 13. This pericope is still concerned with boasting and self-defense, but it is a conclusion and also a transition.

b. *Known Sentences.* In reading 12:11-21 one is struck by Paul's frequent use of the first person singular, especially the fivefold appearance of the emphatic *egō:* see vv. 11, 13, 15, 16, and 20. Furthermore, in this passage there are a number of rather well-known sayings:

> "Even though I am nothing" (end of v. 11);
>
> "I do not seek what is yours but you" (in the Vulgate: *Non enim quaero quae vestra sunt, sed vos,* v. 14b);
>
> "The children ought not to save up for the parents, but the parents for the children" (v. 14c);
>
> "But I will most gladly spend and be spent for your souls" (in the Vulgate: *Ego autem libentissime impendam et superimpendar ipse pro animabus vestris,* v. 15a);
>
> "If I love you more, am I loved less?" (v. 15b);
>
> "All (is done) for your upbuilding" (v. 19c).

The consequence is that 12:11-21 has become one of the best-known Pauline texts.

Regarding the equally well-known sentences of 12:9-10, see p. 208.

c. *Theological Reflection.* In 2 Cor 12:12 Paul speaks of "the signs of the apostle." Although according to this commentary "the signs" in that verse are further explained as Paul's miraculous deeds, one can, as it were, enlarge its meaning and raise the basic question of apostolic legitimation. In 13:3 Paul says to the Corinthians: "you seek the proof that Christ is speaking through me." What is it that truly commends an apostle? How is the authentic apostle identifiable and recognizable for the Christians, distinguishable from the false ones? Nowhere else has Paul brought together so many elements of this proof as he has done in 2 Corinthians, especially in chs. 10–13. Here Paul is pointing to the authenticating signs of his apostolate. These objective signs, visible and verifiable, equally constitute the recommendation of the apostle and, at the same time, his legitimate boast. However it goes without saying that the interpretation of these signs by the Christians is no easy matter. This discernment requires the assistance of the Spirit and will in the end hardly produce "mathematical," once-for-all certainty.

Five irrefutable criteria are present in 2 Corinthians. (1) For his legitimation Paul refers to the visible results of his apostolic work, to the very existence of the Corinthian church: see 10:12-18. The Corinthians are his boast, not only on the day of the Lord Jesus but already now (1:14); they are his work in the Lord (cf. 1 Cor 9:1). They are his true letter of recommendation, written on his heart, to be known and read by all, a letter of Christ prepared by Paul (2 Cor 3:2-3). The children for whom Paul was in the pain of childbirth again, until Christ was formed in them (cf. Gal 4:19), "prove" the authority the Lord gave him, the authenticity of his commission.

(2) More than once Paul also mentions his complete openness: "we are open to God. I hope, however, to be also open to your consciences" (2 Cor 5:11). There can be no doubt: Paul is certain that this honest, straightforward attitude pleads for the genuineness of his apostleship: "we have renounced the deeds one hides for shame; we do not practice cunning nor do we falsify the word of God, but through the open preaching of the truth we commend ourselves to anyone's conscience in the sight of God" (4:2; cf. 2:17, and see also 12:14-18).

(3) Paul is, moreover, interiorly convinced that his way of life and moral conduct are of vital importance for his missionary work: "we give no offense in anything lest our ministry be blamed, but as ministers of God we commend ourselves in all things: with great endurance, in afflictions, hardships, (and) constraints . . ." (6:3-4, and see the whole list of hardships up to 6:10). "For (our reason) for boasting is this: the testimony of our conscience, that we have behaved ourselves in this world, and above all toward you, in simplicity and godly sincerity, not by fleshly wisdom but by the grace of God" (1:12). The integrity of his personal conduct provides a proof for the veracity of his message.

(4) It would seem that Paul speaks only incidentally of the "signs of the apostle" that were performed in Corinth with utmost patience: signs and wonders and miracles (12:12). Nonetheless, one must not deny that for Paul these signs and wonders do possess an authenticating value. In Rom 15:15-17 he states that grace has been given him by God to be a minister of Christ Jesus to the Gentiles in the priestly service of the gospel of God. He has reason to boast of his work for God. In this letter to the Romans he also mentions the "signs": "I will not venture to speak of anything except what Christ has accomplished through me to win obedience from the Gentiles, by word and deed, by the power of signs and wonders, by the power of the Spirit of God . . ." (Rom 15:18-19). Again, it is evident to Paul's mind that both work and wonders authenticate the apostle.

(5) It must have been Paul's heartfelt desire that the fact of proclaiming the gospel to the Corinthians free of charge should be an undeniable proof of the purity and veracity of his apostolic endeavor, but, as far as one can surmise, this criterion had not been recognized at Corinth. It was not received with gratitude; it was even misinterpreted (see 2 Cor 11:7-12 and 12:13-18). Yet Paul emphasizes his making no use of an apostle's right to get a living by the gospel: no one will deprive him of this ground for boasting (see 1 Cor 9:6-18 and 2 Cor 11:10, 12; cf. 12:14). No doubt this particular boast was also a personal supplementary authentication.

Two more criteria: weakness and privileges. (6) According to Paul, it is very much the weakness of the apostle that proves the genuineness of his apostleship. After he has abundantly pointed out his weakness he goes on to write: "I hope that you will discover that we have not failed the test" (13:6). That the apostles are "as deceivers yet truthful, as unknown yet well known, as dying and behold [they] live, as punished yet not put to death, as saddened but always rejoicing, as poor but enriching many, as having nothing yet possessing everything" (6:8-10) is indeed a most convincing proof of apostolic authenticity and godly recommendation. In this way it is made clear that this extraordinary power belongs to God and does not come from the apostle himself (cf. 4:7). The Lord himself has revealed to Paul that, paradoxically, power is made perfect in weakness (cf. 12:9a). Paul adds in a personal reflection: "most gladly, therefore . . . I rather will boast of my weaknesses in order that the power of Christ may come to rest upon me. That is why I am well pleased with weaknesses, insults, hardships, persecutions, and constraints (endured) for Christ. For whenever I am weak, then I am strong" (12:9b-10).

(7) But what about Paul's "foolish" boasting of his Jewish origin (11:21-22; cf. Rom 11:1 and Phil 3:3-6), of his labors, greater than those of the others (cf. 2 Cor 11:23-29; 1 Cor 15:10), of his visions and revelations

of the Lord (2 Cor 12:1-6)? Does all this also belong to his credentials? In 12:6 he denies the foolishness of this action of boasting: "but if I want to boast, I will not be foolish, since I will be speaking the truth; but I refrain in order that no one esteems me above what he sees of me or hears from me." To be sure, in 12:1 he remarks that nothing is to be gained by this sort of boasting, and in 12:2-3, 5 he regards God's extraordinary gifts as not given to him but, as it were, to a different person. Nevertheless, despite all that, he does boast of such things more than once, and he emphasizes that he speaks the truth. Therefore, it would appear that this specific boasting in foolishness—more foolish than other boasting that is always to a certain extent foolish—is not necessarily wrong, although it may be particularly dangerous and not so useful for the legitimation process itself. Still, in the concrete Corinthian situation this boasting could be of some positive help for recognizing the validity of his ministry: "I was in nothing inferior to the super-apostles, even though I am nothing" (12:11).

The best proof: resurrection power. (8) One most important credential has not yet been mentioned, i.e., Paul's strength, often in the midst of weakness. Paul does not deny that his letters are weighty and strong (10:10) and that he is bold toward the Corinthians when he is away. But he adds: "just as we are in word by letters when absent, so (we will be) in action when present" (10:11).

As far as Paul's human-divine strength is concerned, one passage in 2 Corinthians deserves special attention: 13:1-4 (see further the Notes and Interpretation of these verses). In v. 4d Paul announces that he will deal with the Corinthians in a life-filled, powerful way. This particular strength has been and will be experienced by the Corinthians. Paul's anticipative resurrection power is his credential par excellence. In its own way it constitutes a visible proof of authenticity that all believers encounter in their legitimate missionaries.

d. *Actualization.* At the end of this survey one may conclude that Paul appears to have quite a number of legitimating proofs that at the same time are good reasons to be proud and to boast: the existence of the Corinthian church, Paul's openness, his moral conduct, the miraculous deeds, his preaching free of charge, his weakness, the many privileges, and the anticipative manifestation of Christ's resurrection power in himself. Not all of these are equally convincing, but in given circumstances each of them can be useful and may be employed. They function as the rightful self-defense of the apostle and should help Christians to identify him.

What Paul explains in 2 Corinthians 10–13 at great length regarding his apostolic authenticity no doubt applies analogously to the authentic identity of every Christian.

For Reference and Further Study

Bieringer, Reimund. "Plädoyer für die Einheitlichkeit des 2. Korintherbriefes" in Bieringer and Lambrecht. *Studies on 2 Corinthians*. BEThL 125. Leuven: Leuven University Press/Peeters, 1996, 169–173.

_____. "2 Korinther 6,14-7,1" in idem, 568–570.

Court, John N. "The Controversy with the Adversaries of Paul's Apostolate in the Context of his Relations to the Corinthian Congregation (2 Corinthians 12,14–13,13)" in Eduard Lohse, ed., *Verteidigung und Begründung des apostolischen Amtes (2 Kor 10–13)*. Benedictina 11. Rome: Abbazia San Paolo fuori le mura, 1992, 87–105.

Jervell, Jacob. "Die Zeichen des Apostels. Die Wunder beim lukanischen und paulinischen Paulus," SNTU.A 4 (1979) 54–75.

Lambrecht, Jan. "Dangerous Boasting" in Reimund Bieringer, ed., *The Corinthian Correspondence*. BEThL 125. Leuven: Leuven University Press/Peeters, 1996, 339–346.

20. *Stern Announcement and Injunction* (13:1-10)

1. This (is) the third time (that) I am coming to you. "On the evidence of two or three witnesses every case must be established" (Deut 19:15). 2. I said to those who sinned before and to all the others, and now while absent I say, just as (I did) when present the second time, that when I come again I will not refrain, 3. since you seek the proof that Christ is speaking through me, (Christ) who toward you is not weak but is powerful among you. 4. For indeed, although he was crucified in weakness he certainly lives by the power of God. For although we too are weak in him, we shall certainly live with him by the power of God (in dealing) with you.

5. Examine yourselves (to see) whether you are in the faith; test yourselves. Or do you not realize that Jesus Christ is in you? If not, you have failed the test. 6. I hope that you will discover that we have not failed the test. 7. We pray God that you may do no wrong, not that we should appear as having passed the test, but that you will do what is good, though we may seem to have failed the test. 8. For we have no power against the truth, but (only) for the truth. 9. For we rejoice whenever we are weak but you are powerful. What we pray for is this, your improvement.

10. This is why I write these things while absent, that when present I may not have to act severely according to the authority God gave me for building up and not for destroying.

NOTES

1. *This (is) the third time (that) I am coming to you.* "*On the evidence of two or three witnesses every case must be established*": For the first clause and its grammatical construction see the Notes on 12:14. The quotation from Deut 19:15 is also found in Matt 18:16 and may have been proverbial in Judaism. At any rate Paul wants his repeated visits to function as "witnesses." With his third visit his case will be valid without doubt. Paul thus warns the Corinthians.

2. *I said to those who sinned before and to all the others, and now while absent I say, just as (I did) when present the second time, that when I come again I will not refrain:* The construction of the sentence in the Greek text is quite balanced, yet unavoidably heavy in translation. Due attention should be given to the double use of the compound *prolegō* (literally "to speak beforehand"): "I said" (perfect tense) and "I say" (present tense). The people meant by "those who sinned before" are most likely those of 12:21 (sexual sins), and by "all the others" perhaps the Corinthians who side with the opponents (cf. 12:20). For "while absent" and "when present" cf. 10:1-2 and also, later in this pericope, 13:10. Although *ean elthō* is an *eventualis* condition, its sense here is purely temporal and does not suggest uncertainty: "when I come." For "I will not refrain" see 12:6 (here in the matter of boasting).

3. *since you seek the proof that Christ is speaking through me, (Christ) who toward you is not weak but is powerful among you:* With "proof" a terminology that was present in 10:18 is taken up again. In this pericope it will be employed thematically by means of related terms: *dokimē* ("proof," v. 3), *dokimazō* ("to test," v. 5), *dokimos* ("approved," v. 7) and *adokimos* ("not approved," vv. 5, 6, 7). Another thematic cluster of words in 13:3-4, 8-9 is that of "being strong," "powerful," and "power."

   Some commentators claim that Paul uses the title "the Christ." This is, however, not certain. The reader pauses before Paul's self-understanding: Christ speaks through him. Note in v. 3b the shift from *eis* ("toward") to the rather surprising *en* ("among"). Here Paul refers to his own "weak" appearance, which might be misunderstood and used against the validity of his ministry. Through Christ Paul is really powerful and strong among the Corinthians.

4. *For indeed, although he was crucified in weakness he certainly lives by the power of God. For although we too are weak in him, we shall certainly live with him by the power of God (in dealing) with you:* Paul grounds what he stated in vv. 2-3 by comparing his own weakness and strength with those of Christ. Less important variants write "with him" instead of "in him" in v. 4c and vice versa in v. 4d. For a detailed justification of the slightly paraphrastic translation of v. 4 we refer to the Interpretation, c. "We shall certainly live with him" (v. 4d) does not point to life after death, but to Paul's promised boldness of action during his third visit.

5. *Examine yourselves (to see) whether you are in the faith; test yourselves:* Paul rather abruptly addresses the Corinthians. They must not only look for a "proof" in

Paul but also in themselves. Note the emphatic position of *heautous* ("your-selves") at the beginning of the sentence and its threefold repetition in v. 5. "To be in the faith" means to be a true Christian, to stand firm in the faith.

Or do you not realize that Jesus Christ is in you? If not, you have failed the test: In "do you not realize that . . ." the reflexive pronoun *heautous* (employed a third time here in v. 5) is not translated. It might be considered an accusative of respect: "with regard to yourselves." However, it could also be the direct object of *epignōskete* (literally "to know thoroughly"); "that" is then explicative: "Do you not thoroughly know yourselves, namely that Jesus Christ is in you?" The clause "Christ is in you" means the same as "you are in the faith" (v. 5a). If they "have failed the test," then Jesus Christ is not in them. "Having failed the test" is the same as being *adokimoi* ("not approved").

6. *I hope that you will discover that we have not failed the test:* Paul returns to his own case. The future "you will discover" probably points to his third visit: then, during that visit, they will have the opportunity to know—the verb is *ginōskō* (cf. *epiginōskō* in v. 5)—i.e., to find out, to discover. When the Corinthians realize that Christ is truly in them they will at the same time discover that Christ is in Paul, that Paul has not failed the test. The two "discoveries" belong together. However, in v. 7 Paul makes the distinction between his own personal case and that of the Corinthians.

7. *We pray God that you may do no wrong, not that we should appear as having passed the test, but that you will do what is good, though we may seem to have failed the test:* The accusative *hymas* ("you") is almost certainly the grammatical subject of the infinitive "to do wrong." Paul clarifies and explains his real intention, his apostolic care. In order to "be approved" one must live a moral life. Not to do wrong is to do good. Furthermore, in Paul there is no ultimate concern for what others (incorrectly) think of him: cf. the *hōs adokimoi* ("as it were not approved"). In fact Paul is "passing the test" and is, of course, "not without proof."

8. *For we have no power against the truth, but (only) for the truth:* "Truth" lies deeper and is more important than "appearance" (cf. v. 7). In the final analysis it is "truth" that will prevail. Rudolf Bultmann (*Second Letter*) here identifies the term with "gospel," perhaps too easily.

9. *For we rejoice whenever we are weak but you are powerful. What we pray for is this, your improvement:* Paul can be glad in his weakness since it "produces" strength in the Corinthians (cf. 4:12). Yet note again that moral life must be present. One is really strong when restored to good conduct. In the Greek text *touto* ("this") stands at the beginning of the clause in v. 9b and refers to what follows: "this, i.e., your restoration to perfection, your improvement."

10. *This is why I write these things while absent, that when present I may not have to act severely according to the authority God gave me for building up and not for destroy-ing: Touto* ("this") in *dia touto* ("this is why") again refers to what follows. The clause "I write these things" probably refers to the entire letter. For "while absent" and "when present" cf. v. 2 (and 10:1-2). At his third visit Paul would

like to avoid a "strict, severe" way of acting. "Unsparing severity . . . is no joy to Paul; if he can avoid using it by writing a sharp letter he will do so" (Barrett, *Commentary* 340). Paul has been writing this very letter so that the Corinthians prepare themselves. For *oikodomē* ("upbuilding") see 12:9; for the entire clause "according to . . ." see 10:8. The improvement may point to the restoration of the relationship between the Corinthians and Paul, as well as between the Corinthians and God. In Paul's opinion the two forms of disunity may have had the same sinful causes.

INTERPRETATION

a. *Structure and Line of Thought.* A threefold division can be detected in 2 Cor 13:1-10. (1) In vv. 1-4 Paul announces (again, see 12:14, 21) his third visit and stresses once more that he will not be lenient. (2) In vv. 5-9 he urges the Corinthians to examine themselves: Are they in the faith? Is Jesus Christ in them? Are they passing the test and thus approved? Are they really strong and is their life morally sound? He also defends himself; he did not fail the test. (3) Finally, in v. 10 Paul speaks of the letter itself. The mention of its severity, as well as the vocabulary of "absent-present" and "authority," refers back to vv. 1-4. So one has reason to perceive in this pericope a sort of *a-b-a'* structure.

For the numerous connections with ch. 10, both in vocabulary and in content, as well as for the inclusive function that chs. 10 and 13 fulfill, see the discussion on pp. 158–159.

b. *Moral Integrity.* While in 10:18 the recommendation and approval of the Lord have reference to the apostolic authority of the opponents (in a negative way) and of Paul (positively), in 13:5-9 Paul speaks of the approval, surely also of himself, but more specifically of the Corinthians. The subject matter is no longer what ministers have done in their mission field, but the behavior of Christians in daily life. Doing no wrong and doing what is right are needed to pass the test and be approved (cf. 13:7). Improvement, restoration to perfection, is required from the Corinthians. The truth has an innate relation with the way one lives. The building up of Christians consists of the development of their moral integrity. A life in love and peace will be the ultimate proof that the Corinthians really hold to the faith and that Christ is truly in them (cf. 13:5).

c. *Theological Reflection.* Special attention must be devoted to 13:2-4, more particularly to 13:4: the comparison between Christ and Paul himself as far as weakness and strength are concerned. The warning threat of v. 2 lies at the end: "when I come again I will not refrain (or: I will not spare you)." Verse 3a provides a motivation for this warning: "since you seek the proof that Christ is speaking through me." "Christ" is then further explained by the long relative clause in vv. 3b-4a. In v. 3b one reads: "Christ who toward you is not weak but is powerful among you." This reasoning goes farther in v. 4, which provides as grounding two parallel sentences, each of them consisting of two clauses (*kai* is not translated):

> 4a   For he was crucified in weakness,
> 4b   but lives by the power of God.
> 4c   For we are weak in him,
> 4d   but we shall live with him by the power of God (in dealing) with you.

The symmetry between the two sentences is striking indeed, yet the clauses are also different from each other. In v. 4c the verb "was crucified" of v. 4a is replaced by "are weak." The tenses of the verbs also disagree: aorist (past tense) in v. 4a, present in v. 4b, present also in v. 4c, and future in v. 4d. The second sentence (c and d), with the emphatic *hēmeis* ("we") at the beginning and the phrases "in him," "with him," and "(in dealing) with you," is much longer. From the double mention of "in him" (in c and d) it appears that for Paul weakness and strength are christologically conditioned. The most surprising feature, however, is that the phrase *eis hymas* (understood as "in dealing with you") causes a shift from resurrection life strictly speaking in v. 4b (so in Christ and so, one would expect, also in Paul after death) to the apostle's future powerful encounter with the Corinthians in v. 4d. Three philological notes may help us to grasp the correct and full meaning of this theologically most important verse.

(1) What is the exact meaning of the twofold *kai gar* (literally "and for") at the beginning of both v. 4a and v. 4c? In v. 4a the *gar* is connecting and the adverbial *kai* possesses an emphatic force: "for indeed Christ was crucified." In v. 4c *gar* is equally connecting but, notwithstanding the preceding parallel clause 4a, the meaning "also" for *kai* remains the most likely: "for we also (or: we too) are weak in him."

(2) The whole of v. 4 "grounds" (*gar*, "for") what is said in v. 3. More specifically, verse 4d repeats and grounds v. 3a, and through it the warning at the end of v. 2. The formal parallelism between v. 4ab and v. 4cd should in no way deceive us. Paul is not making two separate statements, one about Christ and one about himself. He is not even strictly comparing himself with Christ (so Christ, so we). His conviction that Christ speaks in him, and that as an apostle he is weak in Christ and that with Christ he will prove powerful, i.e., filled with God-given life, sufficiently shows that behind this formal parataxis lies an implication concerning Christ and Paul. Out of Christ's death and life come Paul's weakness and

strength. The argumentation behind the symmetric composition requires that the second sentence (4cd) is understood as consecutive. We may paraphrase v. 4 as follows (*gar* not translated): "Indeed Christ was crucified in weakness but lives by the power of God, *so that* we too are weak in him but shall live with him by the power of God (in dealing) with you."

(3) Each of two sentences, moreover, possesses a *gar . . . alla* ("for . . . but") construction that, most likely, is the equivalent of the well-known *men gar . . . de* ("for on the one hand . . . on the other hand") construction in which the *men* clause often has a concessive nuance and the real reason is to be found in the *de* clause. In v. 4ab Paul expresses the motivation for the fact that Christ is mighty in the midst of the Corinthians (see v. 3b). The logical sense can be brought out by means of a paraphrase: "For indeed, *although* Christ was crucified in weakness, he *certainly* now lives by the power of God." In v. 4cd Paul gives the motivation for his own firm decision not to refrain (or: to spare the Corinthians) at his third coming (see the end of v. 2): "For *although* we too are weak in him, we shall *certainly* live with him by the power of God in dealing with you." In both sentences, v. 4ab and v. 4cd, the first clause (4a and 4c) refers to supposedly common Christian knowledge, i.e., to evidence upon which all readers agree and which, therefore, can easily be conceded. In both sentences, too, it is the second clause (4b and 4d) that brings the motivation properly speaking.

In 13:3-4 there is, moreover, a remarkable and theologically most interesting use of the tenses of the verbs:

3a: Christ is actually speaking through Paul
    (present continuous)

3b: he is not weak now but powerful with regard to the Corinthians
    (present continuous)

4a: the Corinthians know very well that Christ was crucified
    (narrative aorist)

4b: but they should also realize that he is now living by God's power
    (present continuous)

4c: Paul admits that the same Corinthians experience that he himself is weak
    (present continuous)

4d: but he stresses that they must also believe that he will deal with them in a life-filled, powerful way
    (future)

In v. 4 the movement from past to present and from present to future should not go unnoticed; one encounters all three temporal dimensions here. Thus once more the formal parallelism in v. 4 is broken, now by

Paul's wording itself. The differences in time indicate the limits of the real inclusion of Paul in Christ. Christ was crucified long ago, yet the apostle still suffers. Christ is living his resurrection life; in Paul that life is already present but its future manifestation before the Corinthians, forceful as it will be, is but a weak anticipation of the fullness of life after death.

This lengthy and, hopefully, useful discussion should not lead the readers away from the fact that in v. 4 the main point lies in the announcement of clause d: in dealing with the Corinthians during his third visit Paul will be strong with human-divine power.

One more remark should be added. Within 13:1-4 there is an interesting chiastic movement: from Paul (vv. 1-2) to Christ (v. 3); and from Christ (v. 4ab) back to Paul (v. 4cd).

We might have the impression that for Paul there is still a difference between the severe authority with which he does not want to act during his third visit (cf. 13:10) and the anticipative resurrection power always present in the apostle (cf. 13:4d), but if so, the difference is not easily defined.

d. *Actualization.* We Christians today are also addressed by Paul in a twofold way in 2 Cor 13:1-10. First, not to fail the test means to do no wrong; it is through Christian moral life that we will pass the test, that ultimately we will be approved. Second, the anticipative resurrection power with which Paul confidently approaches the Corinthians is, as a matter of fact, present in all Christians, in each of us. This mostly hidden, indestructible strength should at the same time remain deep within us a source of Christian joy.

For Reference and Further Study

Court, John N. "The Controversy with the Adversaries of Paul's Apostolate in the Context of his Relations to the Corinthian Congregation (2 Corinthians 12,14–13,13)" in Eduard Lohse, ed., *Verteidigung und Begründung des apostolischen Amtes (2 Kor 10–13).* Benedictina 11. Rome: Abbazia San Paolo fuori le mura, 1992, 87–105.

Lambrecht, Jan. "Philological and Exegetical Notes on 2 Corinthians 13,4" in Bieringer and Lambrecht, *Studies on 2 Corinthians.* BEThL 125. Leuven: Leuven University Press/Peeters, 1996, 589–598.

21. *Final Exhortation, Greetings, and Blessing* (13:11-13)

11. Finally, brothers and sisters, rejoice, mend your ways, take the appeal to heart, be of the same mind, live in peace, and the God of love and peace will be with you.

    12. Greet one another with a holy kiss. All the saints greet you.

    13. The grace of the Lord Jesus Christ and the love of God and the communion of the holy Spirit (be) with you all.

Notes

11. *Finally, brothers and sisters, rejoice, mend your ways, take the appeal to heart, be of the same mind, live in peace:* Paul concludes his letter with final exhortations. As far as *chairete* is concerned, it is difficult to make a choice between a full imperative ("rejoice," just like the other imperatives that follow and hence more probable) and a Greek goodbye or farewell wish. The following imperative is better understood as a middle with an active sense, not as a passive; hence the translation "mend your ways." The next imperative, *parakaleisthe*, is a middle ("encourage one another") or a passive ("be encouraged, heed my appeal"). For *to auto phroneō* ("to be of the same mind") see the same expression in Rom 12:16; 15:5; Phil 2:2; 4:2. For the verb *eirēneuō* ("to live in peace") see Rom 12:18 and 1 Thess 5:13. Compare, with other vocabulary, also 2 Cor 5:14-21: "reconcile yourselves to God" (v. 20); 12:20: reconciliation of the Corinthians with one another; 6:1; 7:2: reconciliation with Paul.

All the imperatives in v. 11 are in the present tense, pointing to continual action.

and the God of love and peace will be with you: Should we consider v. 11a as a condition? The sense would then be: "If you mend your ways . . . then the God of love and peace will be with you."

The expression "the God of love" is a *hapax legomenon* in the New Testament (but cf. v. 13: "the love of God"). Does "peace" refer to the preceding verb "live in peace" (in which case the meaning is reconciliation) or does "peace" possess its Hebrew comprehensive sense in this instance? The second option appears to be most likely.

12. *Greet one another with a holy kiss:* Did the "holy kiss" already exist in Paul's day as a liturgical gesture (after the homily?), or did the act take its origin from Paul's letters (cf. also 1 Thess 5:26; 1 Cor 16:20; Rom 16:16)?

All the saints greet you: The Authorized Version and hence other translations (cf., for example, the RSV, but no longer the NRSV) number this clause as v. 13 and what follows as v. 14. "All the saints" are all the brothers and sisters, all (Macedonian) Christians who know that Paul writes this letter.

13. *The grace of the Lord Jesus Christ and the love of God and the communion of the holy Spirit (be) with you all:* There is no verb. Supplying "be" as an implored blessing from above seems preferable to "is." In reading this verse today Roman

Catholics recognize the source of the identical blessing at the beginning of their Eucharist.

INTERPRETATION

At the end of 1 Corinthians Paul expands "The grace of the Lord Jesus (be) with you" (16:23) with "My love be with you all in Christ Jesus" (16:24). At the end of 2 Corinthians he expands "The grace of the Lord Jesus Christ (be) with you all" with "the love of God" and "the communion of the holy Spirit." Paul "may be simply reflecting a liturgical formulation already used in his churches"; it is more likely, however, that "these words originated at this point and were expressed in light of what is going on in Corinth and what has been said in this letter—especially so, since nothing like this appears anywhere else in his letters, particularly in letters after this one" (Fee, *Presence*, 362).

If it could be accepted that "of the holy Spirit" is also a subjective genitive (like "of the Lord Jesus Christ" and "of God") one would have here a very early, already beautifully balanced "trinitarian" formula. But "Spirit" may be an objective genitive: participation in or fellowship and communion "with" the Spirit (cf. the objective genitives in 8:4; 1 Cor 10:16; Phil 3:10). Some commentators claim that the genitive is both subjective and objective, which is not very probable.

Note the so-called "economic" order: Christ, God, Spirit. Christ comes first since through his gracious work we came to know the love of God. It should also be kept in mind that Paul's focus seems to be more on the three nouns. Yet grace, love, and communion "relate to 'personal beings' who are called by different names. It is a small step to believe that the 'God of love and peace' of whom Paul spoke comes to us as three 'persons' within the one God" (Barnett, *Second Epistle*, 619). Commentators like to quote the appropriate dictum of Karl Barth: "Trinity is the Christian name for God."

The expression "with you all" stands at the very end. Christ's grace, God's love, and fellowship through (or: with) the Spirit cannot but bring all Christians together into a lasting communion with one another, into an indestructible community.

FOR REFERENCE AND FURTHER STUDY

Belleville, Linda L. "Paul's Polemic and Theology of the Spirit in Second Corinthians," *CBQ* 58 (1996) 281–304, especially 288–290.

Fee, Gordon D. *God's Empowering Presence: The Holy Spirit in the Letters of Paul.* Peabody, Mass.: Hendrickson, 1994, 362–365.

Hengel, Martin. "Das Bekenntnis zum dreieinigen Gott (2. Kor. 13,11-13)," *ThBeitr* 16 (1985) 60–89.

Martin, Ralph P. "The Spirit in 2 Corinthians in Light of the 'Fellowship of the Holy Spirit' in 2 Corinthians 13:14" in W. Hulitt Gloer, ed., *Eschatology and the New Testament*. Peabody, Mass.: Hendrickson, 1988, 113–128.

Riesenfeld, Harald. "Was bedeutet 'Gemeinschaft des Heiligen Geistes'? Zu 2. Kor. 13,13; Phil. 2,1 und Röm. 8,18-30" in Yves Congar, ed., *Communio Sanctorum*. Geneva: Labor et Fides, 1982, 106–113.

INDEXES

SCRIPTURE INDEX

New Testament

INDEX OF AUTHORS

INDEX OF NAMES, SUBJECTS, AND TERMS